VIMY

VIMY

THE BATTLE AND THE LEGEND

TIM COOK

ALLEN
LANE

ALLEN LANE

an imprint of Penguin Canada, a division of
Penguin Random House Canada Limited

Canada • USA • UK • Ireland • Australia •
New Zealand • India • South Africa • China

First published 2017

www.penguinrandomhouse.ca

LIBRARY AND ARCHIVES CANADA CATALOGUING IN PUBLICATION

Cook, Tim, 1971-, author
Vimy : the battle and the legend / Tim Cook.

ISBN 978-0-7352-3316-4 (hardback)
ISBN 978-0-7352-3317-1 (electronic)

1. Vimy Ridge, Battle of, France, 1917.
2. World War, 1914-1918—Canada. I. Title.

D545.V5 C66 2017   940.4'31   C2016-904744-X

Book design by Five Seventeen
Cover image: Canada Dept. of National Defence/
Library and Archives Canada

Printed and bound in the United States of America

10 9 8 7 6 5 4

This book is dedicated to my father, Dr. Terry Cook,
who was a fine historian, a world-renowned archivist,
and an even better dad.

CONTENTS

MAPS viii

CHAPTER 1   Vimy: Battle and Legend 1

CHAPTER 2   Vimy Battleground 8

CHAPTER 3   Preparing the Assault 36

CHAPTER 4   Over the Top 72

CHAPTER 5   Vimy Aftermath 114

CHAPTER 6   Vimy's Impact 138

CHAPTER 7   Commemorating the Fallen 164

CHAPTER 8   Constructing Memory 191

CHAPTER 9   The Great War Contested 218

CHAPTER 10 The 1936 Vimy Pilgrimage 249

CHAPTER 11 Forging an Icon 274

CHAPTER 12 Birth of the Nation 300

CHAPTER 13 Vimy Contested 328

CHAPTER 14 Vimy Reborn 366

ENDNOTES 385

ACKNOWLEDGMENTS 439

SELECT BIBLIOGRAPHY 444

INDEX 479

CREDITS 500

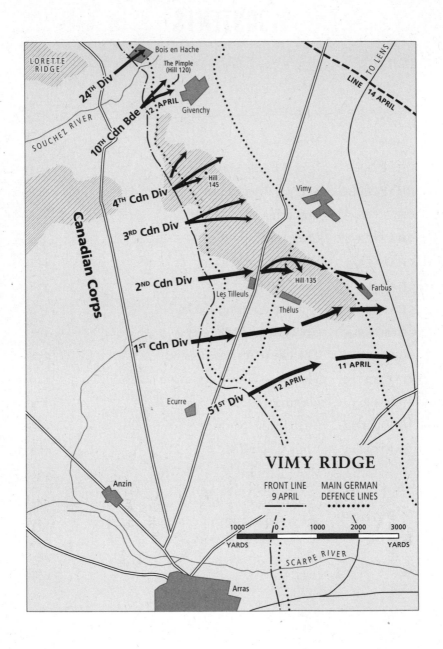

LORETTE
RIDGE

Bois en Hache

The Pimple
(Hill 120)

24TH Div

TO LENS

LINE 14 APRIL

10TH Cdn Bde

12 APRIL

Givenchy

SOUCHEZ RIVER

4TH Cdn Div

Hill
145

Vimy

3RD Cdn Div

Canadian Corps

2ND Cdn Div

Hill 135

Farbus

Les Tilleuls

Thélus

1ST Cdn Div

11 APRIL

Ecurre

51ST Div

12 APRIL

Anzin

VIMY RIDGE

FRONT LINE
9 APRIL

MAIN GERMAN
DEFENCE LINES

1000   0   1000   2000   3000

YARDS   YARDS

SCARPE RIVER

Arras

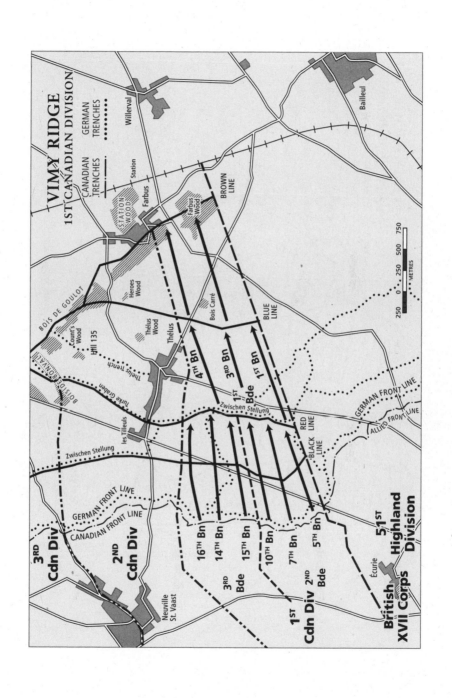

VIMY RIDGE
1ST CANADIAN DIVISION

CANADIAN TRENCHES ———
GERMAN TRENCHES •••••••

Willerval

Bailleul

Station

Farbus

STATION WOOD

Farbus Wood

BROWN LINE

Heroes Wood

Bois Carré

BLUE LINE

BOIS DE GOULOT

Count's Wood

Hill 135

Thélus Wood

Thélus

4TH Bn

3RD Bn

1ST Bn

1ST Bde

BOIS DE BONVAL

Thélus Trench

Turke Graben

Zwischen Stellung

les Tilleuls

Zwischen Stellung

RED LINE

BLACK LINE

GERMAN FRONT LINE

ALLIED FRONT LINE

250   0   250 500 750
METRES

3RD Cdn Div

2ND Cdn Div

GERMAN FRONT LINE

CANADIAN FRONT LINE

Neuville St. Vaast

16TH Bn

14TH Bn

15TH Bn

10TH Bn

7TH Bn

5TH Bn

3RD Bde

2ND Bde

1ST Cdn Div

51ST Highland Division

Écurie

British XVII Corps

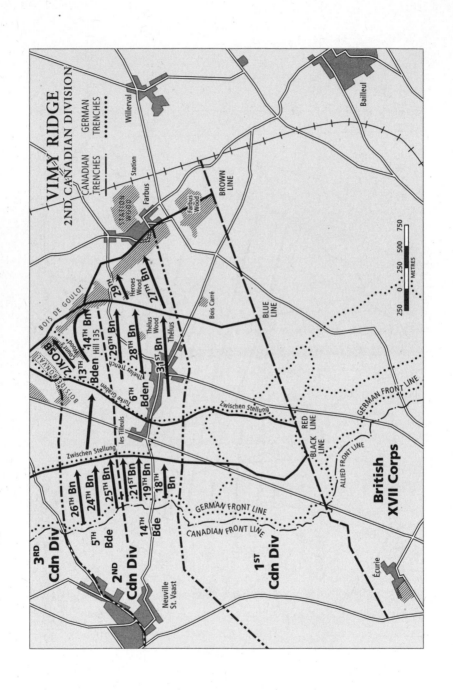

VIMY RIDGE
2ND CANADIAN DIVISION

CANADIAN
TRENCHES

GERMAN
TRENCHES

Willerval

Bailleul

Station

Farbus

STATION
WOOD

Farbus
Wood

BROWN
LINE

29ᵀᴴ

Heroes
Wood

27ᵀᴴ Bn

BOIS DE GOULOT

Bois Carré

BLUE
LINE

BOIS DE GOULOT
2/KOSVAL

Count's
Wood

13ᵀᴴ
Bden

14ᵀᴴ Bn

Hill 135

29ᵀᴴ Bn

28ᵀᴴ Bn

Thélus
Wood

31ˢᵀ Bn

Thélus

Thélus Trench

6ᵀᴴ
Bden

Türke Graben

les Tilleuls

Zwischen Stellung

GERMAN FRONT LINE

RED
LINE

BLACK
LINE

ALLIED FRONT LINE

British
XVII Corps

Zwischen Stellung

26ᵀᴴ Bn

24ᵀᴴ Bn

25ᵀᴴ Bn

21ˢᵀ Bn

19ᵀᴴ Bn

18ᵀᴴ
Bn

GERMAN FRONT LINE

CANADIAN FRONT LINE

Écurie

3ᴿᴰ
Cdn Div

5ᵀᴴ
Bde

2ᴺᴰ
Cdn Div

14ᵀᴴ
Bde

1ˢᵀ
Cdn Div

Neuville
St. Vaast

250   0   250   500   750
METRES

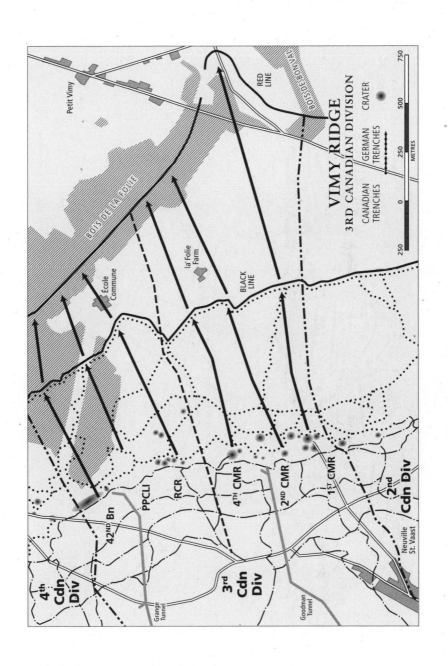

VIMY RIDGE
3RD CANADIAN DIVISION

CANADIAN TRENCHES .... GERMAN TRENCHES .... CRATER

250   0   250   500   750
METRES

Petit Vimy

BOIS DE LA FOLIE

BOIS DE BONVAL

RED LINE

École Commune

la Folie Farm

BLACK LINE

4th Cdn Div

42ND Bn

PPCLI

RCR

4TH CMR

2ND CMR

1ST CMR

3rd Cdn Div

Grange Tunnel

Goodman Tunnel

Neuville St. Vaast

2nd Cdn Div

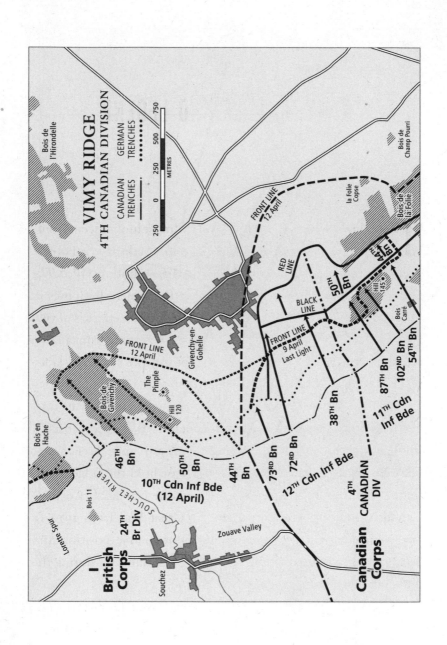

VIMY RIDGE
4TH CANADIAN DIVISION

CANADIAN TRENCHES
GERMAN TRENCHES

METRES
250 0 250 500 750

Bois de l'Hirondelle

Bois de Champ Pourri

FRONT LINE
12 April

la Folie Copse

Bois de la Folie

RED LINE

BLACK LINE

50TH Bn

41ST Bn

Hill 145

Bois Carré

FRONT LINE
9 April
Last Light

FRONT LINE
12 April

Givenchy-en-Gohelle

The Pimple

Hill 120

Bois de Givenchy

38TH Bn

73RD Bn

72ND Bn

87TH Bn

102ND Bn

54TH Bn

11TH Cdn
Inf Bde

12TH Cdn Inf Bde

4TH
CANADIAN
DIV

Canadian
Corps

Bois en Hache

46TH Bn

50TH Bn

44TH Bn

10TH Cdn Inf Bde
(12 April)

SOUCHEZ RIVER

Bois 11

Lorette Spur

24TH
Br Div

British
Corps

Zouave Valley

Souchez

CHAPTER I

VIMY: BATTLE AND LEGEND

The Vimy Memorial, with its white, almost luminescent stone, stands on the ramparts of a ridge in northeastern France, a site of mass killing and myth-making. In a painting called *The Ghosts of Vimy Ridge* that hangs in the Parliament Buildings in Ottawa, the twin pylons reach into the night. The effect is of two swords raised, or perhaps the tip of a cross emerging from a large crossbeam. From the east, the view captures the shattered landscape of mud and shell craters that leads up to the memorial's stone wall, which appears immovable and permanent, a bulwark against invaders and time. Returning to the memorial are the ghosts of soldiers. They are Canadian, although many more French and German soldiers died trying to capture or hold the ridge, more than 150,000. Yet in April 1917, it was the Canadian Corps—Canada's 100,000-strong army in the Great War from 1914 to 1918—that assaulted the seemingly impregnable position and delivered victory. It cost close to 3,600 Canadian lives during the four-day battle that raged from April 9 to 12.

Painted in 1929 by Australian artist Will Longstaff, *The Ghosts of Vimy Ridge* depicts the memorial seven years before it was completed and unveiled. In the foreground, and surrounding the memorial, is a lunar landscape of death and destruction from April 1917.[1] Longstaff painted the wasteland of the battle, but combined it with the future stone memorial of 1936, and he populated it with the spectral figures of fallen soldiers. The past bleeds into the present and interlaces through the future. Vimy has been reframed, reconstructed, and reimagined over time. The presence of the soldiers' ghosts symbolizes the constant return of Canadians to this site of memory and meaning that haunts our history, culture, and society.

Lieutenant Edward Sawell of the 20th Battalion, from Millgrove, Ontario, wrote in his diary on April 9, 1917, the first day of the Vimy Battle, "Canadian soldiers this day, did more to give Canada a real standing among nations of the world than any previous single act in Canadian history."[2] Only days after the battle, Percy Willmot, a Cape Breton staff sergeant with the 25th Battalion, echoed Sawell, writing home, "This is the battlefield that will go down in history as the magnificent achievement of the Canadian Corps."[3] Sawell would survive the war while Willmot never made it home to his family, but, for them both, Vimy resonated as more than just a battlefield achievement. They were certain that the battle would live on in Canadian history. Over the last 100 years, Vimy has become part of the fabric and fable of the nation, though some generations have invested more energy in the symbolism of this historical moment than others, and it resonates far more strongly in English Canada than in French.

"THE CANADIAN CORPS WAS TO WIN other outstanding victories, but none so caught the popular imagination or were so peculiarly identified with Canada as the taking of Vimy Ridge. As is usually the case in such matters, the popular instinct was absolutely right. No matter what constitutional historians may say, it was on Easter Monday, April 9, 1917, and not on any other date, that Canada became a nation."[4] Historian Donald Goodspeed wrote these words in 1969, and he was not alone in believing that Vimy marked, to use a widespread phrase, the "birth of the nation." Yet how did a four-day battle at the midpoint of the war, which had little strategic impact on the larger direction of the Allied war effort, become elevated to a national symbol of Canada's war effort and the nation's very beginning?

This book has two goals: to examine the Battle of Vimy Ridge in detail and then to unravel the constructed legend of Vimy during the 100 years that followed it. The Battle of Vimy Ridge was the most carefully planned operation the Canadians fought during the war. The ridge was the site of several titanic battles, starting in October 1914, and a place where hundreds of thousands of French and German soldiers had been killed or maimed in attempting to capture or hold the critically important geographical position. The 7-kilometre Vimy Ridge protected the coal-rich area around Lens that the Germans occupied and desperately needed to retain to supply their war effort. When the Canadians arrived at the foot of the western side of the ridge in October 1916, Vimy was a vast desert of shell craters and rotting corpses. The Canadians faced one of the most formidable positions on the Western Front. Under the command of British general Sir Julian Byng, the four Canadian divisions, with significant support from British engineers, gunners, and soldiers, prepared for the battle in April 1917. The assault on Vimy was part of a larger British push, the Arras offensive, which was, in turn, a supporting attack for the French Artois offensive to the south. Through meticulous preparation, training, determination, and sacrifice, the Canadians succeeded where the French armies had failed in the past. The Corps' victory solidified its reputation among allies and opponents as an elite fighting force.

But Vimy is more than a battle. The unanswered question of Vimy is how the battle became a focal point of remembrance and an icon of Canadian identity. Why do Canadians remember Vimy instead of the 1915 Battle of Second Ypres or the 1918 Hundred Days campaign? The former was the first major engagement where the Canadians faced chlorine gas and stopped the overwhelming German forces; the latter was hailed at the time as the most important series of battles by the Canadian Corps. To pull back the gaze further, why do Canadians celebrate Vimy more intensely than they mark battles of the Second World War, such as the Battle of the Atlantic, D-Day, or the liberation of the Dutch in 1945? How do we make sense of the proud Canadians in 2007 who returned to Vimy Ridge wearing hats and T-shirts that proclaimed "Vimy: Birth of the Nation." No one would attribute that origin story to the battles of Ridgeway, Paardeberg, or Ortona, to Normandy, Kapyong, or the Medak Pocket. Vimy is unique.

The value that Canadians attach to the battle and the memorial is forever linked to the Great War. For many English Canadians the war marked Canada's coming of age, as its primary land formation, the Canadian Corps, spearheaded a number of Allied offensives and delivered hard-fought victories. The war was perceived differently in French Canada, which had a distinct culture and identity, and by many of the two million immigrants who had come to Canada since the late nineteenth century. Nonetheless, the war was an important transformative event for all. The enormous exertions on the home front saw millions of shells produced for the war effort, crops grown by farmers to feed the Allied nations, and unprecedented patriotic support of the war effort and the soldiers. Major social changes, from industrialization, income tax, and enfranchisement for women to deeper government intervention into the lives of Canadians, were ushered in by the war. Old certainties were swept away.

Death and division plagued the nation. The wrenching losses of life brought grief to every part of the country. Despite the voluntary enlistment of hundreds of thousands of citizens in the first three years of the war, the terrible fighting overseas demanded even more men to keep shattered units up to strength. By 1916, as recruitment faltered, and as fathers and sons were cut down by the thousands in the trenches, life became harder in the Dominion. Canadians turned on one another looking for enemies in their midst. Prime Minister Sir Robert Borden's government's enactment of conscription in the summer of 1917, and the dirty and divisive tactics used to win the December 1917 election over the issue, nearly tore the country apart along linguistic, regional, and class lines. At the war's end, survivors sought to sift through the ashes to make meaning of the horrendous fighting that had killed 66,000 Canadians from a nation of fewer than 8 million.

The idea of Vimy fed into a postwar narrative of the Great War as a transformative event for Canada. At the same time, the extreme exertion demanded during the war effort by patriotic leaders had also damaged the social fabric of the country. That damage was downplayed over time, and Vimy—a victory involving Canadians from across the country—became part of the story of the war as a major event of change. Yet this transformation did not happen at the end of the battle, on April 12, 1917, or even at the end of the war, on November 11, 1918.

The Vimy legend—the conflation of the battle, the ridge's landscape, and the Canadian National Vimy Memorial (as it is officially known)—was created by veterans, educators, writers, historians, and politicians. It took years for the idea to fully emerge in social memory, fed and sustained by commemorative events and the memorial's construction. Vimy, like all legends, is a layered skein of stories, myths, wishful thinking, and conflicting narratives.

Vimy has become an important touchstone that Canadians of multiple generations have employed to tell stories about the country. The idea of Vimy has come to signify Canadian martial strength and unity of purpose. The capture of the seemingly impregnable ridge by Canadians from all regions is a built-in unity story. Vimy has been described as a key event in Canadian history, even the origin of the modern country, but what that means in 2017 is different from what it meant in 1992 or 1967, in 1936 or 1917. Vimy's meaning has shifted with each generation, but it has usually been an important symbol. The Vimy idea is admittedly not universally accepted. Our heroes and legends are rarely all things to all people. Canada is a country—like most—that places little stock in its history, teaching it badly, embracing it little, feeding it only episodically. As Canada developed over time, we cast aside much that grounded us in the past; yet there are some ideas, myths, and icons that persistently carry the weight of nationhood. Vimy is one of them.

"This memorial is not a monument to the capture of Vimy Ridge only, or any other individual victory," wrote Colonel D.C. Unwin Simson, a wartime engineer responsible for reclaiming the Vimy site in the 1920s. "It is a memorial to a nation."[5] We need to understand why so many Canadians think that Vimy is where Canada was born as a modern nation, or wish that to be true. Canada came into being in 1867, a full fifty years before Vimy. In order to understand the heady ideas that underpin the story of Vimy, we should acknowledge that the evolving idea of Vimy is part of the unfolding narrative of Canada and Canadians throughout the past 100 years. Vimy is a battleground of remembrance and forgetting, of constitution and reconstitution, of myth-making and nation-forging. It is a place of past sorrows and future hopes, at once tied to the Great War and to the larger history of a Canada determining its own course and place in the world.

CHAPTER 2

VIMY BATTLEGROUND

The Shield of Arras, Vimy Ridge, runs along the western edge of the Douai plain in northeastern France. Protecting the coal fields of Lens and the ancient city of Arras, Vimy Ridge rises to a height of 110 metres from the chalk plain, offering a commanding view of the flat and low countryside in all directions. At 7 kilometres long and situated on a northwest–southeast axis, the ridge is a natural breakwater. From the south, emerging from the lowlands, the climb is gradual, but it ascends more sharply towards the northern tip. The highest point is Hill 145—its name indicating the number of metres above sea level—where the Canadian memorial stands to this day.

Vimy Ridge was fought over from the first months of the Great War and the bleached bones of tens of thousands of slain soldiers littered its cratered slopes. The ridge was fiercely contested because it was a commanding geographic feature on the Western Front. Whichever army held it had an enormous advantage over the force at its base.

The soldiers of the Kaiser's army had swept to victory up and around Vimy Ridge in October 1914 as the French were thrown back. The French Tenth Army of six divisions launched its first sustained counterattack against the Germans atop Vimy Ridge in December 1914, in the aftermath of British, French, and Belgian forces holding off a massive offensive in the Flanders region to the east of Ypres in late November 1914. It was bayonets and bravado for the French, but they had to pass through the storm of machine guns of the 1st Bavarian Reserve Corps. The six French divisions were turned back, suffering more than 7,700 casualties.[1]

Another French campaign, known as the Artois offensive, was launched over the spring of 1915, fought in conjunction with British attacks to the north around Aubers Ridge and Festubert. For six costly weeks in the summer, from May 9 to June 18, General Victor d'Urbal's Tenth Army attacked near Arras, with the goal of capturing Vimy Ridge and the surrounding region. The Moroccan Division drove some 4.5 kilometres into the enemy lines on May 9, surging up Vimy Ridge and capturing it.[2] But gaining the ridge was different from holding it. The Moroccan Division, consisting of French troops serving in Morocco and large contingents of the French Foreign Legion, was overextended, as French divisions on the right flank had been unable to keep up with the advance as they faced a hail of long-range gunfire. The Germans mounted fierce counterattacks, and within a few days they had driven the Moroccan Division from the ridge. A second, smaller assault on June 16 met with little success, for the Germans had used their time to strengthen their defensive positions. The French suffered a staggering 300,000 casualties, of which 100,000 were killed; the Germans toll was 80,000 killed, wounded, missing, and captured.[3] However, the French attacks ate into the German buffer zone to the west of Vimy, including capturing the strong-point of Neuville–St. Vaast, forcing the Germans to dig in along the ridge. In being forced back to the ridge, the Germans lost the advantage of a defence-in-depth, a series of trenches that dissipated the attackers' blows.

Nine more French divisions attacked in September 1915, and the British forces up the line supported the offensive with their push to Loos. The British failed to capture much terrain, losing some 11,000 British and Indian troops, and the French had only marginally more success. In more devastating fighting, with attack and counterattack, the French suffered under the fall of shells directed by defenders on the ridge. Hounded from the field fortifications, the French left many dead on the battlefield, with total losses of another 40,000 or so bloodied and maimed *poilus*. The Germans, too, had suffered heavily, although they retained the prize. A year and a few months later, when the Canadians arrived at the site of mass execution, Lieutenant-Colonel Joseph Hayes of the 85th Battalion would write, "There is perhaps no place in France where as many men have been killed to the square yard as on this sloping ground."[4]

THE CANADIANS WERE WILD MEN FROM a frozen dominion: tough and resilient, and inured to hardship. Or at least that was their reputation. The prevailing British perception fed this idea, based on literature, travel accounts, and adventure stories that focused obsessively on Canada's "great North-West."[5] Some of this myth-making came from within Canada too. British-born Canadian journalist Arthur Hawkes declared in 1910, "If this country has got any great contribution to make in the future of the Empire . . . it is going to be made because we can show the Old Country that we can raise better men here than she can send us, and it is being done every day."[6]

The 1911 Census had revealed a population of about 7.2 million Canadians, with some 250,000 immigrants arriving each year. Three years later, the Dominion of Canada, fewer than 8 million strong, was spread an astonishing 9.5 million square kilometres across nine provinces—although like a snake's skin, thinly along the southern border with the United States. Canada was also firmly a British nation, taking its political traditions and culture from across the Atlantic, as well as having its foreign policy decided in London and not Ottawa. But not all Canadians embraced Britain. Many French speakers, who formed about 30 percent of the country's population, as well as some of the two million immigrants who had arrived since the last decade in the nineteenth century, believed that Canada would be better off on its own. However, there was no Canadian passport and all were subjects of the British Empire, even though there was an emerging understanding of what it meant to be Canadian. Geography, history, and culture were slowly shaping national characteristics. The process had been slow, and according to historian and public affairs commentator W.S. Wallace, who wrote after the war, "that Canadian national feeling [was] a phenomenon of very recent growth."[7] The creation of a small Department of External Affairs (1909) and navy (1910) had been identifiable signposts in Canada's gaining gradual control over its destiny. At the same time, Canadians defined themselves by what they were not. Despite the close proximity to the Americans and increased trade across the border, most Canadians saw their country as being very different from the republic to the south. The Americans, with their rampant democracy and corruption, with their civil war and their racism, with their swagger and their search for the almighty dollar, were sneered at by many moralizing Canadians waving the Union Jack.

BRITAIN HAD GONE TO WAR ON August 4, 1914, after Europe slid into savagery. The assassination of the Austrian archduke Franz Ferdinand on June 28 sparked war between the Hapsburg Empire of Austria and Hungary against the meddlesome Serbian nation that had supported the archduke's assassins. A series of alliances between Germany and Austria had led to emboldened action, while Russia felt it had to support fellow Slavic nation Serbia in its uneven fight, as well as re-exert its strength in European affairs. A misreading of opponents, be they the intermarried royals or their advisers, led to a headlong rush to war, with little time for diplomatic solutions. Few called for sober second thought before it was too late to reverse the mobilization of massive armies. France, ever fearful of a strengthened Germany that was an industrial and demographic juggernaut, and desirous to restore its honour and lost territory after its defeat in the 1870–1871 Franco-Prussian War, took the opportunity to stand by its ally Russia and oppose Germany. The Germans, under the direction of the maladjusted and at times seemingly mad Kaiser, who sought glory and prestige at the expense of the other great powers, first supported Austria-Hungary; then, when his last-minute effort to avoid war failed, he ordered a rapid mobilization of the army. The invasion of neutral Belgium allowed his forces to sweep down on the French in what was dubbed the Schlieffen Plan. The Kaiser and his generals hoped to secure a lightning victory within six weeks, before turning to the east and confronting the lumbering Russian bear. Like toppling dominoes, the invasion of Belgium brought Britain into the war, supposedly to uphold an eighty-five-year-old treaty guaranteeing Belgium's neutrality, but really to ensure that Germany did not humiliate France and become the sole superpower of Europe. With Britain's declaration of war on August 4,

Canada, as a dominion within the Empire, was automatically at war. But it would be Canadians who chose the extent of their support, and young men would decide if they wished to serve in a voluntary expeditionary force.

Tens of thousands of Canadians rushed to the recruiting stations to serve King and country. With a tiny standing army, Canada initially created its fighting force out of the existing militia units—albeit with new numbered battalions—that were stationed across the country and manned by civilian-soldiers. Prime Minister Sir Robert Borden had decreed that this would be a voluntary army, and that conscription would not be invoked to force men to serve against their will. There were more than enough volunteers in 1914 for everyone to expect that Borden would never have to break his word.

The First Contingent of 31,000 Canadians to go overseas were 60 percent British-born. As the war progressed, more Canadian-born served, eventually reaching about 51 percent.[8] English Canada contributed far more men in numbers and proportionality than French Canada, which, after centuries of isolation in North America, did not have the same emotional links to Britain or France.[9] There were also fewer French-Canadian militia units, the formations from which the First Contingent initially drew upon for much of its strength, and the army was a unilingual formation with few French-speaking officers.[10] All of this deterred enlistment in Quebec. French-speaking Canadians did serve—at least 14,100 out of 300,000 by April 1917, with about half coming from Quebec and half coming from other provinces.[11] More French- and English-speaking Quebeckers enlisted than that number, but the data is inconclusive, with the numbers ranging from about 32,000 to 78,000. However, many of these men were

Anglo-Quebeckers from Montreal, Canada's largest city and the centre of finance at the time.[12] While it is impossible to determine an exact number of French Canadians who served in uniform, there is no doubt it was far below that of English Canadians. About 4,000 First Nations men joined the colours, as did thousands of new Canadians or Canadians who are now labelled visible minorities, especially after racist restrictions were loosened in 1916.[13]

When the Canadians arrived in England in October they were greeted by thousands of grateful British citizens who saw the new world supporting Mother Britain. Yet there was also widespread disappointment that the Canadians were not all "savages," dressed in beaver pelts and arrayed in war paint. After a young boy was visibly disappointed that Gunner Frank Ferguson and his comrades were not Indigenous warriors, Ferguson remarked, "I suppose he shared the popular idea that all Canadians were redskins."[14] The Canadians were also known to play up their supposed frontier heritage of being backwoodsmen and hunters. Some came even to believe in it. As one Canadian veteran writing in a postwar novel was to claim, "No anemic men, these, drawn from office stools or shop counters. No. But men whose clear eyes have that look in them that comes only in the eyes of those whose horizons have been wide. Men of the prairies, of the mountains, of the timberlands. Canadians."[15] Sir Arthur Currie, who would rise to command the Canadian Corps, wrote after the war that "All Canadians are pioneers themselves, or are the immediate descendants of pioneers. . . . The severities of our climate eliminate the unfit."[16] This army of cow-punchers, prize-fighters, and trackers had all, supposedly, been raised with a rifle in hand.[17] In reality, most Canadians came from the big cities. In March 1916, statistics revealed that only about 6.5 percent of the Canadian Expeditionary

Force (CEF) were farmers or ranchers, while 18.5 percent were white-collar workers, and 65 percent were manual labourers.[18] The numbers changed during the war, but the force always had more workers than farmers or hunters, by a wide margin.

One of the distinguishing features of the Canadians was their pride in coming from a less class-conscious society. At the start of the war, many of the soldiers called their officers by their first names, an unforgivable sin in the British army. Yet men who had known their officers through work or church found it unnatural to stand on formalities. The British never quite got used to this, and even though the first-name references became infrequent in the CEF as the war progressed, the Canadians took pride in highlighting their egalitarian ways. In this regard, they were like the Australians in attempting to carve out a separate sense of identity from the British—though they were British subjects and, almost to a man, proud of their link to the British Empire.[19] This Canadian identity required some sophistry, moreover, since about half of the CEF by the end of the war, and more in the first two years, were British-born. Now, some men had come to Canada as children and were, by any stretch of the imagination Canadian, but many had been in the country for only a few years. Unified under the maple leaf cap badges and proud regimental traditions, British men were incorporated into the fighting services, and all were seen as Canadian. The Canadians were particularly chippy about being mistaken for British soldiers, and there were plenty of anecdotes and stories of Canucks going out of their way to distinguish themselves through exaggerated slang and ill-discipline.[20] These accounts were played up in Canadian wartime propaganda, from newspaper stories to instant histories, and further cemented the creation of a unique identity.

THE CANADIAN DIVISION ARRIVED ON THE Western Front in February 1915 and was engaged, two months later, in the Battle of Second Ypres on April 22. There, the untried Canadians faced the first significant chlorine gas attacks in the history of warfare. They even counterattacked the advancing German troops when two French divisions wavered and fled in the face of the death cloud. The four-day Canadian part in the battle cost over 6,000 killed, wounded, and captured, but, according to Canadian Talbot Papineau, a Rhodes Scholar and a decorated infantryman, Second Ypres would become part of Canada's "glorious history." Despite the horrible losses, "These may be the birth pains of our nationality. Great movements are in progress."[21]

The Canadians fought at the costly slaughter of Festubert in May 1915 and then through a quiet summer of trench warfare. Another Canadian division arrived at the front to join the 1st Canadian Infantry Division and form, in September 1915, the Canadian Corps. Eventually there would be four Canadian infantry divisions grouped in the Corps, which was a homogeneous,

There were few photographs of the Battle of Second Ypres in April 1915, but this drawing captures the chlorine gas attack unleashed against the Canadian Division.

semi-permanent, national formation. Unlike British divisions, which were moved freely from corps to corps to meet operational requirements, the Canadian Corps was not to be broken up piece-meal. Canadian politicians and soldiers fought for this, and Sir Douglas Haig, the British commander-in-chief from late 1915, understood over time that the self-governing dominions were not like colonial troops. Brigadier General Ox Webber, a professional British soldier and senior staff officer in the Canadian Corps, remarked, "The Canadian Corps was an organization. It had life; there was a family feeling present. British Corps was a machine to supply the necessary formations . . . the British Corps had no life."[22]

The Corps needed a commander, and Sir Julian Byng was a rising star in the British army. The fifty-four-year-old general looked the part—a wiry man, with a campaigner's lined face, fierce gaze, and piercing blue eyes. As the seventh son of the Earl of Strafford, Byng was a contemporary of Haig and the other senior army and corps commanders. The professional soldier had fought with distinction in the South African War, and had passed through the staff college. A friend to the King, who cheerfully called him "Bungo," he was generally easy-going, especially in relation to some of the martinets who rose to senior command in the British army. Byng made his name by organizing the difficult but remark-ably successful retreat from the Gallipoli campaign in January 1916.[23] While few forge their reputation in overseeing evacuations, all acknowledged that the Allied withdrawal from Gallipoli could scarcely have gone better. Byng cajoled and enthused, and crafted a wily deception plan that allowed much of the materiel and the forces to get away under the noses of the Turks.

Following Gallipoli, Byng was given command of XVII Corps on the Western Front, and seemed to be in line for promotion to

*Sir Julian Byng, the
Canadian Corps'
commander from
May 1916 to June 1917.*

an army command. Having saved the Gallipoli forces, Byng was
tasked in May 1916 with saving the floundering Canadian Corps
that had lost the Battle of St. Eloi the previous month. A bewildered Byng was informed by Haig that he would command the
now three-division-strong Canadian Corps. Byng complained,
"Why am I sent the Canadians? I don't even know a Canadian."[24]
Byng was, however, likely familiar with the political tentacles that
snaked all the way from Ottawa, and especially the mercurial and
meddlesome minister of militia, Sam Hughes, who had made life
miserable for the previous corps commander, Lieutenant-General
E.A.H. Alderson.

General Byng arrived at the Canadian Corps in late May,
where its three divisions were dug in to the southern portion of
the Ypres salient. Canadian infantry battalions were holding the
high ground around Hill 62 and Mount Sorrel in a semicircular

series of trenches. The front was quiet, but the Württemberg XIII Corps opposite the Canadians appeared to be preparing for an assault. Byng barely had time to settle in and meet his staff before he faced his first battle as commander of the Canadians.

When the Germans struck behind a hurricane artillery bombardment on June 2, the 3rd Canadian Division was blown off the ridge. Shellfire tore up the trenches, dismembered the garrison, and buried soldiers alive in their shallow dugouts. "The ground shook like jelly," wrote thirty-eight-year-old Lawrence Rogers, who survived the battle but not the war.[25] When the German infantry surged forward, the shattered front-line units of the 1st and 4th Canadian Mounted Rifles (CMR) were swept aside. One of the Canadians observed, "It was a day of obliteration."[26]

The disorganized and stunned 3rd Division, which had its commanding officer killed in the bombardment, launched two desperate attacks on June 2 and 3, but made little ground against the Germans for the loss of about 3,750 casualties. A desperate Byng was planning another counter-strike when his most experienced divisional commander, Major-General Arthur Currie, intervened. The commander of the 1st Division offered another plan.

Born in 1875, and forty years old in 1916, Currie had a smooth, babyish face with large jowls. Tall at almost six feet, three inches, he was overweight and looked unsoldierly in his uniform, with his pear-shaped body seeming to burst from his trousers and battle dress. Nor was Currie particularly charismatic. He sympathized with the soldiers under his command, but he had a hard time finding the words to put them at ease. Part of the challenge was that he was a fierce disciplinarian. Nonetheless, he had proven himself in battle and although he was quiet, even a bit shy, he had a good mind for modern warfare. And he abhorred casualties.

The big general tried to find ways to ration his soldiers' lives on the Western Front, though this was not always apparent to the men in the trenches, who could only see death and destruction around them.

At Mount Sorrel, Currie argued that the Canadians should hold off attacking again in another rapid strike until a concentration of artillery guns could be brought forward for a prepared assault. Byng was wary of leaving the high ground in enemy hands, but he took Currie's counsel. Over the next ten days, Byng and Currie gathered all the guns available—218 in total, with nearly half of them heavy calibre—and laid down punishing fire, hurling 75,000 shells at the enemy.[27] In the early hours of June 13, Canadian and British guns unleashed a heavy bombardment on the German lines and four front-line battalions routed the enemy. The Canadians paid a heavy price to reclaim the ground, with 8,000 total casualties in less than two weeks. But Byng and the senior staff had evidence of the battle-winning combination of artillery and infantry working closely together to smash and suppress enemy defences in order to give the ground-pounders a chance in battle.

"I KNOW NOT WHERE TO START," wrote Gunner William Ball of the 37th Battery in his diary upon arriving at the Somme. "The ground around here is a mass of shellholes some big enough for a house. . . . Tonight we occupied our hole with a dead German. . . . The firing is continuous."[28] The Canadian Corps was lucky to have missed the first two months of the Somme campaign, although the Newfoundland Regiment, serving with the 29th British Division, attacked on July 1. They were shot down in sickening numbers, with the regiment all but annihilated at Beaumont Hamel.

French troops under shellfire on the Somme. French and British armies mounted an offensive on the Somme to drive back the Germans. They failed to break through, and the battles from July 1, 1916, were an attritional slaughter.

Recovering from the losses of Mount Sorrel, the Canadian Corps, three divisions strong at about 60,000 soldiers, and with a fourth division soon to arrive, marched to the Somme in late August, arriving at intervals. Infantry formations achieved a significant victory at Courcelette on September 15 behind a heavy artillery bombardment, although seven supporting tanks did little to assist other than to terrify the enemy. A final two-battalion assault on Courcelette by the Nova Scotians of the 25th Battalion and the French Canadians of the 22nd Battalion secured the burned-out village. Infantryman Percy Willmot wrote to his sister about the 25th Battalion's heavy casualties, observing, "the marvel of it all is that there are any left to tell the tale."[29] The operation on the 15th cost the Canadians some 7,230 killed, wounded, and taken prisoner.[30] There were no bloodless victories on the Western Front.

The capture of Courcelette and the surrounding trenches brought considerable recognition to Byng's corps, with British general Hubert Gough noting that the capture of the terrain "across the open without any jumping-off place in the nature of trenches is without parallel in the history of the present campaign."[31] But subsequent fighting to overrun a number of fortified enemy trenches to the north of Courcelette met with little success and high casualties. The Battle of Thiepval Ridge on September 26 gained little ground, as did the failed assaults on the heavily fortified Regina Trench on October 1 and 8. Almost 20,000 men in the three Canadian divisions were killed or wounded in the vicious fighting up to mid-October before the Canadian Corps was relieved from the line. Into the breach went the newly arrived 4th Division, which fought with a British corps from October to mid-November, gained a few blasted trenches, and added 4,300 more men to the butcher's bill.

The paralyzed Somme front left hundreds of thousands of dead in its wake. No force—German, British, French, or Canadian—was able to mount a sustained operation that did not lead to crippling casualties or that yielded gains beyond a single day's thrust. On the Somme, enemy front-line defences were smashed by hundreds of thousands of shells, but it was difficult for the guns to register on enemy targets as they fired in the muddy conditions and without suitable forward or aerial observers to correct the fall of the shells. And even after bombardments, there were always survivors who emerged from deep dugouts carved in the chalk, ready to man the guns. Barbed wire was often uncut, channelling the infantry into kill zones. Too often an attacking force lost half its strength simply by leaving its own trenches, climbing from the safety of the subterranean bunkers into No Man's Land, and then crossing the shell-cratered wastes. "It may be taken for granted that in attacking the front system of the enemy's trenches, the first three lines will be wiped out; the fourth may reach the enemy's second line; the fifth may take it," wrote one British doctrinal pamphlet.[32] Such tactics and doctrinal predictions were less than inspiring for the man at the sharp end. Poor communication beyond the original trenches, with telephone wires cut or runners killed, left commanders with little insight into the unfolding battle. Isolated Canadians, low on ammunition and grenades, and lacking reinforcements, were relentlessly attacked by surging German forces and driven back out of the trenches. With a million Allied and German losses on the Somme, new ways of fighting were required if the allies were to break through the enemy trench systems.

THE CANADIANS ARRIVED AT THE VIMY front in staggered marches starting in late October 1916. They soon occupied a line that ran from about 4 kilometres north of Arras to 4 kilometres northwest of Lens, about 15 kilometres in length. The Canadians' entire front was dominated by the Germans on Vimy Ridge, who looked down into their trenches. The smell of corruption pervaded the area. One Canadian gunner, William Ball, wrote in his diary about the hulking ridge: "Never saw anything like it before. I think it is called Vimy Ridge, or the Valley of Sorrows as sixty thousand French men were supposed to have been lost here."[33] More were killed and thousands still lay on the battlefield. With some 430,000 casualties suffered by the French and Germans in this area, and more than 150,000 of those killed, there remained thousands of unburied corpses and fragments of bodies. The shell craters were filled with foul, murky water, and many contained the rotting remains of the fallen who had dragged themselves into the depths and never emerged.

"Vimy was a huge grey mountainous mass of mud," recounted Sergeant Robert Kentner. "It appeared as though nothing had ever or ever could live upon its surface. The absolute negation of beauty, a monument of wickedness, most distorted and repulsive."[34] The ridge rose steadily, culminating in Hill 145. In the centre of the Canadian lines was the ruined village of Neuville–St. Vaast, where soldiers took refuge in shelters and basements. It was marbled with underground tunnels, many dug by New Zealanders starting in May 1916, and other subterranean labyrinths. To the north of the ridge was another dominating piece of ground, the 135-metre Pimple. From there, the Germans perched up high above the Allied lines could strike mercilessly. Harwood Steele, an officer from the 27th Battalion and a staff officer at Vimy, recounted that the Canadian trenches were in a low part of the terrain and "heavily waterlogged; with the Germans looking straight down on it and giving us hell with artillery and trench-mortar fire every day."[35] One of those killed was forty-year-old Francis Cumming, an infantryman in the 46th Battalion and a farmer and father of five. He had enlisted two years earlier, after a freak hailstorm had destroyed his crop near Yorkton in Saskatchewan.[36] A shell took his life in a snowstorm in the trenches opposite the Pimple on January 3, 1917.

THE WINTER OF 1916–1917 WAS THE coldest in Europe in more than twenty years. Hard black frost covered everything. Shivering and shaking, men waited in the trenches for something to happen. "The defence of freedom is not so much dangerous as excessively onerous," wrote an Edmontonian to his mother. "It does not afford me with the remotest opportunity of killing a Hun. Instead, it has converted me into a beast of burden; when I am not bearing loads I am digging, digging, digging. The battlefield is my garden."[37] Soldiers fought boredom as they were stationed in the front lines, and then rotated to the rear and back again. The tours included about six days at the front, another week in the rearward trenches, and a week out of the line before returning to the firing line again. Corporal Charles Cameron, a six-foot-one, 190-pound tough-as-nails Highlander with the 16th Battalion, wrote of the poor bloody infantry's plight, "If we had to go over the top in some big coup then let all the artillery on earth blast forth, but to have thousands and thousands of men living in dirt and slime while batteries of artillery wasted fortunes in endeavouring to blast them to hell with no particular object of any magnitude in view, that was utter nonsense."[38]

When the 4th Canadian Infantry Division joined Byng's Canadian Corps before the end of 1916, the formation rose to a strength of close to 100,000 men. The four infantry divisions remained about 20,000 strong each, and another 20,000 men in uniform were in specialized arms controlled by the corps headquarters, everything from heavy artillery brigades to logistical formations. The post-Somme period was a crucial one for the entire British Expeditionary Force (BEF) and the Canadian Corps. Byng and his senior officers ordered that all commands, down to the battalion level, analyze and report on the fighting experience from the Somme. These reports made grim reading, but it was crucial to know what had happened on the battlefield so that it could be addressed and reformed.[39] All of the divisional commanders encouraged their subordinates to compile lessons-learned documents. Survivors' interviews indicated that much of the failure stemmed from the artillery's inability to cut the barbed wire, from sporadic communication from front to rear, from poor coordination of the infantry and the artillery, and from inadequate time for planning operations. At the tactical level, the importance of carrying extra grenades and ammunition into enemy trenches was emphasized, as the attackers were often cut off there by the German counter-barrage that landed between them and their own trenches, and had to fight on against the rising tide of enemy assaults. The clearing of wounded, the use of weapons in the attack and defence, and even the lack of pre-battle training, rehearsals, and issuing of maps were all highlighted.[40] Things would be different in the next battle.

Byng absorbed the tough teachings generated within his Canadian Corps, but he also knew the British and French were engaging in the same painful process. He ordered his most trusted general, 1st Division commander Arthur Currie, to join a group of British officers on a study tour. Currie knew what he did not know, and he was always keen to learn. After observing and interrogating the French, Currie came back to the Corps with new lessons. He was impressed by the improved French infantry tactics that had emphasized a devolution in command to empower junior officers and non-commissioned officers (NCOs). If officers (majors, captains, and lieutenants) were knocked out in battle, the lower ranks (sergeants, corporals, and privates) were to continue on to their objectives. For this decentralization to work, however, more trust had to be placed in the soldiers, and they needed to be trained to attack around areas of resistance. Added firepower in the form of grenades and machine guns would help. Currie also noted the evolutions in artillery tactics, and the importance of closely integrating the infantry and the gunners to craft an effective tactical union to overcome the German defences.[41] One of Byng's strengths was his willingness to benefit from his wide contacts throughout the British army, from whom he learned evolving lessons of battle. He was also very good at harnessing the talents of his bright subordinates; he studied Currie's report, understood its importance, and ordered that it be implemented throughout the Corps.

BOTH THE FRENCH AND GERMANS HAD been bled white at Verdun, with some 700,000 casualties, but when the battle had staggered to a standstill in November 1916, it was the French who had refused to break and the Germans who had been unable to claim a victory. That same month, the Allies hammered out a new strategy for taking the war to the Central Powers. The French commander-in-chief, Joseph Joffre, had stiffened the backbone of his military comrades and encouraged them all to strike at once: the Russians agreed to attack in the east, the Italians against the Austrians, and the British and French in the west. With fights on several fronts, it would be difficult for the Germans to move their reserves to counter each offensive.

But less than a month later, Joffre had been removed from power. "Papa Joffre" had been a force in his day and was elevated to national hero after the Battle of the Marne saved Paris in September 1914. But he was too old for the war, unable to adapt to the changing nature of warfare, too wedded to a strategy of attrition, and unwilling to communicate his ideas to French politicians. The French already had hundreds of thousands of dead and were well on their way to the total of 1.3 million Frenchmen who would eventually be killed by the time of the Armistice.[42]

The new French commander knew where he wished to strike. Robert Nivelle had proven a smart and aggressive general during the Verdun campaign. He put his faith in the cannon's mouth. He had punished the Germans at Verdun by massing artillery fire and smashing the enemy lines, just as the Germans had done to the French at the start of the nine-month-long battle, and he had captured the symbolically important Fort Douaumont. In contrast to the other drab generals, both French and British, Nivelle was dashing, wildly optimistic, and able to speak coherently to both France's and Britain's skittish politicians. For a war-weary French population, he offered hope and a way forward. But his bluster verged on lies, and he had no more understanding of how to break the deadlock of the Western Front than any other French, British, or German general. Nivelle was, nonetheless, the new man and he seemed to have a solution to the stalemate.

In Britain, there was new leadership too. The uninspiring Prime Minister Herbert Asquith was overwhelmed for much of the time, and was worse when he took to the bottle, which he did more frequently during the dark days of 1916. His coalition government fell in December 1916 and he was replaced by the "Welsh Wizard," David Lloyd George, the former minister of munitions. With his shock of white hair and self-made-man status, Lloyd George turned his considerable energy and wild creative genius to rejuvenating the flagging war effort. The new prime minister had long looked for another theatre of battle to provide an alternative to the Western Front, and he remained unimpressed with the British generals in France, who, in his opinion, had achieved little other than killing off his countrymen with astonishing effectiveness. Lloyd George was particularly harsh in his evaluation of General Haig, who he thought was an inarticulate knuckle-dragger whose only solution to breaking through the Western Front was to keep bashing away at enemy strength.

As France was the senior partner in the alliance with Britain in the land war fought on French soil, and was contributing far more men to battle, Lloyd George, anxious to avoid more ghastly casualties to his soldiers, backed Nivelle's plan. The French general prepared to attack a large German salient that extended into the Allied lines from Soissons to Reims, known as the Aisne front after the river of the same name running through it. "I can assure you that victory is certain," guaranteed Nivelle publicly.[43] The brash Nivelle would squeeze out the salient by attacking its flanks, and destroy the German forces caught within the pincer before driving forward into the disorganized enemy lines, especially the strongpoint of the Chemin des Dames. Mobility would be restored to the stalemated front. While the French would carry the weight of the campaign, Nivelle needed the British to first launch an offensive to the north a week before his own thrust in order to draw down German reserves. The year of 1916 had been one of attrition; now, he promised, it would be breakthrough.

General Haig had his own plan and he hoped to attack in the Flanders region, east of Ypres. The Germans U-boats were launching from pens along the northern coast and wreaking havoc, sinking 150,000 tons of Allied shipping in January 1917, doubling that number the next month, and increasing to a crippling high of 850,000 tons in April.[44] The Royal Navy admirals pleaded for assistance, but Haig understood the importance of coalition warfare and knew that Lloyd George was enchanted with the French plan, or at least anxious to let the French do the attacking and dying. On Christmas Day 1916, Haig agreed to fight the northern Arras battle in support of Nivelle's armies and pin down the Germans. Even with Haig's support of Nivelle, the British prime minister talked of putting the British forces under the French general's command. Haig was aghast. Two hundred years of fighting the French in European and colonial wars, and now a French general at the helm of the largest land war effort ever fielded by the British Empire! Haig would rather have faced court martial than allow such a travesty, and he would likely have been backed by the King, whose power exceeded the prime minister's. With Haig and Lloyd George openly warring, the situation was dire and only saved by an uneasy compromise effected by other concerned senior generals.[45] The British would serve under Nivelle, but only temporarily, and Haig would control operations in his sector; he would also have the right of direct appeal to London in case he should disagree with Nivelle.

As part of the British offensive on the northern part of the line, the First and Third Armies (there were five British armies on the Western Front) would lead off the attacks, which included an assault on the anchor of Vimy Ridge. Knowing the Vimy barrier had been impregnable to date, Nivelle suggested to Haig that perhaps he should start his offensive farther to the south to avoid the ridge and the misfortune it seemed to portend.[46] Haig did not like the prospect of attacking fortress Vimy, with its mounds of corpses, but General Sir Edmund Allenby, the commander of the Third Army, insisted that it had to be captured if he was to push on with his ten divisions to the logistical centre of Cambrai. Without Vimy in British hands, the Germans would be able to see deep into the British rear (and call down artillery fire there), as well as having a place from which to launch a series of attacks and threaten any advance to the south. Vimy would have to be captured. And that dirty job would fall to the Canadian Corps.

NIVELLE'S PLAN OF ATTACK WAS COMPLETELY upset by a radical German manoeuvre: a significant withdrawal from the Arras–Roye–Soissons salient, a retreat of some 30 kilometres ceding about 1,000 square kilometres of territory. In a war where terrain was sacred, and tens of thousands died for muddy ridges and fields, there had been few strategic retreats to date. A German withdrawal from the overextended salient was a canny strategy, albeit aided by the deplorable French intelligence that had leaked plans of the forthcoming operation. In mid-March, the Germans ushered in Fall Alberich, a retreat to new defences and a laying waste of the land in between, including fouling wells, razing buildings, and pitting roads. Lieutenant Ernst Junger of the 73rd Hanoverian Fusilier Regiment described the retreat as "an orgy of destruction."[47] Alberich, named after an evil dwarf in the Nibelung saga, would force the Allies to advance through a wasteland and then devote massive resources to rebuild the infrastructure to support an offensive. In shortening the line, the German senior command also added thirteen divisions and hundreds of artillery guns to its reserve, allowing for the strategic reinforcement of the Siegfried Stellung when it was attacked. That trench system, about 10 kilometres deep, was known to the British as the Hindenburg Line, and all advances against it would result in attacking infantry being caught between interlocking machine guns and artillery fire. The German strategy for 1917 had been to knock Russia out of the war, which they were in the process of achieving, and to fight on the defensive on the Western Front until their armies were ready to strike. All the while, the U-boats would strangle British supplies.

As part of their planned attack on the salient, Nivelle's forces had spent months creating ammunition dumps, laid new light and heavy rail lines, dug kilometres of roads, and situated jumping-off positions. In one fell swoop, all of these had now been left some 30 kilometres behind the front lines. The German retreat disastrously upset the apple cart. However, Nivelle and much of his staff misread the manoeuvre and chose to interpret the German withdrawal as a sign of their willingness to abandon their position and of a loss of their will to fight. Since they could not imagine giving up any more of France, the French high command assumed the Germans must feel the same way, and that their actions indicated that the morale of their armies was crumbling. Nivelle remained suicidally optimistic that the end of the German army was in sight. He would continue with the offensive as planned.

THE GERMAN HIGH COMMAND OF GENERALS Paul von Hindenburg and Erich Ludendorff, aware that their forces were being pounded into oblivion by Allied shellfire, implemented a new defensive buffer zone after the harsh lessons of Verdun and the Somme. Fewer infantrymen grouped around a machine-gun strongpoint could still lay down withering fire, and more soldiers might survive the Allied bombardments if larger forces were kept several kilometres to the rear. A defence-in-depth, ideally up to 10 kilometres, with machine-gun emplacements laid out like the black-and-white squares on a checkerboard, would slow and absorb the Allied attacks, while still making any assault coming over land costly in terms of lives lost and shells expended. It would not be a fight to the death in a forward trench, but a painful extraction of blood from the Allies, whose momentum would be worn down by fire and not flesh. And it was to be elastic, too, so that when the Allies pushed deeper into the German-held territory, there would be a spring-back from counterattacking forces when the invaders were at their most vulnerable. Though these defences were in the process of being implemented farther to the south against the French and British, the relatively narrow Vimy Ridge could not accommodate a deep defence. The French attacks of 1915 had eaten away the western defence-in-depth, capturing strongpoints like Neuville–St. Vaast, and now the Germans held only the ridge.

The German Sixth Army—commanded by Prussian general Ludwig von Falkenhausen—was responsible for the La Bassée–Arras front, which contained Vimy Ridge. Throughout the early months of 1917, as the Canadians prepared for the coming assault, the Sixth Army doubled the strength of the divisions in reserve. Closer to the front and defending Vimy Ridge, General Karl Ritter von Fasbender's 1st Bavarian Reserve Corps of about 40,000 men had spent months strengthening the trenches. Fasbender, a sixty-five-year-old decorated veteran whose gold-rimmed pince-nez partially disguised his ruthless intensity, urged his forces to use the natural strength of the ridge. Every inch of terrain had been mapped, and gunners and mortar teams could fire without seeing the enemy or even exposing themselves as long as forward observers called back target coordinates. His forces had all the advantages, with their multiple lines of trenches protected by barbed wire woven through the area, inter-supporting machine guns, and several deep underground tunnels leading to the front. The only drawback was that the ridge was too narrow to create the elastic defence. While the Vimy defenders had a hard crust but little depth, Fasbender was optimistic that he could hold the ridge because of the natural strengths of the terrain.

The height of the ridge meant that large German counterattacking forces could be garrisoned in villages behind the lines, well away from searching artillery fire. This would allow fresh troops to be cycled through the front, and should a counterattack be required, they had ready access along good roads to throw the weakened attackers from the ridge. Falkenhausen had five reserve divisions at his disposal, although some were as far away as 30 kilometres. They should have been closer, but the general was constrained by the number of villages in the area in which to billet his soldiers, and wished to keep his men out of muddy and frozen trenches.[48] The divisions had also been savaged on the Somme and were rebuilding and undergoing training that Falkenhausen did not want to interrupt. Both the Sixth Army headquarters and General Fasbender felt they had time to strike back against the Canadians if they should have the temerity to attack the ridge.

German forces on and around the ridge were also strong and effective. Because the ridge narrowed from south to north, and was also laid out in a forty-five-degree angle from northwest to southeast, the lower portion had deeper fortifications. The front was defended by three divisions known as Group Vimy: the 1st Bavarian Reserve Division in the south (up to Thélus), the Prussian 79th Reserve Division in the centre (and covering Hill 145 and a sector to the south opposite the 3rd Canadian Infantry Division), and the 16th Bavarian Jaeger Infantry Division in the northern sector (beyond Hill 145 and dug in on the Pimple). Fortified in depth, the three divisions had five regiments at the front, with a regiment consisting of three battalions (a little smaller than a

British brigade). Group Vimy also had access to over 300 guns, most of which were dug in to prepared artillery and better protected than any of the more recent British or Canadian gun sites that were being set up to the west of the ridge.[49]

The fifteen German battalions in forward and reserve positions were echeloned in depth following the contours of the land and manmade obstacles. At any given time, there were around 8,000 Germans on the ridge to defend against any assault, with another 2,500 in immediate reserve, and thousands more to the rear.[50] The Prussians were considered the most fierce and dependable of all the German troops, with the 79th Division winning several significant victories on the Eastern Front against the Russians. The division also had a steel spine of six battalions of Prussian Guards. The Bavarians were thought to be no less resolute in holding the front.

The Vimy defences were constructed around the Germans' heavy-machine-gun teams. The MG-08 machine gun, a belt-fed gun that could fire over 500 bullets a minute from atop its heavy steel-sled frame, was a formidable weapon. There were twenty-four of these in each German battalion—usually reinforced by dozens of additional machine-gunners in independent units—and they were almost always situated in mutually supporting positions so that the bullets swept over the front in overlapping arcs of fire.[51] Attackers had few openings to advance upon the machine-gunners without being shot down. The Germans at Vimy had all the advantages, and the Canadians were forced to slink through the mud at the base of the ridge. Few could imagine a successful assault against fortress Vimy.

CHAPTER 3

PREPARING THE ASSAULT

The Canadian Corps was now close to 100,000 strong, with four infantry divisions. It was a semi-permanent formation, which meant that the four infantry divisions and the multitude of Canadian support units, such as heavy artillery, were not parcelled off to other units. As a result, the Canadian Corps was seen as a small, national army whose commander reported upwards to the army commander and ultimately to the commander-in-chief, Sir Douglas Haig. The unbroken nature of the Corps also meant that it was more readily identifiable by the press, politicians, and propagandists, with Canadians garnering greater coverage than other British corps.

Canadian officers at all levels knew one another due to the Corps' structure. They weren't all friends, but they understood the pressure on commanders and their various peccadilloes, and most tried to work together for the greater good. Staff work, training, tactics, and doctrine were more easily standardized within the four Canadian divisions than in other British corps. The staff, or the "bloody red tabs," as they were sometimes referred to derisively by the rank and file, were essential to running the huge formations, be they the Corps, divisions, or smaller units.[1] These were not easy positions to fill, as the complicated work of setting up training programs, translating commands into written orders, and the organization of logistics in the Corps of 100,000 (everything from finding billets to food and ammunition) were not skill sets that many Canadians had acquired before the war. The British lent superb professional soldiers to fill the staff positions until Canadians could be trained in them.

Three of Byng's four divisional commanders were very good. Byng and Currie, commander of the 1st Division, had an easy relationship, and the two had spent much time together over the previous year. The 2nd Division's commander, Richard Turner, had proven uneven in battle, but he had improved steadily and his division had captured Courcelette on the Somme, to much acclaim. But in the aftermath of the Somme, and with the firing of the erratic and overburdened Minister of Militia and Defence Sam Hughes, Turner had been sent to England as the chief of staff to reorganize the disastrous reinforcement and training camp system. He proved to be an excellent administrator and was too valuable to return to the front.[2] Henry Burstall, a Canadian professional gunner who had proven himself in the previous two years of battle, replaced Turner. Burstall had commanded the Corps' artillery on the Somme, and the forty-seven-year-old had twenty-five years in the army and was a staff college graduate. He was shy, though he knew his mind, and, somewhat quixotically, he kept a cow at his headquarters to have daily access to fresh milk. The 3rd Division was also well served at the divisional command. Louis Lipsett was an Irish-born British professional soldier who had come to Canada to train soldiers before the war, and was known as a tough disciplinarian. He was also brave and charismatic and had a reputation for trekking through the muddy trenches, inspecting front-line positions and querying sentries about the Germans opposite. The general had an aura of toughness, competence, and professionalism.

Only the 4th Division's commander, David Watson, was not up to snuff. A prewar militia officer and owner of Quebec City's conservative *Quebec Chronicle* newspaper, Watson had been a courageous battalion commander and a solid brigadier, but he had gained his divisional command through his friendship with Sam Hughes and one of the minister's cronies, Sir Max Aitken (Lord Beaverbrook).[3] Watson—lean, tough, and with a weathered face— knew how to play the political game ruthlessly, and when Hughes fell out of favour, Watson turned his back on him. But the general never found his footing as divisional commander, in part because his senior staff officer was the fiery, brilliant, and intimidating Lieutenant-Colonel Edmund Ironside. Most soldiers thought that the six-foot-four British professional soldier, who spoke half a dozen languages and had a forceful manner, controlled Watson instead of supporting him. Ironside eventually rose to the highest position in the British military, chief of the imperial general staff, but he was also known for trashing his superiors. Watson's command record would be spotty throughout the war and Ironside had little respect for the general, sniping that, "He had risen above anything that he should have done and was at a loss commanding a Division."[4]

After the Somme, the quiet yet perceptive Byng studied the brigadiers and battalion commanders and removed, promoted, or transferred many of them. Six of the brigadiers he appointed became some of the finest commanders of the war, including wealthy militia officer Victor Odlum, prewar regular officer and future chief of staff James MacBrien, and the lawyer and politician William Griesbach. The brigadiers included a mixture of militia officers and professional soldiers, both British and Canadian, but all had come up from the ranks, with most serving first as majors and lieutenant-colonels. An astonishing forty of the forty-nine infantry battalion commanders would be appointed under Byng's command.[5] Some were replaced, as they were too worn out from the previous year's fighting, while others had failed the test of battle; nine had been killed at Mount Sorrel and the Somme. New officers were elevated to command positions, usually after having proven themselves in combat. By the time of the Vimy battle, commanders of the divisions and brigades had held their positions for an average of nine months, while infantry battalion commanders had held theirs for just over seven months. This was a corps with an experienced and senior high command, and with battalion officers who had risen through the ranks and knew their jobs.[6]

BRITISH CHIEF OF THE IMPERIAL GENERAL staff Sir William Robertson lamented that "each war has its own peculiarities, but one would think that no war was ever so peculiar as the present one."[7] Indeed, the peculiar war required a constant re-evaluation of tactics and doctrine. The Somme had proven that the infantry company of 220 men was too large and unwieldy to control in battle, especially when the firing started and the major was killed or wounded. The devolution of command then had to move to the battalion's lieutenants, who commanded the forty-five-man platoons. One senior Canadian Corps document issued at the end of December 1916 noted frankly, "It is not too much to say that this is the Platoon Commander's war."[8]

The war on the Western Front had proven that specialist fighters beyond the level of riflemen were needed to both successfully

attack and defend positions. On the Somme, the specialist grenadiers and the light Lewis machine-gun teams were pulled out of
the infantry platoon to create hard-hitting formations, although
they were difficult to employ effectively. At the same time, this
reform had denuded the infantry of bombers and machine-gunners,
and in many of the battles, when the infantry had finally closed
with the enemy, they often did not have enough firepower to destroy
strongpoints or hold off German counterattacking forces. After
these lessons were learned the hard way, the specialists were
brought back within the platoons. On December 9, 1916, about
six weeks in advance of the orders from Haig's headquarters, the
Canadian Corps instigated a new platoon structure that reflected
the need for integrated firepower. The platoon became a more
balanced fighting unit, with riflemen, bombers, rifle grenadiers,
and a Lewis machine-gun section.

The rifleman remained the basic fighting soldier. Each infantryman was trained to use the British-made Lee Enfield, a robust rifle
that weighed about nine pounds and fired a .303 round. It was
sturdy and far more reliable than the Canadian-made Ross rifle,
which had jammed in early battles, especially at Second Ypres in
April 1915. When the Ross was replaced in the summer of 1916,
infantrymen breathed easier. The Lee Enfield was a bolt-action
rifle, meaning that a shot was fired, the bolt was pulled back to
eject the casing, and another round was chambered from a magazine. The Lee Enfield could kill from a distance greater than 500
metres, although most men would have had trouble hitting a
moving target at even 200 metres.

The rifle also had a seventeen-inch sword bayonet, attached
to a socket under the rifle muzzle. Advancing in battle with seventeen inches of steel leading the way helped to steady the nerves. It

was also terrifying to be on the receiving end of a bayonet charge. The idea of being run through with a bayonet convinced many wavering enemy soldiers to surrender. Corporal Charles Cameron of the 16th Battalion described the bayonet as "a brutal weapon."[9] Soldiers were often loath to jam steel through another man's body and kill him in hand-to-hand combat. It was far easier to pull a trigger or toss a bomb. However, the bayonet was useful in directing prisoners, for jabbing them in the back or rear end to emphasize a point. While statistics from the war reveal a very low casualty rates from bayonets (far less than 1 percent of wounds), many of the bayonet stab wounds, which usually involved a twisting motion to free the bayonet from muscle and bone, were lethal, and under-reported in official combat records.[10]

Crucial in the attack and defence was the grenade. The mass production of the bombs began in mid-1915, including the British-made Mills No. 5, with its casing of serrated edges that shattered upon explosion, creating a jagged mass of steel splinters to shred flesh. It could be thrown about 30 metres and had a blast radius of about 18 metres, although it was only deadly to about 5 metres. One downside of grenades was that they had become so popular on the Somme that some commanders complained that the infantrymen often forgot to use their Lee Enfield rifles in favour of the bombs, which required less skill as they detonated over a large area. But a bucket of grenades was heavy and only so many of them could be carried into battle. When they were used up rapidly, the infantry were often at the mercy of the enemy.

Rifle grenadiers were another group of bombers, and these infantrymen had specially equipped, wire-reinforced Lee Enfields. Bombs fitted with rods slid into the bore of the rifle, and when fired, the grenade and rod were launched up to 100 metres. They were not accurate and were fired with the butt of the rifle in the ground and reversed (not from the shoulder), but they could be directed by a lieutenant or a senior NCO against a strongpoint, instead of calling back to headquarters for supporting mortar or artillery fire.

The Lewis machine gun was even more important in advancing against the enemy. The twenty-six-pound air-cooled Lewis looked like a rifle, but with a more tubular barrel. It could be fired on the move from the hip, although it was more accurate when resting on something solid. The team of two gunners kept the 137 parts clean and, during battle, the number-one man fired while the number two prepared the next 47-round ammunition drum that was attached to the top of the gun. With an accurate range of up to 200 metres, and stopping power beyond that, the Lewis gunner could unleash hundreds of bullets a minute. One training manual claimed the role of the gunner was to "kill the enemy above ground and to obtain superiority of fire."[11] The Lewis gun provided more firepower than a section of riflemen and was used to pin down the enemy and allow comrades to advance and attack positions from a more advantageous location.

Within the newly decentralized command structure, smaller groups of soldiers—either the forty-five-man platoons or the four ten-man sections—advanced without having to wait for centralized commands, and were now equipped with heavy firepower. The companies, platoons, and sections still moved in groups, but the units were trained to advance in more staggered and broken formations, using the ground and rushing ahead when the fire against them shifted to other targets. The infantry were learning to overcome the inherent power of enemy positions in what would become known as "fire and movement" tactics, and they were trained not to wait for the artillery or even their company commanders. Combat power was both diffuse and flexible enough to concentrate on enemy strongpoints.

ARTILLERY WAS THE HAMMER OF BATTLE. The challenge on the Somme, even with the million-shell bombardments, was to find ways to clear the deep rows of barbed wire that lay coiled in front of the trenches and throughout No Man's Land. The barricade of metal strands, loops, and razors, sometimes 15 metres deep, slowed attackers and channelled them into killing grounds on which enemy riflemen or machine-gunners trained their weapons. The wire could be cleared by high explosive blasts, but shells often burrowed into the mud and soil to explode upwards, creating deep craters that were difficult for the infantry to traverse. At the same time, while the gunners could target enemy trenches— both forward and reserve, with the aid of aerial photographs, maps, and forward artillery observers calling back coordinates by phone—they had a more difficult time harassing the opposing gunners, whose camouflaged gun pits were usually several kilometres to the rear.[12] The Somme had revealed that unless those guns could be silenced, the attacking infantry, even if they were to bypass the barbed-wire defences, would be subject to pitiless shellfire. Somehow, the enemy guns had to be stopped.

The top gunner in the Canadian Corps—the general officer commanding, Royal Artillery (GOCRA)—was Brigadier Edward "Dinky" Morrison, a South African War veteran who had cut his teeth on 12-pounders on the veldt. He had been a brave and inspiring junior officer, but the forty-nine-year-old senior gunner was more of a fire-eating front-line commander than an innovator,

This painting by Richard Jack, The Taking of Vimy Ridge, Easter Monday, 1917, *captures the Canadian gunners shelling the German defences* on *Vimy Ridge.*

and he was out of his depth as the GOC. While Morrison remained aggressive and lived by the motto "Kill Boche," the growing complexity of the creeping barrages and counter-battery work required a more professional breed of officers.[13] Morrison relied heavily on three subordinate gunners: Brigadier Roger Massie, Lieutenant-Colonel Andrew McNaughton, and Major Alan Brooke.

The British professional soldier Roger Massie had fought for years in the Empire's colonial wars. He was often in pain, as he had sprue (celiac disease), which caused terrible indigestion and seemed alleviated, in his case, only by strawberries. The forty-eight-year-old Massie brought important experience to his role as the general officer commanding, Heavy Artillery (GOC HA), beginning with his posting to the Corps in January 1917. As commander of the heavy artillery—siege guns above a 6-inch howitzer calibre—he was responsible for breaking enemy fortifications and trenches. He worked well with his superior, Morrison, as well as with McNaughton, who drew upon Massie's heavy guns and logistical support in destroying the enemy batteries.[14]

Lieutenant-Colonel Andrew McNaughton was a first-class Canadian artillery innovator. The thirty-one-year-old prewar professor of engineering at McGill had a keen mind for scientific gunnery. "Andy," as the men called him, had commanded a battery at Second Ypres and been injured there. Handsome, with dark features and a clipped moustache, McNaughton had an easy way with his men, often sharing a cold can of bully beef with them over a small fire and swapping stories. Byng and Morrison, guided by the senior corps staff officer, Brigadier Percy Pollexfen de Blaquiere Radcliffe, had selected McNaughton for an important new position. In late January 1917, the Canadians followed developments throughout the BEF by establishing the Canadian Counter Battery Office, an artillery headquarters that identified, located, and destroyed enemy guns.[15] Countless lives would be saved among the Canadian infantry if the enemy guns could be destroyed or suppressed.

The third gifted gunner in the Canadian Corps was Major Alan Brooke, a thirty-four-year-old professionally trained British staff officer. Brilliant in mind, sharp in commentary, and with a huge capacity for work, Brooke—in his position as staff officer, Royal Artillery—had been appointed to the Canadians in early February to draw up the complicated artillery fire plan. Thin, angular, and sure of himself, Brooke was unimpressed with his superior, Morrison, who was more than willing to allocate most of the work to him. Brooke was fine with that, but he faced enormous pressure: much of the success of the battle hinged on the fire plan.

Brooke spent February with a small group of officers crawling through the mud to survey the enemy defences on and around Vimy. He studied topographical features and intelligence reports, pored over aerial photographs and raid accounts, and slowly pulled together the complex picture of the enemy defences. The ridge was too large and too well protected to destroy every dugout, every concrete pillbox, and every sniper's nest. Though clearing the barbed-wire entanglements was an important focus, the key to the bombardment during the battle was to force the defenders to go deep into their dugouts to escape the full fury of the shells. Brooke, who would rise to chief of the imperial general staff during the Second World War, would turn to a creeping barrage.

The creeping barrage had been introduced in the later parts of the Somme and had led to some success on that cruel battlefield. On the first day of battle, July 1, the colossal bombardment had stopped firing on the German front trenches at zero hour (before shifting to rear targets), right before the Allied infantry left their trenches, because the gunners believed that if they continued firing they would kill their own soldiers. Unfortunately, stopping the bombardment alerted the Germans to the coming attack and no longer put them in danger. When the cannonading ceased, the survivors rose from their dugouts to shoot down the British Tommies in open ground. In the coming battles, the bombardments continued after zero hour to confuse and kill the enemy, and from mid-September onward the creeping barrage further evolved to keep shellfire on the enemy while the infantry advanced on him. Gunners fired in unison on a target for a number of minutes—usually three—and then the shellfire crept forward, jumping 100 metres to fall on the next target. The hundreds of shells continued to crash forward in steady intervals, clearing barbed wire and then smashing through the enemy lines. As the storm of steel approached, the Germans took to their dugouts for protection, or slipped out into shell crater defences that were, it was hoped, a safe distance from the targeted trenches. If all the Allied guns could fire in unison on the same targets, the attacking infantry could follow behind this wall of shells into the enemy lines. The creeping barrage was a tremendous advance in supporting the fighting troops in crossing No Man's Land, but it was complicated to plan and harder still to carry out by hundreds of gunners. Faulty shells, worn-out gun barrels, and untrained gunners could all result in shells falling short or wide, leaving part of the enemy trench untouched. An effective creeping barrage would be one of the keys to victory at Vimy.

INFORMATION ON THE LOCATION OF ENEMY positions, strong-points, and batteries was central to the gunners' war, and the best intelligence was supplied by the "eyes in the sky." The airplanes ranged far wider and faster than the cavalry scouts of old who had supplied commanders with evidence of troop movement. With planes taking to the skies only a decade earlier, the first wartime models were rickety and slow, and had the disquieting tendency to come apart in midair. But when they were in the air, the pilots and observers could range widely and see for hundreds of square kilometres.

The sleek aircraft were the race cars of the day, and Canadians flocked to join the air arm. Yet during the rush to create a new overseas army in 1914, Minister Sam Hughes had no desire to pour resources into a Canadian air force. Canuck airmen served with the British flying services, either the Royal Naval Air Service or the

Royal Flying Corps (RFC). By war's end, 22,812 Canadians flew in the British air services, and 1,388 were killed.[16]

While the fighters and aces—those with five or more kills in the British air services—would become the most recognizable figures in the air war, it was the observation aircraft that were increasingly tied into the communication network with the artillery. Lieutenant E.P. Charles of the RFC, a former bank employee, wrote, "We do about three hours per day in one flight. The work I am doing is artillery observation. . . . We call it a 'shoot.' I take up an observer who does the shoot, while I fly the machine and look out for Huns."[17] Despite the swirling snow and heavy cloud cover over much of the winter, thousands of photographs were snapped using large plate cameras attached to the outboard of the pilot's cockpit. Experts at corps headquarters carefully examined the photographs for new barbed wire laid in mud or snow, while shell casings revealed where camouflaged guns lay hidden, as did the perceptible tracked movement of horses or tractors.[18] These positions could be targeted with immediate shellfire or saved for a later time when they might be deluged with a hurricane bombardment.

The Canadian Corps worked closely with No. 16 Squadron, RFC, whose slow-moving two-seater reconnaissance planes, the F.E.2b and 2d had observers and gunners. The slow F.E.s were pusher planes, with the engine at the rear, and the gunner, who sat in the cockpit in front of the pilot, scanned the skies anxiously, his Lewis machine gun swivelling. The inelegant and slow spotter planes were outclassed in speed by the German Fokkers and Albatrosses. Even though the RFC outnumbered the Germans, they lost heavily in February and March, and April was worse, as the Germans flew in formation, often engaging in battle only when the odds were in their favour. With new pilots thrown into the air,

British BE2 flying over trenches on the Arras and Vimy front.
Observation planes like this one were vulnerable to enemy fighters, as
they were unable to engage in evasive manoeuvres and had to fly relatively
low if they wished to secure their photographs of the trenches.

it was estimated that the life expectancy for new flyers was about seventeen hours.[19] And still the brave pilots flew on, taking their photographs and compiling crucial targets for the gunners below.

"The German airmen seem to have it all over ours on this front," wrote a concerned Corporal Robert Miller, 27th Battery, Canadian Field Artillery, in his diary on March 22, 1917. "One red plane has come over and brought down two of ours that I have seen right in front of us, and ours did not have a chance."[20] That plane was flown by the "Red Baron," Manfred Freiherr von Richthofen, an aggressive flyer who led his all-scarlet Flying Circus of Albatrosses. As the most famous ace of the war, his fighting formation over the Vimy front was utterly overwhelming, and the Red Baron would destroy thirty Allied planes in the spectacular slaughter that came to be known as Bloody April. During that grim month the Allies lost 245 aircraft, in comparison to the Germans' 66, and 319 RFC pilots and observers were killed.[21] Princess Patricia's Canadian Light Infantry (PPCLI) Lieutenant J.W. McClung, son of the activist and author Nellie McClung, agonized over the Red Baron's mastery of the sky in his diary: "2 of our machines came down in Flames. The red Fritz fairly goes faster. . . . Sheer murder to put ours up."[22] It was crucial that the RFC observation planes fly and get their aerial photographs, and so they went up, day after day, often facing their doom, to assist the ground forces mired in the mud.

THE ASSAULT ON VIMY RIDGE WOULD be largely a Canadian show, but Byng was able to call upon the full support of First Army commander General Henry Horne, within whose army he served. The Scottish Horne was a protegé of Haig and an artillery expert.[23] During the first two years of the Great War, he served as a skilled gunnery officer who embraced new technology such as coordinating artillery with aircraft, and he was recognized by his superiors, and especially Haig, for his forward thinking.[24] Horne was known as the "silent general," but he cultivated a command style of consultation and discussion, of listening to and encouraging subordinates. A safe gunner among generals who recklessly ordered the cavalry to break through the trenches, Horne understood the importance of careful planning and the power of artillery. Vimy was to be his first battle as army commander.

On January 19, 1917, Horne informed Byng that he would lead the attack on Vimy Ridge, and by early March, Byng and his staff had a plan of assault. In Byng's vision, the battle for the heights of Vimy would be a limited attack based on firepower, shock, and a massed infantry assault. The key was careful planning and training, as 1st Division commander Arthur Currie had recommended. The supporting artillery barrage was absolutely crucial to victory. There had been precious few victories on the Western Front to date, but the third phase of the Mount Sorrel attack, with its thorough preparation and massed firepower, was a good base upon which to build for success.

To the gunners—the hammers—everything looked like a nail. But to win at Vimy, the guns needed to not only pummel the enemy lines but also target strongpoints. Accuracy was important, and wind, barometric pressure, and rain could throw off a shell in flight. The gunners were soon accounting for meteorological conditions, using daily weather reports to guide them. There were also new locating technologies: sound ranging and flash spotting. Drawing upon British gunners' success in this field, McNaughton established specialized observers to go forward and set up triangulated microphones to listen for the bark of enemy guns. By triangulating the sound of the shell or observing the flash from the muzzle, they could locate the guns' position over time. All of this was devilishly complicated, but expertise was gained gradually, and when combined with other means of gathering information, especially aerial reports, these scientific advances helped the Canadian gunners locate more enemy artillery targets.

Working from similar maps and grid references, the forward observers in the observation post, known as an O-Pip, were the eyes at the front, while the gun teams at the rear, working off standardized large-scale trench maps, could simply respond to coordinates and "shoot from the map." Telephone wires snaked back from the front, usually buried 2 metres deep. The Canadians eventually laid 34 kilometres of cabled wire that ran in a spiderweb formation laterally and to the rear along the main trench system.[25]

Canadians took to the high ground on Lorette Ridge behind their lines, near Souchez, and in the ruined twin towers at Mont St. Eloy Church. The area was periodically shelled by the Boche (as the Canadians sometimes called the Germans), but observers bit back their fear and used it to study the ridge and peer into the enemy lines. Both sides turned to their artillery to harass the enemy's preparation, to lower morale, and to knock out opposing soldiers. Under the fall of shrapnel and high explosives, the death toll rose steadily.

The Corps' targeting of enemy guns in a sustained counter-battery program increased in intensity through February and March, and was even more effective when the new 106 graze trigger fuse became available. It allowed shells to explode on contact with barbed wire, and assisted in clearing the deep rows of jagged metal that slowed attackers on the Somme. The primary focus was on smashing the German defences on the ridge, and this was very much a British–Canadian operation. First Army commander Horne allocated heavy British siege guns to the Canadian Corps to accelerate the process, and of the nine heavy artillery groups, seven were British. Further British batteries were added to deepen the punch of divisional artillery, with the First Army attaching 30,000 gunners from the Royal Artillery to the Canadian Corps.[26] Even with these resources, there remained a race between the Canadians and the Germans, as the gunners destroyed the wire by day and the German infantry laid new wire at night.

As shellfire claimed Teutonic lives, the Canadians looked for more firepower to drive them into their dugouts. Firing from a fixed platform, the Vickers heavy machine gun unleashed up to 500 bullets a minute. The gun team included a shooter and a number two who fed the belt of ammunition into the gun, as well as three other members to run up ammunition and take over if the shooter and loader were knocked out. Though the Vickers were devastating in a direct fire, defensive position, with the machine-gunners sweeping along fixed and interlocking fields of fire, during the Somme the Canadians had experimented with using them in an indirect-fire role. By tilting the Vickers into the sky, gunners could spray the enemy lines indiscriminately with tens of thousands of bullets. It was difficult to gauge the effectiveness of saturation fire, but with the bullets falling along high-traffic routes to the front, the barrage seemed an effective way to harass and kill the enemy.

From the first week of March onwards, a number of dedicated Vickers machine-gun teams commenced their bullet barrage. Brigade machine guns were grouped together and sixty-four guns fired by day and another sixty-four by night to keep the German front under a hail of bullet fire. "Prisoners taken earlier in the month had testified that our machine gun harassing fire had kept down practically all overland movement and restricted carrying parties almost entirely to the trenches," recounted Lieutenant-Colonel C.S. Grafton, Canadian Machine Gun Brigade.[27]

"WAR LOOKED MORE LIKE A HUGE INDUSTRY than a fight," wrote one Canadian gunner in response to the enormous logistical build-up before the battle.[28] New roads had to be built to accommodate the hundreds of trucks, tens of thousands of men, and 50,000 horses and mules.[29] Often the ruined villages behind the lines provided the stone and bricks to act as a roadbed, further obliterating the places that thousands of French civilians had once called home. Dozens of kilometres of wooden planks were laid down to avoid slipping into the mud or falling into potholes. Railway crews created new rails for light trams and trolleys carrying supplies from the rear. The light trams ran on two-foot gauge, had small engines, and moved at night to avoid enemy shelling. The 30 kilometres of rail saved the road system from being torn up, as horses and mules would have had to carry the 830 tonnes of supplies that the rails transported every per day.[30]

"Horne has been more than helpful and backed me up in everything," wrote Byng to his wife about the pre-Vimy preparation.[31] With the Canadians as the spearhead of the First Army, Horne

Piles of spent 18-pounder shell casings. The Allied gunners fired hundreds of thousands of shells at the German defences on Vimy Ridge. The horses seen here are bringing more shells and supplies to the front.

ensured that the Canadians had access to logistical and manpower support. The army commander's headquarters also coordinated with other corps to pool labour support for the Canadians, especially after an early thaw in March that, according to an official report, "utterly ruined" the road system and required thousands of labourers and infantrymen to work day and night to shore up the "bog."[32] The Canadian Corps required 2,500 tonnes of ammunition a day to meet the artillery harassment program, and the First Army carried out much of this logistical undertaking.[33]

With the roads continually disintegrating under the thousands of tramping boots and horses' hooves, corduroy paths of two-and-a-half-inch beechwood planking were wired together to create something solid under foot, but these were treacherous when wet and slimy. The horses paid for it with broken legs. Fodder, grass, and grain were also in short supply, and the shearing of the horses' coats to protect against mange left the animals vulnerable to the wet and cold.[34] Corporal Robert Miller wrote, "Horses are dying every day, and are in very poor condition owing to overwork, exposure, and poor food."[35] In the muddy fields, emaciated corpses lay in massive piles, most having been mercifully killed to ease their suffering. There was too much work to be done to bury the mounds of glistening carcasses.

Not only did war materiel have to be brought forward, but the entire structure for the underground cities at the front and behind the lines needed to be built. Horses and men consumed 225,000 litres of water a day. Everyone was thirsty in the front lines, an irony not lost on soldiers who often stood ankle-deep in water—albeit water fouled with mud, corpses, poison gas, and all manner of horrors. New waterways were laid, with a long pipe leading up to the Zouave valley from two reservoirs constructed farther to the rear that gathered spring-fed water from hills in the region. In all, twenty-two engines and twenty-four pumping stations pushed water through 70 kilometres of pipeline that snaked 2 metres beneath the earth.[36] When the pipes froze in late January, there was a water crisis in the Corps. An army marches on its stomach and drinks a lake daily—and without either food or water, it dies—but engineering wonders freed the pipes of ice. Though all the soldiers suffered water shortages and severe strain from the cold, Private Bert Cooke, a thirty-six-year-old from Toronto who had owned a small delicatessen on Danforth Avenue before enlisting in the 75th Battalion, wrote in his diary, "We are tough now and think we can stand anything."[37]

WHILE SOME SOLDIERS WERE BUSY DIGGING trench systems above ground, others were engaged in gruelling work beneath the chalky soil. There was a vast underground network of caves in the area. Some of these, like Zivy Cave on the 2nd Division's front, could house hundreds of men. The Canadians found many of the existing caverns filled with the rotting corpses of French troops from two years earlier. The dead, what was left of them, were cleared away and buried; the caves were too valuable for protecting the living to be left as tombs. Amid the fecund aromas, the soldiers took refuge from the enemy shellfire. To pass the time, Canadians carved their names and those of their units into the soft chalk walls and ceilings. The walls were soon festooned with sayings, crests, and drawings by men who had passed through the space. Added to the dugouts and caves were thirteen longer underground tunnels.[38] Many had been dug by the French in 1915, but the Canadian and British engineers extended them beginning in 1916. They were located about 8 metres underground and wound for hundreds of metres. These were no place for the claustrophobic, but they offered protection from searching and stray fire.

In addition to these tunnels created to protect the infantry, mining companies of engineers, sappers, and infantrymen pushed narrow shafts under the enemy lines with the goal of laying high explosives. Even before the Canadians arrived at the front, the British had exploded 750 mines and the Germans had replied with nearly 700.[39] Over the winter of 1916–1917, both sides mined and countermined, pumping oxygen into the dark, closed spaces that were often more than 15 metres below the surface—far deeper than the tunnels that housed the infantry. The sweaty and grimy sappers worked quietly, picking and chipping away at the chalk, stopping periodically to listen for the telltale sounds of similar enemy mining work from off in the earth. It took a special breed of man to work day in and day out underground in the stifling tunnels, but 800 infantrymen were ordered from each division to assist in removing soil and chalk from the tunnels.[40] Private Len Willans of the 60th Battalion later said of his experience, "It was hard work, and scary too."[41] When the underground shafts were dug close enough to the enemy outposts, they were packed with high explosives to be detonated a few minutes before the zero-hour attack and to cause further chaos in the enemy lines.[42]

ENORMOUS LOGISTICAL WORK WAS CARRIED OUT behind the lines, and Allied artillery hurled shells overhead, but it was the infantry who would be responsible for clawing their way up the fortified ridge. The coordination of infantry and artillery was essential, with the creeping barrage moving at a methodical and relentless rate of, for the most part, 100 metres every three minutes. The infantry had to "lean into the barrage" and stay within 35 to 65 metres of the wall of fire. Anything closer meant that shortfalling shells would likely land amid the troops, and soldiers holding farther back would be at risk of being hit by the enemy's counter-barrage. Infantryman Arthur Bonar of the PPCLI described the process:

> The infantry advance in long waves. . . . When the barrage lifts the waves of men jump forward a given distance, keeping close to the barrage until it lifts again, when the same tactics are repeated. The concentrated drumfire from the artillery and machine-guns keeps the enemy in his deep dugouts. When the barrage lifts he hasn't time to come out of his subterranean galleries to work his machine-guns before our infantry are on top of him.[43]

The race was between the Germans, climbing the 6 to 9 metres of dugout steps and filtering into their smoking trenches, perhaps with machine guns working or buried but with riflemen equipped with their Mausers, and the Canadian infantry, surging forward over the smouldering craters and around barbed-wire entanglements to close the distance and throw grenades, snipe the enemy, or spray a trench with Lewis-gun fire. Byng met the troops, encouraging them, letting them know what he expected of them, and even warning them of the coming danger: "Chaps, you shall go over exactly like a railroad train, on time, or you shall be annihilated."[44]

The infantry honed their small-unit tactics. Incorporating lessons learned from the Somme that were now being codified throughout the BEF in infantry manuals, the four ten-man sections

One of the large models of the Vimy Ridge trench system
used by the Canadians to train for the coming assault.

in a platoon practised advancing on the battlefield.[45] These manoeuvres were carried out behind the lines, at army, corps, and
divisional headquarters, where there were detailed topographical,
modelling-clay, and wood dioramas of the Vimy battlefield that
allowed officers to study the terrain they would soon be facing.[46]
Hundreds of soldiers practised their measured advance, moving
towards flags that marked the imaginary methodical trench barrage. Captain S.G. Bennett of the 4th CMR described it as practice
for a "machine-like assault."[47]

"Our fights are won or lost before we go into them," believed
Brigadier Victor Odlum.[48] Such thinking placed too much emphasis on the value of training and failed to account for the chaos of

combat, but thorough preparation was indeed crucial for any future scrap. An astonishing 40,000 maps were created by the Canadian Corps' cartographer section, and issued down to the privates so that men would know the very ground they were to take and hold.[49] This practice of sharing information with subordinates was occurring in British formations too, but it was ramped up in the Canadian Corps. Never before had the Canadians had the same level of intelligence and months in which to undergo such intricate training, nor would they again. Robert England, new to the Western Front but destined to survive and wear the Military Cross, noted, "We had time to learn about Vimy Ridge."[50]

AFTER MONTHS OF PREPARING FOR the coming Battle of Arras, the generals were firming up the details of the operation. British commander-in-chief Sir Douglas Haig continued to grumble about the offensive that would see his forces attack first and act as bait to draw off German reserves, but he had been ordered to carry out this role by British prime minister David Lloyd George. The British Third Army, under the command of General Sir Edmund Allenby—known as "the Bull" for his hard-charging and gruff attitude—would throw ten divisions against the enemy, while General Henry Horne's First Army, with the Canadians in the spearhead role, would launch five divisions. But Horne's forces— four Canadian divisions and one British—faced the most fearsome feature on the British front: Vimy Ridge. One senior German staff officer observed the need to hold the ridge, but noted in writing that it would not be easy: "Committed at the most important spot was the Canadian Corps, counted among the best troops of the opponent."[51]

For the first and only time in the war, all four Canadian divisions would attack together. On the Somme, there had been two-division attacks, and later in the war three divisions would stride off together, but at Vimy all four divisions assaulted, shoulder to shoulder. As the Canadians faced the ridge, the four divisions would sweep forward with Currie's 1st Division on the far right, Burstall's 2nd Division next to it closer to the high point of the ridge, Lipsett's 3rd Division in the centre-left, and Watson's 4th Division on the far left facing the heights of Hill 145. With the geography dictating the advance, Currie's men faced the longest distance, over 4,000 metres to Farbus Wood, while Watson's soldiers would have to charge 700 metres up the highest and best-defended part of the ridge. The two divisions against the southern part of the ridge, the 1st and 2nd, faced the longest advance, and there were four phases to their attack. Up the ridge, where the enemy front narrowed, the 3rd and 4th Divisions would attack in only two leaps forward. All of the objectives, denoted by coloured lines on the soldiers' maps, would be captured behind a creeping barrage that dictated the pace of the attack and included pauses allowing follow-on formations to come forward and continue the drive. These manoeuvres were considered quite complicated and required constant practice, as units passing through other units could become mixed up, lost, and misdirected. All expected it would be a long day of battle.

At the far end of the ridge, the northern slope, there remained a German strongpoint: the Pimple. Overlooked by Hill 145, this prominent feature still commanded a view of the shelled-to-rubble village of Souchez and the Zouave valley, through which Canadian trenches zigzagged, and the western slope of Vimy, which the 4th Division would have to scramble up to reach the pinnacle. The

Pimple was not part of the ridge, but it would have to fall. Up until late March, the Pimple was to have been assaulted by I British Corps on the left flank of the Canadians. But Horne changed the operation on April 1, hoping to save I Corps so that it would be fresh for the exploitation phase of the battle, and he ordered Byng and his Canadians to take the hill. Byng and Watson struggled with what to do.[52] The 4th Division was already fully committed to snatching Hill 145, and there were simply not enough troops to divert a brigade or more towards the Pimple in a new operation. Moreover, to reposition the artillery for the attack, and to pull them off the main operation only a week before the battle was not sound planning. Byng settled on a compromise. He would order the 10th Infantry Brigade to capture the Pimple after attacking Hill 145, while also masking the Bavarian defenders on the hill with smoke and artillery fire. Leaving the assault on the Pimple until after the ridge was captured was, however, an enormous risk to the entire operation.

THE WAR WAS FRUSTRATING FOR MOST INFANTRYMEN. Private Len Willans of the 60th Battalion recounted that, in the leadup to Vimy, "I had been some 19 days in the trenches, hadn't fired a shot in anger, and took what seemed like a lot of punishment."[53] He and most Canadians were anxious to strike at the enemy. To keep the Germans off balance before the big battle, the Canadians sent out patrols to secure intelligence, and larger armed groups to frighten, kill, and impose their will on the enemy. The job of the patrollers, usually a handful of men, was to spy on the enemy, study barbed wire or strongpoints, and gather information about targets that was passed back to the artillery.

The raids were deadlier affairs. D.E. Macintyre, a former scouting officer who spent a lot of time in No Man's Land and survived, wrote in mid-March, "Raids are frequent now. We raid the German partly to get information as to what they are doing and what they think we are doing and also to terrorize them and lower their morale."[54] The Canadians unleashed sixty raids in the three months before the battle, forty-eight of which reached the enemy trenches.[55] These operations netted 338 prisoners, and countless more enemy soldiers were killed.[56] The goals of the raids were to inflict terror and casualties, win control of No Man's Land, hamper the enemy's ability to lay barbed wire, and gather intelligence. Raiding contributed to the Canadian reputation as being fierce warriors; one of these, Private Harold Peat, wrote, "The Indian regiments . . . were the most feared by the Hun. . . . To-day the Canadians in France are known by the enemy as the 'white Gurkhas,' and this, to us, is one of the highest compliments. The Gurkhas are considered bravest of the brave. Shall we not be proud to share a title such as this?"[57] The Germans were slowly beaten back to the point where they feared to leave their trenches. "The Canadians are known to be good troops, well suited for assaulting," observed one German report in March 1917.[58]

The success of Canadian raiding led to more risky operations. With a reputation for fierceness and a long-standing competition between battalions and brigades that was nurtured through regimental pride and even sports behind the lines, raiding became another way to show toughness and dominance. Commanding officers took pride in reporting on successful raids, and the brigade-, division-, and corps-level headquarters believed the litany of raids revealed that the infantry were chomping at the bit to get at the enemy.

Not to be outdone by the other more seasoned divisions, the 4th Canadian Division planned a massive raid against the heights of Vimy Ridge on March 1, 1917. The raid involved four battalions—the 54th, 72nd, 73rd, and 75th—for a total of about 1,700 men, who would attack behind a lethal gas cloud released from hundreds of large steel canisters dragged into the front lines. Reliance on a gas cloud strayed dangerously far from the tested and proven approach of the all-arms battle that saw artillery, machine guns, and infantry working together to shock the enemy lines with fire before, during, and after a raid. Even though several battalion commanders objected to the raid, arguing that their soldiers had no training in advancing behind gas, Watson overruled them.[59] The attack was executed on March 1, 1917, with two waves of gas released. Neither of these harmed the Germans, and the second wave turned back on the Canadians, with disastrous results. Men fumbled in desperation to get their respirators attached. "We were frantic when the green clouds of poison, blowing back over our own lines, cruelly snuffed out the lives of Canucks instead of the intended *les Allemands*," wrote one Canadian who escaped the death cloud.[60]

The element of surprise had been lost and the raid should have been called off, but Watson and Ironside refused to entertain the thought. At 5:40 A.M., the four battalions of Canadians rose from their trenches and advanced up the ridge. The assaulting forces passed through remnants of the deadly gas cloud that remained heavy in places along the ridge, especially in craters where the raiders dived for cover. The Canadians were cut apart and then suffocated in craters filled with gas.[61] When the ghastly mess was finally tabulated, the Canadians had taken 37 prisoners, but at the cost of 687 killed and wounded.[62] Watson, a consummate schemer who was adept at placing blame on others, escaped the debacle, as did Ironside. Both the general and his senior officer might have been sent home, but doing so would have drawn more attention to the gross failure and also further gutted the 4th Division before its major Vimy operation. Canadian soldiers paid the price in blood, but the raids, which continued until days before the battle, kept the front in a state of agitation.

IN THE FINAL WEEKS BEFORE THE assault—which was firming up for April 9—the Germans continued to hurl shells into the Canadian lines in the hopes of disrupting preparation and killing the unlucky. Black high explosive puffs and whitish shrapnel bursts exploded over the front. Records indicate that on April 4, the Germans fired 23,000 shells in comparison to the Allies' 79,000, and on the 5th and 6th, they fired another 54,000.[63] After one sustained German bombardment in early April, Captain Keith Campbell Macgowan wrote of the enemy, "His gunnery was good and he just hammered the trenches and communication lines and the valley behind from end to end."[64] During the last week in March and the first week in April, the Canadians sustained 1,653 casualties from shell- and small-arms fire, and from their own costly raiding.[65] Sachimaro Moro-oka, a Japanese Canadian serving with the 50th Battalion, recounted one grisly sight: "A shell exploded among a group of men and created a terrible mixture of blood, flesh, and mud. We looked on in horror. There were bodies with no heads. One poor soul was blinded, blood pouring from his eyes."[66]

Though the shelling was bad for the Canadians, it was worse for the Germans. The Canadian and British artillery pieces had

Shellfire clearing German barbed wire at Vimy Ridge.

moved steadily to the front throughout March, and spread out to the west of Vimy Ridge in a half-circle called "Gun Valley."[67] The massive stockpiles of shells were now distributed for the first of two phases in the artillery fire plan. The first phase of bombardment ran for fourteen days, from March 20 to April 2.[68] Brooke's plan called for Massie's heavy artillery, along with supporting guns from the four divisions, to continue the process of clearing the barbed wire and smashing fortifications. To deceive the enemy about the Canadians' strength, half of the divisional guns were to be kept silent. But even then the firepower was awe-inspiring, with 24 brigades of artillery: 480 18-pounders, 138 4.5-inch howitzers, 96 2-inch mortars, and 24 9.45-inch mortars. In addition, McNaughton's counter-battery group and

Massie's heavy artillery headquarters controlled 245 siege guns and heavy mortars that alternated between targeting enemy guns, unleashing destructive fire on strongpoints, and harassing troops moving along the lines of communication leading to the front.[69] During the initial bombardment, the gunners had 343,000 shells to fire in a steady disruption of the enemy lines.[70] Of the 212 identified German guns, 83 percent were destroyed, harassed, or silenced by the more than 125,000 shells fired by the Canadians engaged in counter-battery work.[71] According to McNaughton, he, Massey, and Brooke were instructed by Byng and Morrison "to exploit gun power to the limit for the purposes of saving the lives of our infantry.'[72]

A week before zero hour, on April 2, and following a heavy snowstorm, the Canadians blitzed the enemy lines. Over a million shells were available to be fired and most found their way into the enemy trenches.[73] The Germans called it the Week of Suffering. One German *frontsoldaten* wrote of the experience, "What the eye sees through the clouds of smoke is a sea of masses of earth thrown up and clouds of smoke rolling along. . . . How long did this nightmare last?"[74] Those who survived the shellfire were left trapped in their bunkers and climbing the nicotine-stained walls with anxiety. The bombardment was a sonic assault, and shells landing nearby sent a blast through the caves, striking men like a body blow. Terrified rats and trench dogs scurried in terror, often running in circles or throwing themselves at men in their madness. The humans were no better off. Soldiers chewed their nails to the bloodied quick. There was no sleep. Some men shook like they had palsy, while others stared off into the darkness. Candles were lit and then extinguished by the blasts. Slowly the emergency rations and water were consumed. Feces and urine were deposited into steadily filled buckets. And still the bombardment smashed down. Some soldiers collapsed under the mental strain. Other dugouts disappeared in the blast. The worst cases were those dugouts where the entrance caved in, sealing men underground for a slow, asphyxiating death. The cries of those terror-filled men were lost in the cacophony of explosions.

Corporal Adolf Hitler was almost a victim of the shellfire. After recovering from an October 1916 wound to his upper leg (and possible loss of one testicle) on the Somme, Hitler had returned to the 16th Bavarian Reserve Infantry Regiment, which was stationed on Vimy Ridge.[75] But the unit was moved later that month about 15 kilometres north to La Bassée, where the Sixth Army expected a British attack. Had his unit been on Vimy Ridge during the ramped-up Canadian artillery blitz, Adolf Hitler might have fallen victim to the shellfire, as did thousands of his German comrades, and world history might have turned out very differently.

With the Canadian and British artillery assault in full swing and the Germans atop the ridge able to see the massive logistical buildup in preparation for an offensive, there was no chance that the Vimy operation would be a surprise. Even though von Falkenhausen's superiors suggested that the Sixth Army commander move some of his reserves closer to the front, he chose not to because of shortages of billets. And so he left his divisions where they were. The general had faith in the Vimy defences. And the Germans on the hill were indeed ready for what the Canadians might throw at them. Only days before the battle, the commander of the 79th German Reserve Division sent a warning out to his troops: "The Canadians are known to be good troops and are, therefore, well suited for assaulting. There are no deserters to be found amongst the Canadians."[76] The Germans knew the

Canadians were coming and they knew nearly to a day when they would strike.

AS THE BOMBARDMENT CONTINUED TO RAKE through the German lines, the Canadian infantry prepared to move into the front-line trenches and underground tunnels. The total strength of the Canadian Corps' four divisions was 97,184, of which 56,494 were infantry.[77] There were another 14,736 infantrymen in the 5th British Infantry Division attached to the Canadian Corps, and some 30,000 additional British gunners, as well as additional logistical formations. Byng's command expanded to 170,000 soldiers for the Vimy battle.

"Easter Sunday. The lull before the storm."[78] So wrote Lieutenant Victor Nixon in his diary on the night of April 8. Some 15,000 soldiers filtered into the forward trenches and into the thirteen tunnels marked by red-and-white barber poles. The tunnels were lit by strings of electric lights along the tops of the caverns that reached only about 2.5 metres high, although all the tunnels were at least 8 metres below the surface.[79] The longest tunnel, Goodman, ran 1,721 metres in length and the third longest, Grange, was 1,228 metres.[80]

In the underground subways, men smoked and talked. The rumble of artillery never stopped. The chalk walls sweated as men quietly pondered the coming battle. The sharp whiff of wet, woollen uniforms mixed with the body odour of men who had not bathed in weeks. While there were electric lights, they occasionally burst from the shellfire, throwing much of the tunnel into shadow.[81] As in the hours before all battles, rumours ran up the line on all manner of subjects. Many centred on the United States, which had entered the war on the Allies' side a few days earlier on April 6. That was good news and it partially countered the truthful rumours that the Russian czar had abdicated his throne and that Britain's allies in the east were on the verge of civil war. A few of the more optimistic or naive soldiers thought that maybe the offensive might be called off now that the Yanks were in the war. Even those who knew that this was nonsense would later be disappointed to find that the first American divisions would not arrive at the Western Front until late in the year, and that the bulk of the American doughboys would not be fed into the line until the summer of 1918.

As the men waited anxiously for battle, sitting on ammunition boxes or sprawled on their behinds leaning against the chalk walls, all struggled with intruding thoughts. What did the future hold? Would it be a maiming wound or a less serious injury—a Blighty, as the soldiers called it—that would take one back to England and a warm hospital bed? Darker thoughts turned to death and how a man could be reduced in the blink of an eye from a living thing to a corpse. Most soldiers penned a last letter in case the worst should happen. Lieutenant Gregory Clark of the 4th CMR wrote to his father before the battle:

> This is Good Friday, and I am spending the day girding myself for action. For our Easter Sunday, with peace on earth and good will towards men, I take part in the greatest battle in Canada's history and perhaps in the history of the world. So this is to say farewell in case I go down.[82]

Private David McLean wrote to his dear wife, Lettie, a last letter, but could only find the words to remark on the strangeness of killing on Easter Sunday and how he had finally secured some eggs and milk, only the second time since coming to France. He finished by wishing her "lots of love."[83] It was the last letter he ever wrote.

CHAPTER 4

OVER THE TOP

"Tomorrow will make history," claimed the war diarist for the 5th Canadian Mounted Rifles on April 8, the night before the attack. "Everything possible has been done. . . . All ranks calmly confident."[1] After months of planning, the outcome of the battle was in the hands of the infantry. But they were not alone. The concentration of artillery—983 available field and siege guns and mortars—was about three times heavier than at the Somme.[2] Twenty-one first-wave Canadian battalions of around 15,000 infantrymen were set to capture the sinister ridge. Most of the battalions went into the line with between 650 to 700 men in four companies, while about 10 percent of the fighting force was Left Out of Battle, as the official policy was called, to rebuild the battalions should they be savaged. "During 18 months of warfare I have become more or less deadened to feeling & emotion," wrote Staff Sergeant Percy Willmot of the 25th Battalion on the day of the assault, "but I could not prevent the tears from rolling down my cheeks, and the choking in my throat for the cheery lads who were marching away, many of them of never to return.[3]

Soldiers were equipped with the standard-issue Brodie steel helmet, which looked like a saucepan and was sometimes dismissed as a Tommy helmet, tin hat, or battle bowler. It had webbing on the inside to keep the cold steel off the skull and absorb a blow. Soldiers groused about the added weight on their neck, but after the helmet's introduction in early 1916, the number of head wounds dropped significantly. Almost every man who served at the front for any length of time was saved by his helmet from being knocked senseless by shrapnel or other debris. A helmet could deflect a high-velocity round fired from a rifle or machine gun, depending on the angle, although some went straight through the steel and brain. Private Gus Sivetz of the 2nd CMR mused that "very few men are much concerned with fear of death. Fear of mutilation—a shell splinter in the belly, for example—seemed more real."[4]

The soldiers wore their greatcoats, along with shirts and trousers, with the lower legs wrapped in puttees to keep out mud. The hobnailed leather boots were a demon to break in, but durable through bad weather and long marches. Around the torso was a series of straps and pouches known as webbing. Hanging off it or in the pouches was an entrenching tool (detachable and composed of two parts), water bottle, haversack, two days of rations, 170 rounds of ammunition, two Mills bombs, a flare, three empty sandbags, and a few pans of Lewis ammunition. These were not insignificant loads for men who were, on average, five foot seven and about 150 pounds. Some of the bigger men in the secondary waves were also ordered to carry picks and shovels. Infantrymen travelling through boot-deep mud would need every ounce of strength to keep up with the creeping barrage that stopped for nothing.

In the early hours of the 9th, dozing soldiers were awakened in the tunnels and trenches for a meal. Company cooks tried to send up warm porridge, but not all men were so lucky and some munched on cold meat and bread. "The time seemed to pass so very slowly," lamented Lieutenant Edward Sawell of the 20th Battalion.[5] To calm nerves, battle rum was broken out by the officers in most of the units. It was strong and fiery, over-proof and thick, and it burned all the way down. The rum offered some warmth to the shaking men, many of whom had been told to leave behind their greatcoats as they became too heavy when caked in mud. The rum also allowed men to redirect their anxiety into anger. As one Canadian wrote of the rum, "After drinking the stuff, I would have killed my own mother."[6]

AT 5:28 A.M., TWO MINUTES BEFORE zero hour, 230 heavy Vickers machine guns, their barrels tilted upwards, started to fire over the German lines. Curtains of .303 bullets rained down on known roads, crossroads, and trenches.[7] "We could see the tiny lights, like fireflies, of tracer bullets streaming through the air all up and down the line," recounted Private Hubert Morris, a stretcher-bearer with the 10th Field Ambulance.[8] Another Canadian, infantryman C.G. Cook, remembered, "You could hear nothing but the rattle of machine guns."[9] During the course of the battle, the machine-gunners were to fire some five million rounds in support of the infantry, described by one report as serving to "isolate the position attacked and prevent any counter-attacks."[10]

Hundreds of officers' synchronized watches struck their mark at 5:30 A.M. and 863 field guns and howitzers and 120 mortars opened fire.[11] A number of Allied mines detonated, too, adding to the chaos. Massie's heavy artillery rained behemoth shells down on enemy strongpoints, while McNaughton's guns focused on those surviving German batteries that opened up in retaliation. Brooke's artillery plan called for the field guns to fire the complex creeping barrage that crashed down for three minutes on the outer German trenches of No Man's Land before lifting 100 metres to move on to the next position like a hot rake through churned-up mud. A second and third standing barrage thickened up the wall of fire, coming down 135 metres and 275 metres farther on, with all three fields of fire moving in unison every three minutes. The shrapnel barrage partially obscured the attacking infantry, while also allowing Canadian units to follow the bombardment into the enemy lines.

Beneath the roar of the shells sweeping overhead, the underground tunnel entrances were blown out for the infantry to surge forward. Other Canadian infantrymen in the trenches, some standing in mud up to their knees, climbed ladders to emerge into the maelstrom. These actions took a few minutes as soldiers queued up at the limited number of exits. Most Canadians made themselves small, mouthed a final prayer, touched a magic talisman, and told themselves there was no bullet with their name on it.

Soldiers were struck by the unholy roar. The cacophony of shellfire was like a physical assault and the sky seemed a solid ceiling of blurred steel. The weight of sound rushed over the heads of those in the mud. Canadian brigade signalling officer E.L.M. Burns, a lieutenant in this war and a lieutenant-general in the next one, remembered, "The noise of the barrage dominated all other impressions: imagine the loudest clap of thunder you ever heard, multiplied by two, and prolonged indefinitely."[12]

The infantry chased the snow, sleet, and steel, with the darkness of the dawn cut by the blinding light of countless explosions. "The artillery opened up a terrible barrage and shells of all shapes and sizes fell like hail just in front of us on Fritzies trenches," wrote Lieutenant John Albert House, who had broken off his studies at

Queen's University as a geological engineer to go overseas. "And away we went with a rush into the roar and the flash (just what my feelings were about then would be hard to describe)."[13] With shells soaring overhead, along with enemy machine-gun bullets snapping along the front, throwing up bits of slime and sparking off barbed wire, never did these 15,000 Canadians feel so naked. Enemy flare rockets were fired to signal an attack and to call upon their batteries to respond with shellfire. Even though McNaughton's artillery pieces had begun suppressing the German batteries, and would eventually put out of action forty-seven German guns from zero hour, the enemy still shelled the front.[14] There was terrible carnage to the advancing Canadians, who were cut down by the shrapnel blasts.

WHILE THE GERMANS ON THE RECEIVING END of the inferno were often killed, wounded, or buried alive, not all defenders were incapacitated. After the creeping barrage swept over the lines like a tornado, defenders raced up from their dugouts to man their trenches. The Bavarian and Prussian riflemen—some with bleeding ears and concussions from the shellfire—understood that they were in a do-or-die situation. They were no less brave than the Canadians coming over ground at them, and they set to firing their Mauser rifles at the fleeting glimpses of khaki-coloured soldiers dancing like spectres through the destruction. Others madly tossed their stick grenades, which could be thrown farther than the Canadian apple-like Mills bombs but had a less lethal blast radius. Hidden Maxim MG-08 machine guns came to life, often firing from the flanks, where they were hard to locate and harder still to knock out. The five-man teams operating the belt-fed machine guns raked the ground in front of them for hundreds of metres in all directions. The Maxim's fire was constrained only by the number of bullets available in the gun pits and concrete bunkers, and the need every ten or fifteen minutes to change the overheated barrels to prevent jamming or inaccuracy. They were industrial killing machines, and even a single gun could devastate a battalion of infantrymen advancing in the open. The Canadians knew this and concentrated all of their fire on these weapons to silence them. One German machine-gunner contemplated his fate: "When they have found out a machine-gun position . . . they let loose on us with all their weapons, since the machine guns are really terrible arms."[15]

Major-General Arthur Currie's 1st Canadian Infantry Division was on the right of the Corps' front, and it faced the deepest enemy defences at over 4,000 metres. On the right flank was the 51st Highland Division and on the left flank, closest to the heights of Vimy, was the 2nd Canadian Infantry Division. On the 1st Division's front, arrayed from north to south, was Brigadier George Tuxford's 3rd Brigade with three battalions in the line (16th, 14th, and 15th) and Brigadier Frederick Loomis's 2nd Brigade (10th, 7th, and 5th Battalions). These two brigades were commanded to capture the Black and Red Lines, before Brigadier W.A. Griesbach's 1st Brigade (1st, 3rd, and 4th Battalions) passed through them to overrun the final Blue and Brown Lines. While the ridge to the north loomed over the front, much of the 1st Division's terrain was open and flat, although pitted by mines and shell explosions, and the Canadians marched downhill in the far-eastern part of the front that offered an open view of the Douai plain and the villages of Willerval and Farbus.

The 15th Battalion—originally raised in Toronto—swept forward at zero hour towards the enemy's Black Line, known to the

Germans as Zwolfer Weg, the front-line trenches 685 metres away. They had been bombarded mercilessly. "When we reached the German lines," wrote Lieutenant Gordon Chisholm, "we hardly recognized them. What had once been trenches were only mere sunken lines."[16] The smouldering ruins were occupied within about forty-five minutes, the Canadians having met little opposition from the defenders of the 3rd Bavarian Infantry Regiment, although they lost men to longer-range fire. There the 15th Battalion waited forty minutes for the guns to wreak havoc on the enemy trenches in the Red Line. There was some short shelling from some of the Canadian field guns that had trouble finding the range, but good front-to-rear communication from a forward artillery observation officer stopped the guns before too much damage was inflicted.[17] The 15th Battalion continued onwards to the Red Line, and cleared it rapidly after finding the Germans dead or dying. Private Hector Owen, a slight seventeen-year-old, was already bleeding heavily from a wound in his thigh when he came across a German in a rifle pit, covered in a ground sheet. He did not know if the German was alive or dead, or perhaps slow to surrender, but he fired before he had an opportunity to take in the situation. He felt bad about shooting the German in the head, but, as he was later to note, "Life was cheap that day."[18] The 15th's losses were about 20 percent, with three officers killed and six wounded, while the other ranks suffered more than 100 killed and wounded, a relatively low figure for the battle.[19]

The middle battalion in the brigade, the 14th, initially raised in Montreal, faced stiff opposition as they assailed the Black and Red Lines, southeast of Thélus. While the creeping barrage had torn through the front, several strongpoints survived in the Eiserner Kreuz Weg, a deep trench about halfway to the first object, the

Black Line. The bayonetmen and Lewis gunners raced to close with the enemy, their bare muddy legs clearing the barbed-wire strands that snagged their kilts. Four Bavarian machine-gun teams swept the front. The 14th Battalion was caught in the open and the casualties were fierce. Even though both of the company commanders were mortally wounded—and this would have led to chaos six months earlier on the Somme—the well-trained infantrymen continued the advance, with new leaders rising from the ranks to drive forward. Two machine guns were eventually knocked out by grenade fire; the crew of the third was shot dead by Lieutenant B.F. Davidson, leading a small assaulting party that were nearly all killed in the rush; and the last was charged single-handedly by Sergeant-Major J.F. Hurley, who "bayoneted the crew of three men and captured the gun."[20] The Bavarian troops were of stern stuff and, according to one report, they "fought to the last, showing no inclination to surrender."[21] The 14th paid for the obstinate German defence, and the initial reports noted that, in clearing the positions, the battalion lost 287 men killed, missing, and wounded of the 701 who went over the top.[22] Later, when some of the missing were found, the total casualties were reduced to 265: 92 killed and 173 wounded.[23] The Germans died where they stood and the unit was all but wiped out.

On the northern divisional sector, the kilted 16th Battalion, initially raised from four Highland militia regiments in Victoria, rushed the enemy lines. The bombardment had done tremendous damage along much of the front, but it had left unscathed an enemy sector in Visener Graben, a trench line about 30 metres short of the Arras–Lens Road and part of the Red Line objective. The Scottish dashed towards it, shooting and throwing grenades, dropping to the ground to escape scything fire, and moving forward again. Some ran hunched over, others crawled through the muck. At about 50 metres from the objective, after a brief pause to gather a number of men, a motley crew sprinted in a wild bayonet charge. Many went forward in stockinged feet, the mud having gripped and ripped their boots off. No one stopped. Those Germans who did not surrender out of terror of cold steel were soon human pin cushions.

There were other battles along the 16th Battalion's front, and enemy machine guns firing from hardened positions behind steel loopholes held up the right flank of the attack. The Allied advance on these killers was slow, and around the machine guns, stretching out for several hundred metres, was a fan-shaped clump of Canadian corpses and screaming men. One German infantryman wrote of his machine-gun comrades, "It must be a very strange feeling to lie behind a machine gun shooting at infantry troops moving forward. One can see them coming and directs this terrible hail against them."[24]

Twenty-four-year-old Private William Milne from Moose Jaw, Saskatchewan, exhibited astonishing bravery in taking on two machine-gun positions. Milne, with total disregard for his life, stalked the two guns, even as his comrades were shot or took cover in shell craters. When he was within 20 metres, he tossed a number of grenades at the first machine gun. The bombs exploded in their midst, peppering the Germans with metal and killing them with the blast. He did not stop there and assaulted a second machine-gun nest, destroying it too. Milne's bravery saved countless lives, although his own was lost later in the morning. For his uncommon bravery he was awarded the Victoria Cross, the Empire's highest award for gallantry in battle. It was one of four VCs awarded to the Canadians at Vimy, three of which were posthumous. The 16th Battalion surged on to their final objectives at the Red Line, known to the Germans as Zwischen Stellung, but suffered 333 casualties.[25]

On the 2nd Brigade's front, the 10th Battalion advanced next to the 15th. Most of the 10th's casualties occurred in the first fifteen minutes, before they cleared the enemy artillery's predetermined fire zone. As officers were injured, the lower ranks stepped up to lead the charge. One of them was Private John Dunbar, who took over his platoon after the officer and NCOs were downed and led his comrades to clear an enemy position. Dunbar killed nine Germans before he was fatally wounded. By 7:07 A.M., the 10th had pressed through the Black Line and were on the Red, with total losses for the day at 374 men.[26]

In the centre of the brigade, the 7th Battalion reached the Black Line at 6 A.M. with few casualties, but it suffered more as the infantry pushed on the Red Line. Allied shells delivered a terrible pummelling of the enemy trenches, but a number of machine guns survived the shellfire and had to be methodically knocked out. During the scramble to the Red Line, which was reached at around 7:05 A.M., the 7th and 8th Battalions were mixed up and they attacked together. The assault was slower in the southern brigade sector, which bordered the 51st British Infantry Division, where Saskatchewan's 5th Battalion had a very hard go. Even though the commanding officer had wisely ordered some of the lead platoons to sneak into No Man's Land before zero hour, slithering into the thousands of shell holes along the front to be closer to the enemy, when the barrage opened up, enemy long-range machine-gun fire immediately caused casualties. The German machine-gun emplacements, according to one Canadian officer, poured out a "murderous fire" but "one by one they were put out of action."[27]

An official report noted, "Casualties among officers and NCOs were extremely heavy, but at no time were there wanting natural leaders to carry the work forward with speed to success."[28]

By the time the two forward Saskatchewan companies reached the Black Line at 6:10 A.M., they had lost some 200 men of the 300 that had gone over the top. The 5th Battalion soldiers were frustrated and angry, and one official report provides a glimpse into the grim combat at the sharp end that is rarely recorded in the history books: "The tactics of the enemy, as usual, consisted in the use of his machine guns to the very last, and our most effective weapon against them was undoubtedly the rifle grenade. At one or two places, there were smart bayonet fights, in which our men proved much superior. Several cases of treachery on the part of the enemy were summarily dealt with."[29] Surrender on the battlefield was fraught with peril. It was not uncommon for German machine-gunners, often elite troops, to shoot to the last bullet or until the Canadian infantrymen were within spitting distance and then reluctantly throw up their hands in surrender. The decision to accept the surrender was always with the attacker. The politics of this was unwritten yet known to most soldiers. Surrendering soldiers threw down their weapons and raised their arms; in broken English they shouted "surrender" or "*kamerad*." Those Germans with some time to plan their capitulation would gather pictures of their wives and children in a desperate bid to reveal their shared humanity with the men who stood over them with weapons. Others ran for their dugouts, racing into the darkness. While this was a death trap, leaving them vulnerable to attackers throwing down grenades, it bought time for the defenders to allow an assaulting soldier's blood lust and adrenaline to cool. It was not easy to murder an unarmed man in cold blood.

Most Canadians took the surrender, although prisoners still had
to traverse hundreds or thousands of metres of shelled No Man's
Land to reach enemy lines, and many were cut down there. By day's
end, 14 of 24 officers had been left writhing in the mud and some
350 other ranks in the 5th Battalion were killed or wounded.[30]

The front was alive with chaos. Despite all the pre-battle training, on the 1st Division's front, as with all the divisions, brigades,
and battalions, this was no tidy advance. Though the intense prac-
tise and decentralization of the command helped broken units
to fight their way forward without having to rely on commands
from officers they could not find, many soldiers blindly walked
in the general direction of the enemy trenches, stumbling from
crater to crater until they closed in on their objectives. Following
the creeping barrage helped, as it mowed methodically from west
to east. However, there was no stopping Currie's division, even
though several battalions suffered a 50 percent casualty rate in
the single day of battle, and they were on the crucial Red Line by
around 7 A.M.

The second-wave formations, Griesbach's 1st Brigade, prepared to pass through the desolation and the now furiously digging
infantrymen of the lead battalions, but they would have to wait
until 9:35 A.M for the creeping barrage to begin anew. In the meantime, the Allied gunners fired thousands of shells on the German
Blue Line positions, the next to be attacked by the Canadians. Some
of the Canadians who were digging in pleaded with their officers
for permission to go back over the pitted ridge to look for comrades
who were hemorrhaging and in need of assistance. Almost always
the orders were to stay put. Every man was needed in the line.
Corporal Archie McWade, a prewar lacrosse champion from
Havelock, Ontario, recounted years later that the battle was one

of ferocity and barbarity, and the infantry had the toughest job in the line: "You live like pigs, and you kill like pigs."[31]

THE 2ND DIVISION FACED THE HIGHPOINT of Hill 135 and the fortified villages of Les Tilleuls, Thélus, and Farbus. There were also several wooded areas where Bavarian counterattacking forces of the 1st Bavarian Reserve Division could wait out of sight of aircraft and forward artillery observers. Major-General Henry Burstall's division faced an irregular front, with the forces on the right preparing to push to 2,750 metres from the start line while those on the left would advance to only 2,000 metres. This ill-formed battlefield made it difficult for the artillery to lay down comprehensive fire, and the gunners were worried that the creeping barrage lifts might miss key objectives. Because the wide front was well fortified, it was felt that the assault would require two brigades in the first wave of attacks on the Black and Red Lines, and two additional brigades to tackle the Blue and Brown Lines. And so a fourth brigade was added to Burstall's division, the 13th British Infantry Brigade of the 5th British Division. This was the only part of the Vimy front where British infantry would be thrown into combat.

As further evidence of the position's difficulty, eight tanks—all of those assigned to Byng's Corps—were made available on this sector. The Mark 1 tanks were monsters at 28 tonnes, 4 metres wide, and 8 metres in length, with an additional 2-metre steering tail. They moved at the speed of a walking man, but they would be useful in overrunning belts of barbed wire northeast of Thélus that, because of the terrain, were difficult to hit with salvos of shellfire. Tanks made a positive impression on the infantry, but they were not a game-changer. Lieutenant Armine Norris of the machine-gun companies wrote astutely of them, "Those tanks!—the marvellous insolence of them is to me far above their as yet, proved, effectiveness."[32] These were impressive weapons of war but they had been largely ineffective when Norris had seen them on the Somme and they had not improved much in the six months since. Haig's entire Arras offensive had only sixty tanks. When they were unleashed on a front, the Germans quaked in the face of the metal beasts, even though the tanks threw their tracks regularly, were easily knocked out by shellfire, or "bellied" in rough or marshy ground. But these weapons raised the morale of the Canadian and British Tommies, and more would have been welcomed by Haig and his soldiers if production problems in England had not left them in short supply.

The 2nd Division was ably supported by the combined might of the British and Canadian artillery. The division's field batteries and trench mortars were augmented by the 5th British Divisional Artillery (a reserve division that allowed for the stacking of the guns closer to the front), as well as the 28th and 93rd Army Field Artillery Brigades. A battery of British trench mortars were thrown in for good measure to complete the smashing of the enemy lines. In all, the division was supported by 183 field guns, mortars, and howitzers, as well as 102 heavy Vickers machine guns to be used in both a direct- and an indirect-fire role, and another 54 medium and heavy-siege guns.[33]

At 5:30 A.M., the first four battalions went over the top: the 18th and 19th Battalions from Brigadier Robert Rennie's 4th Brigade on the right and the 24th and 26th Battalion from Brigadier A.H. Macdonell's 5th Brigade on the left. The four battalions were to capture a series of German trenches that extended back to the

Black Line situated on the Zwischen Stellung, about 640 metres away, before two more reserve battalions, the 21st and 25th, passed through them and pressed on to the Red Line along the Turko Graben trench. The fourth battalion in each brigade, the 20th and 22nd, would follow behind the lead units as a mopping-up force, bombing sheltering dugouts, disarming prisoners and sending them to the rear under escort, and fighting the bitter-enders.

On the southern part of the front, the 18th and 19th Battalions used 150 scaling ladders to climb out of their deep trenches, and pushed off, hard on the heels of the creeper. There was only a desultory enemy counter-barrage, although some pockets of enemy resistance survived. The deadly German mortars that were dug in close to the front were overrun rapidly, and most only fired for about twenty minutes before being put out of action. The enemy brigadier for the sector later reported, "Where German guns and

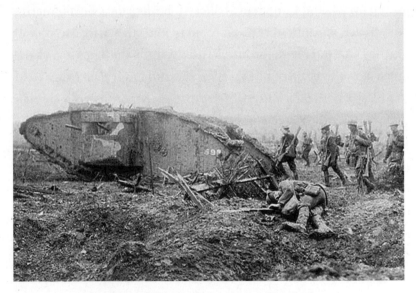

Canadian infantry advance past a knocked-out
tank on the 2nd Division's front.

machine guns were still firing, the attack was stopped, and the dead piled high. Where ammunition and grenades ran out or muddy machine guns gave up the job, they fought with bayonets."[34]

Overcoming resistance with their fire and movement tactics, the 19th Battalion, originally raised from Central Ontario and north of Toronto, arrived at the Black Line at 6:11 A.M. On the 18th Battalion's front, to the right of the 19th, the infantrymen drawn from Western Ontario made rapid advances until a hidden machine-gun nest opened up and sent the riflemen into the mud. Every time the Canadians moved forward, they were shot down. Grenadiers tried to close the distance but were unable to cross the kill zone. The rifle grenadiers lobbed their small bombs, but the notoriously inaccurate grenades could not find the range. Lance-Sergeant Ellis Wellwood Sifton had had enough of the murder. The twenty-five-year-old farmer from Wallacetown, Ontario, inched his way forward in the mud, wriggling like a worm, metre after metre. He pressed his body into the muck when the sweeping arc of fire swept his way, and continued on again when it moved off in search of other victims. At 30 metres, he lurched to his feet and charged the machine-gunners. It took a few seconds for the surprised Germans to comprehend the threat, but then the number-one gunner swept the barrel on to Sifton, preparing to cut him down. He fired off hundreds of bullets, but somehow Sifton remained unscathed. The Canadian closed the distance, jumping over craters and hurling barbed wire, and then emptied his rifle into the enemy. There were no survivors. Sifton's comrades plunged past him to eventually break into the Black Line, but the hero was shot in the head by one of the dying Germans in the position that he had cleared. His Victoria Cross was awarded posthumously.

The 24th Battalion, raised from Montreal, and the 26th Battalion, drawn from New Brunswick, moved forward briskly at zero hour. With little enemy return fire, it seemed at first like a cakewalk. But that easy advance degenerated into a massacre. "In spite of the most violent and concentrated use of artillery," wrote Captain Robert Clements of the 25th Battalion, "the German support and forward reserve trenches were not completely destroyed."[35] The 24th Battalion lost their creeping barrage as enemy machine-gunners swept the front. With the methodical wall of shellfire moving off without the Canadians, they were forced to subdue the enemy positions, according to the official report, "only after sharp encounters, sometimes by rifle grenades . . . sometimes by counter machine-gun fire . . . sometimes by bombing and Mills grenades . . . and again by straight driving bayonet attacks."[36] The Canadian Tommies fought their way forward and the two battalions reached the Black Line a little after 6:10 A.M. Private Magnus Hood of the 24th Battalion, who had survived "withering bursts of fire from hidden machine guns," described the battle, with phlegmatic understatement, as "hard slogging."[37]

All four assaulting battalions had captured their first objective, but they had left behind enemy strongpoints filled with Bavarians. The new tactics practised over the winter of 1916–1917 had emphasized taking down enemy positions with concentrated frontal fire and flanking attacks, but some objectives were too strong and costly to destroy. Reducing them over time would mean losing the creeping barrage as it marched off. The positions were therefore screened by ordering a few riflemen to keep firing to drive the Germans' heads down or to simply bypass them, leaving them for the "winkling out" battalions—as the mopping-up process was sometimes called. Many Germans surrendered, demoralized and frightened to find themselves behind the Canadian lines. But not all. The Germans were trained to sit tight, keep firing, and wait for liberation from their own counterattacking forces.

The mopping-up parties of the Central Ontarians who made up the 20th Battalion and the French Canadians who formed the 22nd Battalion had no easy time. One by bloody one, the remaining positions were systematically cleared. Machine-gun positions were surrounded and blown up; snipers were shot or pinned down with fire and stabbed to death by charging bayonetmen. Many Germans were taking refuge in the dugouts, too afraid to come out and give up. It was not an enviable position for the Canadians to be in—standing at the top of a 10-metre dugout and shouting down for the enemy to surrender. Any soldier going down might get sharpened steel from a bayonet jammed up his bowels. Most Canadians yelled a few calls for surrender; if there was no movement, they tossed in grenades or specially made explosives. Some units took to using flares to burn out the inhabitants. "The wounded," recounted one Canadian involved in these operations, "came running out on their stumps."[38]

AS THE LEAD UNITS DUG IN on the Black Line a little after 6 A.M., the second-wave formations, the 21st and 25th Battalions, with elements from the mopper-uppers caught up in the flow, moved forward from their trenches through the acrid smell of powder that choked and gagged. They crowded into the now captured forward positions in the Black Line as the artillery bombardment kept up its thumping on the enemy. The men from Kingston and Nova Scotia—the 21st and 25th Battalions—had bayonets at the ready when the barrage moved off again at 6:45 A.M. towards the Red Line, 550 metres off. They followed it.

The 21st Battalion, on the right, made a run for the destroyed village of Les Tilleuls. "Never before had attacking troops of any army been supported by so much artillery and machine gun fire," wrote Lieutenant Edward Sawell.[39] The 21st passed through the rubble, destroying five machine-gun nests before arriving at the Red Line at 7:15 A.M. The artillery bombardment had been very effective and little was left standing. But there was a stubborn machine-gun position firing from the direction of Nine Elms that was raking the front. Sawell came upon the scene of carnage and he orchestrated an assault by two Lewis gunners and about thirty-five riflemen. They stole forward along a ditch that offered some protection from the sweeping fire, and when they were about to spring on the enemy, the Lewis gunners and some riflemen opened up from the other flank, forcing the Germans to take cover for a few precious seconds. At that point, in Sawell's words, "We charged exactly as we had done so many times during training. . . . It was a mad scramble during intervals as they changed gunners or ammunition belts."[40] Running, flopping, firing, and moving again, the Canadians timed their rushes when the German fire slowed or temporarily stopped, as ammunition belts were fed into the gun. The machine-gunners were eventually sniped, and Sawell, who was awarded the Military Cross, never forgot the sight of one of the Germans, shot through the forehead, lying in a pool of blood, his life ebbing away, but his mouth still moving, opening and shutting, "in much the same manner as a fish just taken from the water."[41]

It was tougher on the left, where the Kingstonians, Maritimers, and French Canadians from the 21st, 25th, and 22nd Battalions, now mixed up but still surging ahead, captured two 77mm field guns, eight machine guns, six trench mortars, and almost 400 prisoners.[42] The 21st and 25th Battalions, in turn, suffered at least 468 casualties, while the 22nd's Van Doos got off lighter. Their war diary recorded 89 officers and men killed, wounded, or missing.[43] Private Harry Blaikie of the 25th Battalion recounted after the war, "I really expected to be killed at Vimy. In my company we went into the attack with 155 men, and when we were taken out of the line there were 47."[44] Though the 2nd Division paid for its victory, the eight lead battalions had sharply evicted the Germans from their first two lines of trenches.

MAJOR-GENERAL LOUIS LIPSETT HAD TRAINED his division well, and his fighting units faced a far different battlefield than the 1st and 2nd Divisions on the right. Because the ridge climbed significantly on the 3rd Division's sector and then narrowed, the Canadians had only two objectives, the Black and Red Lines. But the front was pitted with countless craters, including some enormous ones made from subterranean mines that were 10 to 15 metres deep in places. Some of these housed German defenders, and Lipsett and his staff had paid special attention to them, ordering them shelled relentlessly.[45] Because of the slimy mud, the unlucky Germans there had few hardened positions in which to seek shelter, with even sandbag defences collapsing, and most were killed and their bodies buried in the sludge.

Across a battle front of 1.5 kilometres, Lipsett put everything he had in the shop window. His front-line forces of six battalions would dash across the 1,200 metres, passing through the Black Line and crashing into the Red Line on the reverse slope of the ridge, to dig into the trenches extending through the shattered trees of Bois de la Folie. From south to north, six battalions would attack: the 8th Brigade's 1st, 2nd, and 4th CMRs, along with the 7th Brigade's Royal Canadian Regiment, PPCLI, and the 42nd Battalion on the far northern boundary with the 4th Division. There were no villages on the heights of Vimy, but on the 4th CMR's front there was a fortified chateau, La Folie Farm, surrounded by hedgerows, and blocking the 7th Brigade's objectives were fourteen large craters, forming almost a barrier.

When the barrage lit up at 5:30 A.M., the six battalions surged into the solid wall of debris, snow, and fire, with several of them emerging from the 1,721-metre-long Goodman and 1,228-metre-long Grange tunnels. In the centre of the 8th Brigade's advance, two companies of the 2nd CMR, men drawn from British Columbia, passed through the smashed German trenches and machine-gun

Canadians attack up the muddy ridge under shellfire.

nests, most of which were still smoking and containing mulched bodies. Sergeant John MacGregor—"Jock" to his mates—led his men forward, closing on the final objectives. One eyewitness chronicled his leadership:

> And follow him we did. . . . Bullets whined, thudded and pinged through our ranks and grenades boomed, splattering mud and shrapnel. Lucky for us, the blowing snow hindered the snipers. Jock led us up the slopes behind, and sometimes in, the creeping artillery barrage, zigzagging and leaping from crater to hillock to crater but always forward. He was nearing our objective when Hun machine guns rata-tat-tatted at his platoon. Yelling at us to lie low, Jock charged the machine gun nest, killed the crew, and captured the guns.[46]

MacGregor, from Powell River, B.C., and one of Canada's most decorated soldiers, would be awarded the Distinguished Conduct Medal and, later in the war, the Military Cross twice and the Victoria Cross. The 2nd CMR bagged over 150 prisoners.

On the 1st CMR's front, in the division's southern sector, the barrage had been extremely effective. But by the time the riflemen reached the Black Line, an enemy counter-barrage was falling throughout their zone of advance. The gluey mud absorbed many of the shells that exploded within the ground, but enough shells dropped near the Rifles to send them pin-wheeling in all directions. The capture of the Black Line at 6 A.M. was rapid, and most of the enemy, according to one official report, "had not time to get into action, and of the two [machine guns] that made an attempt to do so, both were wiped out immediately by our infantry."[47] A German official account noted that the defenders in the 261st

Regiment were buried by shellfire: "Dead lie the crews in their stand-to positions. Now the task is easy for Tommy."[48] Some 350 prisoners were seized, but the 1st CMR lost 365 killed and wounded in the process.[49]

The 4th CMR, mobilized from Toronto, had a much harder struggle. They went forward in strength, with all four companies arrayed in four waves each: two platoons in the lead while a third acted as a mopping-up formation, and a fourth as a reserve force.[50] The battalion faced numerous enemy trenches criss-crossing the front, including Zwischen Stellung, a communication trench named Artillerie Weg, several smaller trenches, and the second line of defence on the Red Line along the crest of the ridge. Lieu-tenant Gregory Clark, a platoon commander in the 4th CMR and a future journalist, described the creeping barrage they followed: "In one sense, it was a beautiful sight. It was still quite dark. Sleet was falling. . . . It blazed, flashed and flickered, the bursting shells; and white and colored flares were fired frantically by a distracted enemy. And the flashing, flickering lights showed an infernal wall of twisting, boiling smoke and flame, against which stood out the distorted silhouettes of men advancing into it. . . . There before us, frightfully close, was the edge of hell."[51]

One German on this front, from the 263rd Reserve Regiment, a farmer from Lüneburg, testified that the German machine guns "in flanking positions had a great effect and struck down rows of Englishmen [but] the German artillery barrage was directed on to the enemy position and went over the heads of the mass of the British [Canadian] infantry and did no harm to it. The enemy artillery . . . was very well placed and as the attack made progress it was always just a little forward of the British infantry. This and the immediate heavy British rifle and machine-gun fire caused very heavy German casualties."[52] The German soldier, Hagemann, was the only member of his 1st Battalion to make it to the rear without being killed or captured.

On the northern divisional sector, the 42nd Battalion, the PPCLI, and the Royal Canadian Regiment encountered a concentration of snipers and riflemen. In the centre of the thrust, two companies of the PPCLI burst from Grange Tunnel on the 7th Brigade's sector, led forward by their regimental pipers on a 225-metre-wide front. "What a noise . . . we were away. Over the craters like 1000000 ants. I bet Fritz thought the whole British Army was coming," recounted Lieutenant Jack McClung in his diary at the end of the long day. A number of German machine guns were met, but the PPCLI "bombed and rifle grenaded them." As they pressed into Bois de la Folie, McClung noted, "all our casualties were from snipers."[53] The enemy sharp-shooters, many of whom were firing from the open flanks on the 4th Division's front, were especially effective in targeting officers in order to disrupt the command and control of the attack.[54] Despite the cutting down of their leaders, the Royals, Patricias, and 42nd Highlanders crashed to their objectives, north of La Folie Farm. By early morning, the 42nd estimated it had 200 casualties and the Royals' initial tabulation of losses was 57 killed, 165 wounded, and 65 missing (although most were thought to be injured and at medical dressing stations). By April 14, the PPCLI had suffered 222 casualties.[55]

The fate of a battalion in battle was often determined by unpredictable factors. It was found that while some had to travel farther than others, leaving them susceptible longer to enemy fire, more often it was chance that decided the fate of hundreds of men. If the supporting barrage smashed enough of the German defences, then a battalion might have a less bloody passage; however, if even one machine gun survived, situated in the right spot to sweep a front, the results could be devastating. As well, the agency of the attackers and defenders could change the pattern of combat, with victory snatched from the jaws of defeat by resolute Canadian infantrymen and sections clawing their way to their objectives, regardless of the losses or the opposition.

"AFTER ALL THE HUNS' BOASTING the Ridge was impregnable, it was ours," gloated one Canadian.[56] The crest of the ridge had fallen at around 7 A.M. to the three divisions to the south, and Canadian patrols were worming their way through Bois de la Folie, attempting to push back German stragglers and advancing to create a buffer zone that would slow an enemy counterattack if it came. Farther away from the front, but with a longer view of the battlefield, General Henry Horne, commander of the First Army, wrote in a letter home to his wife of his pride in the "great success" on the 9th, especially in the capture of Vimy Ridge. "Byng has done very well indeed & the Canadians have fought splendidly!" But, he warned, "Must now take care to *keep* it."[57] But by early on the 9th, a few hours into the battle, the Canadians did not yet hold all of the ridge. Only the first two lines—Red and Black—had fallen to the Canadians, and those only on the 1st, 2nd, and 3rd Division's front. The remaining two lines had to be taken, and the 4th Division remained in a perilous position.

Major-General David Watson's 4th Division faced the steepest part of the ridge. The division had been there before—five weeks earlier in the disastrous March 1 gas raid—and had been soundly repulsed. There would be no more gas attacks and the plan on the

9th was to smash the enemy with artillery and rush the hill hard and fast. Two brigades, the 11th on the right and the 12th on the left, would order six battalions into the line, along a frontage of 1,800 metres. With each battalion plunging ahead with two companies up, each of about 125 men, it was roughly a metre and a bit for each man, although to a depth of around 685 metres.

On the right of the division, Brigadier Victor Odlum's 11th Brigade faced Hill 145, the highest part of the ridge. The 102nd and 87th Battalions would attack on the right and the left, with second-wave units, the 54th and 75th Battalions, set to leapfrog them and push down the eastern side of the ridge. On the other side of the brigade boundary, Brigadier James MacBrien, who would become Canada's chief of staff after the war, hurled the 38th, 72nd, and 73rd Battalions into the line, with the 78th Battalion passing through them. The front was torn with craters and the attackers would face stiff opposition from the defenders around the summit of the hill and from those across the 1,800-metre valley, where defenders on the Pimple could direct long-range fire into MacBrien's flank.

The German 79th Reserve Infantry Division had strongly garrisoned the entire front. The two main defensive lines, labelled Black and Red on the Canadian maps, had four trenches encircling Hill 145. The German commander of the sector, Lieutenant-Colonel Wilhelm von Goerne of the 261st Prussian Infantry Regiment, had walked every inch of the terrain, personally sited machine guns to sweep the open land, located dead ground in which Canadians might hide and taped these out for mortar teams, and had his troops stake out row upon row of barbed-wire entanglements. In the face of the German strength, only the artillery could shoot the Canadians forward onto their positions. When the shells smashed down at 5:30 A.M., the attackers rose from their trenches and charged. But Brigadier Victor Odlum, an experienced and respected commander, had made a crucial error. He had signalled to the artillery to leave unscathed a section of German trench about 100 metres long, 365 metres from the Canadian front lines. The unmolested position, known as Batter Trench, was not struck during the bombardment in the mistaken belief that it could be used as a forward headquarters.[58] While undamaged trenches were easier to operate from, Odlum did not fully weigh the cost of leaving part of the enemy defences untouched. The creeping barrage skipped over the trench and the German defenders in it. In this football-field-length trench, a number of machine-gunners were set up and ready for the assault.

The brave Canadians nonetheless pushed through the enemy fire. On the division's far right, the 102nd Battalion, a unit drawn largely from British Columbia, closed the distance with the German trenches, killing or driving the 9th and 11th Companies of the 261st Reserve Infantry Regiment out of the Black Line by 6:40 A.M. But the enemy fought hard and there was much confusion as most of the 102nd's officers were killed or wounded, and for a period the command of the companies devolved to a company sergeant-major. The 102nd suffered 314 casualties but held the line, although, as Sergeant L. McLeod Gould was to write, the survivors spent most of the day "lying well under cover."[59]

The 54th Battalion, full of tough lumberjacks, miners, and cowboy types from the interior of British Columbia and mobilized at Nelson, had been one of the battalions badly shot up during the March 1 gas raid. Advancing along the 3rd Division's flank to the south, the British Columbians passed through and to the right of the 102nd Battalion and closed to the Black Line, running along the ridge's summit. But when they got there, they found large parts of the trenches enfiladed by riflemen on Hill 145 who fired into their lines, and they got no farther as they caught it in the neck.

The 54th and 102nd Battalions were pinned down by "murderous fire from rifles and machine guns" because on their left the 87th Battalion (Canadian Grenadier Guards) had run into the garrison of the undamaged trench.[60] The Germans fired directly into the lead units of the 87th Battalion, with a hail of bullets so dense that the soldiers from Montreal could barely climb out of their trenches. As the first waves of men were bowled over, many were thrown back into the trenches, landing on top of comrades like bloodied rag dolls. The second and third waves wavered. With Armageddon above, most wisely stayed below ground. After fifteen minutes, at around 5:45 A.M., some of the guardsmen tried to advance again, but they too were scythed down. Attesting to the ferocity of the attackers and defenders, an enemy officer of the 261st Prussian Reserve Infantry Regiment reported that the Canadian "corpses accumulated and formed small hills of khaki."[61]

Most of the 87th Battalion's officers were killed or wounded, with one report noting that they lost 60 percent of their strength from machine-gun fire.[62] Of those who made it into No Man's Land, almost all sought cover in the shell craters and waited for assistance. It did not come. A few brave sections were finally able to fight their way forward into the outer crust of enemy trenches, but all cohesion in the sections and platoons was blown apart. In this confusion, the Grenadiers of the 87th drifted away from the heavy fire and crossed into the 12th Brigade's front on the left, where the 38th Battalion was exchanging fire with the enemy. After a long, agonizing period of combat, during which both sides tossed hundreds of grenades, the Germans were eventually driven back from a few trenches—but at the cost of 303 casualties.[63] Most of the front still remained in German hands, especially the heights of Hill 145, from where the Prussians could fire down into the exposed Canadians. A German officer noted of his soldiers, "They fought like men possessed."[64]

The reserve battalion, Toronto's 75th, could not move forward through the 87th as the line was a shambles. Matters were just as bad with the 78th Battalion, to the left of the 87th, whose courage drained away as they witnessed the slaughter of the guardsmen. Officers tried to encourage the rank and file, to no avail, and there was a minor mutiny as the men of the 78th refused to leave the trenches and charge into certain destruction. Who could blame them? Exhorting calls of King and country paled in comparison to the sight of eviscerated comrades. Some of the officers forced their men out of the trenches by threatening execution with their revolvers, but they were cut down in rapid succession. The commanding officer was informed of the failure to advance and sent his remaining nine officers forward to rally the troops.[65] The 78th did not get far when they finally left the trenches. Their flanks were unsecured and, at 8:30 A.M., they encountered a 200-strong German counterattack. It was defeated by concentrated Lewis-gun fire, but the 78th lost some 75 killed, 261 wounded, and 159 missing, many of whom would later be determined to have been killed. All along the 11th Brigade's front, the Canadian push had been shut down. A Canadian forward artillery observer in the 4th Canadian Siege Battery, moving with the infantry, described the destruction: "Shell hole upon shell hole, some being enough to put a small house in, and most filled with water and mud. A tangled mess of old wire, iron, pit props, equipment, and, here and there, the bodies of friend and foe—a ghastly sight."[66] The Germans were very much in control of the linchpin of Vimy.

THE NORTHERN BRIGADE (on the far left of the division), MacBrien's 12th, faced an equally fearful charge across the open ground below the slopes of Hill 145. Montreal's 73rd Battalion, on the far left of the attack, leaned into the barrage and rushed to the Black Line in half an hour. The trenches were difficult to consolidate because the Germans held nearby positions and the Montrealers were being shot at by defenders on the Pimple, who had only momentarily been quieted by smoke and gas projected over their lines. Even though much of the fire from that position was poorly aimed and simply sweeping the front, bullets still found flesh. One report described two German machine-gunners protected in a concrete bunker who engaged in "great execution" against the 12th Brigade.[67] There was also a German trench over the ridge in front of the main thrust and the 73rd did not have orders to attack it, although its defenders were laying down heavy fire into the flank of the 72nd and 38th Battalions on the right. Here, the 73rd seems to have been content to stay in their protective trenches rather than race forward into an uncertain firefight. As a result, the 72nd was unable to reach the first objective, the Black Line. They were caught in a crossfire from several directions, with the 72nd losing 76 percent of its force.[68]

Ottawa's 38th Battalion was attacking up the slope of Hill 145, to the right of the 72nd Battalion, with some 562 men. Large craters were defended by German infantrymen, and while the lead units bypassed these as per their orders in the push to the Black Line, the enemy held out and shot at the companies advancing behind them. The cohesion of the assault disintegrated, with the lead units separated from those supporting them in the rear. The Ottawans dived for cover in the shell craters, not knowing that some were as deep as houses. They slid down the slick walls, clutching at the occasional root or rotting body to stay out of the slime at the bottom. The muddy walls made it nearly impossible to climb out again, and the piteous cries of men rose and fell as they slowly lost strength and hope.

By noon, the battle on the 4th Division's front had broken down. The right-hand brigade had a toehold in the Black Line on the crest of the ridge, but most battalions had been stopped short of their objectives. Watson had Brigadier Edward Hilliam's 10th Brigade in reserve, but that fresh unit was slated to attack the Pimple the next day and, if ordered against Hill 145, Hilliam's unready men would take several hours to move it forward. The 4th Division was trapped in the Black Line or No Man's Land, and under heavy fire from the German troops on the fortress of Hill 145. Within hours, new enemy reinforcements would be marched in to backstop the Prussians, and the entire Vimy operation might go from a teetering victory to collapse and defeat.

FARTHER TO THE SOUTH, THE SOLDIERS of the 1st Division could see the fierce battle up the ridge, but they faced their own challenges. The first two German lines, the Black and Red, had fallen rapidly to the advancing battalions, but there remained two distant lines to reach, as well as the ongoing consolidation of the captured front. The 13th Battalion, Royal Highlanders of Canada, stalked forward behind the lead waves of the 14th, 15th, and 16th Battalions, clearing enemy dugouts that had been bypassed. Infantryman

Archie McWade, a twenty-two-year-old lance-corporal in the 13th, remembered that his officers had told him to take no prisoners. "Any bugger who stood up in front of me, I shot him."[69]

The 1st Brigade moved forward for the third phase of battle against the Blue Line, about 1,100 metres from the Red Line and on the eastern slope of the ridge. Three battalions, the 4th on the left and the 1st on the right, with the 3rd Battalion in the centre, prepared for the new assault, although moving about 1,800 men through enemy shelling resulted in some casualties. The attackers nonetheless had to hurry to get into position before zero hour at 9:35 A.M., when the barrage would surge forward again, with the Canadians set to take two more lines that encompassed the enemy trench systems.

The three battalions set off at 9:35 A.M., but they did not encounter much resistance. The Germans were demoralized and many of the defenders, witnessing the disaster that had unfolded hours earlier in the loss of the forward trenches, bugged out from their positions. Other Germans had simply been annihilated by the bombardment. Private William Green of the 4th Battalion remembered marching over the entrails of shredded Germans, and passing other men slashed "open right from the head down."[70]

There were a handful of fierce battles, but the 3rd Battalion fought its way into the enemy trenches with relatively light casualties, losing about 150 men by the end of the day.[71] Private Gordon Liddle of the 3rd Battalion recounted one grim event. Most of the German garrison was dead or in retreat, but "one exception was a lone German soldier who was unarmed and in a state of extreme hysteria from shell shock and was getting down on his knees and putting up his hands, over and over again. Somebody said, 'Shoot the son of a bitch,' and somebody did. I concluded that not all sons of bitches were in the German ranks."[72] The Mad Fourth (along with the 3rd Battalion) cleared much of Farbus Wood and captured about 100 Germans at the loss of only 30 casualties. The Blue Line was occupied by around 11 A.M., with the 1st Battalion digging in to ensure a hard right shoulder and protect against any attacks that might come across the southern divisional boundary, where the British were fighting the Germans. The 3rd and 4th Battalions waited to push on.

The final attack on the Brown Line was unleashed by the 3rd and 4th Battalions behind another creeping barrage at 12:26 P.M., and it saw the Canadians drive the demoralized Germans out of their last series of trenches by around 1 P.M. A break in the snowstorm let the sun shine through the thick clouds, illuminating a battlefield of mud and murder. The 1st Division had rushed 4,000 metres from their trenches into the German lines at the cost of about 2,500 men, or one man killed or wounded for every 1.5 metres advanced—the average length of a fallen man. More than 1,200 prisoners were taken by the division, hundreds more killed or wounded, 40 machine guns bagged, and 27 artillery pieces and mortars sent to the rear as trophies.[73]

IN THE THIRD AND FOURTH WAVE of attacks on the 2nd Division's front, the 6th Brigade and the 13th British Brigade pushed on to their objectives on the Blue Line and the final Brown Line. Around 8 A.M., the Iron Sixth moved forward to get into position, with the 31st Battalion on the right, the 28th in the centre, and the 29th on the left, passing through the 4th Infantry Brigade. They were to charge to the Blue Line, overrunning the strongpoints of Thélus and a number of wooded areas. Leapfrogging them, the final reserve unit, the 27th Battalion, was to rush the Brown Line, which ran through Farbus. On the left flank, the British 13th Brigade's 2nd Battalion, King's Own Scottish Borderers, and 1st Battalion, Royal West Kents, faced a narrow front but had to capture the heights of Hill 135 that overlooked the entire division's sector. Once past this second-highest point on the ridge, both the Canadian and British brigades would have to fight through Thélus Trench, a strongpoint cutting along the front.

At 9:35 A.M., the barrage opened up, thickened by the field guns and howitzers from the 5th British Division, which doubled the firepower. There was some confusion, however, and many of the guns started the barrage by firing short, forcing the Canadians on the right back into their trenches as shells smashed down among them.[74] The losses to friendly fire were a discouraging but accepted part of battle. Medical Officer Captain Harold McGill of

Concrete German machine-gun emplacement in Thélus.

the 31st Battalion went over the top with the infantry to set up an advanced dressing post in the German lines to treat the wounded. "Just as we entered the barrage I came across a newly severed human foot lying on top of the mud directly in my path. It was cut off above the ankle as cleanly a though done with an axe. The boot and sock were completely stripped away, and the skin was white and clean as if the owner had just come out of a bath. It was mute evidence that someone had been blown to pieces but a moment before."[75]

Eight tanks were to assist the infantry, but the lumbering steel giants were ungainly, slow, and easily holed by shellfire. The Germans had caught wind that tanks would be used on the 2nd Division's front and had rushed forward a special tank-killing unit of four 77mm field guns firing armour-piercing shells, but two were wiped out by Allied counter-battery fire and the other two retreated in the face of the Canadian advance. The tanks proved of little use, however, as the 28-tonne steel beasts became bogged down in the mud, slipped into large mine craters from which they could not emerge, or were shredded by shellfire. None of the clumsy armoured vehicles had an impact at Vimy, and it would not be until the Battle of Cambrai in November 1917 and the Battle of Amiens in August 1918 that tanks were gathered in enough density to overpower the enemy.

By the time the Albertans of the 31st Battalion arrived at Thélus, little remained but smoking rubble and dismembered corpses.[76] On the left, the 28th and 29th swept forward to Thélus and on to the Blue Line, with the 29th driving forward beyond that to the Brown Line. There were great heroics at the front, but not every soldier was able to stand the strain. Corporal Robert Miller, a gunner attached to the 28th Battalion, wrote about how, late on the 9th, he and a mate found a 28th Battalion infantryman cowering in a dugout. Sympathetic to the infantryman's fear, Miller "kept him till dark, then advised him to go up to his btn [battalion]. He got away with it."[77] Such is the nature of battle. The instincts of self-preservation and fear can override training and duty. However, the vast majority of Canadians drew deep upon their well of personal courage, followed orders, and advanced into the fire.

The reserve battalion—the 27th—with elements from the 29th, raced over the crest of the ridge, through Thélus Wood and a number of trenches, pushing deep into German territory that was part of the flattened crest. Lead elements of the battalions from Winnipeg and Vancouver ran up against a number of forward German 77s—the enemy's light field gun. Cold steel against artillery shells would lead only to slaughter. But the German gunners were in the process of limbering their guns to horses and retreating. The Canadians steadied themselves and rushed forward before the gunners could turn their artillery pieces on them. The bayonet charge took care of enemy battery, and the commander and staff of the 3rd Bavarian Reserve Regiment were also caught in the bag. So too were 250 German prisoners in the area with no fight left in them.

THE BRITISH REGIMENTS FOUGHT SKILFULLY, and the King's Own drove the Germans off Hill 135 and dug in on the eastern forward wooded slope between the villages of Vimy and Farbus. The position gave the Tommies a good firing zone, and in the assault they captured some 250 prisoners, two 21cm howitzers, and four machine guns for the losses of 21 killed, 2 missing, and

138 wounded.[78] As one Canadian officer later recalled in his memoirs of the sterling British contribution to the battle, "I take pains to explain this," he wrote, "because I feel that we Canadians have not been over generous in giving the due and proper share of credit to the men of this fine division from the Old Land for the part they played."[79]

At 11 A.M., as the British were digging in, the commander of the German 79th Reserve Division ordered a three-battalion counterattack to recapture Hill 135. It might have succeeded if the Prussians, as they moved forward, had not been caught in shellfire that dispersed their formations in the rough terrain. The sector commander, seeing his lines on the verge of breaking, had not received word of the thrust through his trenches, and so he used the three battalions to strengthen his position instead of mobilizing them for the counterattack.[80] The fog of war had descended over the battlefield. By the time the 79th's headquarters were informed that the counterattackers had become stationary defenders, the delay had killed any chance of driving the British off the tactical strongpoint.

The final push to the Brown Line began at 12:26 P.M., after a ninety-minute standing bombardment of the German trenches. The surviving defenders—many of whom had already faced shellfire all day and were routed from previous positions—were dazed and docile. With the Allied guns firing at their upmost range, there was much barbed wire left uncut, but the Winnipeggers of the 27th and Vancouverites of the 29th battalions found the gaps. "Fritz lambasted us right till we got right up to him," remembered W.J. Sheppard, an infantryman in the 27th Battalion, "and then threw up their hands and said, 'Mercy, Comrade.'" I don't think they got much mercy."[81] The German positions fell a little before 2 P.M.

With the 3rd Division dug in and consolidating their two lines of defences, and engineers guiding the work of strengthening the front, the only unoccupied portion of Vimy Ridge by late morning was the heights of Hill 145. Here the Germans had made a successful stand against the 4th Division. They threatened to upset the entire Canadian Corps operation with their forward base from which they could launch counterattacks and sweep the southern, lower parts of the ridge with artillery and machine-gun fire. If Hill 145 did not fall, the successful Canadian Corps assault might be reversed.

THE 4TH DIVISION'S OPERATION TO CAPTURE the heights of Vimy had been stopped cold with heavy costs on the Black Line, the first trench system, around noon. There were a few late-morning minor engagements—including the clearing by the 46th Battalion, from South Saskatchewan, and the 47th Battalion, from British Columbia, of at least 150 Germans from a number of craters that had been overlooked in the initial advance—but the front had stalemated. Marksmen on either side sniped anything that moved. A German regimental history recounted that in the grinding warfare, the forward units were "bleeding to death."[82] The Canadians were no better off. Captain Keith Campbell Macgowan of the 47th Battalion wrote of the shelling, "I was busy all afternoon and when we moved up to hold the line, which is more telling than going over because you simply have to stand and take artillery fire."[83]

Major-General Watson was staring down another defeat with little hope of salvaging it. He had one final battalion to throw into the line, and it was an unlikely candidate for delivering victory.

The 85th Battalion from Nova Scotia was a Highlander unit that had never seen combat and had not even been issued its kilts, leading to taunting by other Canadian units. It was deeply humiliating for the proud Maritimers, and to date the 85th Battalion had been a labour battalion that had spent far more time digging with shovels than practising with rifles. Now, in the desperation of the stalled attack, the 85th were ordered to the front.

Into the blaze of battle went two companies of the 85th by late afternoon, with the 300 or so men threading their way to their jumping-off trenches—moving through underground tunnels and new communication trenches in preparation for the assault. The front was strangely quiet, an ominous sign—either the Germans were resting after an exhausting day or they were waiting, guns at the ready. Watson and his divisional staff had the afternoon to liaise with the gunners to lay down a new bombardment, but the commanding officer of the 85th, Lieutenant-Colonel A.H. Borden, surveyed the front and saw how close the lines were to the German fortifications. He made the tough decision to call off the supporting artillery bombardment, fearful that short shelling from Canadian guns would hit the 85th. This did not bode well for any success. Borden did not waver. Nor did his company commander, Captain Percival Anderson, whose men were mostly drawn from Cape Breton; he vowed, "We will take it or never come back." [84]

As the 6 P.M., zero hour approached, the Maritimers waited in the forward trenches for the telltale bombardment. The message of the cancellation arrived and was handed to one of the company commanders, but there was not enough time to spread the news to all officers. Along the line, the untested infantrymen made final preparations, murmured prayers, and cast determined glances at their chums. Then they fixed bayonets. The front-line officers studied their synchronized watches, waiting for the minutes to tick down. A warning went out at thirty seconds to zero. Men hunched their shoulders involuntarily, as protection against the sonic artillery bombardment that was about to begin.

And nothing happened. The officers and NCOs looked at one another perplexed. A bayonet charge over open ground into the mouth of the enemy guns was suicidal. Thirty seconds passed, then a minute. The officers made the gut-wrenching call and gave the order. Over the top. To a man, the Highlanders scrambled up their ladders, over the scattering of sandbags, driving forward. The Germans were initially taken by surprise since it was lunacy for any force to attack without artillery. The Highlanders pushed the pace, gobbling up the ground to close the distance. The enemy's surprised sentries snapped to the danger, Mauser rifle shots ringing out, soon to be followed by machine-gun fire. As the Highlanders charged they let out a blood-curdling battle cry, just as enemy guns began to spew a hail of bullets. Maritimers were punched down by fire, but the survivors refused to go to ground. They tore through the enemy lines on the crest of Hill 145, shooting, stabbing, and clubbing the enemy to death. Grenades were tossed to shred flesh. Lewis machine-gunners fired from the hip. Riflemen found their targets. Captain Anderson was at the head of his troops, leading from the front, and he single-handedly took on and knocked out a machine-gun position. As almost all the officers were killed or wounded, Anderson continued to rally the men under fire. For his gallant leadership and devotion to duty, he was recommended for the Victoria Cross but received the Military Cross. He did not survive the war, being killed a few months later at Passchendaele.[85]

Within ten mad minutes, the enemy folded in the face of the ferocious advance. The heights of Hill 145 fell to an untried battalion in the most audacious Canadian bayonet charge of the war. Some resolute Germans clung to trenches on the eastern slope of the ridge, which in places formed a double lip with dead ground that the Canadians could not observe from their heights, but the Highlanders had reversed the imminent defeat on the 4th Division's front, and perhaps of the entire Corps' operation. "Bodies could be seen protruding from shellholes half filled with water stained

Canadians atop Vimy Ridge looking out over the Douai plain.
The commanding view from the heights starkly reveals the
importance of the ridge that dominates the terrain.

scarlet with human blood," wrote one soldier. "The bodies were in all shapes and shapelessness of sudden death, many on their backs with hands raised and a wild look of terror on their races from the shell or bayonet that had hurled them into eternity."[86] By the end of the day, as reinforcements came forward, the 85th had suffered 56 officers and men killed and almost 300 wounded, many of whom later died of their wounds.[87] The cost was high, but the German backbone was broken on the ridge.

As the sun set on April 9, the Canadians were in command of the ridge line of Vimy, with only some sectors along the lower eastern slope in enemy hands. The battle was a clear-cut victory. But a bloody one. The 9th of April would be the single bloodiest day in Canadian military history. Once the corpse-counters behind the lines tabulated the reports of the injured and killed, it was found that a shocking 7,707 Canadians were casualties, including 2,967 dead, on April 9 and 10.[88] A.F. Brayman of the 50th Battalion captured this grim reality in his diary, observing, "The entire face of the hill was covered with German green and Canadian khaki. Men lay out there in that blood-soaked field, some dead, some dying."[89]

CHAPTER 5

VIMY AFTERMATH

There were many ways to be killed on Vimy Ridge. Major Albert Percy Menzies, a prewar Presbyterian minister who was awarded the Military Cross at Vimy, wrote of his astonishing experiences at the front. He had several near-fatal events, with shells bursting around him and killing men next to him while he remained unscathed. Menzies recalled talking to a man who was killed the next instant by a bullet through the heart. He even survived a shell landing almost at his feet, his life spared only because it was a dud that did not explode. "These are some escapes which I noticed, though I have always contended, that the misses which one failed even to notice, may be the most dangerous. Further, I feel almost sinful in talking about my 'luck,' for there is a superstition among soldiers that the luck will change if you talk about it. They would cry instantly 'touchwood' 'touchwood.' However I will try not to be superstitious." [1] Death was chaotic in the purest sense—there was no predicting how it would strike and little that could be done to avert it. Like Menzies, many soldiers embraced their faith, while also turning to superstition and magical talismans to keep them safe. These charms and beliefs were kept secret: if they worked, men rarely talked about them; if they failed, the secrets went to the grave.

Some 7,000 Canadians were injured on Vimy Ridge. Some broke legs in craters, others were concussed by high explosives. Most often, jagged steel from shell casings or shrapnel balls or bullets tore through flesh. In good wounds, the metal passed through the body without hitting organs and exited, usually taking a large chunk of flesh with it. A man could still bleed to death, but he had a fighting chance. In bad cases, the steel shattered bones, pulped organs, and lodged in the body. A cut artery or a strike to the heart or liver could kill almost immediately. Brain wounds could be ghastly, destroying physical functions and personality, but a surprising number of men survived such traumatic injuries. Stomach wounds tore up intestines and, in the age before antibiotics, usually led to a slow, agonizing death.

The human body could withstand tremendous punishment, and most often the wounds were not immediately fatal. Neil McDougall, a Canadian infantryman from Grand River, P.E.I., wrote home after the battle, "It was a machine gun bullet that got me. It went in on my left side and came out on my right. If it had been one half inch around towards my back it would have killed me instantly."[2] Private Walter Louden, an eighteen-year-old Calgarian who had fought on the Somme, was clipped by a bullet in the head during the 10th Battalion's surge forward, noting, "I can remember getting spun around a couple of times." Knocked to the muddy ground and watching mesmerized as the pieces of red-hot metal rained down and sizzled around him, he pulled himself to his feet and continued the advance, unaware that he was bleeding badly from the face and that he had lost part of his right ear. When his mates finally sized him up, he was sent to the rear with a bloody bandage awkwardly wrapped around his head.

The injury ended his war. Louden was one of the thousands of walking wounded that day, men hit by shell splinters or bullets in fleshy parts of their body and then able to summon up the strength to begin the long trek back to their lines for medical care.

The medical system at Vimy was a multi-tiered structure from front to rear, from initial treatment by stretcher-bearers and battalion medical officers to more intricate surgery behind the lines, leading all the way back to Britain. Closest to the front were stretcher-bearers, non-combatants trained by the battalion's medical officer in how to apply bandages and offer some pain relief. For the Vimy battle, in preparation for the hard fighting to follow, the numbers were augmented, with 100 bearers per battalion. It would not be enough. From the first minutes of fire,

Light rail tram taking wounded soldiers out of the line. Canadians and German prisoners assist in pushing and pulling the rail car.

stretcher-bearers hunted through the ruins for the wounded, often turning over dead men in search of the living. When a breathing man was found, a comforting word was offered under the fall of the shells. A surprising number of bleeding soldiers asked for a cigarette, finding relief in old habits. Morphine tablets were issued for pain relief, although the stores were used up rapidly and not all units had access to them. Most of the stretcher-bearers carried a canteen of rum to ease the pain, and it was administered to the cold, corpse-like wounded men as long as they did not have stomach wounds. Maurice Bracewell, a stretcher-bearer for the 102nd Battalion who would survive the battle and the war, albeit with a serious injury, wrote of his time on the ridge, "It is not an easy thing to go around among your friends . . . lying there face up and in all manner of grotesque shapes. It is not a thing you soon forget."[3]

For those carried off the battlefield, the movement from front to rear along boot-sucking muddy trenches meant that the stretcher-bearers, in teams of two or four, often slipped, tripped, and dropped their patients. Every step was agony for a soldier with a broken femur or whose intestines were spilling out of his abdomen. A soaking-wet man, even with his kit and backpack cut off, who might weigh 150 pounds normally, could be 75 pounds heavier. A deadlift of 225 pounds over several kilometres of broken ground and while under fire was an exhausting affair, and most stretcher-bearers were only good for a few trips before collapsing.

Stretcher-bearers sought to carry their bleeding burdens to the battalion medical officer, who usually had a dugout or cave near the original front lines. Some medical officers, such as Captain Harold McGill of the 31st Battalion, followed their unit into combat and set up a forward aid post in the captured German trenches. Wherever the dugout was located, one could usually find it from the screams and moans of the traumatized men. The medical officers inspected the gaping wounds, changed bloodied bandages, and immobilized broken bones. In only the most extreme cases was more complicated surgery carried out. The chance for infection in the dirty hovels was too great, and there were overwhelming numbers of suffering men. Major Walter Bapty, medical officer for the 102nd Battalion, described how the wounded he treated early in the day had relatively minor injuries, mostly "walking cases," but that later the dreadfully hurt arrived. "I cannot begin to describe all the variety of cases—rifle wounds, shell wounds, but no bayonet wounds. Fractures of all parts, from depressed fractures of the skull down to the bones of the foot. It was just a bloody jumble. . . . It is impossible for you to imagine how plastered they were with muck and corruption."[4]

For those treated by the medical officer, it was still a long way back to a field ambulance. With the shortage of carriers, prisoners were conscripted to transport the wounded. Most accepted eagerly. To have a purpose on the battlefield made prisoners less likely to be executed by some overzealous or revenge-minded Canadian. "The Germans worked hand in hand with us," recounted one Canadian infantryman, "dressing wounds, carrying stretchers over muddy, soaked ground."[5]

Where the terrain allowed for trams and hand trucks on narrow-gauge railways to get close to the front, such as the line that ran from an advanced dressing station at Neuville–St. Vaast to the rear, the wounded could be cleared rapidly. "Worked all night at Ambulance Corner loading ambulances + unloading tram trucks of wounded," wrote Joseph Harrison MacFarlane, who had enlisted at age twenty from Montreal and served in the No. 9 Field Ambulance. "Terrible experience."[6] On April 9, MacFarlane and others like him moved 1,050 lying cases (men unable to walk and confined to stretchers) to the rear, and another 350 were transported the next day.[7] Another 2,000 patients passed through No. 8 Canadian Field Ambulance on April 9, where many succumbed to their wounds. Twenty-year-old Private Andrew Coulter of the No. 4 Canadian Field Ambulance wrote in his diary on April 9: "At one time nearly 500 dying on stretchers in the open."[8] Coulter eventually returned to Canada, where he studied to be a doctor, practising in Weyburn, Saskatchewan. But he never escaped the war. He was plagued his whole life by nightmares and took his own life in 1960.

Even trained doctors were shocked by the carnage. Captain Bellenden Hutcheson, an American surgeon serving with the Canadians and a future winner of the Victoria Cross, wrote to one friend about the wounded whom he encountered. "The whole thing seemed rather unreal. . . . I remember one man who had a ghastly wound which would obviously prove fatal in a short time, pleading with me, amidst the turmoil of explosions, to shoot him."[9] Lieutenant Howard Scott, a combat engineer who witnessed the bleeding mess of men, penned in his personal diary, "Worst battle in history of war to date. Hundreds blinded, arms and legs off. One man without any arms and legs still living."[10] Amos Mayse, a veteran of the South African War, wrote to his wife and children about the human wreckage: "At the present time we are on a part of a battlefield which will be for ever famous in British history, & which will stand out as among the bloodiest of the whole war. . . . the horror of it all can never be described, it's worse than hell."[11]

With the field ambulances overwhelmed by the wounded, difficult choices had to be made by the medical officers. "Casualties were lying on stretchers in rows," wrote Private Hubert Morris of the No. 10 Field Ambulance, a twenty-one-year-old schoolteacher from Lambton, Ontario. The commanding medical officer examined the men, triaging those who were to be treated first and those who could wait. A smaller number who were too badly wounded to survive—or whose treatment would take up hours and therefore consign to death other men who were left without care—were untreated. "Occasionally, he gave us a nod to carry one outside," noted Morris. "These were ones he thought could not survive and it made room for one that could. We heard no protest from those removed and they were probably unconscious."[12] Morris and his fellow medical orderlies helped to transport some of the critically wounded out into the cold air. They tried to make them comfortable by putting blankets over them, but soon the falling snow covered them like a shroud.

"One poor fellow, a big chap, was crying like a baby with shell-shock," wrote Lance-Corporal Donald Fraser, a machine-gunner in the 31st Battalion. "His nerves and control were absolutely gone."[13] The broken soldier was sent to the rear. Along the front, the ordeal of battle left men with mental injuries. The strain of combat, both the anticipation and fear before the assault, and the chaos and awfulness of the clash, could shatter the mind. Sometimes a traumatic trigger event set a man off—watching a friend dismembered by a shell or a near-death experience. Even the best leaders succumbed to the strain. Captain Thain MacDowell of the 38th Battalion led from the front, captured dozens of prisoners, and organized his depleted company to defend against counterattacks, all of which earned him a Victoria Cross for his inspiring leadership. But he would break down and suffer from shellshock in the battle's aftermath.

"BODIES COULD BE SEEN PROTRUDING FROM shellholes half filled with water stained scarlet with human blood, and many of the various Canadian regiments and numerous Germans lay scattered everywhere over the ground," recounted Captain Joseph Hayes of the 85th Battalion.[14] The stretcher-bearers had focused on the living, while the dead were left for the grave-digging teams. It took several days to clear the battlefield of corpses, but it was a necessary task to prevent contamination of the water sources. Lime was spread liberally to quell disease. It worked, but for Vimy veterans the sharp smell of lime would forever be associated with mass death.

Rare photograph of Canadian dead on the Vimy battlefield.

A roll call for the front-line battalions in the days following the battle was a sombre affair. The survivors were called to attention and an officer read out the names of the missing. Men answered when present; too often there was silence. Occasionally a private asked for permission to speak and recounted seeing a chum shot or wounded, or decisively killed with a bullet through the head or heart. Some of these stories were confused and wrong. Men with frightening wounds survived in rear hospitals, while others, perhaps suffering a minor injury, were killed by a shell or bullet further down the line. It took days and sometimes weeks to compile the true casualty lists, and even then, many of the dead were listed as missing, their bodies swallowed in the mud or dismembered in shellfire. On the Somme, many of the missing had, in fact, been taken as prisoners in enemy counterattacks as the Canadians were pushed out of their trenches. But at Vimy, where the enemy was thrown off the ridge, the Canadians lost only fifty-one prisoners to the enemy. The fate of a disappeared man was almost always death.

Before the battle, the Canadians had prepared for the mass loss of life. They had dug large pits behind the lines and prepared grave registration teams to identify and bury the dead.[15] But with badly dismembered corpses, that was no easy task. Burial teams collected information on the Canadian dead, especially the two-part identification disk (known as a dog tag in the next war) that provided key information and religion. The religion was important to make sure the padre said the right words over the bodies. With so many bodies to inter, many teams buried the corpses in shell craters on the ridge to avoid the grisly transport of the slain to the rear. Corporal Fred Maiden of the 10th Battalion, who would be awarded the Military Medal, recalled, "We tried to identify some of the boys to try to get their identity discs off them. But we couldn't do it. See, the boys were blown to pieces."[16]

The seeping bodies and body parts were collected and catalogued, but that took time, and guards had to be posted around the mountains of corpses to keep away the thousands of rats. It was a losing battle, and within the layers of dead the rats feasted. When the trains and trams finally brought their grim cargo out of the line, they moved the corpses to the graves. Wilfrid Bovey of the 8th Brigade wrote decades later that he had never forgotten a "trainload of corpses, piled on top of another on light railway flat cars. They had to be checked over to see that the necessary identification tags had been left in place, not removed as had often been done. Still limbs, white faces, gaping bloodless wounds were sights we all remember only too well, but these dreadful carloads had a peculiar horror."[17] Of the 10,602 casualties over the four-day battle, 3,598 were fatal.[18]

THE 9TH OF APRIL HAD BEEN a long day, and by its end most soldiers were near collapse. Storms swirled around the ridge, with great gusts of icy wind lashing the exposed infantrymen. Some of the infantry units were cycled to the rear, but most had to tough out the night. The Germans sought to discomfort the Canadians with shellfire throughout the period, and the occupiers on the ridge, according to one eyewitness, "got badly mauled."[19]

A wave of Canadian Vickers machine-gun teams had accompanied the second and third waves of infantry. The Vickers were too heavy to drag into combat to engage in direct fire, with that role left to the Lewis machine-gunners, but 104 Vickers came into the front lines throughout the day to act as a powerful force to

*Canadian Vickers machine-gun teams dig into the mud on
Vimy Ridge and prepare to hold it against enemy counterattack.*

defend against potential counterattacks. On the 3rd Division's
front, a number of Vickers assisted the beleaguered 4th Division
by firing into the rear areas of the Germans, and a party of 300
reinforcing enemy troops was caught marching exposed along
the bottom of the eastern slope. The Vickers mowed them down,
leaving dozens of corpses in the mud.[20]

Above the battlefield, RFC observer planes circled the front,
providing information to the commanders in the rear and searching for enemy targets. At least two German battalions were marching towards the ridge in mid-afternoon on April 10, when the
observers in the planes above caught sight of them and reported
their location to the gunners.[21] Both enemy forces, the first at

Willerval, and the second opposite Thélus on the 2nd Division's front, were broken up by shellfire.

While some of the Allied guns could still hurl shells into the enemy lines from their positions to the west, the mass of artillery would have to be dragged up the ridge for any further advance into the German lines. New roads were built and duckboards laid over the mud for the infantry, but the horses struggled to make any headway. Major Cyrus Inches, commander of the 1st Canadian Heavy Battery, wrote that "the ground was so bad that in some places sixteen horses were used to move a gun."[22] Corporal Leonard Cuff wrote, "rain + snow + mud to the horses bellies, there were hundreds of them shot which had got stuck in the mud."[23] In such conditions, few guns moved forward on the 9th.

The enemy, in turn, shelled the Canadians on the ridge, claiming dozens of lives. Others were left mangled and mutilated. Ethelbert "Curley" Christian was a private with the 78th Battalion, running up supplies to the sharp-end forces. The thirty-three-year-old prewar labourer was an African American who stood five foot six and acquired his nickname from his dark, textured hair. Curley was delivering supplies to the front when a shell landed near him, injuring him badly and throwing him into the foul muck. He somehow escaped suffocation, but lay near death for two days before being discovered. Surgery saved his life, but gangrene had set into all of his wounds and the doctors were forced to amputate both his hands and his legs below the knees. Curley beat the long odds, the only Canadian quadruple amputee to do so in the war.[24] He returned to Canada, married the volunteer aide in Toronto who cared for him, Cleopatra (Cleo) McPherson, and devoted his life to serving other veterans.

WHILE MOST OF HILL 145 WAS in Canadian hands by the end of the 9th, Germans were still dug in along the eastern slope. They had to be cleared out. On April 10, Major-General Watson ordered Brigadier Edward Hilliam's 10th Brigade of the 4th Division to drive the enemy back. Hilliam had been preparing to strike against the Pimple, as per the original plan, but the need to seize all of the ridge overrode it. The Pimple would have to wait.

The torn-up ground and terrible weather delayed the operation as infantrymen struggled to the front-line trenches. But the 44th and 50th Battalions swept down the ridge at 3:15 P.M. behind a creeping barrage, heading to capture the Hangstellung, a line of trenches at the bottom of the ridge. "Heavy shells from well-targeted guns hidden in the valley began to level our officers and men," wrote Private Victor Wheeler of the 50th Battalion. "Down went a dozen of Canada's finest chaps in the first sixty seconds." With bullets and shells tearing men apart, Wheeler noted that the soldier in battle, in pushing himself to advance in the face of heavy fire, "finds himself staring alone into the face of the Almighty. A breath of blackness blows cold on his innermost soul." The Manitobans of the 44th took their objectives, but the Albertans in the 50th on the left were held up by machine-gun fire from the Pimple, and from at least one 77mm field gun firing over open sights below them on the cratered ridge. Wheeler observed his comrades "impaled like grotesque scarecrows on rusty concertina wire, splashed into water-filled craters, scattered over the lower slopes of the hill in gruesome fragments."[25]

As in so many battles over the previous twenty-four hours, it fell to small groups, sometimes even a single man, to tip the balance. Forty-two-year-old John Pattison, a British-born engineer from Calgary, advanced alone against a live machine gun, sneaking to within 30 metres of it. Judging the distance, he lobbed his grenades and leapt up in a bayonet charge. The stunned Germans were slow to react and he ran them through with cold steel. The way was opened up, and Pattison's men followed him. Pattison was awarded the Victoria Cross but was killed in fierce fighting six weeks later. By late afternoon, the German lines east of Hill 145 were cleared of the enemy, and another 200 prisoners were captured and hundreds more killed or wounded.[26] More importantly, the danger of the Germans counterattacking was much reduced as they no longer had a firm base to the east of the ridge from which to strike.

One strongpoint remained. The Pimple, a high point of about 135 metres, was a bastion from which to mount an effective thrust into the Canadians' open flank. It was a heavily defended position with two large concrete emplacements. While the enemy high command was in turmoil over the loss of Vimy, they had kept their heads and reinforced the Pimple with two battalions of elite Prussian units from the 4th Guards Infantry Division. No one expected it to fall easily.

The final battle for the Vimy sector was launched at dawn on April 12. After a postponement from the previous day because of the challenges of situating the guns and getting ammunition to the front along the muddy, rutted roads, and through snow squalls, the Westerners of the cut-up 50th, 46th, and 44th Battalions were ordered to drive the Germans from their fortifications. As the three attacking battalions waited in their trenches for the barrage along a 1,000-metre front, the enemy engaged in searching fire and relentless flares that lit the landscape in ghostly shades of white. The crump of high-explosive shells was an ominous sound for so early in the morning, and the Germans seemed ready. Experienced

Canadians were visibly nervous, with men shivering from the cold and nerves. The clouds became denser and the moon disappeared. Large snowflakes fell and boots were soaked through from standing in the icy slush.

At 5 A.M., the barrage lit up the enemy lines and the darkness. "Where all had been quiet a moment before," wrote Private Robert Kentner, "there was a bursting hill of death, a screaming, savage, devilish thing let loose upon us, maddeningly hungry for our destruction."[27] A German officer of the 2nd Reserve Infantry Regiment later wrote of being on the receiving end: "Insanely violent drumfire came down on our trenches."[28] Private Neil McLeod, a tall farm boy from Turtleford, Saskatchewan, was advancing as part of a rifle-grenade team. They pushed forward, stopping to fire their grenades when they saw a target through the snow and shellfire, and then shuffling off again into the blinding storm and enemy fire. "We hadn't gone three or four steps when the little fellow who loaded the rifle grenade for me had his head blown off. I was looking right at him and all of a sudden his head just vanished. I had bits of his brains splattered all over my tunic."[29] The stunned McLeod steadied himself and continued the advance. He was destined to survive the war.

Private Victor Wheeler of the 50th Battalion struggled to lift each boot out of the clinging mud to keep up with the storm of shells, marvelling at the German trenches exploding skywards. All around him, within the blizzard of shells and driving snow, his friends were falling to the ground. Others were already dead, their lifeless faces staring up at the sky or submerged in water-filled craters. Wheeler's breath caught in his throat as he came across Harry Waller, a friend of two years. "He was in great pain, his back twisted out of shape. His left arm and right leg were broken, and his shin bone was sticking through the flesh. Pieces of shrapnel stuck out of his head. His eyes filmed greyly and shut out the past—and the present."[30] Wheeler took this all in, along with the piteous sight of Harry's brother, Art, weeping over his brother's writhing body, and then continued to push forward into the madness.

Two hidden concrete pillboxes containing Prussian machine-gunners and infantrymen were firing into the Canadians as they struggled over the muddy ground. With little cover, the Canadians fell in sickening numbers but continued the advance, stumbling forward behind the creeping barrage as it moved on, going to ground when it smashed down in front of them. Stabbing, shooting, and bombing their way forward, they felt the resistance crumble. Within two hours, the Prussians were either in full flight, heading towards prisoner camps, or dead. Maritimer Laurence Colpitts, serving with Saskatchewan comrades in the 46th Battalion, recounted that "Small groups could be seen running for safety towards their own lines. I was firing on these as fast as I could work my magazine and take aim when a sniper on our right got me in the shoulder."[31] Colpitts was one of 108 casualties suffered by the 46th in the attack on the Pimple: 26 killed and 82 wounded. Atop the Pimple, the Canadians now dominated the Souchez River and ridge, and held a nearly continuous front with their comrades on Vimy.

"CAPTURED VIMY. HUN IN FULL RETREAT," wrote Sergeant Victor John Nixon in his small red diary on April 12.[32] The brief entry was all the combat soldier had time to write, but it encapsulated the success of the day. The German final defences had been broken decisively. While isolated pockets of defenders held on to

This cartoon by Bruce Bairnsfather, the most famous
British cartoonist of the war, celebrates the Canadian
victory. The text states rather cheekily, "Vimy! And
the next thing Please." The triumphant Canadians
are ready for more battles.

the southern part of the eastern ridge, the three German divisions, and backstopping reinforcements, had been routed. Most of the front-line German regiments were annihilated.

The Canadian soldiers took enormous pride in their victory, and they had every right to it. But they also noted that thorough planning, intense training, evolving tactics, and the crushing artillery bombardment had eased the way to victory. Some believed there was nothing left to do after the bombardment but occupy the smoking ruins, but the brutal fighting and horrendous casualties revealed that assertion to be misguided. It might have been an easy march up the ridge on a few fronts, but most sectors required intense combat. Success also went to the generals and staff officers, who had put the plan in motion, gathered resources to assist those in the forward units, and thrown reinforcements into the line when they had to. Byng and his divisional commanders had all risen to the occasion, and even Major-General David Watson, a weak commander, had done right by his men.

The Canadian victory was aided by the poor generalship of Sixth Army commander General Ludwig von Falkenhausen, who had acted with insufficient urgency in the critical hours on the 9th. Information coming into his headquarters was confused and conflicting, but he seemed stunned and unable to function when word arrived that his troops had been ejected from the ridge in a single day of battle. He had based his whole defence on holding the ridge for several days, long enough to march up his counter-attack forces, especially the 1st Guards Reserve Division and 18th Infantry Division, both of which were ready to spring against the invaders. The shock and speed of the Canadian advance had destroyed his plan. The few failed desultory counterattacks that were broken up by Allied artillery and infantrymen, with heavy casualties to his troops, provoked the dispirited von Falkenhausen to cut his losses. On the 12th, he ordered a withdrawal of about 7 kilometres, out of range of Allied shellfire, to his existing line, and waited for a renewed assault.

Crown Prince Rupprecht, von Falkenhausen's commanding officer, wrote despondently in his diary in the days following the battle, "I doubt that we can recapture Vimy ridge. . . . This leads to the question: is there any sense in continuing the war?"[33] There was, as the loss of Vimy was only a tactical defeat. Nonetheless, it weighed heavily on the Germans since Vimy Ridge was a symbol of the German occupation throughout northeast France. The ridge shielded the crucial Lens coal mines that had to be kept running to feed the German war machine. Being driven off the ridge represented more than simply the yielding of a few kilometres of muddy, cratered farmers' fields. Ludendorff cashiered the seventy-two-year-old von Falkenhausen from command of the Sixth Army in Vimy's aftermath and he was appointed governor general of Belgium. The German high command of Hindenburg and Ludendorff, the latter whose birthday fell on the 9th, was shaken by the defeat—"deeply depressed," in Ludendorff's words. "The impact of the news throws a sombre picture," lamented the normally phlegmatic Hindenburg. "Many shadows, little light."[34]

If despair blackened the German command, there was exhilaration at Haig's headquarters. The commander-in-chief wrote in his diary on April 12, "When I think over the fine work of the 4th Canadian Division in taking the Pimple notwithstanding the mud, shell holes and snow, I come to the conclusion that no other people are comparable to the British race as downright hard fighters."[35] A triumphant Byng was no less pleased when walking the ruins on the Pimple. "It is a sight: The dead are rather ghastly but a feat of arms that will stand for ever. Poor Old Prussian Guard. What a mouthful to swallow being beaten to hell by what they called 'untrained Colonial levies.'" As Byng and Haig knew, the Canadian Corps were hardly untrained colonials. They had spent months practising and planning the operation. They had built roads, dug gun pits, and marshalled guns. They had introduced new weapons and found ways to wield them into a coherent, hard-hitting formation. And all of that had helped to level ground that was firmly tilted in favour of the German defenders. Vimy had fallen to the Canadians in four days of fighting through combat of the most intense and violent kind. Forward-thinking leadership, dogged-ness, and courage had carried the battle. Careful preparation based on good intelligence, gathered over months, had contributed to victory and was, somewhat ironically, the antithesis of the repu-tation for wild dash and reckless élan of the supposed natural frontier warriors who formed the Canadian Corps. At the same time, heroes had emerged, been shot down, and been replaced by new ones stepping up. The cost had been terrible, but the Canadians, against all odds, had driven the Germans from their fortress.

THE VIMY VICTORY WAS NOT ACHIEVED in isolation from the British offensive to the south. Allenby's Third Army bore the brunt of the Arras campaign and ten divisions launched the initial assault, with two more in close support. On April 9th, the British made deep gains as artillery shattered the enemy's forward defence, and some 9,000 German prisoners were captured and thousands more killed on the first day of battle. But like the Canadians on the ridge, the British had grave difficulties in moving forward their artillery to keep up with the advancing infantry whose momentum was taking them out of range of protective shelling. Major-General Tim Harrington, chief of staff to General Sir Herbert Plumer's Second Army, remarked on the challenge of fighting: "The further we penetrate his line, the stronger and more organised we find him . . . [while] the weaker and more disorganised we are liable to become."[36]

General Allenby was wildly optimistic that he had the Hun on the run. Though "the Bull" was inarticulate at the best of times,

Allenby was now frothing with excitement at the prospect of a breakthrough. Anxious to see greater advances, he issued wild orders to attack, attack, attack. While his staff tried to translate these orders into coherent objectives, the divisions at the front were already flailing blindly. Poor weather had grounded many of the aircraft that had been supplying intelligence to the infantry and gunners. Although the British continued to make impressive gains on the 10th, the enemy line was stiffening and the gains were limited. The next day, April 11, Allenby tried to whip his men forward, claiming that the Germans were beaten and urging that "risks must be taken freely." He achieved little other than working himself into a lather, and his brave Tommies increasingly ran up against uncut barbed wire and undamaged defensive positions, with disastrous results.[37] On that same day, the Germans found firmer footing and began limited and localized counterattacks that further slowed the British advance. The advantage soon shifted to the Germans, who fell back on their lines of communication and the protective screen of artillery, machine guns, and reinforcements. The BEF had shown that it could fracture the enemy line behind massive artillery barrages, but that they could not break through or out of the German defence-in-depth. The initial high hopes degenerated into an attritional slugfest.

THE BATTLE TO THE SOUTH WENT completely off the rails when the French Aisne offensive was launched on April 16. Due to an appalling lack of control over information, leaked French plans revealed to the Germans exactly where General Nivelle planned to strike at the 180-metre highpoint of Chemin des Dames and the surrounding region. Moreover, the German retreat in March had severely disrupted French planning and they had not recovered, despite having had six weeks to advance into the abandoned zone. Some 54 French divisions supported by 5,300 guns attacked 21 German divisions, who were backed by another 17 counter-attacking divisions.[38]

The French forces, already worn out from the Verdun battles the year before but puffed up by Nivelle's promise of an assured breakthrough, wilted in the face of concentrated German fire and suffered tens of thousands of casualties in the first two weeks of combat, with some 30,000 killed and 100,000 wounded.[39] Even though the stoic French soldiers were no strangers to grisly blood-lettings in the pursuit of liberating their country, the losses were particularly crippling to morale since Nivelle had guaranteed victory. As the French push floundered, Haig continued to press the offensive in the north. April 9, 1917, had ended in stark contrast to July 1, 1916, and Haig had been thrilled by the initial victories in the early days of the Arras campaign. Haig suppressed his early reticence to push the offensive too far, and now became fully enamoured with the campaign. An attritional battle on the Arras front might write off enough German divisions to hamper the enemy's ability to vigorously defend the forthcoming Flanders campaign. Haig wrote in his diary on April 18, "Great results are never achieved in war until the enemy's resisting power has been broken."[40] In Haig's mind, Arras was now a wearing-down campaign, much like the Somme, and the breakthrough would happen in Flanders. With optimistic reports fed to him and his own stout faith that God was on his side, Haig believed victory was only a battle away. He was wrong.

The British launched another major offensive on April 23, known as the Second Battle of the Scarpe, in which five British divisions pressed the assault. Wet and cold weather made life miserable for the British troops, but the initial thrust achieved a significant advance of up to 1.5 kilometres and far surpassed anything on the Somme. Yet there was no decisive blow, and the German defences around the coal-mining town of Lens could not be breached. The Third Army, to the south, engaged in even more futile battles that accounted for another 8,000 casualties for few gains.[41] A half-hearted push on April 28 offered few tangible triumphs, although the Canadian Corps captured the strongpoint of Arleux, and further added to its reputation as shock troops since most of the other British formations floundered in defeat.

The French offensive was far worse off. A desperate Nivelle fired generals and encouraged his battered forces to continue to press the enemy, but they were exhausted and even the lowest ranker could see there was no chance that the enemy would break. By the end of the battle, the French casualties had risen to around 160,000. The politicians in Paris, feeling tricked and used by Nivelle and his earlier sanguine claims of victory, now denounced him. Closer to the front, the *poilus* shuddered at the losses, made worse by their callous treatment by uncaring officers, bad leave policy, and unsympathetic leadership. One staff officer described the French force as an "army without faith."[42]

In early May, a few units refused to enter the line to continue fighting. The infection spread, and by the time the Nivelle offensive was shut down on May 15, a quarter of the army was in mutiny.[43] The French soldiers would not abandon the line, which would lead to France's defeat in the war, but nor would they continue to throw themselves into the enemy guns with their usual reckless abandon. Nivelle was packed off to North Africa in disgrace. Philippe Pétain, an army commander at Verdun, replaced Nivelle as commander-in-chief. The new high command gradually restored order in France's hollow armies by instigating reforms to ease the infantry's anger, including better food and leave policy, but also by executing about fifty of the mutiny's ringleaders. The reforms stopped the hemorrhaging, but the patient remained on life support. The French army was a shaky force for the rest of the year.

Haig knew his Gallic allies were faltering, and so he felt compelled to continue attacking and keep up the pressure on the Germans. Further British operations on May 3 made little progress, although the Canadians again captured their objective at Fresnoy, and the next two weeks saw limited engagement and battles along the line until Haig shut down the offensive on May 15. During the thirty-nine-day campaign, Haig's forces had inflicted an estimated 120,000 casualties on the enemy. In turn, they had suffered 158,660 casualties.[44] The French nation and army was traumatized by the grand failure, while Haig's army had too little to show for its massive bloodletting. Only the capture of Vimy Ridge was an identifiable victory in a sea of slaughter and stalemate.

CHAPTER 6

VIMY'S IMPACT

"You have no doubt heard before this of the big advance of the Canadians and the capture of Vimy Ridge," wrote P. Winthrop McClare of Mount Uniacke, Nova Scotia, an underage soldier who arrived at the front on April 8, 1917, and was immediately sent into combat with the 24th Battalion. "I was in the whole of that battle and it was Hell. I got a small splinter of shrapnel through the fleshy part of my shoulder. It was very slight and I went through it all with it. It was some battle and I am glad to say that I was through it, as it will be one of the biggest things in Canadian history."[1] Winnie, as he was known to family and friends, survived the battle but was killed less than a month later. He has no known grave, and he would never know for certain that Vimy would indeed become one of the most momentous events in Canadian history, or that his name would eventually be inscribed on the Vimy Memorial as one of Canada's missing.

Canadian soldiers were proud of Vimy in a way that was different from the previous two years of battle. The tone of the letters after Second Ypres, the April 1915 battle, was one of battered pride and of duty done. In the days following the battle, the War Office announced, "The Canadians had many casualties but their gallantry and determination undoubtedly saved the situation."[2] The losses had been crippling—at one third of the force—but Canada had stood its ground in the face of shells and gas, and had forged its reputation. No soldiers wrote in such terms of the defeats at Festubert and St. Eloi, in May 1915 and April 1916, except again to express a gritty pride in having stood a terrible test. That was also the sentiment on the Somme, although there was significant celebration of the 2nd Division's victory at Courcelette in September.

But from the start of the Vimy battle, the Canadian reaction was different. Vimy was understood by those who were there as a significant victory. "The morning of the 9th saw the greatest artillery barrage since the War began and under its intense course the Canadian Infantry won undying glory in the capture of one of the greatest of the enemies strongholds Vimy Ridge," enthused Major Horace Hubert Forster Dibblee in his diary.[3] While some Vimy victors admitted to the important role played by British artillery, logistic, and infantry support, the battle was framed as a Canadian victory. Sergeant Walter Draycot of the PPCLI was not alone in claiming, "It was Canada's day."[4] Lance-Corporal G.H. Tripp, from Huttonville, Ontario, wrote, "I guess you know by now that we attacked the Germans last week at Vimy so you can tell by the papers what success attended our efforts. We certainly did better than we expected."[5] Tripp was killed in battle less than three weeks later, but he knew that Vimy was a victory, partially because, as he noted, the Canadians did better than any could have predicted. Vimy mattered because the Germans had seemed to be in an impregnable position. The French had tried in the past to capture it and failed, and the Canadians, through careful planning and tenacious fighting, had taken it. The Canadian

Corps, continually remade by new units and reinforcements, but four divisions strong and consisting of men from across the Dominion, could claim Vimy as an unqualified victory, in a way that the Somme, Mount Sorrel, or even Second Ypres were not.

"I AM NO HERO, MOTHER," WROTE thirty-three-year-old Private Percy Holden of the 75th Battalion, who was awarded the Military Medal. "I did what I could not help but do and what I have seen many another man do."[6] There were countless acts of bravery on Vimy Ridge, but most went unrecorded. In the hierarchical British and Canadian armies, an officer had to witness an act and write a citation for a soldier to be recommended for a gallantry award. Many deserving men were overlooked, especially because the horrendous casualties to officers meant that the recording of courageous actions went to the grave with them. Artillery officer F.A. Pile wrote disgustedly, "I don't know on what system they do these things, but there are an awful lot of good deeds that are never rewarded and many who do get honours do not deserve them."[7] Most combat soldiers agreed with this and few put much stock in trying to secure a gallantry medal. Four Canadians received the Victoria Cross during the battle, the Empire's highest award for gallantry, three of them awarded posthumously. No one would deny the extraordinary valour of these men, but many more could have been recognized with awards in the mad and costly scramble up the ridge.

As the heroes were honoured, the Canadians also counted the battle's spoils. The Corps captured 63 enemy guns, 104 trench mortars, 124 machine guns, and 4,081 prisoners of war.[8] The records for two German divisions, the 79th Reserve and 1st

Bavarian Reserve, indicated total losses up to April 11 of 6,604 soldiers, and likely another 1,000 men were killed, wounded, or captured on the 12th.[9] War trophies had always been a tangible sign of victory over the enemy, and the enormous number of captured guns and prisoners were proof, if more was needed, of the Canadian triumph. Major C.B. Topp of the 42nd Battalion wrote of the trophies, "There were great stacks of machine guns, curiously futile looking jumbled together as they were like so much old iron, huge parks of artillery of all sizes, each gun jealously chalked with the name of the unit by which it had been captured."[10] The Imperial War Museum, founded in 1917, had first dibs on the trophies, as it was to display the Empire's war effort, but after the war thousands of trophies were sent back to the Public Archives of Canada in Ottawa. From there the trophies were distributed across the country to cities, towns, and villages, where they were displayed prominently at city halls, parks, and libraries.

On the battlefield, for the first time in the war, many of the Canadian units erected memorials. What was it about Vimy and not the Somme, or Mount Sorrel, or Second Ypres that compelled the creation of these memorials? At the most basic level, Vimy was a clear-cut victory. At the battle's end, the Canadians were left with the ridge in their hands, and they held it for several months before moving off to another sector of the Western Front. At the time, the Germans had retreated to the east and it seemed unlikely that they could mount any sort of effective counterattack. A memorial built on the ridge might therefore survive the war. No one could say that of memorials on the Somme or in the Ypres salient, where see-saw battles raged over battlefields won and lost. But there was more to it than the question of perseverance. Vimy had also been a costly battle, the most devastating to that point

This memorial, erected by members of the Canadian Artillery,
was one of many unit monuments to mark the victory
and sacrifice at the Battle of Vimy Ridge.

in the war in terms of soldiers lost per day. The 10,602 casualties over the four days of fighting equated to almost 2,700 a day, and were far more than the Somme's 24,000 casualties spread over the three months of September to November.[11] And even more deaths were attributed to Vimy as soldiers succumbed to wounds after the battle. Private Leo LeBoutillier of the 24th Battalion, who wore the Distinguished Conduct Medal for his bravery on the battlefield, was one of them. Shot in the stomach during the battle, his wound appeared clean, but "Boots," as he was known to his friends, died on April 18, 1917, likely of infection. Many more followed him to an early grave after the battle's official dates of April 9 to 12. Statistics show, for instance, that the Canadian Corps suffered 13,660 casualties from April 1 to 24.[12]

In the aftermath of the battle, Major-General David Watson wrote to a correspondent about his pride in how the Corps drove the enemy from their strongpoint, especially at Hill 145. He believed that an "all-Canadian Memorial Monument should be erected at this point to testify to the valour and sacrifice that has been made in the struggle for the famous Vimy Ridge."[13] There was a need to mark the sacrifice. While the creation of a national memorial was some time off, individual units set to building their own monuments. The 21st Battalion resolved to put up a cross on Vimy as a memorial to its fallen soldiers, using material salvaged from the battlefield. One of the battalion's privates, George Williams of Cornwall, was an adept carpenter and he was temporarily transferred to the 4th Field Company of Canadian Engineers. There, he had access to woodworking tools and supplies. He constructed a handsome cross and painted it white, while the officers pooled their money and purchased a steel plaque.[14] The memorial stood in the Canadian Cemetery during the war and was brought back to Kingston after the armistice, where it found a home at the Royal Military College of Canada and eventually, in 1994, at the Princess of Wales' Own Regiment armoury in Kingston. "It is some satisfaction to know that those lads who had gone out never to return had not made the sacrifice in vain," recounted Canadian Lieutenant A.K. Harvie.[15]

There were other regimental memorials, like the crosses erected by the 44th and 46th Battalions and the Canadian artillerymen's large stone cairn at Les Tilleuls crossroads, east of Neuville–St. Vaast. The 1st Division also built a stone cairn supporting a white cross, south of Thélus, while the 3rd Division created a cross on their fighting front.[16] Captain T.C. McGill was there in early July with about 100 men for the unveiling of the division's memorial. At noon, twelve of the big guns fired three volleys, and all the men presented arms. Pipers lamented with a dirge and padres preached. "I have never seen men stand straighter or with their heads more proudly lifted," wrote McGill, "for each felt that a little bit of his own heart was buried there too."[17] The Canadians stood with their back to the Germans, but they turned to face the front when they sang "God Save the King."

NEWS OF THE VICTORIOUS BATTLE REACHED Canada in time to appear in the late editions of many newspapers on April 9, 1917. The *Edmonton Journal* crowed, "Whole German Line Wavers Under First Spring Attack."[18] The next day, *The Globe* informed its readers, "Canadians lead in triumph," while the Vancouver *Sun* exclaimed on its front page, "Famous Ridge the Scene of Many Gory Battles was Stormed and Carried by Warriors from Canada."[19] *L'Acadien* from Moncton led with the story, "Brillant fait d'armes canadiens. La fameuse crete Vimy, theâtre de tant de combat metriers, est enlevées aux allemands par un irresistible assault de gars du Canada."[20] *Le Devoir*, the Quebec paper that was critical of the extent of the Canadian war effort, also repeated translated accounts from the English papers that extolled the Corps' victory.[21] The headlines and stories continued to unfold, with the *Halifax Herald* reporting on April 11 how the Canadians had inflicted on the enemy, "A terrible if not disastrous defeat." Even American papers such as *The New York Times* declared that the battle, "would be in Canada's history . . . a day of glory to furnish inspiration to her sons for generations."[22]

The news of the Vimy victory provoked immediate jubilation across the Dominion, followed by a wave of fear. The casualty lists were published a few days after the battle, and even before the long columns of the dead appeared, there were widespread

=HE WOULD LIKE TO KNOW=

VON HINDENBURG—"Iss dose United States-ers relation any to der Canadians, vot?"

This Canadian newspaper cartoon depicts the battered German general Hindenburg asking a German-American sympathizer if the Americans are as strong and powerful as the Canadians. The general, the cartoon suggests, hopes the Americans are not as good as the Canadians, who have just handed him a defeat, or the German army is doomed.

rumours that the ridge's capture had been a costly one. Survivors at the front, tired and heartbroken, took to writing to their killed mates' families, and these letters arrived two to three weeks after being posted. Letters were almost always couched in the language of cheerful sacrifice and a clean death in battle. They were what the families wanted and needed, although they were not always an accurate reflection of the final minutes of a dying soldier's experiences.

Those at home worried as they waited for news. Will Antliff, a commerce student at McGill who enlisted with No. 9 Canadian Field Ambulance in January 1916, was at Vimy. As early as April 9, his mother wrote, almost pleadingly, that, "the papers are about the taking of Vimy Ridge." Three days later, as the casualty lists were printed in the papers, she was more anxious, querying in another letter, "Were you at Vimy Ridge? It is all so terrible. . . . It is very sad though that so many fine lives must be sacrificed, the latest one we have heard of whom we know is young Symonds."[23] Will Antliff survived the battle, and the entire war, to be reunited with his family in Montreal.

Thousands of Canadian families were not so fortunate. The mother of infantryman Shinkichi Hara, who was killed at Vimy, committed her grief to paper, writing, "Since the death of my son, I feel very lonely, but I am well. My son's ambition was to fight for his country and help bring world peace. It is very difficult for me to realize that he was killed in France. He was my only child."[24] Hara was one of fifty-four Japanese Canadians killed serving with the Canadian Corps during the war. Mrs. Duncan Ross of Waldegrave, Nova Scotia, received official notification that both her sons—Major Arthur Ross and Lieutenant William G. Ross—were killed.[25] She was stunned by the horrendous news but soon settled herself, writing notes to loved ones, finding comfort in her neighbours and friends. A few weeks later, a letter arrived from her son William, dated after his reported death. She frantically tried to find out if he was alive or if the letter was misdated, sending off telegrams and letters to Ottawa. Perhaps Arthur was alive, too. More weeks of agonizing waiting and frantic missives to the Department of Militia and Defence revealed that William had indeed survived the battle. She received no reprieve for Arthur, who had fallen at Vimy.

Some parents were unable to accept the anguish of never seeing their sons again. Lieutenant Clifford Wells of the 8th Battalion wrote to his mom and dad of the Vimy battle on April 20, noting that, in his mind, "the greatest victory of the war has been gained, and I had small part in it." He was killed eight days later. His mother, Frances Moule, who, according to her husband, had before the news been "the embodiment of health, strength, and an abounding and radiant life," took to her bed in grief.[26] She died twenty-two days later. The Vimy battle claimed more than just soldiers.

VIMY WAS ONE OF THE FEW bright spots in the otherwise bleak Arras campaign. After years of defeat, death, and stalemate, the British Empire was in desperate need of a win—and a dramatic one at that. It received this from the First Army and the Canadian Corps. The King wrote to Haig, "Canada will be proud that the taking of the coveted Vimy Ridge has fallen to the lot of her troops."[27] The French, too, after the bloodletting of Verdun and their own trials in the Aisne region, could celebrate "Canada's Easter Gift" to their nation, as newspapers extolled it in headlines across the Republic.[28] That was not just hyperbole: the French knew of Vimy Ridge and the blood sacrifice there by their own troops. For two years, Vimy had rarely been out of the French papers, and the contested site was always in German hands; now it had been returned to France by the Canadians.

Vimy also had its own geography. It was an identifiable site on maps, looming over the countryside, and it stretched even further in the mind's eye. This warscape was significantly different from the terrain farther to the south that the British captured, which was largely eviscerated farmland. One British soldier, Den

Fortescue, wrote to his father, "the papers really give a very fair idea of the show apart from the fuss that is made of the Canadians: their share of it was really very small though they did very well."[29] On the 9th, there were several British divisions who drove deeper into the German lines than the Canadians, but the ridge dominated the region and the imaginary landscape too.

The strategic picture of the war did not change with Vimy. The war did not end on April 12, 1917. It would go on for nineteen more months, minus a day. But Vimy mattered at the time to the Allies, and it mattered far more to the Canadian Corps. The martial history of the Corps, to April 1917, was a spotted one at best. No one would denigrate the heroic stand of the Canadian Division at the Battle of Second Ypres in April 1915 against overwhelming German forces, firepower, and chlorine gas. But the battles since then—Festubert, St. Eloi, Mount Sorrel, and the Somme—had been a mixture of costly victories, draws, and defeats. Vimy changed all of that. "We sure have our chests stuck out these days," wrote Corporal Leonard Cuff in the aftermath of Vimy.[30] With a newfound confidence and a battle-honed attack doctrine, the Corps never lost another major engagement. In this sense, Vimy made the Canadian Corps' reputation, which it would build upon in future battles.

Vimy also cemented General Horne's status as a careful planner, a shrewd judge of what soldiers can do in battle, and a solid leader who backed his subordinates. In contrast, Third Army commander Allenby had failed and was banished to the Middle East, where it was thought he could do little harm. Surprisingly, in the open warfare of the desert and in a far different campaign, Allenby proved an adept commander and a victorious general. Vimy made Byng's career, too, as Haig elevated him to command the Third Army. When the general was raised to the peerage, he took as his title Baron Byng of Vimy. The thorny issue of who would command the Canadian Corps remained. In Byng's mind, Currie was the only Canadian who could succeed him. Haig agreed, and the Canadian-born militia officer was knighted in early June and then given command of the Corps on June 9. Currie would be the final corps commander and he was a symbol of how the Canadians had matured as a fighting force.

The Canadian way of war had been established at Vimy, and it involved the melding of weapons and men in a combined-arms set-piece engagement. The carefully planned battles that involved artillery, machine guns, and infantry, supported by engineers and logistical units, were predicated on biting off a chunk of enemy terrain and holding it with firepower against counterattack. The Vimy victory also revealed that constant study of success and failure; learning and improving through training and reforms; and meticulous preparation and good intelligence contributed to victory. Later, starting at the August 1917 Battle of Hill 70, the Canadians would add "destroy" to their combination of bite and hold: first capture ground—the *bite*—and then *hold* it, using firepower to *destroy* expected German attacks. In 1918, the battle-hardened Canadian Corps, working together as an efficient formation, increased the tempo of decision making and decentralization in the series of battles known as the Hundred Days campaign; units were empowered to fight their way forward and exploit the enemy's weaknesses, all behind a combined-arms approach to battle that added airpower, chemical warfare, and mobile mortar and machine-gun units to the tested combination of infantry fighting with artillery. From Vimy onwards, the Canadians were the shock troops of the British Expeditionary Force.

THE YEAR 1917 WAS THE WORST of the war for the Allies, even though the Germans lost heavily on all fronts. Suffering from massive casualties, faltering military and political leadership, and rising bread prices, Russia was driven from the battlefield in the east and retreated to fight its vicious internal revolution. French army morale was shattered after the Artois offensive in the Chemin des Dames, and it took the better part of the year for it to recover. The Passchendaele offensive, from July to November, was a disaster for the British, chewing up men and ruining the army's morale amid horrific conditions that exceeded the horror of the Somme. The Italians also achieved little in a series of battles against the Austro-Hungarians except to run up the losses in their fruitless assaults along the Isonzo River, and then in their stark defeat at the Battle of Caporetto in November 1917. The Vimy victory seemed all the more poignant in this sea of defeat. While the Canadian Corps' success could not compare with the massive exertions of the major powers, it was an undeniable bright spot.

Back on the home front, three long years of grief and strife had worn away at Canadians, who faced growing financial hardships and deepening pain from the unending losses overseas. As the recruitment of young men dried up in the latter half of 1916, the mood of crusading Canadians turned darker. Prime Minister Robert Borden and his government were under tremendous pressure to enact conscription to support the boys overseas. If able-bodied men would not enlist, declared the recruiters, then they must be forced to serve. Was the war not a just one? Was this not a crusade in defence of civilization? Britain was bleeding badly and had brought in conscription at the end of 1915. Many agreed that Canada had to do the same.

The hyper-patriotic and fractiously angry began to ferret out those who were not pulling their weight. With the cost of inflation hurting all—but especially those on fixed incomes, like soldiers' families—Canadians sought to expose profiteers, who were supposedly making money while the nation suffered. There were few identifiable figures, and that resulted in even more rage. Farmers were an easier target, though only a year earlier they had been told they were important contributors to the war effort. Now they were roundly condemned as unpatriotic parasites and blamed unfairly for the rising price of food.[31] The country was coming apart, but the greatest wrath was reserved for Quebec. Low recruitment figures in francophone Quebec were singled out as an example of how the French had let down the nation. They were accused of disloyalty and, in extreme cases, of traitorous behaviour. The war overseas was poisoning Canada.

THE BRITISH PRIME MINISTER, THE FIERY Welshman David Lloyd George, took office in December 1916 and was dismayed at the stalemated front and the terrible slaughter. More men were needed to make good the losses of the Somme, and Lloyd George felt he could not ask the dominions to dig deeper without offering something in return. He invited the dominion leaders to London for the Imperial War Cabinet (IWC). Borden jumped at the chance to be a part of the strategic direction of the war effort, perhaps too anxiously, since Canada was roiling in turmoil, but he felt the need to be at the table if he was offered a seat. Lloyd George and the British cabinet fêted Borden and the other dominion prime ministers. Borden was especially proud to be in London on April 9, when the Canadian victory at Vimy was all the talk. He was later to write, "The great achievement of the Canadians in capturing Vimy Ridge, which has been unsuccessfully attacked on several occasions, has aroused a universal tribute of admiration not only in the United Kingdom but in France and Italy."[32] Borden also witnessed the wreckage of the battle, as thousands of injured Canadians, some still mud-caked from the ridge, were sent back to Britain. The prime minister visited his young countrymen in dozens of hospitals, talking to the shattered Canadian heroes. They had given so much for the country and the Empire. He was angered at the injustice when military authorities told him that many of the patients, despite their wounds, would have to be sent back to the front. Borden brooded over this and saw no fairness in these brave boys sacrificing all while other able-bodied males remained in Canada.

At the Imperial War Cabinet, Borden was a hawk, demanding that the Empire prosecute the war to the finish. Lloyd George took to him immediately. But Borden also wanted something from London in return for Canada's sacrifice. With Borden taking the lead, the IWC crafted Resolution IX, an agreement that the relationship of the dominions to London would change, with the dominions becoming equal partners within the Empire. The midpoint of a deadlocked war was not the time for constitutional debates, but the leaders agreed to return to the negotiations after victory was won. The innocuous-sounding Resolution IX was an epoch-making agreement, stating that future talks "should be based upon a full recognition of the Dominions as autonomous nations of an Imperial Commonwealth."[33] In effect, Canada and the other dominions would fully control their own foreign policy. It would be a long road to full nationhood, but an important milestone was agreed upon that spring. For Borden, the victory at

Vimy was intertwined with the victory at the negotiating table in London, and he was to tell Lloyd George early the next year that "the idea of nationhood has developed wonderfully of late in my own Dominion."[34]

DESPITE HIS SUCCESS ABROAD, BORDEN CAME back to Canada in May 1917 in a dark mood. A grim-faced prime minister stood in the House of Commons on May 18 and told Canadians that the crusade was too important to be left to volunteerism. Even though in late 1914 he had promised no conscription, the situation had changed. There was a duty to the nation's soldiers, and to those who had fallen. His government would bring in universal service. Large parts of English Canada roared their approval, but in Quebec there was widespread unrest. Many felt betrayed; in turn, the hyper-patriotic pointed out that the burden of war had not been borne evenly.

In Montreal, the largest city in Canada and with a majority of French Canadians, there were nightly demonstrations throughout the summer by crowds ranging from a few hundred to several thousand. On May 23, some 3,000 Montrealers congregated in Champs de Mars and roamed the streets, eventually breaking windows at *La Patrie*, a pro-conscription newspaper. The next night, more than 10,000 protesters gathered to listen to speakers denounce conscription. Streetcar windows were broken, police were attacked, and three soldiers in uniform were sent to hospital.[36] When conscription was passed in late August with the Military Service Act, the Montreal *Gazette* reported on August 29 that several thousands marched through the city shouting, "Down with Borden" and "Long Live the Revolution."[37] A group dubbed the

Dynamite Gang blew up one of the residences of Lord Atholstan, the pro-conscription newspaper owner, and they also planned to assassinate Borden before they were caught. This was serious business—an armed revolution was not implausible. Spies and eyewitnesses reported the agitation to Borden and the cabinet, along with information gathered on supposed secret societies in Quebec and the West (the latter filled with Communists) that were plotting revolution.[38]

This cartoon of Arthur Meighen, Borden's chief proponent of conscription, depicts him placing a helpless Canadian soldier, with thousands more to follow, into the blood-soaked hands of British imperialism.

The fury and angst over conscription was not just confined to the English and French. There were many Canadians who despaired over the terrible losses overseas and the hardship at home. The farmers felt ill-treated as city folk continued to condemn them for rising food prices. Organized labour was increasingly unhappy with wage disparities; if there was conscription of men, why was there no conscription of wealth? That criticism was beyond the pale for a government that was uneasily watching the Bolsheviks in Russia carry out a Communist revolution.

As Canada was tearing itself apart in the aftermath of the Vimy victory, Borden sought to win the December election that was to be fought over conscription. As the prime minister wrote in his diary, electoral victory would be achieved "at any cost."[39] He believed, along with several million Canadians, that this was a war to preserve civilization. An even greater motivator was the Canadian fallen. At this point in the war, more than 30,000 Canadians had been killed in battle. It was a staggering loss of life, and everyone in English Canada knew a family who had felt the sting of death. Could the war effort be scaled back in the face of such trauma? Borden thought not, and in such a bitter and desperate climate, his government used every means at its disposal to mobilize support.

Borden's government, with the clever, sharp, and at times vicious minister of the interior, Arthur Meighen, in the lead, used its majority to ram through legislation that would cement victory in the December 1917 election. New legislation gave votes to women—mother, wife, sister—with a link to a soldier overseas while disenfranchising about 50,000 Canadians from Germany and Austro-Hungary, labelled enemy aliens, who had come to Canada after March 31, 1902. Meighen glibly told the House his rationale: "War service should be the basis for war franchise."[40]

The end—victory—would justify any means to achieve it. Outside the House, the English newspapers condemned Quebec as a pit of traitorous vipers. The accusations were shrill, vile, and at times hysterical. Both sides traded freely in hatred and bigotry. The unity and pride engendered by the Vimy triumph had led to the shattering disunity of the December 1917 election.

Borden and his Unionists (a new party of Conservatives and Liberals) took 153 seats to the Liberals' 82 in the bruising electoral victory, although almost all of Quebec stood behind the Liberals. The Unionists had won using every means possible, and they had left the country fractured, angry, and bitter. The heated passions surrounding the debate over what was to be done in the name of the war effort and the soldiers overseas set community against community, neighbour against neighbour. And the immediate problem of manpower overseas was not solved. Though conscription was now law, drawing first upon young single men, aged twenty to twenty-four, Borden rightly noted that there had to be a process by which those called up for service could appeal for exemptions. Some had to care for their elderly parents or younger siblings; others were the only able-bodied workers left on farms or were engaged in war-winning work in factories or on rail lines. A surprising 94 percent of those called up applied for exemptions.[41] The tribunals began the slow judging of men for overseas service or exemption. Those who did not want to take a chance fled their homes, and thousands of men were sheltered in the big cities or smaller communities by sympathetic friends and families who refused to let their boys be dragged off to war.[42] Across the country, the Dominion Police hunted fellow Canadians; those who were caught were imprisoned and soon sent overseas, usually with no little brutality and less sympathy.

THE MONTHS OF PROTESTS IN MONTREAL were a popular show of discontent against conscription. In Ottawa, they were seen differently, with some worrying that they were the thin edge of a coming civil war. The uprising in Ireland the previous year had reverberated throughout the British Empire. Moreover, the public protests in Quebec occurred against the backdrop of the Allied overseas war effort taking a dramatic turn for the worse. The Russians had exited the war in late 1917, surrendering to the Germans who had imposed a harsh victor's peace. With Russia in revolution, the Germans were able to transfer several dozen fighting divisions to the Western Front, where they sought to attack before the new American combat divisions could reach the front in sufficient numbers to make a difference. On March 21, 1918, the Germans struck behind a hurricane bombardment of shells and chemical agents, with new *stormtruppen* units charging forward and around areas of resistance. Some 38,512 British soldiers were captured on the first day of battle, and it looked, for a few desperate days, as though the British Third and Fifth armies might collapse.[43] Borden's cabinet became unhinged. All the bloodshed and conflict at home over conscription appeared for nought. The Hun might win the war.

In Quebec City, the Dominion Police had spent much of the winter on the lookout for young men avoiding service. It was a regular occurrence for the police to stop the able-bodied in the streets and demand to see their exemption papers. This humiliation led to rumours that the vengeful police had quotas to fill in finding men for overseas service, and that they filled them by ripping up exemption papers to arrest the innocent. There was little trust and much unease among the population.

On March 28, 1918, the police stopped and detained Joseph Mercier in the working-class neighbourhood of Saint-Roch, Quebec

City, for not having his exemption papers on him. He was handled roughly and taken to the local police station. News spread and an angry crowd set off in search of trouble. Mercier was soon released, but the crowd, now numbering 5,000, stood menacingly outside the station. Angry catcalls gave way to hurled bottles and chunks of ice. Cascading broken windows only added to the frenzy.[44] The mayor arrived to address the crowd, but his pleading had little effect, and somewhat surprisingly, he went home. In the meantime, the police, vastly outnumbered, fled the station. A number were caught by the rioters and assaulted before the crowd dispersed.

The authorities were worried about the next day, Good Friday. The mayor, the police, and the military authorities gathered to plan for further disturbances. There was talk of calling out the military to enforce civil authority. That was a drastic measure and could have led to new violence, and so the army units remained at the ready at their armouries. The day was quiet, but another mob formed at around 7 P.M. in Saint-Roch and then moved to Upper Town. As darkness fell, about 200 rioters stormed the registrar's office at the auditorium, which kept records, including those related to the administration of conscription. Several thousand onlookers cheered them on. The building burned, with military and surveillance records stoking the fire. The mob moved off again, singing and shouting revolutionary slogans and breaking windows for several hours before dispersing.

In Ottawa, Borden and the cabinet were apprised of the situation. The prime minister was angry, feeling that the authorities in Quebec had not done enough to maintain peace or enforce the law. He had let the civil disobedience and protests go largely unanswered in Montreal the previous summer, even when some extremists called for his own assassination, but now he chafed at the idea of riots in the streets while Canadian soldiers were dying on the Western Front as they tried to hold back the German onslaught. Even worse were the imagined threats that gnawed at the prime minister. For months, Ottawa had been sent word by police networks and spies that a Bolshevik and antiwar insurrection was a real possibility, especially in new-Canadian enclaves in the West and in wavering French Canada. Without a strong French-Canadian lieutenant to help him take the pulse of the provinces, Borden was left to his own worries.[45]

On Easter Saturday, March 30, the federal authorities stepped in after the Quebec City mayor signed the documentation required to call out the army. Borden had told Brigadier J.P. Landry, the commander of the military district, to stop the outbreaks of violence by any means necessary. Uneasy with the degenerating situation, Landry asked Ottawa for another 1,500 troops, and those were sent from Toronto and Hamilton under command of Major-General J.L. Lessard, the highest-ranking French-Canadian officer in Canada and widely regarded as being efficient and skilled. As federal troops sped towards Quebec City, another crowd formed in Lower Town that night and marched to the military drill hall where the crowd shouted abuse and threw snowballs, frozen potatoes, and chunks of ice. A number of soldiers were hit in the head and knocked to the ground. Tensions mounted. The commanding officer eventually ordered a troop of cavalry to break up the crowd, which it did, moving at a trot. While this was far from a full charge, a number of civilians were injured as horses knocked them aside.[46] The crowd dispersed, but a number of agitators broke into hardware stores and stole guns and knives. Reports that some of the rioters were arming themselves reached the army, and were carried the next day in Le Devoir.[47]

Monday, April 1, was a warmer day, leading to heavy mist over the city and its mounds of snowbanks, but the soldiers were uneasy in the combative and combustible environment, having heard that the mob might be armed.[48] Around 8 P.M., another crowd formed at the Place Jacques Cartier in Saint-Roch. Soldiers monitored the thousands of milling civilians, listening to inflammatory incitements to storm buildings and oust the Toronto invaders. Many in the crowd were carrying bricks, stones, and ice, and some of these were hurled at the soldiers. Few in uniform were hurt but, at one point, a rioter fired a revolver at one of the soldiers who was trying to apprehend him. All five shots missed, but authorities' fears of an armed mob were realized. The Royal Dragoons arrived on horseback and dispersed the crowd with drawn sabres, but only temporarily. Several civilians were hurt and two soldiers were shot by snipers hiding on the rooftops. The situation was slipping out of control by 10 P.M.[49]

In a show of force, the civil authorities read the mob the Riot Act. While most of the rioters could not see or hear what was happening, word spread. The Riot Act gave the army the right to fire on the crowd if it did not scatter. Few Quebeckers left the scene, some kept there by curiosity, others by anger at having to flee the streets of their town. The soldiers stood in protective ranks, rifles at the ready, staring down the French-Canadian civilians. Insults were hurled back and forth. The crowd surged forward and backwards, as the infantrymen prepared for a breakthrough. Sometime before 10:30 P.M., another soldier was shot by one of the rioters, either from within the crowd or from a rooftop. Confusion reigned. Fog and the high snowbanks added to the sense of uncertainty. The order went out for the soldiers to shoot and they opened up with their Ross rifles. A Lewis machine gun fired for a few seconds, although largely, it would appear from later evidence, into the ground or against brick walls. The rifle firing went on for several minutes, even after the crowd broke in terror. Most of the riflemen were deliberately not targeting the crowd—otherwise, the casualties would have been much higher—but there were still bleeding and dying civilians on the ground and in the snow. Sixty-two rioters were arrested and dozens of revolvers and other weapons were seized. Four lay dead and several dozen were injured. English Canadians were killing French Canadians in the streets of Quebec City.

THE SHOOTINGS SHOCKED THE NATION. In Ottawa, parliamentarians called for calm and the restoration of law and order. Somewhat unexpectedly, French-Canadian MPs condemned the rioters, and even Ernest Lapointe, a Quebec MP who opposed conscription, said there was "no justification for rioting or unlawful resort to violence."[50] The key French papers, *Le Devoir* and *La Presse*, were more guarded, lamenting the rioting but also the actions of the army. However, the word on the streets across Quebec was far more damning. Rumours and stories circulated of cavalry trampling women and children, of multiple machine-gunners raking the crowd, and of cold-hearted bayonet charges into the flesh of innocents.

Borden's iron-fisted reaction stemmed from a number of factors. He remained out of touch with Quebec. With no credible French-Canadian leader in the cabinet to guide him, Borden simply did not recognize the outrage in French Canada over conscription. And it must be said that he did not care. The war was going badly on the Western Front, with the sharp reversal brought by the

German offensive carrying into April, and he was receiving reports that the British might be routed. After so much sacrifice and so much strain, Borden felt there was a far more important issue at stake than what he saw as grumbling in Quebec. He had shown remarkable restraint in dealing with the extremism in Montreal in the summer of 1917, but now the collapsing British armies on the Western Front were a potential cataclysm for the British Empire. At the same time, the killing of Canadians in the streets of Quebec City should have been seen as a similar existential threat to Canadian unity. Further damage to English and French relations occurred when a coroner's inquest found—wrongly—that the federal soldiers had used explosive dum dum bullets. There was festering anger in Quebec.[51] The despicable and unlawful explosive bullets had not been used, and while this finding was later corrected by a second autopsy, the rumours spread that the English soldiers had used the illegal bullets to maim their victims. Over the coming weeks, several Quebec MPs in Ottawa accused the government of poorly handling the situation and described the Dominion Police as little more than thugs. Member of Parliament Thomas Vien predicted in the House, "Many will come to Quebec to visit the spot where it occurred, to see the places where the machine guns were laid on the mob and to see the streets where the men fell. But we Quebecers who live there shall constantly have a remembrance of the disgrace that took place."[52] Indeed, the memory of the Quebec riots would live on, acting as a powerful counter-narrative to the story of Vimy as a nation-building event.

BY THE TIME THE GERMAN OFFENSIVES were finally ground out by the Western Allies in late May, the enemy had absorbed a staggering 800,000 casualties. The Kaiser's homeland was starving because of the British naval blockade, and the first wave of the Spanish influenza was claiming lives. The Allies prepared a counter-attack, starting with a Franco-American offensive in July at the Battle of Second Marne, to be followed by a British and French offensive at Amiens on August 8, 1918. Spearheading the second of these attacks were the Canadians and Australians. Larger, organized efficiently, and ready for battle, the Canadians would punch far above their weight in the half dozen major battles of the Hundred Days campaign. In a series of brutal bashing affairs, the Canadian Corps drove the Germans back at Amiens, on the Arras front, at the Canal du Nord, and in other set-piece battles. While the Allied armies hammered the Germans up and down the Western Front, the Canadian Corps was thrown into some of the most difficult battles to deliver victory. The Corps' assaulting power was unmatched, and its experienced officers led well-trained infantrymen in relentless battles behind hurricane artillery bombardments and in combination with tanks, armoured cars, and machine-gun units. But there were no easy battles on the Western Front. The Canadians suffered some 45,000 casualties during the Hundred Days, almost 20 percent of the total Canadian losses—killed and wounded—of the entire war.

The Great War ended at 11 A.M. on November 11, 1918, only a few hours after the Canadians captured the Belgian city of Mons. It was where the British army had started its retreat in the face of the overwhelming German forces in August 1914. Four years of war had seen unimaginable destruction, the dissolution of empires, and the slaughter of nine million soldiers. The British armed forces, with the Canadian Corps in the lead, ended the war where it started.

CHAPTER 7

COMMEMORATING THE FALLEN

The Great War armistice on November 11, 1918, ended the killing on the Western Front, but the reverberations of those deaths, the mass trauma of more than 66,000 lost Canadians, has echoed through history. Canada was a nation of fewer than eight million and today, with a population more than four and a half times as large, the equivalent losses would be about 300,000 dead in a four-year period.[1] One can scarcely imagine the grief, as every city, town, village, and hamlet mourned for the boys and young and middle-aged men who marched off to war, never to return.

One might have expected a seething population, demanding answers, looking to blame their leaders—politicians, military, business, or church—for having tricked its youth into serving in a faraway war, and then having done nothing to protect them from the maniacal generals who ordered them day after day into the maw of the roaring guns. But that was not the case for most Canadians in the 1920s, who believed that the dirty job of fighting the Germans had been just and necessary.

The legacy of the war would be felt strongly throughout the 1920s, but would then fade. The nation had been fractured from the extremity of the war effort, which had set region against region. French Canadians, farmers, and organized labour felt aggrieved by the accusations that they had not pulled their weight in the struggle. The working class roiled in anger against those who they felt had profited greatly during the war and refused to share the wealth; it led to widespread strikes that culminated in the 1919 Winnipeg General Strike. As during the Easter Riots, Canadians witnessed strikers clash with authorities, this time the Royal Northwest Mounted Police. Two demonstrators were killed and more than two dozen wounded during one nasty contest on June 17, 1919. The Borden government, which had sent several thousand Canadians to fight in Russia against the Bolsheviks, felt it had to strangle the first signs of Communism in Canada.[2] Yet many more Canadians pushed back against this heavy-handedness now that the urgency of the Great War had passed. Was Canada to fight another far-off crusade, this time against Communists? Few wanted Canada to be engaged in such mad adventures, and the force of some 4,000 returned home in the summer of 1919.

Victory had been more costly than anyone could have imagined. The crushing three-billion-dollar debt accrued in unfettered wartime spending would not be easy to pay down. The country was further fractured by the hardship imposed by inflation and the pitting of city folk against farmers, with the former believing erroneously that the latter had reaped money during the war from high crop prices. Everywhere there was rupture; community was set against community, veterans against perceived slackers and new Canadians. Added to this potent mix of rage and resentment were the hundreds of thousands of veterans who were demobilized and filtering back to Canada in early 1919. They expected a country that had changed for the better, one that would reward them with stability and jobs. Instead, too many veterans found unemployment and disillusionment. After the war, Canada was a far harder country to hold together, let alone govern. But it was not one that would turn its back on the fallen.

TWO MINUTES OF SILENCE. IT REVERBERATED like thunder through the busy streets across Canada, as people stood, hats in hands, minds cast back to the war that had ended a year earlier. King George V had made a formal request throughout the British Empire that the eleventh hour of the eleventh day of November in 1919 be observed as Armistice Day, marking the successful end of the war.[3] This stillness was no call to victory but a deep reflection on those who never came home. "The wheels of commerce

Canadians grieved for their slain. This elderly woman wears the medals of a loved one killed during the war.

ceased to turn, trains and tram cars stopped dead, the work of the thousands of office workers halted, and the tools of craftsmen were silenced," reported one Toronto journalist.[4] Anguish and loss over the death of a loved one are usually private and cloistered; now, that loss was shared in public by a nation.

Remembrance Day, as Armistice Day was renamed in 1931, went through cycles of observation and gathering. There were debates about whether it should be a holiday or not, and on which day it should fall, but it remained a day quite unlike any other in the calendar. Another important symbol, one twinned with Armistice Day, was the red poppy, worn on the lapel as a sign of remembrance. The scarlet poppies, first adopted by Canadians in 1921, were inspired by the words of John McCrae's poem "In Flanders Fields," with its vivid imagery of the fallen lying among the red flowers.[5] McCrae's piece, first published in 1915, had been a martial poem, in which slain Canadian soldiers demanded that the survivors keep up the fight against the enemy—"To you from failing hands we throw / The torch; be yours to hold it high"—but during the postwar years, it was transformed into a poem of keeping faith with the fallen. It was inscribed on memorials around the world, a poem that resonated with the grief-stricken.

The war's dead were honoured in Canada and overseas. After the armistice, the Imperial War Graves Commission (IWGC), which was established in 1917 and continues to this day (as the Commonwealth War Graves Commission), began in earnest the arduous process of exhuming the dead and reinterring them in new cemeteries. It was exceptionally difficult work. Grave-digging teams dug up and reburied 128,577 bodies in the first fifteen months after the armistice, followed by another 114,000 bodies over the next three years.[6] When combined with those fallen soldiers already in marked cemeteries, within a few years the IWGC oversaw half a million graves in over 1,000 new cemeteries.

Those cemeteries were to be austere in nature and devoid of large-scale statues or sculptures. Reginald Blomfield, an IWGC architect, wrote, "Many of us had seen terrible examples in France, and were haunted by the fear of winged angels in various sentimental attitudes."[7] Each cemetery would have a Cross of Sacrifice and a Stone of Remembrance. The cross has a symbolic sword of bronze fixed to its face, which poet Rudyard Kipling described as "a stark Sword brooding on the bosom of the Cross." Designed by Sir Edwin Lutyens, the Stone of Remembrance, twelve feet in length and lying raised upon three steps, created a sense of permanence, strength, and majesty. It was inscribed with "Their Name Liveth for Evermore."

The IWGC demanded uniformity of headstones and equality of treatment regardless of rank, meaning that a private would receive the same recognition as a general.[8] It was a radical vision at the time, especially in class-stratified Britain. In death, all were equal. One might have expected the Christian nations to adopt the symbol of the cross, as the French did, but the IWGC chose a non-denominational rounded headstone that allowed for both uniformity and a personalized inscription along the bottom. The Canadian headstones are engraved with an iconic maple leaf, and Newfoundlanders' with a caribou.

Canada followed the British policy on burials: if a soldier fell in Europe or on other foreign battlefields, he would be buried there. There were a few exceptions of the dead who were returned home early in the war, and two cases of mourning mothers robbing the graves of their sons to smuggle the remains back to Canada.[9] While the Americans repatriated many of their dead,

Headstone of Private Harold Kennedy of the 102nd Battalion, killed on April 9, 1917.

Canada was content to leave its casualties overseas for practical reasons, not the least being the challenge of returning tens of thousands of rotting corpses.[10] Most of the cemeteries were created and beautified between 1920 and 1922, and would be important symbols of unity in battle and death within the British Empire. In battle, the Empire had fought together; in death, the fallen armies would forever be, as one contemporary noted, the "Empire of the Silent Dead."[11]

"OUT HERE IN FRANCE AND FLANDERS we men meet on the same platform, worship in the same church, fight in the same trenches, sleep in the same dugouts, and 'ere long, in God's own time and way, we hope to share the same victory. Brothers always, and all brothers."[12] So wrote N.H. McGillivray to his family from the Western Front in July 1917. The brotherhood of the trenches remained a powerful impetus for the returning soldiers. For the first time, Canadians from across the vast Dominion had a chance to meet each other. The value of interactions between men of different faiths, classes, races, and regions should not be underestimated. It was a radical change from the parochial relationships of prewar Canadians, who rarely travelled the country, and it forged new friendships and better understandings of Canada.

There was also a strong desire of the soldiers to find meaning in their service. The idea that the soldiers had fought together for a better Canada, where all men were equal and some of the more petty political arguments were put aside, was an appealing belief for many returning men. The fierce emotional investment of veterans was summed up in the phrase "a land fit for heroes," even though no Canadian politician seems to have uttered these words.[13] Yet the idea, which was spoken by Lloyd George in Britain, was simple: those who had sacrificed so much for King and country should not want for anything when they returned to Canada. Many soldiers had taken to heart the words of Prime Minister Borden. He had promised Canadian soldiers before the Battle of Vimy Ridge that, "The government and the country will consider it their first duty to . . . prove to the returned men its just and due appreciation of the inestimable value of the services rendered to the country and Empire; and that no man, whether he goes back or whether he remains in Flanders, will have just cause to reproach the government for having broken faith with the men who won and the men who died."[14] To vow not to break faith with the returned men was a powerful sentiment, and Borden laid out a social contract between veterans, the state, and all Canadians. But the postwar Canadian government faced financial ruin and was not sure how to follow through on this promise. What was to be offered to the veterans to compensate them for their lost years and suffering?

Aside from government programs or stipends—which were fairly generous, especially in comparison to what Britain gave its veterans—the returned men wanted jobs.[15] There were precious few for them, however, though the women who had been lauded during the war for stepping up to fill white- and blue-collar jobs were pressured to give up their positions.[16] Not all veterans wished to return to their old employment. How could they go from the fear and exhilaration of combat, and of commanding men in life-and-death situations, to working in a shop or stocking shelves? While some men slipped back into positions left open for them, others found that their jobs had been filled for years by a man who had not gone overseas but who had done the work well. In many cases, managers and foremen were not willing to turf the current worker out for a returned man who may have been scarred by his wartime experience or might be bitter at his postwar treatment. Disillusioned veterans resented the "slackers," as they called those fit men and new Canadians who had not risked their lives in the war and who, in some cases, had done well out of it.

While most veterans returned to their loved ones and settled back into society, with thousands more trying to make a go of it on farmland as part of a soldiers' settlement plan, wounded combatants faced other challenges. These citizen-soldiers—former clerks, farmers, students, and bankers—had served the nation and now needed care. By war's end, the federal government oversaw, through the new Department of Soldiers' Civil Re-establishment, the creation of more than fifty hospitals across the Dominion, along with rehabilitation centres, vocational training, specialized facilities for the blinded or shell-shocked, and even prosthetic-limb factories. Tens of thousands of veterans were cared for, although many never left those centres, broken forever in body and mind, missing legs and arms, paralyzed or hacking through gas-corrupted lungs, plagued by the horrors of war.[17] Others developed mental wounds in the 1920s, what we now call post-traumatic stress disorder, and thousands of those "burned-out" soldiers received pensions.[18]

Anticipating the need to fight for their rights, veterans banded together to exert influence. The Great War Veterans Association was formed on April 10, 1917, during the Vimy battle, and it was the largest group of veterans, but there were many other associations across the country. In the first decade, most of the leaders of the organization came from the rank and file, and they did not want officers to be a part of the organization. Those ill feelings only intensified shortly after the war when organized veterans groups demanded a $2,000 bonus for every surviving veteran (a considerable amount considering privates were paid $1.10 a day when serving overseas), partly so that every man would get something out of the war and not have to deal with Ottawa's bureaucratic red tape.[19] The tight bonds forged in the trenches were strained as men turned against their officers, and officers against their men. Sir Arthur Currie felt that the soldiers were led by radicals and he all but cut ties with veterans' groups for half a decade. They, in turn, felt the high command had sold them out. Even respected leaders such as William Griesbach, commander of the 49th Battalion and then of the 1st Infantry Brigade, were ostracized. In one fiery postwar meeting, he was "shouted off the stage and his remarks [in defence of the government not being able to pay $2,000 to each veteran] were so bitterly resented that Edmonton's most distinguished soldier was voted OUT" of the 49th Battalion's regimental association.[20] The governments of Sir Robert Borden, Arthur Meighen, and, after 1921, William Lyon Mackenzie King, all refused to entertain the idea of a universal bonus, believing that the country could not afford it. A large segment of the veteran population felt betrayed.

IT WAS EASIER TO PUT UP stone monoliths to the fallen than to deal with the anguish of the living, and easier to honour the silent dead than the angry living. Without the bodies of loved ones, families struggled to find closure. There was no opportunity for ritualized mourning, and thus it became harder to accept the loss. Moreover, mourning an individual among more than 66,000 deaths seemed wrong for some. Sometimes wealthy patrons or families donated enormous sums to ensure that a son or brother was not forgotten. Commemorative books, named spaces, even specially erected structures would carry the name of a loved one. One of the largest was at McGill University in Montreal, where Molson Stadium was built in honour of a fallen son, Percy Molson, who was killed at Second Ypres. More often, communities built monuments to all of the soldiers from that area. Pavilions, fountains, and libraries marked the dead; cairns, gates, and towers were erected in the name of the fallen. There were plaques and tablets in tribute to those killed who were associated with businesses, churches, and schools. Trees were planted or gardens dug in honour of those who did not return.[21] In Newfoundland, a

separate dominion from Canada, Memorial University was established as a living memorial to the war and its veterans, and to those
who had served at home.

The war was represented in local communities in other ways.
Thousands of captured artillery pieces, machine guns, and small
arms were sent to Canada after the war as representations of
victory. Brigadier Victor Odlum, who would later become a prominent Vancouver politician and a divisional commander in the
Second World War, believed, as many did, that the war trophies
served as "physical and tangible reminders of the courage, forti-
tude and skill of Canada's sons."[22] War trophies were a physical
link to battle, and mounting these relics near schools, libraries,
and town halls across the country provided a constant reminder,
in cold steel, of the sacrifice and victory of Canada during the long
and terrible war.[23] Distributed across the country, the trophies
remained in pride of place up until the Second World War, but
eventually most were melted down to forge new guns to be used
against the Nazis. Some survived, however, saved in museums
and by the historically minded.

There were other memorials from overseas, from battlefield
temporary wooden crosses to regimental markers raised during
the war. The 44th Battalion from Winnipeg erected a cross at
Vimy, about ten months after that battle in early 1918. H.B. Rugh,
a prominent architect in civil life, designed the monument on
Hill 145, and a nominal roll of men killed and missing was etched
into cement. When the memorial was to be torn down in the early
1920s, hundreds of 44th Battalion survivors, spread across Canada
and around the world, donated funds to bring the cross back to
Winnipeg, where it was erected in St. James Park. It remained,
according to one officer in the late 1920s, "a rallying centre where

44th men gather to do reverence to their comrades who have gone before them."[24]

The most important community memorials were those that encompassed all of the dead. Prominent citizens, patriotic groups like the Imperial Order Daughters of the Empire (IODE), veterans, and the parents of the fallen all had a say.[25] With many interest groups, there were fierce arguments over the nature and structure of these landmarks to grief and service. In New Zealand, one chief proponent of a commemorative project observed ruefully, "I am satisfied that no subject on earth is more fruitful of controversy than that of war memorials."[26] It was no easier in Canada.

Monuments were complex sites of anguish and pride, of silence and of gathering to give voice. The community—and especially the close survivors of the fallen—had to be reassured that their boys, fathers, brothers, and husbands had not died in vain.[27] Their battles were glorified and their names etched on the memorials, providing a link between the ideas of sacrifice and victory. In a different vein of memory construction, a memorial also revealed that a community had done its bit, and it was a reflection of duty, civic pride, and having answered the call.

Organizing communities fundraised for the projects with a vigour and aggressiveness similar to the wartime zeal of selling war bonds and collecting money for soldiers' families. As McCrae's poem counselled, faith had to be kept with the dead. Yet sculptors, artists, and architects were in short supply in Canada, and every community wanted a memorial. Some of the memorials, especially that of a Canadian soldier with an arm raised in victory, were mass produced, as was *Winged Victory*, long a staple monument. Some of the memorials were austere, while others were architectural monstrosities. Almost every one, however, was traditional in design and message, and many were infused with symbols of Christian righteousness.[28] The war, some believed, had ushered in a new, modern period, a sharp break with all that came before it. That was the case with some forms of artistic expression—with new movements developing in dance, poetry, and painting—but in memorializing the dead, there was no break with the past. Sculptors met the demands of citizens who sought solace in embracing the "big words" that were supposedly blown away in the war—duty, fealty, honour, and sacrifice.[29] In the early 1920s, when many of the memorials were conceived and being constructed, the communities that had contributed men to fight for King and country had not soured on the tremendous loss, but instead sought to elevate it to justify the sacrifice. The war was made to have profound meaning—a just cause against militarism, a defence of the British Empire and Canada, and a conflict in which Christian soldiers had given their all in the name of righteous victory.

Quebec, too, had its memorials. Despite the clash of nationalities during the war, the French-Canadian 22nd Battalion was greeted home in Montreal in May 1919 by thousands of supporters, as were individuals who served with other units. War trophies were sent across the province, accepted by francophone and anglophone communities. Cities, especially Montreal, tried to bury the crisis of conscription by raising memorials to the dead. Throughout the 1920s, at least 103 memorials were erected, although many were in the Eastern Townships and anglophone enclaves in southwestern parts of the province.[30]

A crucial component of almost all the memorials, regardless of their design, was the inscribed names of the fallen. The engraved names were a mnemonic device to remember those who had served and whose bodies remained lost to their loved ones and their communities.[31] The names were compiled in Ottawa, with the assistance of the IWGC, but deciding who to include on a memorial was difficult. Some local men who had enlisted in other communities, perhaps where they worked or went to school, usually had their names added to the hometown memorials, although sometimes they were captured in two or more places.[32] To allow a name to be lost or left off memorials was to lose a man again to the war, and perhaps to history. One angry citizen in Saint-Hilaire, Quebec, took dynamite to the town's monument in 1922 because some of the fallen had not been included on the memorial.[33]

With the bodies gone, the names lived on. The memory of the fallen was never to be relinquished to the dust. The lost again

Bearing witness to the war's dead, a large crowd surrounds Toronto's war memorial, in front of City Hall, for its unveiling in 1935.

occupied space, even if it was limited and prescribed. Sometimes the memorials included those who served or were wounded, including nurses. Farmers or organized labour at home were excluded, even though they had been told during the war that they, too, were fighting from the home front. Organizations like the IODE or local patriotic groups often published texts recounting their good war work—with detailed compilations of socks knitted or funds raised—but they too were left off the memorials. But, of course, with Canada in a total war, there would have been few who could not make a claim for having served in the war. Understandably, service overseas—and usually death—trumped all in the remembrance process.

The local memorials, empty graves represented as cenotaphs, cairns, and obelisks, remained crucial to honouring the dead and the returned in communities. Without a national memorial in Ottawa or overseas—with these being delayed until the late 1930s—the community memorials became the focal points of bereavement and pride. The memory of the war remained very much at the local level, and, as such, it was unfocused and difficult to harness into a useable meta-narrative that would see the war transform Canada from a colony to a nation. That important story would not fully take shape until national memorials were constructed, creating new icons of memory and myth-making.

THE COMMEMORATION OF DEATH WOULD BE done in communities, but also at the national level in order to represent all those who served and fell in the war. While the IWGC would care for the mass graves of the Empire's fallen, Ottawa also believed that Canada must mark its own battlefields. This show of independence was a subtle but crucial revelation of Canada's refusal to let Britain dictate the way in which the Dominion would remember, honour, and mark the momentous war effort.

As early as February 1919, Borden's government appointed Brigadier Henry Thorsby Hughes as Canada's representative on the Battle Exploits Memorials Commission in England. Hughes, a prewar railway man and a senior engineering officer during the war, worked with the British to select a number of battle sites for memorials to the Canadian forces. Corps commander Sir Arthur Currie, still overseas as an adviser to the Canadian government at the Versailles peace treaty talks, was informed that the government planned to single out a number of the battlefields for commemoration. The general—who had an eye on his own historical record, which had increasingly been under attack by Sam Hughes and others, especially with regard to casualties in the Hundred Days campaign—demanded to be involved in the selection process.[34] Currie worked with Brigadier Hughes to identify the eight sites that were important to the Canadian Corps (although sites relevant to Canadian units outside the Corps, such as the Cavalry Brigade or Canadian airmen in the RFC, were not considered). Five sites were in France, at Vimy Ridge, Bourlon Wood, Le Quesnel, Dury, and Courcelette; and three were on Belgian soil, at St. Julien, Hill 62 (Sanctuary Wood), and Passchendaele.[35] Bourlon Wood, Le Quesnel, and Dury were all battles in the Hundred Days, while St. Julien represented the Battle of Second Ypres and Hill 62 stood for the Battle of Mount Sorrel.

Hughes travelled to Europe in September 1919 to survey the battlefields and to liaise with the Belgian and French officials to purchase land for the memorials, just as other dominions were doing. South Africa secured the land at Delville Wood on the

Somme, the location of their most costly battle; the Australians had several memorials planned, including one for each of their five divisions and a central monument at Villers–Bretonneux; while the Indian government had allocated funds to mark the 1915 battle of Neuve Chapelle. The Newfoundland government, through its wartime padre Thomas Nangle, secured the shattered farmland around Beaumont Hamel, the site of its greatest wartime disaster, on July 1, 1916. The Belgian government gave small patches of the ruined battlefields to the Canadians for free, and the French did the same with government-owned land, while other parcels were purchased from farmers.

In April 1920, a special committee was established in the House of Commons to determine what types of memorials should be erected "to commemorate the gallantry of the Canadian troops."[36] Percy Nobbs, head of McGill's School of Architecture and a well-known Montreal architect, prepared a report a month later. Nobbs moved in the highest circles, but he was volatile, opinionated, and could unleash scandalous profanity. He was also a polymath, able and willing to comment on almost any subject; he had, for instance, written a scholarly treatise on salmon fishing.[37] The Nobbs report argued for marking the eight memorial sites identified by General Currie, either in a similar manner or by singling out one, "in a central position" that would be "a more imposing design than the other seven."[38] Vimy might be a unique spot, thought Nobbs, because of its geographical location as a prominent ridge and because of its importance as Canada's first large-scale victory on the Western Front. Not all veterans agreed. The most important of them, Currie, who had recently been appointed as principal of McGill University, objected to elevating Vimy above all others. "I do not think it was the most outstanding battle, or had the greatest material or moral effect on the winning of the war."[39] The general instead recommended erecting eight of the same memorials on the Western Front, with no one more important than the other.[40]

Worried about upsetting Currie, who could be prickly in defence of the Canadian Corps' collective memory, the House of Commons created the Canadian Battlefields Memorials Commission in September 1920.[41] The commission was allocated an initial budget of half a million dollars (it would climb to $1.5 million) and was to oversee the erection of a number of memorials.[42] Chaired by Major-General the Honourable S.C. Mewburn, a former minister of militia and defence, the commission also consisted of the Honourable Rodolphe Lemieux (member of Parliament and later Speaker of the House of Commons), Lieutenant-General Sir Richard Turner (a recipient of the Victoria Cross and chief of staff in England during the latter half of the war), and several other prominent Canadians.[43]

The first meeting of the commission was held on November 26, 1920, and its major order of business was to examine the competition rules to find an architectural memorial design for the overseas sites. Less than a month later, the competition was opened to Canadian architects and artists. The planning document offered information on the eight sites and the battlefields, including terrain and history, and the commission's regulations suggested that one memorial might be repeated in all eight sites to "create a cumulative effect due to similarity in scale and general form as landmarks."[44] It was hoped that the memorials—the cost of each anticipated at $120,000—might be erected by November 11, 1922.[45] Even with the tight deadline, some 160 designs were submitted. An international jury, consisting of a French and a

British architect, and Toronto's Frank Darling, who had designed churches, colleges, and banks, selected a short list of seventeen artists in April 1921, and the finalists were paid a stipend to produce models.[46]

At the same time, Brigadier H.T. Hughes, the chief engineer for all Canadian sites in Belgium and France, was sending back updates to the commission. Hughes was not surprised to find that the battle sites needed to be cleared of barbed wire, bodies, and unexploded shells before anything could be built on them. Vimy Ridge was in appalling shape, with all of the roads leading up the ridge severely damaged, the terrain pocked by millions of shell craters, and a mass of unexploded high-explosive, shrapnel, and chemical shells buried in the earth. Hughes wrote, "I am of the opinion that our road programme may need revision [and] with special reference to Vimy Ridge in fact it may even be advisable and an economy to select another site close to the Arras–Lens road and dispose of our property at Hill 145."[47] The costs of preparing the sites had already begun to mount, and the commission's expert overseas even recommended that the Vimy Memorial site might be moved off the heights to a lower position and closer to the few roads not destroyed by shellfire and mining.

In September 1921, the jury studied the seventeen models that were put on display in the Railway Committee Room of the Parliament Buildings. Many of the designers sought to capture the emerging sense of national destiny that was forged in the war. Most of these single-shaft visions saw the memorial reaching for the skies, a burst of nationhood captured in stone. Architects Duke Rowat and R.T. Perry's tall shaft with an eternal flame atop it was one of the most impressive designs. Yet one model, by Toronto architect and sculptor Walter Allward, was stunningly different.

The seventeen finalist models for the overseas memorial, as displayed in the Railway Committee Room of Parliament. In the background, Allward's model can be seen. Clemesha's "Brooding Soldier" is centre-right.

It had a long, heavy base, giving the impression of a bastion of stone standing firm against time, with two austere pylons rising from it. An empty tomb lay in front of the memorial, and over-looking the tomb, a motherly figure, *Canada Bereft*, mourned her dead. Across the memorial were other allegorical figures, clusters identified as the *Defenders*, who were breaking the sword of war and offering sympathy for the grieving and helpless, while another group of figures were identified as the *Spirit of Sacrifice* and *Passing of the Torch*. These and other allegorical figures did not gloat over victory, with the memorial instead exuding loss and sorrow. It was a work quite unlike any of the British memorials being planned overseas.

On October 4, 1921, Allward was announced as the winner. The commission observed that his memorial had "a design of such individuality and complexity that its character precludes it from the possibility of repetition."[48] There could not be eight of them to mark the selected sites. This necessitated a secondary design, and Frederick Chapman Clemesha's memorial was selected. It was a striking shaft of granite from which a soldier emerged, head bowed and hands resting on his reversed rifle. Over time, it has become known as the "Brooding Soldier," and the commission felt that it might mark the remaining seven battle sites. But as Great War official war artist and Group of Seven member A.Y. Jackson wrote in *Canadian Forum*, Allward's design was truly supreme and, "It went beyond and above anything that the framers of the competition conceived of." This created a problem, identified by Jackson: "As there is to be one dominant memorial, the other memorials should be designed in relation to it. The second prize design bears no relation to the first, fine as it may be by itself.

Allward's model of the Vimy Memorial that
won him the government's commission.

When one tries to form a conception of the Allward monument and the four or five replicas of the Clemesha monument along the battle line, one is acutely conscious of discord."[49] The plans for the overseas memorials were losing focus.

MATTERS SOON WENT FROM DISJOINTED to delusional. The three-person jury recommended to the commission that Allward's memorial be placed in Belgium, on Hill 62. This was a bizarre choice, as Hill 62 was the site of the Battle of Mount Sorrel, a hard-fought engagement in June 1916 that was, in its first two phases, a resounding defeat. The assessors' reasoning had more to do with aesthetic values than with marking a key battle. In speaking of Allward's memorial, they noted, "It is a design suited to a low hill rather than a continuous lofty bluff or cliff like Vimy Ridge, where its delicacy of line would be lost in the mass of the ridge."[50] Hill 62 was also accessible by a new road, although this seemed at best a parochial reason to select it for Canada's primary over-seas memorial.

Amid these competing battle sites of memory, it was still believed throughout 1920 and 1921, at least by the commission, that Ypres would be the primary battlefield to highlight for future generations. The Canadians had fought at Second Ypres in April 1915, at St. Eloi and Mount Sorrel in 1916, and at Passchendaele in 1917. The Second Battle of Ypres had been Canada's first major engagement, its fighting men's desperate stand against overwhelm-ing odds and the nefarious use of chlorine gas. Newspapers had praised the Canadian defence there, even as the casualty lists were a shock to the country. Posters used the imagery of Second Ypres to recruit more men, with one of them claiming that the list of battles around Ypres were "new names in Canadian history."[51] Second Ypres was also where John McCrae penned "In Flanders Fields," and the battle was infused with the rallying cry to take up "the torch"—first to wield it against the foe and then, later, to use its light to keep the memory of Canada's dead alive. On the battle's anniversary, both during the war and afterwards, journalists enthused about its importance: "St. Julien: A Glorious Page in Canadian History," claimed Toronto's *Globe* on April 22, 1916. The battle was the place where "Canada was christened into nationhood."[52] Second Ypres's iconic status continued after the war, with veterans' parades on April 22 and textbooks from the 1920s, such as B.A. Garnell's *History of Canada* (1926), asking young readers, in the spirit of the *Boys' Own* adventure stories, "What Canadian does not thrill with pride at the name of Ypres!"[53] W. Stewart Wallace's *A New History of Great Britain and Canada* (1929) also placed more emphasis on Second Ypres than Vimy as a sign of Canada's emergence during the war.[54]

Just as the Australians celebrated their forces' gritty fighting at Gallipoli—where the Australians, New Zealanders, British, and French landed on April 25, 1915, and failed to break through the Turkish lines before retreating at the end of the year—Canadians extolled Second Ypres as their nation's baptism of fire. It occurred at almost the same time, from April 22 to 25, albeit thousands of kilometres from the rocky beaches of Gallipoli. The Australians suffered 26,111 casualties at Gallipoli, but they had proven themselves tough and independent, and out of the campaign came an active enthusiasm for myth-making. Journalist and later official historian Charles Bean wrote of the natural qualities of the Australian digger, who, through innate skills shaped by the nation's outback and frontier society, had supported his mates in battle and carved out a similar "birth" of the Australian nation, which was even younger than Canada, having confederated in 1901. Even though Gallipoli was a clear-cut defeat, the Australians found meaning in it, and it marked the start of a foundational legend that was not dissimilar to the Canadian constructed meaning of the war.[55] Second Ypres was comparable to Gallipoli in that it was a tenacious trial-by-fire fighting retreat that was elevated into a moral triumph. Vimy was different: a victory by all four divisions. If Canada's overseas memorial had been built in the Ypres salient instead of Vimy, the meaning of Vimy would have been very different than it is today.

When Allward signed a five-year contract in 1922 to begin work on the sculptures and memorial, Hill 62 remained the location of choice for Canada's overseas national memorial—although it should be noted that the Hill 62 site represented the June 1916 Battle of Mount Sorrel and not the Battle of Second Ypres, making its selection all the stranger. That same month, the commission's fifth meeting recorded some dissent on the Ypres site, with the members reconsidering where to place the memorial. "The name of Vimy Ridge was more closely associated with Canada not only in the minds of Canadians but of the people of other lands."[56] And Vimy would soon have an unlikely champion.

Prime Minister William Lyon Mackenzie King, who had come to power in December 1921, had not served during the war. He was forty years old in 1914, and therefore really not suited for the trenches, through some older men had donned the uniform. Having lost his seat in the 1911 election, King returned to working as a respected labour negotiator. During the war, he went south to the neutral United States in the employ of the Rockefeller family. In return for a considerable paycheque from one of the richest families in the United States, he had put his talents as a fixer toward easing violent labour battles. In King's mind, his work in reducing labour problems assisted with American production, which ultimately aided the Allied war effort. When King stood for the 1917 election he was taunted for his lack of wartime service, and after the war he was often the butt of accusations of not having done his duty to Canadians. The sensitive King agonized over these slights and slings, and his protests to the contrary rang hollow. King was desperate to contribute to the war effort, even if it was in the aftermath, by propagating the war's memory.

King spoke in the House of Commons on May 22, 1922, on the placement of the overseas memorial: "I hope the commission will consider very seriously indeed—I know in fact is considering it—the advisability of acquiring a very considerable tract of land along Vimy Ridge as a permanent memorial. Whilst sculpture may do a great deal to commemorate the sacrifices of our men, Vimy itself is one of the world's great altars, on which a perceptible portion of our manhood has been sacrificed in the cause of the world's freedom. As a national memorial, nothing can equal the preservation of the ridge itself."[57] Urged on by King, and with the commission's agreement, Rodolphe Lemieux, the charismatic Speaker of the House of Commons, began negotiations with French local politicians in Lille and Arras, where he had a number of contacts among influential politicians. The Vimy sector had been so thoroughly ploughed with shellfire and abandoned by residents that the French government had labelled it a red zone, useful only for reforestation. Lemieux slowly worked his way through the Byzantine structure of local and regional politics, using his contacts, charm, and command of the French language to plead Canada's case. By December 1922, he had reached an agreement between France and Canada, in which the gift of land was formalized: "The French Government grants, freely and for all time, to the Government of Canada the free use of a parcel of 100 hectares located on Vimy Ridge."[58] Canada agreed to develop the memorial and a park (some 250 acres), and France resolved to waive all taxes. It has sometimes been mistakenly noted that Vimy became Canadian soil. French officials, no matter how generous a mood they were in to reward their liberators, would not give away parts of their country after having just spent four years and more than a million lives to oust occupiers.

Mackenzie King crowed about his success in his diary, when word came of the agreement on December 5, 1922:

> ... a cable from Lemieux says French Govt. has presented Canada with 250 acres of Vimy Ridge. This is the outcome of my agitation & persistent effort to secure this land for Canada. It is a great national possession and has been acquired at just the right moment. ... I know this would have never been acquired by Canada but for my efforts. It gives me real happiness that this achievement has come about.[59]

King gave himself too much credit ("persistent effort" seems a stretch), but he had played a role in securing the land. The prime minister believed that Vimy Ridge was the site that should stand above all the others. His support seems to have eased his own troubled conscience over his lack of wartime service, and it was a small gesture to aid the veterans who remained unhappy with his government. Regardless of King's motivations, Allward, veterans, and all Canadians now had the site for their principal overseas memorial, which was moved from Ypres to Vimy. As King expressed it to the House of Commons, "History will look upon the battle-grounds of the Great War as the places of sacrifice. Among the number, no altar will be more conspicuous through the years than that of Vimy Ridge."[60]

CHAPTER 8

CONSTRUCTING MEMORY

The Vimy Memorial emerged in part from sculptor Walter Allward's dream of a ghost army of Canadians on the battlefields:

> I had gone into a troubled sleep after thinking of all the muck and horror over there. I found myself overlooking a tremendous battlefield. Division after division of our army was being swallowed up in this smoke, din and destruction. Everything was disappearing, but as I looked down a long avenue of poplars lining one of the main roads, I saw armies of the white dead coming out to relieve the dying armies of the living. When I awoke, and for long, long afterwards, the poignant impression remained and finally became a part of this work. Without the thought of the dead we could not have carried on, during the war, or afterwards. It is this feeling that I have tried to express.[1]

So spoke Canada's most famous sculptor in the early 1920s in describing how deeply Canada's killed soldiers had shaped his concept of the overseas memorial.[2] The dead weighed heavily on Canada, and on Allward. He constructed a memorial to the fallen to keep those dreams and nightmares alive for all eternity.

Allward's parents had immigrated from Newfoundland, then a separate colony, to Toronto, where Allward was born on November 18, 1876. He had learned carpentry from his father and, by 1890, was studying painting in William Cruikshank's Toronto studio. The next year, he enrolled in evening modelling classes and joined the Toronto Art Students' League, a group of like-minded souls who sketched and shared their passion for art. During this time, from 1891 to 1895, Allward was a draughtsman for the firm of Henry Gibson and Charles Simpson but, like most apprentices, he engaged in much mundane work, receiving little formal instruction in the craft.[3] However, good artists pick up skills by watching, studying, copying, and doing, and Allward was one of the most talented among the staff.[4]

Allward's memorial to the 1885 Northwest Rebellion at Queen's Park in Toronto was his first major commission. He had only completed a few busts of historical figures up to that point, but his superior design convinced the judges. While parts of that memorial were sub-contracted out, particularly the base, it was Allward's elegant figure of *Peace* that stood out prominently. Stark, simple, and powerful, it was well received when it was erected in 1896.

Sculptor Walter Allward in 1914.

Allward achieved another major coup in 1904 when he won the commission for the South African War monument to those Canadians who had fought for Queen and country from 1899 to 1902.[5] Canada had committed close to 8,000 soldiers in support of the Empire's war against the Boers, and more than 270 of them died. Their graves were scattered across the veldt, grouped in small numbers and with few guardians to care for them. The memorial on University Avenue in Toronto, funded by public donations, was erected to mark the soldiers' sacrifice and Canada's participation in a war in which the nation's battlefield prowess prompted the prime minister of the day, Sir Wilfrid Laurier, to declare, "A new power has arisen in the west."[6]

Allward laboured on the monument until 1910. His sculptures were in the Beaux-Arts style, which featured allegorical figures, often composed in a pyramidal structure leading upward to a figure on a raised pedestal. Allward's *Peace* figure for the Rebellion monument, a draped woman with delicate features extending an olive branch, is very similar to the South African War memorial's female figure, *Winged Canada*, holding a crown (the symbol for England) and a sword, high atop the monument on a 22-metre granite pillar. Two Canadian soldiers stand at the base of the pillar, an infantryman and cavalryman, and between them, representing Canada, is the figure of a young mother, for whom Allward used his own mother as inspiration and model.[7] This was a victorious monument, reflecting none of the grief or shame associated with a dirty war in which thousands of Boer civilians had died in concentration camps through neglect, a war in which Empire soldiers had undertaken a widespread farm-burning campaign, and a war in which more men had been killed by disease than by Boer bullets. Nonetheless, when the memorial was erected, Toronto's *Globe* reported on May 28, 1910, that it was, "The tallest, most dignified monument in Toronto."[8]

Allward took on other monuments, including the Robert Baldwin and Sir Louis-Hippolyte Lafontaine commission, which he started in 1907 and finished eight years later in Ottawa, as well as the Alexander Graham Bell memorial in Brantford, Ontario.[9] All were positively received by critics and the public. Walter Allward had been profiled in *Sons of Canada*, a 1916 hagiography about Canada's best and brightest, and largely filled with the political and business elite.[10] Attesting to his fame and influence, Allward was contracted to sculpt war memorials in Peterborough, Stratford, and Brantford in the Great War's aftermath. For the Stratford memorial, he chose not to display Canadian soldiers, but instead carved two allegorical figures, *Spiritual Triumph* and *Brute Force*, one on high ground, looking upward to a new future of peace and prosperity, while the second figure, that of strife and war in defeat, is banished. The other two memorials would drag on for the decade, weighing on Allward and leaving citizens in Peterborough and Brantford increasingly angry that their sons were left without recognition in stone.[11] Allward's attention was instead directed to wrapping up his affairs in Canada and moving overseas to begin work on the national memorial at Vimy.

Before Allward left for Britain, journalist Anne Perry interviewed the forty-six-year-old sculptor in the summer of 1922, enthusing that his face and figure "reveal a tall, well-built body, with broad chest, yet with an air of fine strength rather than of rugged robustness, a strong, high head, crowned by a heavy crop of fast greying hair which softens the somewhat austere lines of an almost sad face, from which look out a pair of blue grey eyes, with a brooding quality, but lightened frequently by a humorous smile, which also curves into pleasantness, a mobile, sensitive mouth which might well be that of a poet."[12] Clearly, Perry had been enthralled by the charismatic Allward. The married sculptor, whose wife, Margaret Kennedy Allward, was a known poet, and whose two sons would assist him with the memorial, had a gentle voice and a slight hesitation before he spoke. "Life isn't very easy for artists of any kind in Canada," he observed in the interview with Perry.[13] Indeed it was not, although it would become easier for Allward after he was awarded the Vimy commission. He was paid about $25,000 initially, and $12,000 per annum throughout the project, a small fortune for the time.[14] His contract ensured that he was both architect and sculptor, and had final say in all matters relating to the memorial. Before he left to go overseas, the sculptor had been fêted on April 12, 1922, at the Arts and Letters Club, presided over by Vincent Massey and other luminaries of the Toronto arts scene. No one was sure how long it would take Allward to complete the memorial, and he guardedly gave no time frame. The *Military Gazette* guessed that it might take five years and cost $1 million.[15]

MEANWHILE, IN YPRES, OTHER MEMORIALS were being erected. "They wrote here their first page of that Book of Glory which is the history of their participation in the War," intoned Marshal Ferdinand Foch, the supreme Allied commander during the last year of the war, at the unveiling of Canada's memorial at St. Julien on July 8, 1923.[16] Second Ypres was Canada's test of fire; bowed but unbroken, it had emerged stronger. "The wave that fell on us round Ypres," wrote Sir Max Aitken during the war, "has baptized the Dominion into nationhood—the mere written word, 'Canada,' glows now with a new meaning before all the civilized world."[17] Second Ypres had been embraced by Canadians after the April 1915 battle, and it was a watchword for Canadian martial prowess and pride, and even after the victories at Vimy, Hill 70, Passchendaele, and the Hundred Days, Second Ypres held a special place in the war history of Canadians.

Frederick Clemesha's granite soldier memorial was selected to mark the heroic stand of the Canadians. A wounded veteran and architect from Regina, Saskatchewan, Clemesha carved a Canadian soldier from granite. Known as the "Brooding Soldier," he represents the survivors mourning their fallen comrades. The striking figure was unlike any other memorial on the Western Front and seemed to capture the anguish of the millions of soldiers for their comrades. Upon the erection of Clemesha's powerful soldier, the Canadian Battlefields Memorials Commission in Ottawa decided that it was too unique to be reproduced in the other six sites, as had been the plan. The next year, the commission's secretary wrote, "It was considered by some that to repeat the monument would be to detract from its importance; by others that the erection of too tall monuments along the battlefront would savour of ostentation; by others that the design (a soldier resting on 'arms reversed') while suitable for certain sites was not suitable for others where quick victories were obtained."[18] How to mark the six other sites, then? The commission turned to a third, more modest design that had not been one of the seventeen shortlisted models. Fourteen-tonne blocks of grey Canadian granite, cube-like in appearance and bearing inscriptions in English and French, would be erected at the remaining six sites.[19] Inspired by Lutyens's Stone of Remembrance, the memorials would be carved with maple leaves and would incorporate pavilions.[20] The stone blocks were subdued, even as the "Brooding Soldier" remained a poignant presence as it stood sentry for Canada's dead at Ypres. A British journalist described the St. Julien Memorial: "There is a mysterious power in this brooding figure drawing you from the things that are to be to things that were. It does more than command the landscape, it orders the spirit . . . this is the soul of those who fell."[21]

The "Brooding Soldier" marks the Canadian stand during the April 1915 Battle of Second Ypres.

AT VIMY, ALLWARD, TOO, WAS TRYING to capture the soul of Canada's war effort. He would be assisted—and occasionally hindered—by three Canadians. Allward had the critical role as architect and sculptor, but the chief engineer, Brigadier Henry Thoresby Hughes, oversaw the eight overseas memorial sites. Before the war, Hughes had worked for the Canadian Pacific Railway company and laid out the terminals at Fort William. On the Western Front, he served in many capacities in the Royal Canadian Engineers, including commanding the engineer brigade of the 4th Canadian Infantry Division. Hughes was an important conduit back to the commission in Ottawa, but he had little patience for Allward, whom he regarded as a dilettante with no sense of the urgency of his project.

The second key figure was Colonel Henry Campbell Osborne, a wartime staff officer in Military District Number 2 in Canada.

He was a lawyer and a prominent Liberal, a friend to Prime Minister Mackenzie King, and the first secretary of the Canadian Agency of the IWGC. Osborne was also the efficient secretary of the Canadian Battlefields Memorial Commission, which meant he carried out much of the business of that commission. Cheerful and unflappable, he was a firm defender of the Vimy Memorial even as the cost overruns and delays brought criticism. Finally, Captain (later Colonel) D.C. Unwin Simson, also a veteran of the Canadian Engineers, was specifically responsible for the Vimy site. Simson had stayed in the Canadian army after the war and jumped at the opportunity to work with the commission. He went overseas in September 1923, and with his wife set up a residence over a bakery shop on the Ypres–Abeele Road.

Vimy Ridge was a few kilometres from Arras, but all the major roads leading to it and up the ridge had been thoroughly destroyed during the war. Though the Vimy land had been given to the Canadian government for its use, the main road passed through several farms, and so Hughes worked with the French government to run a new cut on Canadian land, which was along the old front-line trench of Bois de la Folie. During the building season of 1922 and 1923, the road to the east of the ridge was linked up to an existing railroad track with a thought of accommodating the huge slabs of stone that would later be used to build the memorial. Labour was difficult to find, as the local citizens were busy rebuilding homes or farms, or helping others do so. Moreover, hundreds of thousands of unexploded shells were buried in the soil and liable to detonate at any movement. According to Simson, "To lessen as much as possible the danger of explosion, three men, each armed with a four-foot long steel probe, started off along the proposed road allowances. One had a mine detector, the other two carried probes."[22] When a bomb or shell was discovered, it was marked and another group removed it. Thousands were removed this way, through painstakingly slow work. Discovered dugouts were filled with concrete, and many bodies were exhumed and passed on to the IWGC.[23]

ALLWARD SPENT MONTHS IN 1923 GOING over every inch of the Vimy site, studying it and paying particular attention to how the memorial would sit on the ridge. Part of his process was to erect telegraph poles to visualize the placement of his future monument.[24] He wished for it to emerge, almost naturally, from the ground. Drilling tests were conducted to determine the strata of rock, and many bodies were found buried in the honeycomb of dugouts and graves. The stench of rotting flesh pervaded the ridge. Deciding to put the memorial on the highest ground, the former battle site on Hill 145, Allward planned to cut away the ridge to level the ground and to remove sight-line obstructions. His memorial would look eastward, out over the Douai plain and towards the rising sun, facing the same direction as the Canadians who clawed up the ridge on April 9, 1917. Simson's workers excavated huge amounts of soil to "give the impression of the walls growing out of the ground."[25] Once the site for the memorial was levelled, there was more digging, outwards in a fanlike direction, with the end closest to the memorial ploughed 8 metres deep in an area extending outwards some 275 metres, to create what Allward called the amphitheatre. In the end, the excavation required removing 65,000 tonnes of soil, chalk, and clay, intermingled with shells and corpses.

The work was difficult, and an architectural firm was required to lay 15,000 tonnes of steel-reinforced concrete for the foundation.

Moreover, finding the proper stone for the memorial proved a significant challenge. Throughout 1923 and 1924, Allward was increasingly troubled as he visited one quarry after another with no success. The delays were testing the patience of the commission in Ottawa. Matters were not helped when Osborne arranged for the prickly Allward to hold a meeting with Percy Nobbs, an architectural adviser who was sent to visit him overseas in January 1924. During a stormy meeting, Allward felt that Nobbs was second-guessing his memorial, telling him what stone to select and that the amount of excavation was far in excess of all the other Canadian memorial sites combined. Allward would not stand for it and complained to the high commissioner in London, Peter Larkin. A friend and benefactor of Mackenzie King, Larkin warned Osborne that it had been a mistake to send Nobbs. He wrote that, while Allward was "one of the nicest gentlemen one could meet, he is temperamental to the extreme and if anything crossed him he is the type of man to drop the whole thing and go home without a moment's notice, not in wrath but in sorrow."[26] Allward the mercurial artist was to be treated carefully, and Osborne ensured that Nobbs made no more visits to the sculptor.

The inability of Allward to find the right stone left Simson and his crew without work. So the engineers set to refurbishing and rebuilding the front-line trench system and Grange Tunnel, which was excavated first in 1926. In Simson's words, his goal was to restore "places recognized by ex-service men."[27] The Grange Tunnel exited to the Canadian trenches around a crater, and opposite it, only 35 metres away, were German trenches and a deep German dugout. Yet the trenches, less than a decade after the battle, "were gradually disappearing from the effects of the weather." To preserve them, according to Simson, "wet cement

*The preserved Vimy trenches, with concrete sandbags
and duckboards. Note the concrete sign reading "Grange,"
which directs visitors to the tunnel.*

was poured into gunny sacks and laid wet upon the other, taking
the imprint of the sacks." The sacks rotted away, but the concrete
sandbags remained. To find the right height of the trenches, the
crews dug down until they discovered "relics of the sandbags,
trench mats, etc."[28] Trench mats were also poured in concrete to
offer a firm foundation upon which to stand.

Grange Tunnel, one of thirteen used by the Corps during the
battle, was 10 metres below ground and stretched back some
1,200 metres to Neuville–St. Vaast. Much of the tunnel had fallen
in over the years, but it remained a labyrinth of passages, enclaves,
rooms, and storage areas. Smoke from candles set along the walls
had blackened the chalk. Mills bombs, ammunition boxes, and
all manner of weapons remained in varying degrees of decay and
danger. "It was as though we had been switched back to April,

1917," wrote one visitor to the tunnel. "Nothing had changed."[29] Simson found a collection of rusting artifacts, including weapons, tools, and equipment, and he decided to leave it in the tunnel as a "small museum."[30] It remains to this day.

Throughout the tunnels were the names of soldiers inscribed into the soft chalk with their bayonets. There were also sculptures and carvings. One of the more striking sculptures was a series of soldiers wearing steel helmets, bearing the inscription "Canada 1917."[31] They were a poignant legacy of the men who had passed through the tunnels. Simson discovered names and sayings from before and after the battle, as many of the tunnels were used following the capture of the ridge, especially in May 1917 when the Canadians remained close to the ridge on the eastern slopes.

The Vimy tunnels were filled with soldiers' carvings and graffiti. This is the crest of the 48th Highlanders of Canada, a Toronto militia unit that formed the 15th Battalion in 1914.

"103234—James Burton, A company, Royal Canadian Regiment, 8 May 1917: 'Still alive and kicking.'" And "670080—W.J. Auchincloss, A Company, Royal Canadian Regiment, 8 May 1917, 'Untouched by whizz bangs as yet.'" Both men survived the war. Many other names marked Canadians who were not so lucky.

IN THE WAR'S AFTERMATH, THE IWGC planned to raise several memorials to the missing soldiers with no known graves. A staggering 526,816 of the Empire's buried soldiers had no identifiable name on a grave, or were simply listed as a name on a memorial, a figure that included the dominions' forces. There had been early talk by the Australians of creating "dummy graves," a headstone over no body, but the IWGC expressed reservations, fearing that fake graves would shake faith in the work of the IWGC. The idea was discarded, but it was felt important that the missing, lost, and unidentified soldiers were somehow all accounted for.[32]

Hughes, Osborne, and Rodolphe Lemieux met with Sir Fabian Ware, head of the IWGC, in the autumn of 1922.[33] They had already been in talks, since the Vimy site included several cemeteries cared for by the IWGC. These included Givenchy Road Canadian Cemetery, which contained 111 Canadians who fell during the battle, and the larger cemetery, Canadian Cemetery No. 2, which was located near the Vimy Memorial, on lower ground, and held some 2,904 Allied soldiers, of whom 695 were Canadian. There were other cemeteries around Vimy with Canada's dead, many from the Vimy battle, and these IWGC cemeteries joined dozens of other French burial sites around the region, including the massive Notre Dame de Lorette, which interred the remains of more than 40,000 soldiers.

Echoing New Zealand's decision to put their missing soldiers' names on their own memorial, the Canadians favoured inscribing the names of their missing countrymen on Allward's Vimy Memorial. This was in contrast to Australia, which had agreed that its names would be inscribed, along with those of many other imperial forces, on the Menin Gate at Ypres, a memorial gateway and arch to be unveiled in 1927. Tens of thousands of Canadians had marched from Ypres through the ruined Menin Gate during the war, and the Canadian baptism of fire at Ypres in April 1915 had been followed by fierce fighting in the Ypres salient in 1916 and 1917. The Canadian commission struggled with the difficult choice, but in late 1922 it was decided that the Vimy Memorial, as Canada's primary overseas site, must hold the names of all of the fallen who were missing (believed at the time to be around 20,000), although this policy would later change.[34] However, the Menin Gate could not be ignored, and therefore it would include the 6,998 names of Canadians with no known graves who fell in the Ypres salient, joining the 54,896 others who are listed there for the British Empire and its dominions—in effect, double naming these Canadians on the Menin Gate and Vimy Memorials.[35] Yet because the Menin Gate ran out of space for all the names of the missing, a number of Canadians who were killed after August 1917 were also commemorated at the massive site at Tyne Cot near Passchendaele, which has 34,887 names of the Empire's missing. The last missing groups of Canadians, those lost at sea, are commemorated on the CWGC Halifax Memorial, while airmen are commemorated at the Airmen's Monument, part of the Arras Memorial. The dividing up of the names of the dead among different memorials was surely not a well-conceived idea, but the politics of death was wrapped up in the question of reputations and representation.[36]

Though the commission had established in late 1922 a policy that the names of the missing Canadians should be commemorated on the Vimy Memorial, it was not until September 1926 that Osborne seriously raised the issue with Allward.[37] During those four years, the commission, worried about how to fit 20,000 names on Allward's memorial, had decided to include only the 11,285 names of the dead with no known graves in France, while the remaining dead would be memorialized on the Menin Gate or Tyne Cot. Nonetheless, the sculptor understandably reacted with shock when he learned that his memorial was responsible for displaying thousands of names.[38] Allward mulled over where to put the names, not liking the idea at all and feeling they would detract from his sculptures. Every surface of the memorial was studied, from the low-lying inside terrace's parapet to the rear buttresses. Osborne did not want them spiralling up the two pylons, as Allward suggested. The sculptor even floated the idea of engraving the names on the floor stones, although he must have realized it would never do to have visitors walking on the nearly sacred representations of the fallen.[39] The memorial's front wall, a critical interpretative element for Allward and the symbolic shield of strength, had a long flat surface, but Allward resisted putting the names there, warning of the "danger of having it look like a huge sign board."[40] However, with nowhere else to inscribe the names, Allward relented and offered up his walls, along the front and up the staircases. But he demanded that the names not be arranged in columns and by units, as on the Menin Gate, but engraved alphabetically, running in continuous bands without interruption from stone to stone, left to right, including name and rank but not military unit.

The names were sandblasted in continuous bands, across both vertical and horizontal seams. This was to signify a continuous

The inscribed names of Canada's fallen in France with no known graves.
There are 11,285 Canadians honoured on the Vimy Memorial.

flow, to tie the memorial and the fallen together as a single entity. Allward even designed his own lettering, and it took four years and much expertise to blast to an even depth for each name, even with the use of specially constructed rubber templates. Allward's desire to run the names across seams would later make it difficult to re-engrave them, but those were problems for a later generation to fix. And it would be the names that most affected later generations. The thousands upon thousands of names speak to the grief and loss of war. These are the fallen with no known graves. These are the dead whose bodies were obliterated or swallowed by the mud to forever disappear. These are the fallen who lived in a twilight world between the living and the dead. Here, on Vimy, the fallen were being numbered and named. Here, the survivors could run their hands over the names blasted into stone and know that the lost had been found.

"I WISH TO MAKE IT VERY plain that I feel the responsibility regarding the stone," wrote Allward to Mewburn in November 1924, "and you must be prepared to find me extremely cautious."[41] He had penned a masterly understatement: the stone was essential to his monument, and Allward would not compromise on a lesser type. At one point, the sculptor had planned to construct the Vimy Memorial from Italian Seravezza marble, but Percy Nobbs objected, believing that the harsh weather of northern France would erode it over time, and feeling that its white, almost translucent glow, was too "ghost-like."[42] There were few other appropriate substitutes. The stone blocks for the sculptured figures had to be flawless and large: the figure groups were carved from stone no less than 2.5 metres in depth, and the central shrouded figure of *Canada Bereft*, also known as "Mother Canada," required a perfect block of stone 4 metres high.

Allward pursued a stone that he had dreamed about. It had a luminescent quality to it, a glow from a flame within. He visited quarries throughout France, but failed to find a suitable stone.[43] Allward set off to inspect other memorials, hoping that the finished products would lead him back to a source. He walked through castles and cathedrals; he studied in detail the monuments to the great men of the past. Nothing moved him. Too many had weathered badly. He set his sights on the horizon, travelling first to Italy, the land of ancient memorials and sculptures, and then to Spain and further afield to northern England. Two years and tens of thousands of dollars were consumed in the hunt, drawing his attention and inspiration away from his sculptures.

A bewildered Ottawa urged Allward on. The commission found their sculptor's delays infuriating, but they were still anxious to support him.[44] Rodolphe Lemieux wrote to one member of Parliament who was inquiring about the memorial, advising him, "Allward is a great artist—but as my father often said of a lazy fellow—he is a slow coach."[45] The stone weighed on Allward day and night, and he despaired over finding the right type for his monument. As 1925 gave way to the new year, Allward heard of the ancient quarry near Split in Yugoslavia, the site where stone had been pulled from the ground in the late third century for Diocletian's Palace. The limestone was known as Seget, and it had a fine-grained look. He found several of the large stones in London and he worked on them, thrilled to find them durable and uniform in quality. The stone, after weathering, had turned a light cream colour.[46] The rough blocks proved supple to his tools and remained soft and warm. Allward might have, finally, unlocked the secret of the stone.

The Split quarry had been closed for centuries, trapping the stone in the ground where it had lain since the earth cooled. Could it be coaxed into the sunlight? Allward set off by train. The sculptor knew he was running out of options; he had tried the patience of Ottawa and now he was seen as a troublesome artist, perhaps even one who did not know his own mind. As the hundreds of kilometres slipped away, he read and sketched, but he also brooded. This might be his last chance. He arrived at Split sometime in midsummer. Despite his fatigue, he demanded to see the quarry. The stone was there, washed and ready, the owners of the quarry waiting in anticipation, mouths almost salivating over the potential windfall. Allward approached the stone with trepidation. It was pure. It was warm. He ran his hand over it. This was it.

The emotional satisfaction of finding the stone soon led to new frustrations over how to extract enough for the enormous memorial. A British contractor, Walter Jenkins, had the vexing job of overseeing the quarrying work. After Yugoslavians chased away the experienced Italian stoneworkers whom they saw as taking their jobs, local incompetents took over who often broke the stone during the difficult process of extraction. Jenkins fretted, as he was losing enormous sums of money, and in desperation he sent along blocks to the Vimy site that were too small or were flawed with marks. Allward refused them. Jenkins accused Allward of being unreasonable, and wrote pleading letters to Ottawa. Allward, in turn, labelled Jenkins a scoundrel and a swindler. Allward wrote of years of "ceaseless controversy with Jenkins. . . . It is difficult to erect beauty under such conditions."[47] While Osborne sided with Allward, and even prepared papers to sue Jenkins for delivering poor pieces of stone, the price of the operation spiralled out of control. Fear gnawed away at Allward, as no one was sure what remained buried, and when the good stone would exhaust itself. But, gradually, over the next year, large pieces were dragged from the earth, and eventually 6,100 tonnes arrived at Vimy in June 1927.

A HANDFUL OF SCULPTORS, GUIDED BY Allward, began the process of carving the stone, using a number of maquettes designed by Allward in his studio. Allward's technique was to sculpt the figurative elements in clay. He then made plaster moulds of the figures, which were transferred to Vimy, where they were placed in position on the walls of the memorial. Using the maquettes as guides, the sculptors, led by Italian master carver Luigi Rigamonti, took the blocks of stone and carved them at twice the size. To do this, a pantograph was used to transfer the maquette designs to the stone by doubling the distances between pencil marks on the maquettes. Buried metal markers provided depth measurements.[48] To work through the winter months, studios were built over the monument to provide enclosed areas.[49]

What to make of Allward's twenty sculptural figures of idealized values arranged in clusters and around the monument, at key corners and even atop the two pylons? *Truth*, *Justice*, *The Defenders*, *Hope*, *Faith*—they were allegorical clichés of everything that was seemingly lost during the Armageddon of war.[50] The terrible destruction of war had, some critics argued, buried these "big words," and now they were not only accepted and praised, but would form the very heart of Canada's overseas memorial. In honouring the fallen, the nations of the world found solace in the traditional.[51] The "just war" idea was affirmed through Allward's sculptures. But the underlying anguish conveyed by the memorial

The Grieving Woman, *as she was called by Allward, is in the process of emerging from the stone through the sculptors' carving. In the top right of the image, Allward's maquette can be seen, which the sculptors are using as a reference, enlarging it to double the size.*

undercut this traditional depiction. Many of Allward's figures are gaunt, their rib cages showing. They suggest suffering, and some are contorted to illustrate pain. The monument's central sculpture, *Canada Bereft*, stands with head bowed, holding wilting lilies, as she weeps for her fallen sons. She is alone in her grief, in front of the sheltering pylons and peering at a sarcophagus below. The bereaved mother represents the tragedy of war and the unending emptiness of families facing a future without a loved one. There are no allegorical sculptures symbolizing martial strength, and Allward dropped a planned figure that had stood with its foot on a German helmet—signifying victory in battle. Many of the twenty figures, placed on the pillars and around the monument, are grieving or deliberately railing against war as they pass on the torch or break the sword. Allward described the symbolic sculptures:

> At the base of the strong impregnable walls of defence are the Defenders, one group showing the Breaking of the Sword, the other the Sympathy of the Canadians for the Helpless. Above these are the mouths of guns covered with olive and laurels. On the wall stands an heroic figure of Canada brooding over the graves of her valiant dead; below is suggested a grave with a helmet, laurels, etc. Behind her stand two pylons symbolizing the two forces—Canadian and French—while between, at the base of these, is the Spirit of Sacrifice, who, giving all, throws the torch to his Comrades.[52]

This would be a monument to peace, not victory, an homage to loss and death, and a call to remembrance.

The story of the stone made news across Europe, and soon architects and artists, not to mention several thousand curious tourists, visited Vimy. None other than Edwin Lutyens, the creator of the Thiepval monument with its 73,000 names of the missing from the Somme, would later travel to inspect the Seget stone. He remarked that "he had never seen finer [stone] in his life."[53] The memorial, too, was awe-inspiring: staggering in its size, scope, and beauty. It has a base 72 metres long by 11 metres high and 37 metres deep, supporting two vertical pylons 30 metres in height. The long wall facing the Douai plain, according to Allward, was meant to suggest a bulwark—"a line of defence."[54] The immovable wall was critical to the memorial, not only to evoke the Canadians' attack and hold of the ridge, but also to suggest that the ridge and memorial would forever stand against weather and time.[55]

Allward had generally resisted talking about the allegorical significances of his memorial, especially the pylons. But after feeling some pressure to explain its meaning to the French, who were increasingly wary of the many and large memorials erected on their soil, he wrote in 1926 about his vision: "The long walls are intended to suggest a line of defence, and also to be in harmony with the long and clean cut line of the Ridge. The two pylons were an endeavor to create an outline against the sky, that would not be easily confused with towers or other landmarks." Allward believed that in the afternoon a shaft of sunlight would break through the space between the pylons, and, illuminating part of the memorial, would suggest a "cathedral effect."[56] The pylons also work at another symbolic level; they rise from the ground, the very terrain where soldiers were mired during the fighting on the Western Front. The war was one of mud and trenches, with the soldiers either looking into sandbags or, more often, peering up at the blue sky, tracking the graceful flight of birds and occasional airplanes. The Vimy monument, large and powerful, is elongated but also reaches for the sky with its twin pylons. The horizontal is cut by the vertical; the battlefield is intersected by the search for greater meaning. The pylons, too, could be mistaken for a buried cross, with the lower part embedded in the ground, the cross arms running along the ground, and the pylons forming the top. Such imagery evoked the Easter Monday battle of Vimy that was celebrated by Christian Canada. The sky was a symbol of escape and hope for soldiers in the trenches; after the war, the pylons would evoke similar feelings for veterans. Or perhaps they were simply large and magnificent in conception and execution.

What the pylons were not was a call to militarism, military victory, or even national pride. Allward emphasized that his memorial was not about celebrating a martial triumph, or, it would seem, the birth of the Canadian nation.

THE COMPLETION OF ALLWARD'S MEMORIAL WAS delayed by years. Throughout the 1920s, members of Parliament would occasionally raise the issue of Vimy in the House of Commons, but it was not a burning question, even though each year appropriations had to be voted on for the Canadian Battlefields Memorials Commission. But as the years wore on, the delays to the Vimy Memorial were commented upon more frequently and became something of a thorn in the side of King and then R.B. Bennett, who became prime minister in 1930. While the deepening financial crisis from late 1929 dominated Question Period, the delays to the overseas monument niggled.

To meet the mounting interest from the public, the commission published a commemorative history in 1929, filled with text and images of the overseas memorials, but Vimy's presence was conspicuously missing. Despite much pleading from Osborne, Allward had not allowed his sculptures to be displayed. Only Allward's 1920 model was shown, although the accompanying text predicted that when the monument was unveiled, "Vimy will be to Canada what Agincourt is to England."[57] Newspapers frequently alerted visitors to Allward's monumental work, claiming it would soon be completed; in 1930, for instance, *The Globe* noted the memorial would be unveiled in 1932.[58] But in the House of Commons, the government's spokesmen were necessarily vague, refusing to be pinned down on an unveiling date.[59] The delays to Vimy were proving increasingly embarrassing to Bennett's Conservative government.[60] While Canadians struggled through the dark days of the Depression, when hundreds of thousands of Canadians were out of work and countless families suffered, the Vimy Memorial continued to cost the government about $50,000 a year—with no end in sight. Prime Minister Bennett had more things to worry about than an overseas memorial, but he was anxious to avoid angering veterans, who were pressuring his government for sweeping changes to pensions. He expressed his displeasure at the rolling barrage of delays and the cost overruns that would eventually reach $1.5 million.[61] Bennett had periodically asked about the memorial since 1928, first as leader of the Opposition and then, from 1930, as prime minister, and he inspected the unfinished memorial later that same year. He was impressed, but ordered sharply in early 1931, "This work must be completed in 1932."[62] The prime minister's demands were ignored.

The commission in Ottawa could do little to urge on Allward other than to work diligently. Osborne remained a shield for Allward, and he took the prime minister's wrath. He wrote and responded to editorials in newspapers—especially one in September 1932 in *The Globe* that claimed there was "official indifference" to completing the memorial—and he claimed in print, "No effort is being spared to expedite the work."[63] When that seemed too close to pleading, he bolstered his case by leaking a letter in December 1933 from British architect Sir Edwin Lutyens, who had visited Vimy and called it a "great masterpiece."[64] Obviously aware of the pressure on Allward, Lutyens warned him not to rush the memorial, declaring, "I am sure that when it is unveiled it will make a great impression for all time; and the time you spend now is small in comparison to the centuries through which it will stand."[65] Despite Lutyens's endorsement, Allward continued to be pressed to give a completion date. The sculptor settled on 1934.[66] He would miss it by two years.

A DECADE EARLIER, IN 1925, ALLWARD had claimed that he "saw the memorial as a way of remembering the sacrifice of Canadian soldiers in a Christian sense."[67] Over time the memorial took on new meanings, even before it was completed. Responding to the terrible bleakness of the Depression and the new militarism of Europe and the Pacific, Allward shifted away from the "Christian sacrifice" of the early 1920s, and the need to find significance in a just war, towards positioning the monument to be, in his words,

The sculpted figure Grieving Man *reclines at the back of the base of the monument.*

a "protest in a quiet way against the futility of war, challenging humanity to hate war instead of being proud of it."[68]

The Vimy monument was not infused with military triumphalism. Perhaps most striking is that there is little evidence in the memorial of the Vimy battle being perceived as a "coming of age" event. Among its rich stone images and supple figures, there are almost no nationalistic symbols or patriotic iconography to suggest the "birth of a nation." The memorial does not indicate how Vimy contributed to the emergence of national consciousness, except that perhaps the Canadian pylon might be interpreted as symbolizing a country that was reaching to new heights. The one plaque inscribed with text, above the tomb, reads in English and French, "TO THE VALOUR OF THEIR COUNTRYMEN IN THE GREAT WAR AND IN MEMORY OF THEIR SIXTY THOUSAND DEAD THIS MONUMENT IS RAISED BY THE PEOPLE OF CANADA." While Allward had been instructed to include only the names of the fallen with no known graves in France, the inscription made it clear that the memorial was in memory of all of Canada's dead. The Vimy monument was not, at this point in history, a symbol of Canada's coming of age.

Senator Rodolphe Lemieux, an occasional critic of Allward for his perfectionism, reported to the Canadian Battlefields Monuments Commission shortly before the memorial's unveiling, "My candid opinion is that we will have there the finest monument of the whole French battlefields. I have watched very closely the marble carving of the various statues, and I declare that they are most artistic and appealing to one's soul."[69] The unveiling was set by Ottawa for July 26, 1936. The question was whether, nineteen years after the battle, the memorial would appeal to the collective soul of the nation.

CHAPTER 9

THE GREAT WAR CONTESTED

I n the aftermath of the terrible war, *Manitoba Free Press* editor and influential commentator J.W. Dafoe wrote in March 1919 about how Canada's sacrifice and strain had carved a path forward to full nationhood. "We have won a new status among the nations of the world; which is the outward sign of that strong nation spirit, evoked by the war which is today vitalizing our common life in all its manifestations—politic, commercial, intellectual, and spiritual."[1] Dafoe was not alone in believing that Canada had risen to the war's challenge. Though it had suffered grievous loss of life and damaged relations between English and French, farmers and city folk, labour and government, the Dominion had done its duty and would be rewarded.

No one knew what that reward might be or how Canada's leaders would position the country to achieve it. Were Canadians simply British subjects in North America, or had they been fundamentally changed by the war? At the level of international relations, nothing appeared to be different: as part of the Empire, Canada had entered the war automatically at Britain's side and ended it there too. Canada gained no new independence on November 11, 1918, although there had been significant steps forward during the war, with Prime Minister Sir Robert Borden holding a seat at the Imperial War Cabinet. Towards the end of the fighting, Field Marshal Sir Douglas Haig grumbled that the Canadians had come to see themselves as "junior but sovereign allies."[2] The wartime patriotism aroused a national sentiment that was further cemented by the Canadian people's mass sacrifice in the name of a just crusade. Too much blood had been spilled to simply bury the war in the past.

An optimistic Borden returned to London in November 1918 to press Canada's claim, aching to have some influence at Versailles, where the Allies would impose a peace on Germany. Though the great powers of France, Italy, and the United States had no desire to see any of the British dominions represented at Paris, Borden refused to accept such an insult, and he stiffened British prime minister David Lloyd George's backbone to insist that the dominions be present. Canada's and Australia's wartime dead of 60,000 for each nation eventually swayed the French, but not before Prime Minister Georges Clémenceau wrote to Lloyd George, "Come— And bring your savages with you."[3]

While the Canadian Versailles delegation was small under Borden, it had an impact by assisting Britain, through sitting on minor committees such as those establishing Greece's borders or international rules for waterways. It was the great powers that decided all of the major issues, from the redrawing of countries' borders to the punishment to be meted to Germany. Nonetheless, Canada signed the Treaty of Versailles on June 28, 1919, but did so within the confines of the British Empire and under Britain's signature on the treaty.[4] Canada's presence at Versailles was widely interpreted as a symbolic triumph for the nation. As contemporary Canadian historian W.S. Wallace wrote, "This diplomatic victory means, if it means anything, that the nationality of Canada is now recognized, not only within the circle of the British Empire, but also within the circle of international politics."[5] That overstated Canada's role at Versailles, but Wallace's was a common belief among those searching for emblematic victories. Versailles was upheld as an acknowledgment of Canada's coming of age.

ENGLISH CANADA HAD STIRRINGS OF NATIONALISM before August 1914, and these were amplified by the war, as they were in many other countries.[6] Canada's war effort had created new Canadian heroes and unifying stories. In battle, the Canadians had done as well as the British, often better. There were the heroes of the sky—Billy Bishop, Raymond Collishaw, and William Barker— who were heralded as aces, with two of the three earning the Victoria Cross. But it was the men of the Canadian Corps who had clawed their way to victory on the Western Front. From early in the war, propagandists and publicists had emphasized how different the Canadian warriors were from the British fighters, that the Dominion's soldiers from the northern wasteland were more effective because of their harsh environment and frontier instincts. In spring 1919, Lieutenant-General Arthur Currie told William Lyon Mackenzie King, who would soon be elected leader of the Liberal Party, that, "The Canadians are going back to Canada with feelings for England and affection for her; but with a feeling also that they are just as good as any men they have found on this side."[7]

Symbols like the maple leaf were important to Canadian soldiers. Many men commented that they came from a more egalitarian society, especially in comparison to Britain, with its deep social stratification. That the Canadians fought under one of their own, Sir Arthur Currie, as of June 1917, was another indication that the young Dominion had earned its laurels on the Western Front—although corps commander Sir Julian Byng was also much beloved by veterans. The string of victories and the immodest acknowledgment by soldiers, from Vimy onwards, that they were elite troops, contributed to a sense of the Corps' distinctiveness. A.Y. Jackson, a war veteran and already on his way to becoming one of Canada's most recognized artists, declared, "We are no longer humble colonials. We've made armies. We can also make artists, historians, and poets."[8] The war, in all its struggle and sacrifice, had forged the conditions for a new nation to emerge. Arthur Lower, a Canadian who served in the Royal Navy and a future historian, captured the pervasive feeling in a simple but powerful statement: "I came back from the war much more of a Canadian than I went to it."[9]

This spirit of independence did not mean that Canadians wanted to cut ties with the British Empire. In fact, the war strengthened that bond. Since the 1890s, Canadian nationalism had developed as a counterforce to imperialism, but still within the framework of empire. To contemplate leaving the Empire was to invite national suicide, it was thought: the United States would eventually gobble up Canada unless it held fast to the Union Jack. By the 1920s, this did not mean having a protective British army at Canada's call, but it did entail a rich interweaving of Canadian and British history, politics, and tradition, all threaded with ties of blood and belonging. The monarchy, Westminster parliamentary traditions, the Royal Navy, and cultural products from the heart of the Empire were all held up as defence against the allure of the United States and its crass materialistic attractions. Canadianism and Britishness were braided together, and most

Canadians could hold multiple identities, seeing themselves, for example, as Haligonians, Nova Scotians, Canadians, and citizens of the British Empire.

These were widely accepted views in English Canada, although far less so in religious and rural Quebec, where the Catholic Church continued to hold sway over the lives of French Canadians. The war, moreover, had led to anger and frustration in French Canada, although these feelings were directed less towards London than Ottawa. In the Canadian capital, the architects of conscription—Borden and his ministers—were seen as having broken the promises of compromise that underpinned Confederation. Quebec withdrew further from the rest of Canada, and even flirted with the idea of independence.[10] Though Vimy was occasionally celebrated in French Canada, mostly in Montreal with its large component of English Canadians, the legacy of conscription was divisive. It challenged the idea of the Great War as a nation-defining event among French Canadians, who made up almost a third of the population. Other new Canadians had been harassed during the war, with some losing the right to vote, while others were simply viewed with suspicion. The war was no nationalizing event for either group. The war had led to an attack on civil liberties, had aroused nativist and racist beliefs, and had damaged unity. The Great War would never be a symbol of national unity and shared sacrifice in French Canada, and the war, in its aftermath and with scars still raw, was as much a divisive event for Canada as it was a stepping stone to full nationhood.

DESPITE FIFTY YEARS OF CONFEDERATION, English Canada had remained a nation in search of itself. In no small degree, the war from 1914 to 1918 had shaken and nearly shattered Canada, but it had also forced Canadians to come together in a national project in a way that they had never done since 1867. After the inferno of war, with its agony and loss, and its patriotic exertions, Canada was never the same. Yet knowing the country had changed and articulating such a change were different things. The embrace of nationhood was a complex process involving shifting perceptions and emerging symbols, rather than a single cataclysmic moment.

For Canadians under fire on the Western Front, for those who had left behind comrades, the sacrifice had to have meaning. The prewar status quo could not remain. Brooke Claxton, a wartime gunner and later a prominent Liberal cabinet minister, was in the forefront of several burgeoning Canadian nationalistic movements in the 1920s. "We emerged from the war with a clean honest record of service," he wrote. Claxton, and many like him, ached to build on that service and martyrdom to forge a more equitable, confident, prosperous, and independent country.[11] The mimicry of Britishness by much of Canada's elite, in Claxton's mind, was no longer useful and was a barrier to Canada achieving its full nationhood.[12] He was not alone in holding this opinion, with intellectuals like Oscar D. Skelton, Escott Reid, and Arthur Lower hoping to reposition Canada in relation to Britain and put the two countries on a more equal footing. Driven by the elite—whether academics, businessmen, or artists—a number of Canadian movements emerged to help guide the nation to maturity. The Association of Canadian Clubs, the Canadian League, the Canadian Institute of International Affairs, and the League of Nations Society were all nationalistic groups that debated the country's role on the world stage. The lure of empire was powerful but, as Skelton, who would serve as undersecretary of external affairs from 1925 to

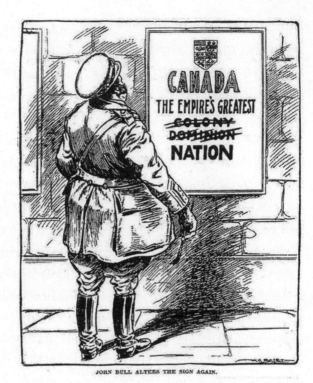

JOHN BULL ALTERS THE SIGN AGAIN.

"John Bull" (Britain) confers nation status on Canada because of its war effort, as captured in this wartime cartoon.

1941, was to write, he and like-minded Canadians sought "ultimate independence."[13]

At a profound level, the war was both a nationalizing and a deprovincializing event that forced Canadians to see themselves differently. Some of the parochialism of Canadians dropped away as the soldiers fought in foreign fields of Western Europe, in the Dardanelles, and even in northern Russia. There were also identifiable political changes throughout the 1920s in the measured march to full nationhood under the leadership of long-serving prime minister William Lyon Mackenzie King. During the 1922 Chanak Crisis, when London pressured Ottawa to send troops to the Dardanelles to protect a threatened garrison from Turkish soldiers, King had set the precedent that Canada's Parliament and not London would decide whether to send soldiers overseas. King reaffirmed Canada's right to determine its own fate at the 1923 Imperial Conference. He fought hard for Canadian autonomy, and refused attempts by the British to re-exert control over defence and foreign policy.

The 1920s were filled with slippery negotiations as Canada slowly gained autonomy, often through symbolic utterances or by resisting imperial flattery or bullying. Ottawa signed treaties without London's influence, contributed to the League of Nations, and built up its Department of External Affairs. Saying no to London was never easy, as every decision went against tradition and expectations. At the 1926 Imperial Conference, former British prime minister Lord Balfour concluded in a special report that the dominions were autonomous communities, no longer subordinate. Five years later, the 1931 Statute of Westminster affirmed that Canada, and all the dominions, would have full control over their foreign policy. Never again would Britain inform Canada that it was at war. However, as Charles "Chubby" Power, a Great War veteran and Liberal MP and minister from Quebec, would later observe, the constitutional changes through the Balfour Declaration and the Statute of Westminster, while recognized, debated, cheered, or lamented by intellectuals, were "not well understood [by the general public], and it was something that had occurred far beyond the borders of Canada."[14]

Constitutional battles are rarely glamorous, although Canadians seem to take perverse delight in them, given how many have occurred since Vimy. In the 1920s, these negotiations, in good and bad faith, were done with little flare or fervour, and it was difficult for anyone to get too excited about a fish treaty or one of the many British documents that cautiously ceded power to the dominions.

Even after the passing of the Statute of Westminster, English Canada remained British at heart. The country was a work in progress, with few symbols and touchstones. There was no national anthem, the flag was still an imperial one, and Canadians remained British subjects. Canadians still needed to find something to fire the nation's soul. Vimy offered a spark.

THE BATTLE OF VIMY RIDGE HAD caught the imagination of Canadians since news of the victory had broken. By July 1917, the capture of the ridge had become the central theme of an official Canadian photography exhibition in London, with tens of thousands viewing photographs of the "historic battle." [15] In that same year, Lieutenant-Colonel J.N. Gunn, in recording the history of his unit, No. 8 Canadian Field Ambulance, wrote:

> What is there for Canadians in the name of "Vimy Ridge"? Or is it a useless question, because all are so familiar with what it means? Does it not mean glory? Yes, but it means death. Does it not mean gain? Yes, but it means suffering. It means all these things and much more, and probably the greatest of these is that it means history unrivalled for Canada, marking an epoch which the children of this and future generations shall cherish as a sacred possession handed down to them by those who fought and won on that Easter Monday morning in April 1917. [16]

Vimy inspired poets, too, who waxed on in verse and song, in clumsy rhyming couplets and heroic stanzas. [17] In the immediate postwar years, Vimy was setting in the memory of Canadians. In 1922, Toronto's *Globe*, on the fifth anniversary of the Vimy battle,

This enormous photograph of the Vimy battle was the centrepiece of the 1917 official Canadian photography exhibition in London.

decreed that the ridge was where "Canadian boys made history that is still gaining lustre."[18]

The 1921 Census revealed that at least twenty-one babies born since 1917 had been named Vimy, most of them girls. The name Vimy was conferred on streets, schools, and community structures, such as the 1937 Vimy Memorial Bandshell in Kiwanis Park, Saskatoon. Advertisers drew upon Vimy to sell clothing and commercial goods, and there was a brand of canned salmon in the 1920s that was named Vimy Ridge, with packaging that depicted a stylized assault by Canadians up the ridge.

Vimy also found its way, not surprisingly, into history books. The first generation of writing was steeped in patriotism and adventure, and sometimes read like travel narratives of mass murder. A Canadian publisher estimated that more than a thousand war-related books were marketed in Canada during the war,

The Vimy legend was commercialized. This can of salmon was offered for sale to Canadians during the 1920s.

and that sales of this type of book increased tenfold over prewar sales. Some had print runs of up to 40,000 copies. Books about the Great War were still strong sellers throughout the 1920s.[19]

Newsman J.W. Dafoe visited the Western Front in March 1919, a mere four months after the armistice. The battlefields were closed to most visitors because of the vast reclamation project underway to disinter the bodies of the fallen and rebury them in war cemeteries. The area was also swarming with gangs of criminals and desperate civilians digging out the buried treasure of brass shell casings and other scrap metal that could be sold for profit. At that time, very few of the British and dominion burial grounds had been taken over by the War Graves Commission, but Sir Arthur Currie acted as Dafoe's patron and facilitated what he described as a "pilgrimage."[20] The prolific Dafoe wrote a little book, *Over the Canadian Battlefields* (1919), as he felt compelled to share his experiences: "For while the memory of the Great War endures. . . . Canadians, generation after generation for centuries to come, will follow the Canadian way of glory over the battlefields of France and Flanders." In the future, there would be sightseers and pilgrims, the curious and the grief-stricken. Vimy was not "in its actual achievement nor in its military consequences the greatest feat of the Canadian Expeditionary Force," but Dafoe observed that the battle "holds, and it may continue to hold, a unique place in the Canadian consciousness." As the first major victory by the Canadians, along with the previous failures there—"white with the unburied bones" of the French—Vimy was "holy ground."[21]

There were a handful of other contemporary accounts of Vimy, although most of the wartime and postwar histories were of the broader Canadian experience in the entire war. A contemporary history, written in 1918 by British veteran and journalist Frank Fox, *The Battle of the Ridge Arras–Messines*, complained that already the capture of Vimy Ridge had overshadowed the larger Arras offensive. The Canadians, he was at pains to point out, were only a small part of the larger operation, but their victory obscured all others: "Indeed, to many casual students of the events of the Great War, the seizure of Vimy Ridge was the Battle of Arras, its beginning, its end, and its whole accomplishment. That is very far from being the case."[22] The next year, in 1919, American writer George Ralphson offered *Over There, with the Canadians at Vimy Ridge*, part of the *Over There* series of novellas. The story featured an American serving with the Canadians—of which there were some 40,000 during the war—but it had little to do with Vimy Ridge, and its later chapters evolved into a spy adventure. Nonetheless, the selection of Vimy as a backdrop of a story for an American audience was a sign that Vimy was known in a way that few other battles were.[23]

Canadian journalists wrote their own heroic accounts of the war, although all were eclipsed by Sir Max Aitken's (Lord Beaverbrook) three-volume *Canada in Flanders* series. The mischievous and flamboyant Canadian millionaire was a kingmaker in British politics, and he used his influence as a newspaper baron, friend to Conservatives, and British MP to get what he wanted.

And what he sought to do during the war was to raise the profile of the Canadian soldiers. In 1916, his account of the Canadian battle at Second Ypres became an Empire-wide bestseller, going through more than a dozen editions and selling a quarter million copies.[24] The other two volumes, the third of which was written by poet G.D. Roberts, took the war effort up to the Somme. The *Canada in Flanders* series celebrated the Canadian soldiers, raising their profile among British and dominion troops and highlighting their heroic stand at Second Ypres.

There were other early histories, like J.F.B. Livesay's *Canada's Hundred Days* (1919) and George Nasmith's *Canada's Sons in the World War* (1919), which provided heroic accounts of the Canadians in battle. While Vimy was prominent in these books, there was no evocation of nationhood.[25] Attesting to the public interest in the Great War, from 1917 to 1921, United Publishers of Toronto commissioned several dozen journalists and veterans to contribute to a six-volume history of the war. The books covered all of the major battles, as well as chapters on services like the medical corps and logistics. It was a significant body of work, and given that the authors had no access to the official records, many of the offerings are surprisingly detailed and accurate. Volume IV of the series, *The Turn of the Tide*, contained a seventy-page chapter on Vimy Ridge by Allan Donnell. His credible account of the pre-battle planning and the engagement contained few errors or even hyperbole, and his restrained conclusion was that "Important as the capture of Vimy Ridge undoubtedly was, it is perhaps as well for Canadians to realize that it was only one of a series of actions designed to dispossess the Germans of a number of outstanding positions, which, by skilful generalship, they had secured early in the war. The action was a step—a very valuable step—in the policy of attrition, which the Somme battles seemed to prove was the wisest method at that time."[26] His was not a grandiose claim about how Vimy won the war or how a battle forged a nation.

School textbooks praised the war and its impact on Canada, but Vimy was not elevated over the other battles in that first post-war decade. Instead, it was the entire war effort that was important, as described by W.L. Grant in his *History of Canada* (1923), where he claimed that the nation's wartime deeds "give Canada forever her place among the nations of the world."[27] The Battle of Second Ypres, argued D.M. Duncan in his 1919 school textbook *The Story of the Canadian People*, was unparalleled, and "Probably no event during the past century has sent a greater thrill throughout the Empire."[28] Almost all of the contemporary histories and school textbooks in the 1920s noted that Vimy and Second Ypres were Canada's finest wartime accomplishments, but it was the war writ large that had ultimately changed Canada.

THE IDEA OF VIMY AS AN epoch-changing event began to take hold when it was decided that Vimy and not Ypres would be the site of Canada's major overseas memorial. And the appointment of Lord Byng as Canada's governor general solidified that motion. It was a celebrated occasion for Canadian veterans. Their beloved general had ended the war as a successful army commander and had taken his title as Baron Byng of Vimy (later Viscount Byng). The battle was deeply associated with his name.

Upon Byng's arrival at Rideau Hall in 1921, he made an immediate impact. Byng always had the common touch and he made many cross-country tours to adoring crowds. He professed

Lord Byng of Vimy, governor general of Canada, 1921–1926. Byng's presence in Canada stimulated interest in the Battle of Vimy Ridge as Canada's singular, representative battle from the Great War—the moment that marked the country's transition from colony to nation.

publicly his support of Canadian books and plays, but also, much to his canny credit, a newfound love of hockey. The Byngs were often seen at the Ottawa Senators hockey games, and his wife would eventually donate a trophy to reward fair play and sportsmanship, which still bears her name.

Byng retained a special place in his heart for his Corps' veterans. Old soldiers visited him at Rideau Hall, and he went out of his way to speak of the memory of the Canadian Corps wherever he went. He was the living embodiment of what had been accomplished by the Canadians under his command on the Western Front. On the anniversary of the Vimy battle in 1922, Byng held the first Vimy dinner in Toronto, with more than a thousand officers present.[29] During the next four years, Canada's most prominent veterans and serving officers, now involved in politics, business, and the academy, took part in the annual dinners, which were reported on by the newspapers.[30] The 1923 Vimy dinner was described as "one of the largest reunions of officers of the corps that has ever been held in this country."[31] With the battle associated closely with Byng, and its memory re-consecrated each year by the banquet, Vimy became more firmly grounded in the Canadian psyche. In 1925, General Currie gave voice to a sentiment that was growing in strength: that the soldiers had gone up the ridge as residents of the nine provinces or as British immigrants, but that they died or emerged as Canadians at the top.[32] "There was no Quebec and no Ontario," Currie said of the Canadians who captured Vimy, "no Nova Scotia and no Alberta— but one great country—that beloved Canada."[33]

Despite Byng's success in reaching out to Canadians, he soon became a casualty of the ongoing political war between W.L.M. King and Arthur Meighen. In the October 1925 election, the resurgent Conservatives won more seats than the Liberals—116 to 101—but not enough to take majority control of the House of Commons. The wily King refused to relinquish power, making the case to Governor General Byng that he could govern by enlisting the support of the left-leaning Progressives, who represented the West and still carried deep wartime grievances from farmers against Meighen. It was strange for Canadians to see King lose to Meighen and remain prime minister, but he survived for almost a year before his government unravelled in scandal. When King went to Byng in June 1926 and asked for a dissolution of Parliament and a new election, Byng refused, saying that Meighen had earned the right to form a government.[34] King was outraged, resigned in a huff, and carried his anger into the election that soon followed after Meighen's government itself dissolved.

King campaigned on the idea that Meighen was unfit to rule, but one of his arguments was that the governor general was part of an imperial conspiracy to curb Canadian independence. It was a broadside blow that had little merit, but Canadians resented the notion of an unelected official dictating to the people. Byng had done no such thing; instead the hero of Vimy had encouraged the development of Canadian institutions and even suggested the nation was ready for a new flag. King backed away from directly attacking Byng, but the smear campaign took hold across the country, amplified on the hustings by Liberal candidates who accused the imperial overlord of meddling in Canadian politics.[35] It seemed that Canadians, though respectful of veterans and Byng, resented the idea that Canadian political authority was undermined. King won the 1926 election in a landslide and vanquished his hated nemesis Meighen. Byng left the country a few months later, despondent at the thought that his desire for fair play—expressed in giving Meighen his chance—had been used against him in such a crude manner by the victorious King. Many outraged veterans, and especially former officers, were furious with the King government, but the prime minister survived the backlash. Even in Byng's absence, the Vimy dinners continued across the country in large cities, and the idea of the battle's importance gained in strength.

IN 1921, THE DEPARTMENT OF MILITIA and Defence funded an official history program, under the direction of an artillery staff officer, Archer F. Duguid. Codifying the Canadian war effort and making sure the Dominion received due credit for its wartime achievements was important to many of the survivors and their families. To produce the eight-volume history, Duguid and his staff first had to sort through and classify the overseas records, which comprised millions of pages of documents. It was an enormous job, and Duguid, who would become Canada's expert on the war, was forced to concurrently engage in multiple other tasks. He and his staff had to sort out battle honours for units; answer inquiries related to history, heritage, and even pension claims; deal with the British official historians who were writing the Canadian story into their own books; and protect the reputation of senior commanders and the soldiers of the Canadian Corps.[36] Little progress was made on the official written history throughout the decade.

By the late 1920s, veterans complained that the delay of an official history—which carried at the time the assurance of being the "true" story supported by official records—was allowing other nations to downplay or misconstrue the role of the Canadians on the Western Front.[37] Duguid refused to make the records available to the public or a few academic historians—except for regimental historians writing accounts of units—arguing that other versions would detract from his own writing. It seemed to others that he was hoarding the records, and the complaints became more vociferous. The Legion, an amalgamation of most of the veterans' groups that came together in 1925, pressured the government from 1929 onwards to find a new historian, suggesting journalist-veterans Will Bird or George Drew.[38] There was no change. A few years later, Bird, a voice for veterans who wrote about the war, complained of the shameful delay in 1932. When the histories were finally published, he lamented, the veterans would all be dead or forgotten. "Then who will read them? . . . We, the men who served, want them NOW."[39]

The Americans were especially jingoistic in suggesting that they had won the war, and almost single-handedly at that. In reality, when President Woodrow Wilson brought the United States into the war in April 1917, the nation's armed forces were deeply unprepared for the sophisticated fighting on the Western Front. Most American divisions did not arrive at the front until the summer of 1918, and then did not contribute much to battlefield success until the late fall of that year. While there was no denying the tremendous psychological impact of having the American million-man army flood into Britain and then France, the U.S. ground forces were almost always bested by the battle-hardened Germans until late in the war. But that did not stop the American propagandists and politicians from smugly claiming victory. The British and French were angered by the American hubris, amplified by Wilson's prominent role at Versailles.

Canadians also felt the sting of the American claims. The bold and inaccurate declarations were another insult to add to the persistent Canadian worry that American culture was seeping north into the Dominion. Hollywood film moguls destroyed the Canadian homegrown industry, although Canadians played a part as they embraced the films.[40] Popular American radio drowned out the fledging Canadian stations, and Canadian magazines were buried in the avalanche from south of the border.[41] Survival was only possible, cultural nationalists claimed, with government intervention—it had to be "the state or the United States."

Throughout the 1920s, American films, books, and even comics claimed that it was Yankee New World troops who had won the war, showing the exhausted Europeans how to drive back the Germans. Canadians were infuriated. One of the more acerbic Canadian writers commented that the United States was neutral for much of the war, during which "America counted her profits while Canada buried her dead."[42] In 1928, responding to a series of egregious American claims to have beaten Germany alone in the last year of the war, George Drew, a veteran and a future premier of Ontario, struck back in print to defend Canada's honour. He penned a fierce rejoinder in *Maclean's* on Dominion Day; in it, Drew lined up a barrage of statistics supplied by official historian Duguid on the Canadian contributions to the war, while showing how the American armies were late to arrive and largely ineffective. The article was republished as a pamphlet called *Canada in the Great War*, and it struck a chord, selling over 100,000 copies.[43] Drew was celebrated for his robust defence of the nation, with one newspaper noting that he had become "one of the most discussed men in Canada."[44] Canadians everywhere refused to let the Americans downplay their wartime contributions.

"THE WAR THAT WILL END WAR," was the powerful phrase coined by writer H.G. Wells to describe the events of 1914–1918, a phrase that would, over time, shift to become "the war to end all wars." Confronted with the more than nine million battlefield dead, a fragmenting Europe, and the collapse of global empires, there was a fervent hope among survivors that the terrible slaughter of the Great War had banished militarism. The worst war in centuries, would, it was deeply wished, bring a lasting peace. Yet that desire for peace did not always sit easily with the need to commemorate and venerate the war as a just one.

By the mid-1920s, that tension began to increase. In the half decade since the war's end, communities across the country had built memorials to the fallen, and would continue to do so, to a lesser degree, for many more years. But postwar pacifism was on the rise. In Britain, still reeling from its 750,000 dead, the No More

War Movement of left-wing intellectuals and organized labour was a presence, albeit a small one. In Canada, too, organizations pressed the government to cut defence spending and to push for disarmament at several international conferences. The Quebec wing of the Liberal Party was particularly fierce in its demands for slashed military funding.[45] Churches also returned to their prewar role of promoting understanding and peace rather than demanding the war be prosecuted to full victory, as had been the case from 1914 to 1918. Militarism, imperialism, and capitalism all became the targets of vocal opponents, who ranged from feminist journalist Violet McNaughton to social activist J.S. Woodsworth, and from student organizations to the Women's International League for Peace and Freedom.[46] Some groups went so far as to protest Armistice Day as a militarized event that celebrated war and should therefore be discontinued. Meanwhile, in 1933, a white poppy was issued to honour peace, promulgating a deliberate counter-narrative to the Legion's red poppies. Most veterans were not amused. Many rejected war as a useless waste, but they would not stand for the denigration of the memory of their fallen comrades. When representatives of the Working Class Ex-Service Men's League laid a wreath in 1933 at the Toronto cenotaph that read "In Memory of Those Who Died in Vain," it enraged many fellow veterans. However, it was clear that the veterans' movement was fragmented and did not speak as a single entity, with the Legion consisting of less than a quarter of all veterans at the time.[47]

Pacifist groups protested against school textbooks in the 1920s that provided heroic accounts of war. "Unless our children are taught the futility and suicidal tendency of modern war," warned Woodsworth, "they will as adults find themselves engaged in another war which experts tell us will almost certainly wipe out western civilization."[48] There were other objections against the cadet movement in schools—the training of young boys in marching, shooting, and military drill—although it had little impact and the cadets gathered in strength and size throughout the decade.[49] More successful were the many peace rallies and "no more war" conventions. In one high-profile challenge in the House of Commons, in 1926, Agnes Macphail, an ardent pacifist and the first woman to become a member of Parliament, questioned a reference to the Vimy Memorial as honouring the "nobility" of the sacrifice of young Canadians. She saw, instead, the war as a wasteful slaughter of youth. "Will the Honourable Member admit," she asked George Nicholson, a CEF veteran, "that what caused the late war is the cause of all wars? Will he admit that the prime cause was an economic one, and that the protection of women and children was no part of it?" Nicholson responded with outrage that he would admit to nothing of the kind.[50] Such a question would have been unthinkable immediately after the war.

The late 1920s also saw the abandonment of the plan for a Canadian war museum. Lord Beaverbrook had established the Canadian War Records Office to motivate officers and units to create better war records; as well, he had established an official war art, photography, and film program to leave a historical legacy of Canadian records for future generations. He had also hoped for a postwar museum in Ottawa to chronicle the country's war effort. During and after the war, there had been a number of successful art exhibitions in London, and then a travelling show of images and artifacts on a multi-city tour throughout Canada and the United States that drew hundreds of thousands of visitors.[51] The Toronto *Globe* reported that the exhibition "seems to express on canvas the thousand emotions which have thrilled Canadians through the war years, as they saw, heard or read of the heroism, the horror, and the never-ending destruction of Armageddon."[52] In Britain, the Imperial War Museum, established in 1917, drew more than three million visitors in its first half decade.[53]

As artifacts were sent back to Ottawa and stored at the Public Archives of Canada, several competing ideas arose for a memorial museum, art gallery, and archives in Ottawa overlooking the river.[54] The museum was to be a memorial to display relics, photographs, and art, but postwar Canada's political indifference was greater than Lord Beaverbrook's considerable drive and the resources from Britain. As the idea lacked an influential political champion in Ottawa, successive governments put off the museum, and it slowly withered and died by the late 1920s.[55] The failure to build a museum to the nation's war effort was one more indication that the memory of the 1914 to 1918 struggle had begun to fade.

THE WAR SURGED BACK INTO CANADA'S consciousness when the nation's most identifiable wartime hero, Sir Arthur Currie, faced a severe attack on his reputation in late 1927. While the Hundred Days campaign saw the Corps' greatest series of victories, it also brought more than 45,000 casualties during the brutal and relentless effort to break the enemy's trench systems. Currie was celebrated throughout the British Empire as one of the finest corps commanders in the war, but some of his own soldiers thought their general was too willing to accept crippling casualties in the pursuit of victory. Others sniped that his glory had been won on the backs of his dead soldiers. They were wrong. Currie always sought

A wartime image of Sir Arthur Currie, the final commander of the Canadian Corps.

victory through shells rather than flesh, but there were no easy wins on the Western Front.

In March 1919, Sir Sam Hughes, the misguided and angry old warhorse who had been cast from Borden's cabinet for his unstable behaviour, stood in the House of Commons and accused Currie of being a murderer of his men during the Hundred Days campaign—especially in his ordering of the capture of Mons on November 11, 1918. It was a shocking charge. And while many stepped up to Currie's defence, the government did not, fearful of becoming embroiled in the controversy and unsure about the merits of Hughes's attack. Currie was exhausted from the war, suffering from what we would now call post-traumatic stress disorder, and he offered a poor defence of his war record.[56] The charges lay heavily, and once made, they were hard to refute. How many casualties were too many in industrial warfare? For those Canadians who wanted answers for the deaths of loved ones, or to blame someone for their loss, Currie was an easy target. The government of the day accorded him no special honours, even as other nations fêted their senior generals with titles and cash gifts. Soon thereafter, Currie exited the military to become principal of McGill University in 1920. He was a resounding success as principal and became one of the country's most distinguished figures. Yet for some Canadians, the "butcher" had slunk from his carnage to take up a cozy university appointment.

On June 13, 1927, a small-town Conservative paper, the *Evening Guide* of Port Hope, Ontario, published a scathing editorial repeating the substance of Hughes's charges in 1919. Currie was portrayed as a callous killer for ordering the attack on Mons on the last day of the war, which was "a shocking useless waste of human life."[57] Currie had lived with these ghosts and the unanswered charges for nearly a decade, and he struck back against the paper, hoping to put an end to the rumours. He sued for libel of character, and the court trial in Cobourg lasted sixteen days, from mid-April 1928 to early May.

The trial was among the most controversial cases ever held in a Canadian court, and Currie's reputation hinged on a victory. If he lost, he would be destroyed. Moreover, the memory of the Great War would forever be cast as a blight on Canadian history—a conflagration in which young boys had been murdered by their general. The newspaper's defence team tried to marshal evidence to show Currie's guilt, but the records did not reveal what they had hoped—callous orders or even significant losses on November

11. The war was refought in the courtroom, and when Currie took the stand he was lashed by the defence, who questioned his every decision. Though Currie suffered under the onslaught, he was backed by almost all of the surviving officer corps, hundreds of whom offered to testify on his behalf. Currie's health was compromised during the trial, but the verdict came down in his favour—awarding $500 in damages, although not the $50,000 he asked for. The general emerged a battered hero, and the survivors of the Canadian Corps felt vindicated. The newspaper's attack seemed one more slight against the memory of the war that had to be battled back. "I think every man who was in the CEF owes you a debt of gratitude," wrote Gregor Barclay to the commander he had served with on the Western Front.[58] Veterans had banded together to protect their corps commander and the memory of the Great War that was, in their minds, never to be sullied.

THE FIGHT FOR CONTROL OVER THE memory of Canada's Great War in the Cobourg court—the justness of the cause versus the wastefulness of war—coincided with a sea change in how the war was being recast internationally. The mass trauma naturally diminished over time from a sharp stab to a dull ache. As life returned to normal, or other challenges stepped to the fore, Armistice Day ceremonies became more poorly attended in the second half of the 1920s, and battlefield tours from Britain to the Western Front declined significantly from 1927 to 1932. Across society, in Britain and Canada, an interest in propagating reverence for the war dropped significantly.[59]

In 1929, the publication of German veteran Erich Remarque's *All Quiet on the Western Front* shifted how the Great War was positioned in the landscape of memory. The book became an international bestseller, and the film of the same name the next year won the Academy Award for Best Picture. The novel and film revealed the squalor and violence that plagued all soldiers on the Western Front, where individual heroism was impossible in the face of the grinding gears of industrial warfare. Remarque and other veterans questioned the war and how it was fought, and some even asked how it should be remembered.[60] Was it right to put up monuments to mark a futile war? Did the act of commemoration give war meaning and perhaps justify the slaughter?

In Canada, James Pedley's *Only This* (1927), Peregrine Acland's *All Else Is Folly* (1929), and Will Bird's *And We Go On* (1930) were dark memoirs and novels, but not disavowals or condemnations of the war. Pedley, a prewar newspaper editor wounded at Amiens, offered a detailed account of the fear and violence of combat, and how soldiers acted at the front, from collecting souvenirs to grumbling about their lot. The retelling was neither heroic nor antiwar, but a realistic glimpse into the soldiers' experience. So, too, did Acland and Bird provide a view of the war at the sharp end in all its raggedness and banality. One reviewer wrote that *And We Go On* reveals "no glamour of patriotism . . . but rather the horrid facts of war are exposed with no attempt to either magnify or belittle them."[61]

The most damning account of the war was a novel by the American-born CEF veteran Charles Yale Harrison, *Generals Die in Bed* (1930). Harrison's work was especially rancorous, and the title—a volley at the generals who led from the rear and would never be killed by bullet or shell—angered many Canadian officers. "His book is a mass of filth, lies and appeals to everything base and mean and nasty," raged Arthur Currie.[62] Others condemned the war book genre, including one reviewer in the 49th Battalion's regimental association paper, *The Forty-Niner*, who blasted Harrison's novel, and books like it, describing them as fixated grossly on the "brutality, cowardice, drunkenness, death and debauchery, fear, favoritism, filth and greed, horror, hunger, lice and muck, manure, misery, mutilation, venereal disease and everything else nasty that the writer can think of. The nastier it is the better the book sells."[63] This type of frank writing struck a nerve with veterans because it seemed to question the very memory of the war that many veterans held so dear. To challenge the war's meaning was to destabilize that constructed narrative; worse, it denigrated the dead.

DURING AND IMMEDIATELY AFTER THE WAR, survivors, citizens, and veterans refused to wallow in the horror of the Western Front, and so the war was ennobled and justified. In the trenches, soldiers had justified their own suffering in the name of a better tomorrow. But when Ottawa and the provinces or municipalities were unable to live up to the ideals of the veterans, many of the ex-servicemen became disenchanted with the war. The struggle against German militarism had not been a waste for most veterans—and certainly few residents of occupied Belgium or France would have accepted that claim—but the chance for a better world in its aftermath had indeed been wasted.

The postwar disillusionment lodged deep during the calamitous Depression from 1929 to 1935, which extended for many to the end of the decade. All nations suffered, but Canada was especially vulnerable as an exporting and farming nation succumbing to the double blow inflicted by drought. Jobs disappeared, dreams followed. Veterans sought solace in one another. Reports by the Legion noted that an estimated 40,000 veterans had their lives cut short in the decade following the war and that more were succumbing to health problems as they aged.[64] Thousands of men were broken by their war experiences—lost to society, and even to themselves. Currie's early death at the age fifty-eight in November 1933 was seen by many as one more lost wartime symbol.[65]

If the Great War dead were revered in Canadian society—and the Remembrance Day ceremony on Parliament Hill in 1931 (the year the occasion's name was changed from Armistice Day) was attended by 50,000 people—it was more difficult for the state to offer hope to the war's still living survivors.[66] All Canadians suffered terribly during the hard years of the Depression, and as much as a third of the country's workforce was unemployed or underemployed. Those veterans who lost farms or businesses carried extra grievances that all their sacrifices during the war had been for nought, and that the war to end all wars had led to economic ruin and a plague of uncertainty. Combat veteran Frank Iriam, a sniper for years at the front, wrote bitterly in 1933 of how Canada had failed to reward him and his comrades:

At this time, 15 years after the war, they are still dropping off one by one. Lingering half sick and wholly sick both in body and spirit. Occasionally we hear of one of them taking his own life and immediately we hear some wise-cracker suggesting that these returned men are sort of nutty anyways. There is a strange and terrible contrast between people's attitude toward the dead soldier and the live one. It seems as though it was a serious mistake for any of them to come back to their home land.[67]

In the face of worldwide economic collapse, dictators in Europe, especially Adolf Hitler in Germany and Benito Mussolini in Italy, offered visions of strength and promised a return to greatness through military might. New wars seemed to rise from the ashes of the old, and the young League of Nations was impotent to do anything to stop the bitterness and anger in countries facing economic collapse and political demagoguery. In Canada, wartime veteran and University of Toronto professor Frank Underhill excited outrage in 1935 when he argued publicly that the British Empire and the League of Nations ought to be scrapped, and that those soldiers who fought in the last war were "suckers." In a much commented-upon and reviled statement, he observed, "All these European troubles are not worth the bones of a Toronto grenadier."[68] Underhill had become cynical and angry at the postwar turn that his nation had taken, even though he had written in the early 1920s that the war was "the greatest national achievement of the Canadian people since the Dominion came into being."[69] While the professor was condemned widely for his callous remark referring to his fellow veterans as suckers, there were many who, like him, felt that the returned men had never been properly rewarded for their sacrifice, and that the war had indeed been fought for no good reason.

The war's relevance and importance—the liberation of Belgium, the response to German militarism, the united stand with Britain—had faded from immediate memory and been replaced by the notion that the war had been a tragic and perhaps even useless conflict that led to the rise of monsters like Hitler and Mussolini. It was best left forgotten in the barbarous past. But most veterans could not do that. The legacy of service, sacrifice, and pride was clung to, propagated, and revelled in over the decade,

and then in the years that followed. That the war had meaning—
that the sacrifice of the soldiers had contributed to a greater good
in a just conflict—was a belief not easily shunted aside by veterans,
families, and next of kin. Those Canadians who perceived the
memory of the war as under threat were desperate for a symbol
to rejuvenate the idea of the war. They would find it in Vimy.

CHAPTER 10

THE 1936 VIMY PILGRIMAGE

Reconnecting with the war, remarked journalist and veteran W.W. Murray, was only possible "in France and Flanders."[1] Even though they were spaces saturated with hardship and horror, a return to the battlefields gave veterans a chance to exorcise demons. Tours to the Western Front began soon after the armistice, with veterans and civilians from Britain making the short and inexpensive trip across the English Channel to France and Belgium. One Canadian commentator noted, "Hardly had the 'Cease Fire' call sounded before sorrowing relatives of French and British soldiers were seen wandering among the simple wooden crosses which marked the resting place of a father, son or brother."[2] These pilgrims, as they often called themselves, went for a number of reasons: to find the grave of a loved one, to accompany a veteran anxious to show where he had spent several years of his life, or perhaps to simply walk over the desolate landscape before it disappeared and returned to farmland.

Tour books, guides, and maps directed the curious and bereaved alike in the footsteps of the soldiers. In the three years from the war's end to January 1922, the Michelin Company sold 1,432,000 battlefield guidebooks.[3] Veterans complained in their newspapers and correspondence that there were two types of visitors: the near-sacred pilgrims and the nosy tourists. The tourists were often derided by veterans for trivializing the war. They sneered at the "curious and disrespectful day-jaunters, sallying out from their comfortable hotels in fast motor cars," buying gaudy souvenirs, and generally demeaning the war experience.[4] The Western Front was not a place for mere sightseeing; there had been too many lives lost, too many dreams buried. However, pilgrims were regarded differently as they engaged in more solemn acts of remembrance. There was a sacredness ascribed to their sojourns. They often travelled with fellow grievers, stopping to place flowers or wreaths in the newly created cemeteries, speaking of their memories in hushed voices. For anguished family members and war-haunted veterans, those reverential trips were about pursuing answers and finding closure.

It was much more difficult and expensive for Canadians and Newfoundlanders to make the trans-Atlantic voyage. In 1923, Thomas Nagle, a former chaplain of the Royal Newfoundland Regiment who had played a key role in rallying support for the erection of a memorial at Beaumont Hamel, attempted to organize a veterans' pilgrimage to the unveiling of the site scheduled for 1925. Unfortunately, the expense of the trip and the length of time away from jobs made it impossible for the majority of Newfoundland's veterans to contemplate the voyage to the former battle site on the Somme. Despite pleas for financial help in newspapers and veterans' magazines, plans for a 500-strong pilgrimage had to be cancelled. Only a few Newfoundlanders were present when Field Marshal Sir Douglas Haig unveiled a caribou statue on June 7, 1925.[5]

Despite the challenges of distance and cost, Canadians made the journey overseas individually or in unofficial groups. These small trips of veterans or next of kin, often reported on in local papers, were overshadowed in 1927 by the pilgrimage to the Western Front of 15,000 American veterans and their families, who were fêted in Paris, where they paraded down the Champs Elysées.[6] The next year, 11,000 veterans of the British Legion paid their respects at the unveiling of the Menin Gate Memorial at Ypres.

Spurred on by these high-profile visits to the Western Front, including the sting of the American trip that garnered such high praise from the French, Canadian Legion delegates passed a unanimous resolution during the 1928 national convention, asking that a Canadian pilgrimage be organized to the Western Front battlefields.[7] Some of the divisive scars from the war had healed, especially that resulting from the alienation of farmers and workers—though not the one caused by conscription in Quebec, which was dredged up for every election. The veterans, too, had put aside many of their grievances over failing to secure the $2,000 bonus and got on with their lives. More than a decade after the armistice, the Legion and veterans were moving into a phase during which they more fully embraced remembrance and honouring, and cemented the ties of camaraderie, although they also did not like being shown up by the Americans. The concept of a pilgrimage—as it was to be known—began to take form, and the Legion aimed to coordinate the return to the battlefields with the unveiling of Allward's memorial, which was expected to take place sometime in 1931 or 1932.[8]

The stock market crash of 1929, and the high unemployment and financial uncertainty that followed throughout the decade-long Depression, was a blow to the Legion's hopes. The delays in the building of Allward's memorial also postponed any pilgrimage, but the planning proceeded, in the words of decorated Great War veteran W.W. Murray, "quietly but with a dogged determination to see it realized."[9] There was growing excitement for the Vimy Memorial's unveiling. In 1931, the veteran and journalist Will Bird enthusiastically wrote in *Maclean's* magazine, "Europe, when viewing the finished work, will change her impressions of the Canadians as a people."[10] A year later, celebrated sculptor Frances Loring, in a public lecture in Toronto, called the Vimy Memorial the "greatest conceived since the Egyptian period."[11]

FROM THE TROUGH OF THE DEPRESSION, there was a surge of interest in Canada's Great War, with the bleak financial collapse compelling many veterans to cast their memories back to the war. In November 1933, the death of General Arthur Currie was broadcast nationally, and tens of thousands lined the streets of Montreal to pay their respects to Canada's most famous general. In the summer of 1934, old soldiers converged on Toronto for the largest reunion of Canadian veterans ever held. For three days and nights, some 75,000 veterans gathered in the streets and pubs to meet old comrades, sing familiar songs, and relive the best parts of the war.[12] One veterans' pamphlet observed, "Those days of Ypres and Vimy Ridge and the Somme are unforgettable. As in shadowy procession they pass and re-pass, each awakens memories in the men who knew them. And once more we travel down a road that is twenty years away and share again its friendship, romance, laughter and tragedy."[13] While there was much to lament about the terrible loss of life in the war, the camaraderie of service remained an important bond that kept veterans together in the difficult postwar years.

Early in the next year, the Legion worked with the Department of National Defence (DND) and the Canadian Government Motion

Picture Bureau to issue the official film of the Great War, *Lest We Forget*. Lord Beaverbrook's wartime cameramen had filmed the Canadians at the front, creating a number of commercially successful films and shorter pieces that were shown in Britain and Canada during the war. But during the 1920s, that valuable footage had been held at the Department of National Defence in Ottawa and kept from the public eye, despite many requests from veterans' groups for them to be screened. When the film collection was finally examined in the late 1920s, it was found to be incomplete and scratched, and, in many cases, the originals had been lost.[14] It was not until the early 1930s, when 7,600 more metres of the film was discovered at the Ontario Motion Picture Bureau—"virtually a resurrection from the dead," according to one journalist—that a new push to produce a film for veterans and Canadians emerged.[15]

Lest We Forget premiered in Ottawa in March 1935. Advertisements claimed, "After 20 years the truth can be seen."[16] The film told the story of the Canadian Expeditionary Force through its raising in 1914 to the momentous battles on the Western Front. But it was not a film that glorified the Canadians or revealed how the war had propelled Canada to nationhood. The film was very much a product of the uncertain 1930s and it questioned the very nature of war, expressing hope that humankind might strive for peace. There were scenes of dead Canadians on the battlefield, and of the wounded in hospitals, although critics complained that the horror of the war was largely absent. One reviewer in *The Legion* observed that the film's main theme was "the propagation of a spirit of Peace by displaying the rigors, the privations and the tragic cost of war."[17] While veterans flocked to see it, its poor showing at the gate seemed to reveal that Canadians were largely uninterested in the history of the war.

Perhaps the greatest champion of the Canadian Corps was official historian Colonel A.F. Duguid. By 1935, the first volume of the official history, covering the period up to mid-1915, was nearing completion, although it would not be published until 1938. At the request of Canada's small group of professional historians, Duguid published an article on the Battle of Vimy Ridge with the Canadian Historical Association in 1935, later republished in the *Canada Year Book, 1936*. At that point, there were almost no academics in Canada writing about modern military history, and Duguid's contribution on Vimy was welcome. "Vimy was the greatest British victory since Waterloo," claimed Duguid, a sentiment sometimes expressed by Canadian journalists but certainly not by British historians of the time.[18] Later, in another article in *The Legionary*, Duguid expanded on Vimy's meaning: "Of all the battles in which Canadians took part, Vimy is the most famous. The fame cannot be altogether justified, either from the historical or military standpoint. It was not the hardest fought, nor the most fruitful of immediate results; but it was almost exclusively a Canadian battle, for the first and only time all four of our divisions attacked simultaneously."[19] Vimy may not have been Canada's greatest battlefield victory, but by the mid-1930s it was already established in Canadian history as the nation's most important battle, even before the memorial was unveiled. Vimy had distanced itself from the other Great War battles in terms of recognition and relevance, and that perception would only gather in strength with the Vimy pilgrimage.

THE LEGIONARY FINALLY PUT AN END to years of rumours when it declared in its July 1934 issue, "The Canadian Legion is definitely organizing and conducting a Pilgrimage to the Battlefields for all ex-Service men and women in Canada."[20] Although the exact date for the unveiling was still not set, the Legion approached the organization of the pilgrimage as if it were a military operation. Captain Ben Allen would handle the day-to-day responsibilities of administration, and he would be ably assisted by the chief transportation officer, a former Great War intelligence and staff officer, D.E. Macintyre.

Ottawa selected the official delegation, as well as the program for the memorial's unveiling, but getting the veterans to the memorial was the Legion's task. More than 6,000 veterans from all parts of Canada had to be moved across an ocean, and then driven to ceremonies and cemeteries in Belgium and France. Then they would participate in the official unveiling ceremony on July 26, to be followed by more visits and commemorations in Britain and France, before returning to Canada. It was a dauntingly complex undertaking—the largest ever peacetime movement of people from Canada to Europe.

Five ships were contracted for the trans-Atlantic voyage. Canadian Pacific Steamships provided *Duchess of Bedford*, *Montrose*, and *Montcalm*, and two ships, *Antonia* and *Ascania*, came from the Cunard–White Star Line. Although the Legion's plans were assisted by sympathetic groups and governments, the veterans stressed that the pilgrimage would be funded by its members without subsidies or financial aid from the Canadian taxpayer.[21] By early 1935, the Legion had calculated the price of the three-and-a-half-week trip to be $160 per veteran.[22] Yet with about 30,000 veterans out of work, and tens of thousands more suffering from the devastation of the Depression, many could not afford the cost.[23] *The Canadian Veteran* pointed out the unfairness of ex-soldiers being denied the right to return to the battlefields because of "lean and empty purses which [made] it seem impossible for them to go." [24]

Speaking in the House of Commons near the end of April 1936, the minister of national defence, Ian Mackenzie, confirmed that the memorial would be unveiled a few months later, on July 26, and that King Edward VIII would preside. [25] With the announcement of the King's presence, the Vimy unveiling was elevated to an Empire-wide tribute. It marked the King's first appearance on the international stage since the death of his father, George V, in January of that year. The Prince of Wales, who had served on the Western Front briefly with the Canadian Corps, had been greeted by adoring Canadians on his tour of the Dominion in 1919 and 1927, during which the attractive bachelor carried his own magic. Now, as King, he lent enormous prestige to the unveiling of the memorial.

Prime Minister Mackenzie King, who had been returned to power in 1935 after five years in the political wilderness, was never one to pass up a chance to be seen with royalty, but he had already made the decision not to go to Vimy for the unveiling. He felt "a little badly" about not being "at this event," he wrote in his diary, "but with my fatigued state, I do not see how it is possible." [26] What King left unsaid was that he was never comfortable around veterans, and that his lack of war service had led to attacks on his supposedly unpatriotic character during and after the war. Moreover, the rancour caused by King's harsh treatment of Governor General Byng during the political and constitutional crisis of 1926 caused many veterans to despise King. [27] The prime minister wisely stayed home.

"VIMY RIDGE HAS BECOME A SYMBOL in Canadian life, a symbol of high endeavor, of great endeavor, and a noble self-sacrifice in the name of Canada and humanity," claimed the Montreal *Gazette* in anticipating the importance of the pilgrims' return to the Western Front.[28] The veterans were set to return to the battlefields that they had left behind them, but the voyage would take the pilgrims back to a Europe plagued by new wars and conflicts. A vicious civil war was to break out in Spain in only a few weeks, which would last three years and kill hundreds of thousands. Even worse, a revitalized Germany, now firmly under Nazi control, had reoccupied the Rhineland in the spring of 1936, challenging the governments of France and Britain to push its armies out. Unprepared in all respects for another war, the wartime allies offered no resistance beyond statements of outrage. Germany remained in place, and its dictator, Adolf Hitler, was emboldened by his unpunished actions. That same year, the Fascist Italian army conquered Ethiopia after a short war and, once again, military aggression was met by a failure to act by the toothless League of Nations. With Fascist nations at war, rearming, or intimidating neighbours, it appeared that the "war to end all wars" had done little more than set the stage for another worldwide conflict.

In mid-July, veterans and their families from across the country boarded special trains bound for Montreal and, coast to coast, newspapers reported on the pilgrimage with breathless anticipation.[29] It was the main topic among ex-soldiers at the Legion Halls, at church, and in their workplaces. One pilgrim writing in *The Legionary* had asked readers about their most vivid memories of Vimy. "Was it the towers at Mont St. Eloy, the billets behind the lines, the 'stupendous bombardment,' or the assault as the 'Byng Boys' advanced up the ridge?" The writer, identified as A.G.R., believed the most prominent feeling of returning veterans was "that old home-sick feeling, not for the War, not for the mud and filth, but for the COMRADES, men one met and loved and lost."[30] A.G.R.'s sentiments captured the tenor of the trip, in which nostalgia mixed freely with the sacred nature of returning to visit the dead. No one spoke then of Vimy as a nation-building site or as the birth of Canadian consciousness.

Some 6,200 veterans and their families boarded the five ocean liners at Montreal. The pilgrims included 50 nursing sisters and 31 ex-servicemen who were doctors to care for the frail.[31] It was later determined that about 100 to 200 veterans came from each of the major cities, but only 7 came from Quebec City.[32] The opposition to the war remained strong in Quebec. There were also 50 Silver Cross mothers and widows, women who had lost sons or husbands in the war. "For over twenty long years the constant thoughts of many a Canadian mother and widow have been in Flanders Fields," wrote one journalist in reference to the Vimy pilgrims.[33] Agnes Wrenn of Bowmanville, Ontario, was 73 years old, but wanted to make the trip to see the grave of her two fallen sons, Alexander and Edward.[34] Many of the elderly women travelled alone, although they found solace in each other's company on the ships. Also among the pilgrims were a number of journalists, most of whom were veterans. The *Toronto Star* sent Gregory Clark, a recipient of the Military Cross, and many of Clark's stories were carried in papers across the country.[35]

On July 16, the Montreal docks were lined with thousands of cheering well-wishers while bands played martial music, airplanes performed stunts above the crowds, and fireworks exploded nearby. Herb Morden described the scene as "pandemonium."[36] Florence Murdoch, from Amherst, Nova Scotia, whose two brothers, Ward and Alfred, had served at the front, was a passenger on *Antonia*: "My, but what a send-off we had. It was 'royal' alright, but then our whole trip was along the same line."[37] At 11 A.M., *Montcalm, Montrose, Antonia*, and *Ascana* set sail, with *Duchess of Bedford* casting off four hours later. As the ships made their way down the St. Lawrence River, HMCS *Saguenay*, a Royal Canadian Navy destroyer, steamed along as their trans-Atlantic escort. Archdeacon F.G. Scott, a much-loved wartime padre, felt the "spirit of the Pilgrimage had taken hold of the heart of Canada."[38]

During the first day of the crossing, kits were issued, containing a haversack, a beret (khaki for the veterans and blue for all others), an identification disk, a Vimy Pilgrimage Medal, and a specially prepared guidebook. The berets became prized possessions, and the medal, worn on the right breast, opposite service medals and gallantry awards, was displayed with pride. Kathleen Murdoch, Florence's sister, enthused that it was "an honour to wear the beret and we never had a hat on until we left the Pilgrimage. The old soldiers and war nurses wore khaki berets with green maple leafs on the sides, and we wore navy blue with green maple leafs. Then we had a very lovely Vimy badge that we wore at all times and a white company pin."[39]

The Canadians were going to Europe, wrote Legion president Alex Ross, "as an Army of Peace, bearers of a message of goodwill, bent on a sacred mission."[40] The language of the sacred demanded that the pilgrims honour the dead. No one needed prompting on that matter. "The years have passed, but time has not obliterated the memory of those who went away and did not come back," intoned Ross.[41]

There were no expressions of disillusionment among the pilgrims, although it's safe to assume that those who preferred to forget the war would not have paid to go back to the battlefields. Aboard the ships, the passengers reunited and drank, shared old stories, and told tall tales. One woman observed how many of the "old soldiers sang from morning until night," reliving their old camaraderie and basking in the shared emotions of time long gone.[42] The songs that had sustained the soldiers during the war—"Mademoiselle from Armentières," "It's a Long Way to Tipperary," and "Keep the Home Fires Burning"—raising morale and binding men together in a period of terrible strain, were now the songs ringing out from well-lubricated throats two decades later. Rank dissolved as all were now veterans in a new army. Saburo Shinobu, one of several Japanese veterans on the ships, wrote:

> there was no such thing as an officer or a private now—all were ex-war buddies. . . . There were an orderly and his battalion commander who had not seen each other for eighteen years now standing silent and staring at each other with tears streaming down their faces.[43]

Amid such bonhomie, old and new comrades relaxed, played games, and danced. Seasickness was blessedly absent for most pilgrims, although one green-faced sufferer aboard *Ascania* told everyone who would listen that he was having "eight meals a day—four down and four up!"[44]

NINE DAYS AFTER LEAVING MONTREAL, THE five ships docked during the early hours of Saturday, July 25: *Antonia*, *Ascania*, and *Duchess of Bedford* at Le Havre, France, and *Montcalm* and *Montrose* at Antwerp, Belgium. "The whole place was lighted with colored lights and every ship in the harbour; really it just looked like a fairy land," wrote a thrilled Florence Murdoch. "Everyone got up and listened to the bands and I for one can never forget the picture."[45] There were shouts from hundreds of French civilians of *Vive le Canada!*[46] Amid bands and an honour guard, journalist Gregory Clark recounted that he witnessed veterans disembarking excitedly from *Antonia*, but was most moved by "the ranks of elderly mothers, women of 60 and 70, wearing berets on their heads and carrying haversacks slung from their shoulders, marching in fours to the waiting trains on the quay. These, the mothers of the men who died twenty years ago, marching in fours. If I wept, I was not the only one."[47]

The veterans converged on the Vimy battlefield like a multi-pronged army, and another 1,365 Canadians joined them from Britain, for a total of about 7,500 pilgrims. Passing through the old battlefields stirred memories. Mary Botel, who was travelling with her husband, Harry, and daughter, Frances, was deeply affected as she rode in a train to Vimy, passing the countryside and listening to veterans "explain where important engagements were fought and places now historic where they were in action or training or billeted during the war. Hard to believe that these beautifully cultivated fertile field had twenty years ago had been shell torn desolate war territory."[48] With some 235 buses hired, many of the drivers spoke no English and some had no idea where the battlefields were located. Veterans directed them to the memorials at Ypres, St. Eloi, Hill 62, Passchendaele, and the Somme. Anxious to see the places where they had fought as young men, many veterans were disappointed that, as former gunner Herb Morden lamented, "the battlefield areas [were] unrecognizable."[49] The graves were the true destination of some of the pilgrims. Here, they finally had a chance to say goodbye to a son, a father, or a brother. Even those who did not have a personal connection to a fallen soldier were overwhelmed by the countless crosses. Nova Scotian Florence Murdoch wrote soberly in her diary of "the horror of so many graves."[50]

"THE MEMORIAL ON VIMY IS A beautiful and impressive structure," commented Mary Botel in her diary. "We saw it from various points of vantage as we drove along the road, and gleaming white in the sunlight, it seemed to dominate the landscape for miles and miles."[51] Another veteran described how Vimy "soared up gleaming white into the blue sky, a mighty picture in stone. The effect left one almost breathless."[52] Archdeacon F.G. Scott recounted that the memorial, as he had seen it in pictures to date, "had not appealed to me. I didn't understand it but the whole impression was changed when I saw it with my eyes." At that moment, Scott believed that Allward's genius was his ability "to interpret in stone the living spirit that ought to be commemorated on that great ridge."[53]

Sunday, July 26, was a warm, sunny day, and the pilgrims—drawn from across Canada and Britain just like the Canadian Corps nineteen years earlier—moved "up the line." They walked or rode along the main road to the memorial, which was lined with 650 maple trees that had been sent from Canada a decade earlier. During the morning and early afternoon, the pilgrims explored the ruined landscape, still pitted and cratered from the hundreds of thousands of shells that had crashed into the terrain during the war. Unlike most of the other former battlefields along the Western Front, Vimy continued to display the war's scars, with

*Thousands of Vimy pilgrims surround the
Vimy Memorial for its unveiling on July 26, 1936.*

thousands of grass-covered shell craters and strange undulations
to the land evident, a result of mines or trenches.[54] Tens of thousands of replanted pine trees were beginning to repopulate the
landscape, but it was untrue, as myth would later suggest, that a
tree was planted for each Canadian soldier who fell in the war.
Walking among the new growth, a few of the Manitobans from

the 44th Battalion trekked up the Pimple to the memorial that had been erected there after the battle, which was now crumbling. Some of the gunners wistfully looked into the distance for the artillery memorial at La Tilleul Corner, but it was too far to walk there from the memorial. The restored trenches, with their concrete sandbags and parapets, offered a tangible link to the bitter warfare that lingered in the veterans' imagination. There were long lines to make the descent into Grange Tunnel. Some of the pilgrims had been in Grange nineteen years earlier and, according to one eyewitness, "They saw the names of their comrades pen-knifed into the chalk, memorials to Canadian youths long since dead, but who unconsciously perpetrated their memory in the careless scratching and the crude carvings on the walls."[55]

With at least 50,000 French civilians honouring their liberators of old, the pilgrims were escorted forward to a privileged spot in the large amphitheatre in front of the memorial.[56] Before that, some took the opportunity to send letters and postcards from "somewhere in France" (invoking the oft-written phrase from the war), taking advantage of a temporarily constructed French and Canadian post office erected on the site. At the amphitheatre, companies of veterans formed up around tall, numbered banners and emblems intended to guide veterans to their prearranged groups. The khaki-beret-wearing veterans were placed in front of the memorial, while civilian pilgrims were on the veterans' flanks.

Some 500 French children were gathered in a place of honour, a request made by the Canadian organizers so that, according to one document, "these children would remember the Canadians with kindly feelings" and would continue to care for the monument over the years.[57] As part of the ceremony, an honour guard from

HMCS *Saguenay* stood on the south side of the pathway that runs across the memorial, while a party of 120 veterans stood to the left of the sailors. The Royal Canadian Horse Artillery Band and a composite band from various Canadian Highland regiments, as well as buglers, were also on parade.

French-Moroccan cavalry men, wearing their traditional blue-and-scarlet uniforms and mounted on white Arabian horses, added to the pomp. Though the bearded warriors represented the French who had fought hard for Vimy in 1915, there was little place for them at the ceremony. Vimy had long since been seized by the Canadians as a national site of significance. There would be little sharing of the glory with other combatants at Vimy previous to the Canadian capture of it, other than a small plaque in tribute to the Moroccan Division erected in 1924 near the memorial.[58] The Germans, despite losing tens of thousands of dead defending the position, had almost no presence on the ridge after the war. Like the Australians and New Zealanders who edged out the British and French at Gallipoli in the constructed memory of that 1915 battle, the Canadians had long since driven other European powers—who had contributed many more troops to the campaign—from the ridge's memory.

Shortly before the King arrived at the monument, the Canadian Radio Broadcasting Commission (CRBC), the forerunner of the Canadian Broadcasting Corporation, began a one-hour-and-thirty-five-minute live broadcast. The CRBC used the shortwave facilities of the British Broadcasting Corporation to transmit the ceremony to Canada over the national radio network, while the British shortwave broadcast was heard worldwide. A bilingual announcer was demanded by the Canadians, so that the ceremony could be presented in both languages and by an announcer without a British accent.[59] The program, according to the *Winnipeg Free Press*, enabled people in Canada to be "present not only in spirit but as auditors."[60]

At 2:15 P.M., King Edward, accompanied by Ernest Lapointe, the Canadian minister of justice, and Philippe Roy, the head of the Canadian Legation in Paris, arrived at the Canadian park and proceeded to the monument. The handsome King, in black suit and tie and without a top hat, strode forward, his long row of medals displayed on his left breast and a gold Vimy Pilgrimage Medal over his right. After the playing of "God Save the King" followed by "O Canada," and then a twenty-one-gun salute, the King inspected the guard of honour. He then strolled further along, stopping occasionally to exchange words with a proud Canadian veteran, before making his way to the memorial to be introduced to such distinguished pilgrims as Lady Byng, Lady Currie, Sir Robert Borden, and Walter Allward. Mrs. Katherine de la Bruère Girouard, whose husband was a Legion official and the designer of the Vimy Pilgrimage Medal, was seated on the memorial with the special guests and official parties. From her vantage point, she thought it was "a marvellous sight to look down and see the thousands of navy and khaki berets"[61]

Although the waiting Canadians had heard the anthems and the artillery salute when the King arrived, they had not yet seen their monarch. When the King stepped from the memorial into the amphitheatre to greet the veterans, the Canadians, according to one eyewitness, offered "such a roar you never heard in war or peace."[62] The parade came to attention and the colour party dipped its standards and raised them again. The King walked among the veterans, stopping for a few minutes to talk with a group of disabled and blinded men. He also stopped to say hello

King Edward VIII meeting the Silver Cross mothers.

to Curley Christian, a war veteran injured at Vimy and the only quadruple amputee to survive his horrific wounds.

One of the most poignant moments of the day was when the King took time to welcome Mrs. C.S. Woods, an elderly Silver Cross mother from Winnipeg. Mrs. Woods had twelve children, many of whom had served in Canadian and British forces. Two of her sons were killed in the war and three others later succumbed to their injuries.[63] Holding her hand as they talked, the King said, "I wish your sons were all here." Her sorrow was evident when she replied somewhat haltingly: "Oh, Sir, I have been looking at the trenches and I just can't figure out why our boys had to go through that." The King's response was one of hope: "Please God, Mrs. Wood, it shall never happen again."[64] Mrs. Wood died in October 1939, a month after Canada went to war again.

THE THREE CHAPLAINS REPRESENTING the Church of England, the United Church of Canada, and the Roman Catholic Church began the unveiling ceremony with prayers. The spectre of the dead and the ongoing grief of their loss were ever-present. The Reverend George Fallis of Toronto recalled, "On these slopes of Vimy a deathless army urges us on. To us they throw the torch. This monument is a fresh pledge that we shall not break faith."[65] Together the padres spoke of the strength of the Canadian nation, her soldiers' sacrifice, and the duty the survivors had to ensure everlasting peace.

Ernest Lapointe, leader of the official delegation, followed the chaplains, speaking on behalf of Prime Minister Mackenzie King. The Vimy Memorial would "preach a new ideal of humanity in which recourse to force shall be abolished before the cries of mothers, the revolt of conscience and the right of the weak," he said. "Humanity suffered too much during the War. . . . Humanity desires . . . justice and truth, and is eager for a Peace founded in conscience and international solidarity, on the will of nations to co-operate for the greatest good of the greatest number of men and peoples."[66] It was a statement that was suitably pious and oblique, especially since Lapointe and the King government had run away from League of Nations sanctions against Italy for its invasion of Ethiopia.[67] Lapointe also claimed that Vimy revealed that in "their hour of testing, the souls of Canadians revealed themselves gloriously at the summit of their national ascendancy."[68] The Canadian soul had been uncovered at Vimy for all to see.

Following his ministers, King Edward moved towards the dais draped in national colours, and with his fair hair tossed by the wind, he began his address in French. Grey clouds had temporarily overcast the skies, but the sun broke through as the King turned to speaking in English, creating a near-holy effect for the thousands of pilgrims who listened in rapt attention. The King said that the memorial "crowning the hill of Vimy is now and for all time part of Canada." Summoning powerful sentiments, he told the British Empire listening in on radios that the world "will long

King Edward VIII's dramatic unveiling of Canada Bereft.

remember" what happened here, "and Canada can never forget." The Dominion during the war stood shoulder to shoulder with France and Britain, as an equal: with this monument, "Canada shall stand forever."[69] The final dramatic action by the King was to reveal *Canada Bereft* by letting drop a Union Jack flag that draped her.

Notably absent from the speakers' roster was Walter Allward. The artist was an old man now, with thinning hair, glasses, and a deep curve to his shoulders. The death of his son Donald in 1934 at age twenty-eight had revealed to him the grief that thousands of wartime parents carried with them. Allward was not asked to speak at the unveiling of his own memorial. He was mentioned by all the dignitaries only a single time, and almost as an afterthought. The official records offer no explanation as to why he was excluded, and Allward did not commit his feelings to paper. But the slight must have wounded him. Perhaps the many cost overruns and delays had made him something of an embarrassment; perhaps artists will always be shoved aside when politicians and a King are involved in solemn national rituals.

Amid the talk of sacrifice, death, and Canada's soul being revealed on that ridge, one wonders what the returning veterans thought of the experience. A contributor to *The Canadian Veteran* wrote that during the ceremony, "the mists of time momentarily [lifted], and once again [veterans stood] in the jumping off trenches waiting for the zero hour. . . . Even the soft splash of snow and rain on steel helmets [could] be heard—then that crashing crescendo of a tornado of bursting shells, with the obligation of a thousand machine-guns the attack [began]."[70] These words seem a bit dramatic, but no doubt those veterans who had been at Vimy nineteen years earlier were drawn back to the battle as they stood on that same ground—ground that the speakers described, over and over again, as being haunted by the war dead. Forty-two-year-old Jimmy Crossby, a wartime sergeant in the 27th Battalion, remembered years later hearing the King's speech but having his mind wander to the battle he had fought in years earlier: "Furtively at first, but then with an overpowering rush, memories of . . . companions, of dirty days and worse nights, came back."[71]

When the official ceremony came to a close, veterans moved forward to inspect the memorial. Hundreds of wreaths representing units, Legion Halls, and communities from across the Dominion were laid against the cold stone. Perhaps even more powerful was the act by dozens of mothers who took off their silver crosses, issued by the government after the war to commemorate their fallen sons, and stacked them upon each other. The grieving mothers, some choking back sobs, then formed a circle around the tower of crosses and stood in silence.[72] Soon the memorial was thronged with pilgrims. They searched for the names of the missing, running their hands over the sandblasted letters that represented friends, uncles, sons, husbands, and fathers. This was their Canada captured in stone. And PPCLI veteran Bill Garvock reflected on the fallen with no known graves "who came from many other lands besides Canada and the Mother Country. Represented on the monument are names of men from the steppes of Russia, the rice fields of Japan, the vineyards of Italy, the dairies of Denmark, the forests of Sweden, the ranches of Australia, the bustling cities of United States and the factories of Belgium. There are names of German-Canadians whose next-of-kin resided in Germany, while they were serving in the Canadian Corps."[73] There was immense power in those names, and pilgrims took photographs or made tracings of the characters to bring home and cherish. For many pilgrims this was their emotional closure for a death two decades in the past. The scattered dead were reconstituted: a silent army of names in waiting. Lost men had finally been found. One of the pilgrims was to write, "Each has gained a glorious grave."[74]

THE VIMY PILGRIMAGE, IN THE WORDS of veteran Walter Woods, a civil servant who had devoted much of his life since the war to aiding his fellow veterans, was "by far the most momentous event in the lives of Canadian ex-service men."[75] In France and Britain there was intense interest in the expedition. The King's presence was instrumental in making the unveiling an Empire-wide event. Canadians were no less enthralled by the unveiling, the memorial, and the pilgrims, countless numbers having listened to it live on the radio. Others read about it in newspapers that highlighted the accomplishments of the Canadians, specifically at Vimy and more generally in the war. The strong Canadian contingent of ministers, the playing of "O Canada," and the prominent place of Canadian veterans and their deeds at the ceremony validated the idea expressed by many of the speakers that Canada had come of age at the ridge in 1917.

In the shadow of the Vimy Memorial, the battle was recast as an iconic, nation-changing event. While no one used the phrase "birth of the nation," the sentiment was stark and clear, even though the memorial itself was infused with themes of grief, loss, and elegy. The idea of the Great War as the fulcrum upon which the nation had matured may have been present for some time, but there had been few opportunities to allow for the expression of such ideas in such a public way. Now was the time.

Canadians would build on the July 1936 ceremony and continue to remake Vimy in the coming decades, grafting new meanings onto the battle and the memorial. The monument at Vimy was distinguished forever from all the others, even the moving "Brooding Soldier" at Ypres, and soon the battle, too, would be elevated above all others, with Vimy cementing its place in Canadian history while the Battle of Second Ypres faded in relevance. With the past seeping into the present, and the present into the past, a new Vimy legend was born on that battle-haunted ridge.

CHAPTER 11

FORGING AN ICON

S ir Robert Borden, Canada's wartime prime minister, preferred his visit to the war's cemeteries along the former Western Front to the unveiling on Vimy Ridge. "It brought back so vividly my visits to the hospitals and long agony of the war," he wrote. "As I walked through the silent ranks of the dead, in the simplicity, beauty and quietude of each cemetery, there seemed to be a brooding peace. And I felt that God was there."[1] The pilgrimage had not ended at the unveiling of the Vimy Memorial and marking the "deathless deeds" of a people there. Buses transported veterans to the battlefields, with most of the pilgrims moving north to Ypres, visiting cemeteries on the way. Not all could stomach a return to the killing fields. Stuart Armour refused to walk the site of the 1916 Battle of the Somme "blood bath" in which he had fought. His experience as a company commander had left him "wearied of it forever."[2] But though the memories of carnage kept some from returning to the old battlefields, most veterans were drawn to the sites where they had served. At Ypres, thousands of pilgrims took part in the ceremony at the Menin Gate. There, a bugler sounded the haunting "Last Post," as had been done since November 11, 1929, every night at 8 P.M., and has continued up to the present day—except in the years of German occupation during the Second World War. Afterwards, the Canadians searched for their comrades among the names of almost 7,000 Canadians inscribed on the gate who had died on Belgian soil and who had no known graves.[3]

After the Western Front tour, the pilgrims crossed the English Channel and were taken to London by trains, arriving on July 28. British veterans welcomed them with cheers and songs at the station. This portion of the trip was organized by the British Legion, which sought to highlight the bonds of empire for which both groups had fought during the war years. *Our Empire*, the British Legion's magazine, honoured the pilgrims of the "Second Canadian Expeditionary Force," observing that this act of unity would "rebind the Imperial brotherhood in awakened memories of a common sacrifice." And it declared that in the likely coming war with Germany, "they can do it again."[4] Such sentiments were no doubt welcomed by many in the Canadian Legion, but that imperial message was all but absent from formal discourse surrounding the pilgrimage.

After a speech by British prime minister Stanley Baldwin at Westminster Hall and a ceremony at Lutyens's memorial to the Empire's dead, the pilgrims were welcomed that afternoon at Buckingham Palace by King Edward, who had made a special trip back to London from Scotland.[5] The King was greeted by ovations and cheers as he mixed freely in the adoring crowd of pilgrims. After an enormous garden party offering cakes and tea, the veterans and their families were allowed to walk through the palace. They sent home postcards with the heading "From Buckingham Palace," and at least one old soldier, according to journalist Greg Clark, collected a handsome bit of silverware.[6] The pilgrims revelled in the royal treatment, and while "O Canada" was sung with gusto, so too was "God Save the King." Canadians could and did hold multiple identities, and while the Vimy Memorial had been reframed as a nationalistic icon where Canada's soul had been revealed, those patriotic ideas would take time to lodge deeply in the Canadian consciousness.

THE OFFICIAL TOUR ENDED IN BRITAIN, with about a third of the pilgrims leaving for Canada on August 1 while several thousand veterans returned to France as honoured guests for another week of travel. After arriving back in Canada, the pilgrims returned to their communities across the country, ready to share stories of the nationalizing epic. Many were invited to local Legion Halls, clubs, schools, and churches to recount their experiences. Although opinion polls did not exist prior to the Second World War, it is clear that word of Vimy spread. "The Pilgrimage is a great National event—probably one of the greatest in our lifetime," declared The Legionary.[7]

The most venerated of the pilgrims was Archdeacon F.G. Scott. A famous poet and inspirational figure who served during the war as the 1st Division's padre, he was much beloved by Canada's veterans. As pilgrim number one, his voyage was much remarked upon in newspapers, and when he returned home, he had many invitations to speak. On October 22, 1936, he addressed the Empire Club of Canada in Toronto—his subject, the power of Vimy: "I feel that the unveiling of that monument and all that was connected with it was really something more than a simple display of a great memorial. It has a tremendous bearing on our whole national development."[8] Scott admitted Vimy was likely not the greatest

Canadian battle, with that grim honour falling to the slaughter on the Somme or "the terrible fighting through mud at Passchendaele," but Vimy "stood out as a clear cut action of the Canadian Corps." As he talked to the audience of old soldiers, Scott hit upon an emerging theme of the Vimy Memorial. Canada's sacrifice and its fallen soldiers were intertwined with the glory of the nation's war effort; in his words, "The mourning Canada will stand for all time as an uplifting symbol of our national life and in our national memory. . . . The monument with its sublime symbolism will always be an uplifting power in the life of Canada."[9] The "uplifting power" that had an impact on Canada's "whole national development" was in a similar vein to Lapointe's comment, in his speech on the ridge, that the battle had revealed the soul of the nation.

The Legionary had already highlighted the pilgrimage in its August 1936 issue, with several articles of passionate prose, reprinted speeches, and spectacular images.[10] The next four issues contained numerous stories by the pilgrims on all aspects of the trip, from travelogues to sacred screeds to humorous accounts. The several hundred thousand readers of the magazine were exposed to Vimy again and again, reinforcing the effects of the early newspaper coverage during the leadup to the trip and the national radio program on the day of the unveiling. F.G. Goddard listened to the broadcast and was so moved that she wrote to the Department of National Defence, "I hope to go one day to Vimy to see the Memorial and to find my brother's name."[11] Veteran Bill Garvock, who served with the PPCLI from 1915 to the end of the war, and who went on to become a bond dealer in Ottawa, wrote of the pilgrimage that "the name 'Vimy' will have an imperishable place in the hearts of all Canadians and in the proud annals of the Dominion."[12]

In the aftermath of the visit, the Legion published a commemorative history, commissioning Captain W.W. Murray, M.C., to write *The Epic of Vimy*. Murray was a parliamentary correspondent for the Canadian Press in Ottawa and "official eye witness" for the Vimy tour. He had long been involved in veterans' activities, authoring the regimental history of the 2nd Battalion, his wartime unit in which he was awarded the Military Cross twice for his gallantry at the front. He also co-wrote the 1934 official film *Lest We Forget*. To augment the written history and involve the readers, the Legion ran a competition to find the most interesting photographs taken by pilgrims, which would be published in the souvenir book.[13] The pilgrims continued to contribute ideas as to how the unveiling, the memorial, and the memory of Vimy would be constructed, as they actively created the visual memory through their photographs.

The blue linen souvenir book decorated with gold was available less than three months after the return of the pilgrims. Lavishly illustrated and containing a list of the names of all the pilgrims, the book sold out its initial run of 3,000 copies before the first one had been shipped; a second edition moved off the shelves nearly as rapidly. Most of these likely went to veterans, but they were also purchased and available in Legion Halls, regimental associations, and public libraries. Like the pilgrimage, the book was not a triumphant celebration of victory over the Hun, but a sombre reflection on the importance of the return to Vimy to honour the fallen. In fact, the frontispiece of the book contained a poem by G.R.L. Potter of Ottawa that warned, "'War to end War!'—the bitter, haunting phrase! / Lies that piled high the holocaust of youth!" Like the film *Lest We Forget*, the book showed that the looming prospect of another war in Europe had veterans questioning the terrible exertions that had been required to deliver victory. To fight a second war within a generation was to insult those who fell in the last one, the war that was to have ended all war.

Despite the growing global angst, the Vimy trip resonated and had to be marked. In addition to purchasing the official history, pilgrims turned to scrapbooks to preserve this once-in-a-lifetime experience, putting together elaborate binders and books full of collages of souvenirs, postcards, letters, and published material.[14] Material was curated carefully, with photographs and captions, additional notes, and ephemera illustrating key events, personalities, or themes. The Vimy passports, medals, and berets were archived and treasured, and some pilgrims published travel accounts.[15]

It is tempting to wonder if the pilgrimage would have been such a success if it had been organized a decade earlier. At that point, many of the veterans' organizations were angry and frustrated with the government. The scars of the war were largely unhealed, with divisive memories still fresh among farmers, labourers, and new Canadians, and in French Canada. Would there have been an impetus for veterans to travel overseas for the unveiling, or had the assault on the war's memory—from the Americans, the war books, pacifists, and the Currie trial—been necessary to impel them to return to the battlefields, honour the fallen, and make new meaning of the war through Vimy?

An official film of the pilgrimage, *Salute to Valour*, was released in the summer of 1937. Filmed by Captain Frank C. Badgley, a decorated wartime officer in the artillery and director of the Canadian Government Motion Picture Bureau, it was shown across the Dominion.[16] The film's production process was torturous, with the Legion, the DND, and veterans all involved. In the hope of securing a hit, experts were called in to offer opinions, which led to the cutting of many speeches and the interspersing of war footage to enliven it. When the film finally premiered in July 1937, many prominent Canadians and veterans were perplexed that Allward had not been included in a celebratory production about the unveiling of his monument. Badgley's defence was that he had secured no shots of Allward, since the sculptor had been all but invisible at the unveiling.[17] *Salute to Valour* attracted some additional attention by critics because it contained the last official footage of King Edward VIII prior to his abdication, a worry among some of the senior politicians and military commanders in Ottawa that almost led to the cancellation of the film.[18] The King's abdication had been so shocking that Canadians were quite unsure about what to do about the footage of his last public speech. The producers eventually found their courage and the movie was released. Though one reviewer gushed that "the whole picture is a priceless record," and another felt that it "should be among the most successful film offerings of the year, not only for ex-servicemen, but for all Canadians," the movie's gate receipts were fairly weak, at only $22,000.[19] The failure of the film to live up to expectations was perhaps an indication that the Vimy idea had not taken hold beyond the veterans' community, by whom the film had been well received, although there was acknowledgment by the Legion and the DND that the film was a poor product, too short for a feature-length film, and out of step with more commercial films emanating from Hollywood.

One of the few Vimy-associated products issued by the government was a register sent to all of the next of kin of soldiers whose names appeared on the memorial. The register was mailed in the fall of 1936 to more than 10,000 next of kin (not all of the

11,265 next of kin could be located), and the names contained within it were compiled from a 1931 Imperial Commonwealth War Graves Commission booklet. Letters of gratitude poured in to the DND in response to the unexpected and moving memorial booklets. Ethel Middleton wrote in late September of her pride in the booklet that contained her son's name: "This beautiful memorial certainly is a great consolation to us who have lost our dear ones and whose graves are unknown." No less poignant were the words of Lilian Staines in memory of her brother Francis Knott, whose name was captured in the registers. "I will treasure them as long as I live. . . . I was pleased that his name was not forgotten," wrote Lilian, who lost four brothers in the war. Twenty years later, her grief was still palatable: "We gave our share."[20]

WHILE THE BOOKLETS WERE A LOVELY but ephemeral reminder, the Vimy Memorial was an enduring symbol. Group of Seven painter A.Y. Jackson, a frequent commentator on art and culture in Canada, described Allward's memorial as "beyond and above anything that framers of the competition conceived of."[21] The *Halifax Weekly Courier* exclaimed that Allward's memorial was "majestic."[22] A women's association in Toronto, the Heliconian Club, enthused that the memorial "carried the spirit of Canada."[23] *Saturday Night* magazine was no less effusive: "There is in the symbolism of this monument no suggestion of that characteristic element of the shallower popular philosophy of our post-war day, the emotional rebellion against all forms of human strife, the strident clamour for the immediate establishment of the millennium on the basis of the present division of the world's surface among the existing sovereign states."[24] This turgid bit of prose seemed to suggest that Allward had made the monument into not just a memorial dedicated to peace but one that delved deeper, into the sacrifice and grief of a nation.

Yet not everyone was in favour of the grandiose memorial. Harold Hesler, a wartime driver in the 3rd Divisional Ammunition Column who served at Vimy, found the memorial's size distasteful. "I am sure that the Canadians who lie in the many beautiful cemeteries along this line believe that they are the true memorial, and that the huge pile of granite costing millions is ostentatious."[25] Garnet Hughes—son of Sir Sam Hughes, a major-general during the war, and generally unhappy with his treatment during the conflict—dyspeptically labelled the memorial a "waste of money as well as being a tribute to vanity."[26] There had also been periodic griping and badgering in newspapers over the years about the cost of the memorial, which had risen to $1.5 million over the fifteen-year ordeal of its creation. But as one Vimy pilgrim snapped back in *The Legion*, "this sum would about pay for half a day's shelling in the great attack."[27]

And there were those who wanted no memorials to the dead, hating the hypocrisy of sending men out to their deaths in the trenches and then elevating them into stone icons as their bodies lay rotting in the ground. War poet and veteran Siegfried Sassoon angrily wrote of the Menin Gate Memorial at Ypres, "Well might the Dead who struggled in the slime / Rise and deride this sepulchre of crime."[28] We can never know how many veterans and survivors Sassoon spoke for, but his message must have resonated with some.

Walter Allward had devoted fifteen years of his life to completing the Vimy Memorial. Yet at the unveiling he had unceremoniously been pushed aside, all but written out of the historic

An older and wearier Walter Allward returned to Canada after the unveiling and received modest rewards for his fifteen-year-long work on the Vimy Memorial.

event. While Allward had been paid handsomely for his work, he must have wondered how his fellow Canadians would greet him when he sailed home in February 1937. When Allward returned to Toronto, as reported by *The Globe and Mail*, there was "scarcely a corporal's guard to welcome him."[29]

While it might have been too much to expect that Allward would be elevated to some sort of celebrity status, he was recognized with fellowships, awards, an honorary doctorate of laws from Queen's, and an honorary LL.D. from the University of Toronto. He was also made a Fellow of the Royal Architectural Institute of Canada. At his ceremony, Colonel Henry Osborne spoke of their work together. He defended the delays as predictable, saying they were not out of the ordinary, and then pointed to Allward's unwavering vision in the selection of the stone. "It was inevitable that, as the troubles multiplied and time pressed, he should be urged to reduce the severity of his specifications and accept stones that were less than perfect. To this he presented an inflexible front, and it is fair to say that apart from his qualities as a great artist, Allward's courage and determination on the point mentioned are responsible for the high quality of the monument as it stands today."[30] Osborne, who would continue to serve the King government in many ways, went on to praise the memorial and how it had built upon, and added to, a heightened awareness of the Battle of Vimy Ridge: "It was the first appearance of the whole nation of Canada in arms, and I think Canada's greatness will date from that time. . . . Dating from April 9th, 1917, there has been a quickening of national consciousness in our country and a new sense of our individuality as a people."[31]

Allward had reached the pinnacle of achievement for a Canadian sculptor. What was to be done now? He soon won a new contract from Toronto Liberal supporters of William Lyon Mackenzie King, who were erecting, with considerable behind-the-scenes prodding from the prime minister, a memorial statue to King's grandfather, William Lyon Mackenzie. King liked the idea of Canada's most famous sculptor, the creator of the powerful memorial overseas, crafting a work of art in memory of his grandfather, whom Mackenzie King liked to think had ushered in democracy in Ontario. Although all were wary of Allward's long history of failing to meet deadlines, money was raised among the Liberal elite; King watched and noted who had given and who had snubbed his grandfather's memory.[32] The sculptor's commission was a princely $25,800, or about $350,000 dollars today.[33] Allward took to his sculpture with new fire. The Mackenzie statue, unveiled in

1940 at Queen's Park in Toronto, was greeted with much praise. Yet no more public commissions came Allward's way, and his artistic style fell out of step with the emerging modernism of the postwar years.[34] Vimy would remain his masterwork.

ON THE FIRST ANNIVERSARY OF THE pilgrimage, in June 1937, veteran and pilgrim Harold Davidson claimed that the journey had "caught the imagination of every Canadian."[35] That was too grandiose a claim, but the overseas travel of 6,200 veterans and their families, the King's speech, the pageantry of the unveiling, and the magnificent memorial itself had been reported upon extensively. Another pilgrim, Bill Garvock, wrote that while standing before the memorial, one could not help but feel that "the name 'Vimy' will have an imperishable place in the hearts of all Canadians and in the proud annals of the Dominion."[36] The memorial on the ridge was unique to Canadian history, and Vimy was now firmly imprinted in the Canadian imagination as a place of pilgrimage, a tribute to the dead, and a place where Canada had bled for King, Empire, and country. After 1936, it appeared that something indeed had been born at Vimy. A space of death and destruction was transformed into a symbol that changed Canada; Vimy was elevated above other battles, displacing even the Battle of Second Ypres as the key wartime event that marked the emergence of a nation.

The success of the trip to the 1936 unveiling provoked speculation about a second trip in 1937. With the support of the Legion, but organized by Cunard–White Star Shipping Company, the tour planned to have three ships sail from Montreal direct to France during July, and three more leave for England, in what was billed as the "Vimy Reunion 1937."[37] But the number of applicants was disappointingly small, with insufficient passengers to fill a single ship, and so the event was cancelled.

Canadians were increasingly wary of visiting Europe, which seemed again to be descending into barbarity. The next year, 1938, saw Germany aggressively rearming itself and threatening its neighbours. In Spain, the civil war revealed a renewed savagery, leading to the deaths and displacement of tens of thousands. Plans for a tour of Vimy were postponed indefinitely. There were also likely a large number of veterans who, like Dr. Francis Scrimger, a medical officer during the war and a recipient of the Victoria Cross for his bravery under fire during Second Ypres, had no desire to revisit or commemorate the slaughter they had witnessed. Of the Vimy Memorial, Scrimger was to remark, "It will probably be the first thing knocked down in the next war!"[38]

Though some veterans had no desire to return to the battle-fields, Vimy had emerged, in only a short period, as an important icon. Pilgrimage organizer D.E. Macintyre wrote around this time that "VIMY" was a "name that is today familiar to every schoolchild in Canada."[39] Macintyre was hardly a disinterested observer, but with the wide coverage and acclaim directed towards the pilgrimage and the unveiling of the monument, Vimy had lodged far more deeply in Canadian consciousness than any other battle of the Great War. Where once the local stone memorials and commemorative plaques had been the focal points of remembrance, a new national symbol now reigned overseas. The fragmented memorials across the country were not displaced, as they remained crucial gathering places on Remembrance Day, but an overarching narrative was emerging as the focus for the nation's grief and pride. Vimy took the disparate local strands of memory and bound them together in a national story, one driven by the very real event of the wartime attack up the ridge by Canadians from across the Dominion.

The Vimy narrative also gained strength at a time when some Canadians felt they needed to protect the memory of the war. The motivating ideas of the "great war for civilization" and the "just war" that had been invoked during the war had been transformed by the early 1920s into the idea of a "great war of necessary sacrifice," as revealed through the local memorials. But there was a growing sense of antiwar disillusionment in the air. The worldwide success of *All Quiet on the Western Front* and, closer to home, the American claims of having won the war and, more damaging, the attack on Sir Arthur Currie's reputation in a 1928 libel trial, shook many veterans. They and like-minded Canadians wanted to keep alive the memory of what Canada had done during the war. The components of the Vimy pilgrimage—the theme of honouring the dead and finding meaning in the battle, the sublime memorial, and the elaborate military pageantry—all combined to revitalize the idea of Vimy. The memorial atop the ridge increasingly became the physical embodiment of how a nation was transformed by war. "The spirit that prevailed at Vimy Ridge is not dead," wrote one journalist in April 1939—"not even weakened."[40]

IN MAY 1939, KING GEORGE VI and Queen Elizabeth came to Canada on a Royal Tour and were greeted by adoring crowds. An estimated half of all Canadians flocked to see their majesties on their cross-country tour. The connection to the monarchy was rock solid, according to sociologist S.D. Clark, who had written a year earlier that, among English Canadians, "imperial and national patriotism reinforce one another." This imperial-national identity remained a common front against the influx of American mass media and culture, a fortification grounded in shared history and sacrifice, and exemplified by the King and Queen.[41]

During the Royal Tour, the King unveiled the National War Memorial. Deep crowds gathered in Ottawa on the morning of May 21, 1939. The new memorial was at Confederation Square, across from the Parliament Buildings, which had been rebuilt after the wartime fire of 1916. The principal architect of the new Gothic buildings, John Pearson, had a grander vision. In 1920, he had prepared plans for a memorial room in the Peace Tower, itself a memorial to the Great War. It would be a shrine to Canada's fallen soldiers, along the lines of the chapel at Westminster Abbey, and would be placed at the heart of the Dominion's most visible icon of democracy.

The memorial built upon Ottawa's other national monuments to the Great War. A decade earlier, on August 3, 1927, the debonair Prince of Wales—before he became king, lent his star power to the Vimy monument, and then abdicated his throne to his brother—had unveiled the Altar of Sacrifice in the Memorial Chamber of the Peace Tower to thousands of Canadians. The *Globe* reported that the solemn crowd, in reflecting upon the momentous events of the Great War, "set the course 'through dust of conflict and through battle of flame' to build for Canada, as nothing else could build, her present-day status of full nationhood."[42] Within the Peace Tower, the Memorial Chamber carried the story of Canada's war effort on elaborate stained glass windows, tablets, plaques, and inscriptions.[43] An engraved verse from McCrae's "In Flanders Fields" reminds visitors, "To you from failing hands we throw / The torch; be yours to hold it high. / If ye break faith with us who die / We shall not sleep, though poppies grow / In Flanders Fields."

There was talk of inscribing the names of missing soldiers on the chamber walls, but the space was too limited. Instead, ornate Books of Remembrance were produced from 1932 onward, with the last Great War volume opened to the public in 1942. Housed in the Memorial Chamber, the books contained the names of the 66,651 Canadians who died during the war and in its aftermath up to April 30, 1922, and their contents have been added to over the years as new names were revealed.[44] Similar books would be compiled with names from the Second World War, Korea, the South African War, and modern peacekeeping and peacemaking operations. In all, some 118,000 names are recorded, with pages turned daily to ensure all names are displayed over the course of a year.

In May 1939, as Canada's King George unveiled the National War Memorial in Ottawa, it was a reminder that while the war had ushered in a terrible urgency—to raise troops and treasure, to grow wheat and manufacture shells, to fight on every front—the commemoration of the war had been deliberate, even slow. The official history, a multi-volume project, had been delayed time and time again, with the first and only volume appearing in 1938. It was supposed to have been an eight-volume series, but the remaining seven volumes would never be written. The Vimy Memorial had experienced many delays. Even more dispiriting, the plans for a war museum, archives, and art gallery in Ottawa had been still-born, first because of penny-pinching and later, indifference. But finally, after two decades, Canada could boast a national memorial on Canadian soil. The King told the enormous crowd and the country that *The Great Response*, as the memorial was called, revealed the "very soul of the nation."[45] Indeed, with another war seemingly unavoidable, the message was unmistakable: peace is often only achieved through sacrifice. Canadians might be called upon again by their king to respond to another war.

The national memorial in Ottawa would take on greater importance over the years, especially as it became the centre of remembrance for the nation. After the Remembrance Day ceremony was first televised in 1954, it became the monument Canadians turned to on November 11 to see their veterans, dignitaries, prime minister, and governor general.[46] But it has always paled in comparison to Allward's memorial overseas. The Vimy shrine remains unique, and its distance from Ottawa creates an additional mystique. Vimy remained a more powerful draw on the imagination as it stood sentry-like on Canada's ridge, overlooking the nation's dead. As the years passed, the complexities of the war faded and blurred. Events receded and lost their poignancy. But the importance and meaning of the war, with its related notion of sacrifice and its link to an emerging nationalism, continued to evolve over time and to coalesce around a single focal point: Vimy.

ON SEPTEMBER 1, 1939, AFTER YEARS of threatening its neighbours and annexing weaker countries, Germany invaded Poland. Just two days later, Britain and France declared war on Germany. After his convincing victory in Poland, Hitler turned his sights on France to rapidly knock it out of the war before striking in the east, where he hoped to destroy the Soviet Union and occupy land to expand a new greater Germany. Canada, after a short parliamentary debate, declared war on Germany on September 10, 1939.

Britain's oldest dominion was its ranking ally, with the United States sitting on the sidelines until December 1941.

Canada sent the 1st Canadian Infantry Division to England, with the bulk of it arriving by early 1940, and it trained there for the coming battle. In France, elements of the British Expeditionary Force dug in to a series of fortified trench systems along the Arras front, as it had done a generation before. In preparation for sending the Canadian division to France, several advance guards visited the British. Divisional commander Major-General Andrew McNaughton, the counter-battery staff officer at Vimy in 1917 and destined to command the First Canadian Army in this war, was among the first Canadians to revisit the Vimy Memorial. Other Canadian dignitaries followed suit. The minister of national defence, Norman Rogers, a Great War veteran, travelled with Canada's high commissioner to Britain, Vincent Massey, and Brigadier-General Harry Crerar, another Vimy veteran, to meet with British generals. The group took time to pay homage at the memorial, and on April 29, 1940, Massey noted, "It looked most impressive in the morning mist. I remembered that I had said when it was dedicated four years before that the memorials of the last war might prove the victims of the next."[47]

Barely two weeks later, the Germans unleashed their forces against the Western Allies. On May 10, 1940, behind lightning strikes of armour and light bombers smashing ground forces, the German divisions surged through weak French defences. The French army collapsed and France was defeated in six weeks, surrendering in late June 1940. Britain was thrown back to its island kingdom and began to prepare for an aerial onslaught and invasion. The situation could not have been more dire. The momentous fall of France and the defeat of the BEF vastly overshadowed the occupation of Vimy, but perhaps a few Great War veterans who had fought there shed a tear for the ridge that was lost without a struggle.

Before the final surrender, but in the midst of the BEF's evacuation from Dunkirk—where Britain was trying to save as much of its army as possible from the impending disaster on the continent—Canadian newspapers reported on June 1 that the Vimy Memorial had been blown up in the fighting by the jack-booted Germans. Canadians were outraged. "Famous Memorial Blasted by Huns," reported the *Montreal Daily Star* on June 1, 1940. "New heights in deliberate fiendishness have been reached in Flanders Fields where Canada's great memorial on Vimy Ridge rises above the graves of Canadian heroes of the last war. German

Canadians were shocked to see this image in their papers in early June 1940. German dictator Adolf Hitler visited the Vimy Memorial with his conquering generals.

fliers smashed the beautiful remembrances to bits. Bombs tore dead Canadians from their graves."[48]

Two days later, *The Globe and Mail* ran the headline "Vimy Memorial Bombed: Sculptor Sad and Bitter."[49] Allward was understandably distraught. A secret fear had gnawed at him throughout the 1930s, as Europe had seemed to be moving again towards war, that his memorial might be in the path of invading armies. Allward had gone so far as to carve pieces of the memorial in stone rather than casting them in bronze, for fear that they might be melted down for munitions in a "future war."[50] When newspapers asked him for his comments, he remarked, "The Hun have gone quite mad."[51] The news that Vimy lay in ruins stiffened the resolve of many Canadians. Brigadier W.W. Foster, a key player in the Vimy Pilgrimage a few years earlier, swore that the memorial's destruction "will serve to strengthen this country's determination to carry this through to the end and vanquish a foe which would stoop to such useless destruction."[52] The *Montreal Daily Star*, having drunk deeply from the cup of anger, asserted, "The Hun is always the Hun. . . . Such fiends are surely unfit to live."[53]

Canadians were ready to ascribe any outrage to the Nazi forces, but within a few days it was revealed that the memorial had not been destroyed. And more than a few Canadians must have been stunned when several Canadian papers reported that Hitler had visited Vimy on June 2. There was even photographic evidence of the Führer, in his greatcoat and peaked hat, inspecting the memorial with his entourage of generals.[54] Hitler was a decorated Great War veteran and was sympathetic to those who had served in the war, both with and against him, but it was still a shocking sight to see the dictator at Canada's memorial to its overseas dead. For the next four years, the Vimy Memorial remained standing in occupied France, unseen and unvisited by Canadians.

Vimy caretaker George Stubbs, who had been appointed by Ottawa before the war to look after the memorial, was imprisoned as an "enemy alien" at St. Denis, near Paris, where he spent the war with other British gardeners and caretakers of the IWGC cemeteries. Stubbs's wife, a French citizen, was left to care for the memorial, and she lived at the site in the couple's small cottage, selling postcards to German soldiers who visited the ridge and memorial.[55] A Belgian expatriate and Great War veteran, Pierre Piroson, who lived in nearby Neuville–St. Vaast and had worked at the site since the mid-1920s, tended to the grounds. Piroson was harassed by Gestapo agents who thought he was a French Canadian, especially when partisan attacks on the occupying German soldiers intensified during the war. One warned him menacingly, "We know you are trying to help the Allies, but so far we haven't been able to prove it."[56] When they did, the Gestapo officer said with a smile, Piroson would be executed.

Curious German soldiers poked around the Vimy battlefields of old. The excavated Grange Tunnel was a popular destination. The memorial suffered little damage, but some of the Canadian soldiers' graffiti in the tunnel was vandalized by German soldiers, and artifacts on the site were looted. At the same time, French civilians in the Arras area continued to honour the dead at Vimy by laying wreaths at the memorial on Vimy Day and Remembrance Day. The French Resistance, partisans fighting the German occupiers and a group to which Piroson owed allegiance, also used the kilometres of Vimy tunnels to store weapons and explosives. When the Germans discovered these stores, they blew up a few of the tunnels and caved in the entrance to Grange.[57]

Back in Canada, Vimy was occasionally invoked to stimulate the war effort or as a plea for greater patriotic support. In June 1941, while Winston Churchill was visiting Ottawa, he drew upon Vimy, declaring, "And when the test comes—and if the test comes—and come it may—I know that they will prove worthy sons of those who stormed Vimy Ridge twenty-four years ago— as an inspiration for the next generation of warriors."[58] On the twenty-fifth anniversary of the battle, in 1942, more than 1,100 Great War veterans gathered at St. James Cathedral in Toronto in a show of moral force

This Canadian Second World War poster combines two important Great War icons: the Vimy Memorial and John McCrae's words from "In Flanders Fields."

and to draw a link from the old war to the new one.[59] The next year, in April 1943, *The Legionary* carried a full-page advertisement for Victory Loans placed by the National War Finance Committee. The Vimy Memorial was featured under a giant boot with a swastika on the sole that was set to stomp on it. "What Price Vimy?" queried the caption. Supporting text invoked memories of the battle: "Well *you* remember the mud, the blood and the glory that made Vimy forever Canadian . . . that dawn of April 9th that bought Vimy at such terrific cost. Your bit of Canada in France was bought too dearly to leave now in the hands of the Nazis."[60]

WHAT PRICE VIMY?

THE bloody boots of the Hun are goose-stepping over Vimy... *your* 2000 acres of sacred Canadian soil is now part of the Nazi New Order!

What price Vimy? Well *you* remember the mud, the blood and the glory that made Vimy forever Canadian... that dawn of April 9th that bought Vimy at such terrific cost.

And now—the shadow of the swastika dims the glory of the Canadian Maples that line the road to Vimy! The call comes again "Vimy must be taken!". *And your sons are on the march!*

Veterans—answer that call! You did it in 1917 —you can do it again. Your bit of Canada in France was bought too dearly to leave now in the hands of the Nazis. Remember, we are on the offensive— *back the attack.*

Yes, *back the attack!* Get ready to go "over the top" once again when the call comes. Answer Canada's Fourth Victory Loan with every dollar you can spare. Your purchase of Victory Bonds will bring the Boche to his knees in unconditional surrender.

Remember "V" stands for Victory... and VIMY!

V   V   V

TODAY—You Can Still Fight for Vimy—with Canada's Victory Bonds

This Second World War victory bond poster uses an image of the threatened Vimy Memorial to urge Canadians to support the war effort. Some of the text reads, "The bloody boots of the Hun are goose-stepping over Vimy. . . . The call comes again 'Vimy must be taken!'"

"ALL OVER CANADA, VETERANS OF THE First Great War are rejoicing at the welcome news from overseas that Vimy Ridge has been captured . . . and that the great memorial . . . is safe."[61] So claimed *The Legionary* with a photograph of First Canadian Army commander and Vimy veteran Lieutenant-General Harry Crerar, standing proudly at the memorial in its October 1944 issue. After defeating the Germans in the Battle of Normandy, the Welsh Guards, a British armoured regiment, recaptured Vimy Ridge and the surrounding terrain on September 1, 1944.

Richard Malone, the editor of the *Maple Leaf*, recounted that he arrived at the site just as Field Marshal Bernard Montgomery was being photographed. He gave the roll of film to Malone, assuming he would want to publish it in his paper for the Canadian soldiers, but Malone was intercepted by Crerar, with his staff, who were racing to the memorial. Malone told him about the film and Crerar erupted in rage. "That will never do. You can't have the papers back in Canada publishing the first pictures of the Memorial with an English General standing in front of it." Malone was pressured to delay publication until Crerar was photographed at the memorial, as the recently released caretaker George Stubbs led him through the site. Malone followed the order and suppressed Montgomery's photographs.[62] The Vimy incident was an insignificant event in the context of a great war, and did not even merit mention in Montgomery's memoirs, but it mattered to Crerar that he, a Canadian, be the first to be photographed at Vimy. Crerar was not just being petty. He understood the importance of promoting Canadian identity and he understood the value of Canadians being seen as the liberators of Vimy.[63]

The memorial had escaped the war largely unharmed, although the figure *Sacrifice* had some damage to its toes. The Canadians

A Canadian soldier and friend visit the liberated Vimy Memorial.

cleared away the rubble to reopen Grange Tunnel, and Simson reported that the memorial became a "site of mecca for Canadian soldiers who come almost daily. Many are sons or relatives of those of 1914–18."[64] Sapper W.E. Ellis was one such soldier, and he and his company took a detour to Vimy to see it. "I shall never forget it," he wrote decades later. "The statuary seemed wrapped in the most ineffable sadness, which was enhanced by the thunder of the guns in the distance. There was a 'Presence' there! I am sure every man in our company felt it."[65] In November 1944, a special Remembrance Day ceremony was held at the memorial by Canadian representatives and the people of Arras, at which the memorial was decorated with flowers and some 500 school children were present. Another ceremony, on April 9, 1945, brought out General Crerar and hundreds of Canadian soldiers and French civilians.[66]

The period of 1914 to 1945, from the Great War through the Depression and the Second World War, was a period of change, repositioning, sacrifice, and sorrow. But a new nation emerged after the Second World War, and it carried with it a maturing sense of identity, shared stories, and manufactured myths. It was not clear if Vimy would be in the foreground or the background of the new Canada's social fabric.

CHAPTER 12

BIRTH OF THE NATION

"From experiences of the Book of Remembrance 1914–1919 and of the Official History, it would appear that less than 1% of next of kin or participants are interested in any national project recalling war," wrote a discouraged Colonel A.F. Duguid, the author of the first volume of the official history, in March 1947. "Such apathy may be inexplicable, but it is widespread."[1] Canadians, he lamented bitterly, were not interested in the Great War, although critics of Duguid could argue that Canadians would have been more able to know their own history if the historian had completed his eight volumes. Since Duguid failed to do that, there were precious few histories of the Canadian war effort, even thirty years after the armistice. Duguid's laggardly pace led in 1947 to the cutting of the Great War history program, leaving Canadians without a foundational official history that other writers could use to write their more specialized studies. Even the official war records would be closed for the better part of two decades.

Soon after the end of the Second World War, Viscountess Byng of Vimy published her memoirs, *Up the Stream of Time* (1946). While the wife of Viscount Byng displayed good judgment in keeping some of her more acerbic thoughts of Canadian politicians to herself—including her hatred of Mackenzie King for his callous treatment of her husband—she provided a voice to General Byng, who had passed away in 1935. In *Up the Stream of Time*, Lord Byng is quoted as saying at one of the Vimy dinners, "There they stood on Vimy Ridge that ninth day of April, 1917, men from Quebec shoulder to shoulder to men from Ontario, men from the maritimes with men from British Columbia and there was forged a nation, tempered by the fires of sacrifice and hammered on the anvil of high adventure."[2] Yet Vimy had little relevance in the new Canada. There were new heroes from the Second World War and more recent battles that seemed to matter more, from Dieppe to D-Day, from the war at sea to the bombers over Germany. Children played with Spitfires, not Sopwith Camels; they re-enacted storming D-Day beaches, not Vimy Ridge. The Second World War veterans slowly supplanted those of the Great War in leadership positions in the Legion, and even the name of the war—the Great War—was changed to World War I or, as officially instated by the government in the late 1940s, the First World War. American and British Second World War films flooded the Canadian market. The memoirs and histories of senior British, American, and later German generals and politicians were eagerly read, but the Canadian high command—Harry Crerar, Guy Simonds, Bert Hoffmeister, Percy Nelles, and Clifford McEwen—were unwilling to commit their stories to paper.[3] The Second World War seeped into culture and society, but it was the American, British, Japanese, and even German stories—not the Canadian one.

The idea of the Second World War as a good and necessary war against Hitler's evil regime pushed the Great War further into the recesses of history. Even Vimy had faded from relevance in the

1950s. Vimy Day was rarely celebrated except by veterans' organ-izations; the thirtieth and thirty-fifth anniversaries of the Battle of Vimy Ridge elicited little interest and few newspaper articles across the country.[4] In 1955, veteran C.T. Sharpe visited Vimy on a cold, wind-swept November 11, and was upset to find that he was the only Canadian present. The issue was later raised in the House of Commons, and in 1957 the Legion asked the government to hold a mandatory ceremony each year at Vimy on Remembrance Day.[5] It complied, but the ceremony did little to raise the profile of the battle or the Great War in society. In the decade following the "Great Crusade" against Hitler and the Nazis, there was no significant Canadian Great War cultural output, whether movies, documentaries, plays, novels, or history books, save for Colonel Hugh Urquhart's biography of Sir Arthur Currie, which was pub-lished in 1950 but written before the Second World War.[6] The Great War had faded into obscurity.

"Allward's masterpiece was hailed as the noblest memorial in Europe," claimed *The Globe and Mail* in the sculptor's obituary.[7] Allward had lived out his last fifteen years without a major project until his death on April 24, 1955, but one obituary writer predicted that he would "remain secure in his place as dean of Canadian sculptors by the common consent of fellow artists and the public alike."[8] There was a momentary focus on Vimy with Allward's passing, but the memorial was largely forgotten in the post–Second World War years in Canada. The estimated 250,000 annual visitors to Vimy during the 1950s were largely British. The official grounds-keeper at the time, Paul Piroson, gave private tours to British sightseers, many attracted to the trenches and tunnels still intact on the Western Front. Most other battle sites had regenerated, covering over the scars of war. He spent much of his time chasing away French kids drinking at the site or looking for a place to make out.[9] There was also a period during which gangsters from Arras, along with warring Algerian factions, used the shell craters as a dumping ground for murdered bodies. Other than those Canadians serving in NATO (the North Atlantic Treaty Organization), few Canadians made the trip to the site, partly because the cost of international travel was prohibitively high. One journalist around this time wrote that, while Vimy would "always remain the special symbol of a terrible and glorious chapter in our national history, . . . with the passage of years, and the coming of new wars, its memory has perhaps become a little blurred."[10] The story of Vimy no longer pulsed in the same way with Canadians.

IN 1954, GEORGE STANLEY, A MILITARY historian at the Royal Military College of Canada, penned the first comprehensive history of the impact of war on the nation in *Canada's Soldiers: The Military History of an Unmilitary People*. He worried that Canadians did not know more about the accomplishments of the Canadian Corps, attributing the deficit to "our sense of inferiority, our lack of pride in our national achievements, and our failure to appreciate history as a road map through the treacherous and rugged terrain of world politics and war."[11] In Stanley's subtitle, he also coined what remains the most famous phrase describing Canadians and their relationship to war: they were an unmilitary people whose history was filled with wars and conflict.

Two years later, Canadians took a significant step towards reaffirming their national character as a people who sought peace instead of war. Lester B. Pearson, the minister for external affairs in the Louis St. Laurent cabinet, played a prominent role on the world stage during the 1956 Suez Crisis. That ill-conceived adventure saw the British, French, and Israelis conspire to invade Egypt and seize the Suez Canal—a crucial international waterway that had been nationalized by President Gamal Nasser. The European powers' blatant act of aggression and intrigue, clothed ineptly as a mission to rescue the Egyptians from the already-invading Israelis, had blown up in the faces of the British and French in late October 1956. The Americans were taken by surprise and were outraged at the plot, while the Soviet Union, looking to distract the world from its own brutal invasion of Hungary at the same time, threatened atomic war. It was no small mis-step to anger and alienate both superpowers. The Canadians were dismayed by the clumsy intrigue, but Pearson, a career diplomat for two decades before he was a politician, worked his contacts at the United Nations (UN). With the assistance of the Americans, he was able to broker a calming ceasefire, and then insert a peacekeeping force to intervene between the warring sides.[12] It was a tour-de-force for Pearson, earning him the Nobel Peace Prize the next year. While some English Canadians snarled that Pearson should have stood by the Union Jack regardless of the cost, many others took pride in seeing Canada play such a strong international role to avert conflict.[13]

After Pearson's Nobel Prize, the world seemed to expect more of Canada. What the country offered was a new commitment to using UN-sanctioned armed forces to intervene between nations that asked for assistance in keeping warring sides apart. Canadians wanted to be relevant on the international stage, and peacekeeping, relatively cheap and high profile, was one way to make an impact. Canada would sign on for nearly every UN peacekeeping mission over the next three decades.[14] It did so to help other nations, but also acted out of self-interest, to keep conflict from boiling over into war and at the same time have a voice in the international community. While Canadian history was filled with war's red tooth and claw, Canadians rapidly pushed this image aside from societal memory and embraced the notion of Canada as a peaceable kingdom.

THE PURSUIT OF PEACE WAS VERY MUCH in line with how Canadians liked to see themselves in the 1960s. At the same time, that decade was marked by activism, nonconformity, and even confusion. The all-encompassing American popular culture surged through the country, as films, television, and magazines brought the story of the United States to Canadians. The bleeding ulcer that was the Vietnam War was increasingly sending American soldiers home in body bags, which Canadians watched with growing despair on their televisions. The race riots and the assassinations of the Kennedys and Martin Luther King seemed to portend a breaking point in the divisive and fragmenting American dream. And yet Canada was tied ever more tightly to the United States, bound inexorably through finance and culture, and was in danger of being sucked into the vortex of war, inequality, and violence.

"Canada is at a crossroads," wrote historian W.L. Morton in 1964. "Either we go forward in the community that has come into being over three and a half centuries"—referring to Canada holding fast to British traditions—or, he warned, "we disappear as Canada and as Canadians."[15] The desperation of his plea was an indication of how many Canadians felt that the country was adrift. Up until the mid-1960s, there remained strong links in English Canada to Britain and what it stood for. Speaking for other like-minded intellectuals, George Grant, in his *Lament for a Nation* (1965), struck a chord with Canadians when he mourned the increasingly frayed ties with Britain and the loss of the stabilizing effect the Commonwealth had had on Canada, which balanced out the unequal relationship with the United States. Pearson's Liberal government, in power since 1963, had sold out the nation, in Grant's opinion, in its quest to share in American prosperity. Right or wrong, there was no reversing the North Americanization of Canada that had been in effect since at least the Second World War. But there was much concern that Canada was losing itself in its measured march away from the British Commonwealth as it struggled to find its own place in Cold War ideological politics and the new geopolitical blocs of influence.

If change was difficult to manage in English Canada, a different upheaval was under way in Quebec. The Quiet Revolution of the 1960s saw progressive segments of French Canada firmly shed the Catholic Church's encompassing influence over almost all aspects of society. The dead hand of the past was being loosened from Quebec's throat. As part of this process, and sometimes driving it, French Canadians strove for more financial, business, and cultural autonomy within a province that was dominated by an English elite. Quebec's ongoing demands were met with some mystification by the rest of Canada, though there was a desire by some to accommodate. But Quebec's need for change was a catalyst for all Canadians to think about what it meant to be Canadian. Pearson was determined to meet the challenges of French Canada in a turbulent decade. The Royal Commission on Bilingualism and Biculturalism identified past grievances and symbols of oppression, noting that Canada was "passing through the greatest crisis in its history."[16] Pearson's government reached out to Quebec and sought to find ways to better allow French Canadians to feel at home in the Confederation project. Some of these measures included hiring more francophones within Ottawa's senior public service bureaucracy, bringing key figures into the cabinet, such as Pierre Trudeau, and allowing Quebec to create its own pension plan. There was no shortage of critics who fumed that the government was purchasing peace at a high price, but there was no other clear way forward for English and French if the country was to be kept.

With Canada closing in on its one hundredth anniversary in 1967, Canadians were taking stock. The country's Red Ensign flag, under which Canadian forces had fought in two world wars, was a powerful, visible link to Britain, but Pearson and the Liberals sought a new, unique standard for the nation. Pearson, a Great War veteran who occasionally referred to himself as "1059 Private L.B. Pearson," announced his desire for a new Canadian flag at a Legion Hall in his riding of Algoma East on May 1, 1964.[17]

Most of those who had served under the Red Ensign were loath to let it fall, and they fought a stubborn rearguard action. The leader of the opposition, John Diefenbaker, the only other Great War veteran to serve as prime minister, condemned what he sneeringly called the "Pearson Pennant." He raged that Pearson and the Liberals were "a government determined to bring down all of our traditions."[18] Pearson stood his ground, adeptly manoeuvred committees to select a suitable flag, and eventually settled on the single red maple leaf on a background of red and white. After months of parliamentary posture, debate, and mania, Canada adopted the flag on February 15, 1965, another sign that the country was distancing itself from Britain.

The fierce and prolonged battle over the flag in the media and in the House of Commons revealed that in many parts of the

Allward's evocative sculpture reclines in the agony of loss,
while another holds high the torch of remembrance.

country Canada remained a British nation. The Red Ensign was
a powerful symbol for older Canadians, and especially for veterans
who had fought in the world wars.[19] Many of those British-
identifying Canadians who had seen the Red Ensign as a vital
symbol looked for a new icon to replace it. They found it in Vimy.

The idea of Vimy now represented far more than a battle: it embodied the sacrifice of the young nation as it stood shoulder to shoulder with Britain, and it encompassed the wider service that had led to a stronger and more independent nation. The Vimy idea was malleable enough to be used to support even opposing positions. In the 1930s, Canadian nationalists had employed it as a symbol of nationhood within a British imperial context. And now, in the 1960s, it was used by some Canadians as an enduring symbol related to a particular kind of nationalism, one linked to the old ways. For those Canadians, Vimy was an important bastion against the lashings of modernity—one rooted in a historic place of service and sacrifice, as codified in Allward's memorial. Vimy was an anchor in a changing Canada.

Pearson and his cabinet sought to invent other symbols and icons, too. In 1967, Parliament approved "O Canada" as the national anthem (replacing "God Save the Queen"), although it was not officially adopted until 1980 due to copyright issues. That year, Canada also established the Order of Canada, a series of awards given annually to Canadians to honour their distinguished service. The Liberals were crafting new symbols for an emerging Canada, while dislodging and replacing existing ones that had served the nation for nearly a century. This was another, less visible "quiet revolution," one that saw the weakening of emotional ties with Britain and the creation of a new multitude of fragmented identities.[20] The remaking of the old order continued forcefully under the leadership of Prime Minister Pierre Trudeau, who was ushered into power in 1968 on a wave of excitement about his new, modern style.[21] Out with the old, in with the new. His first three years of governing saw the passing of important legislation related to homosexuality, divorce, and abortion, and the implementation of bilingualism and multiculturalism policies. The French-Canadian Trudeau had little interest in propping up British symbols that he saw as a throwback to an older time; colonial connotations had to be shed. Trudeau's new images were a continuation of those introduced by previous Liberal governments, stretching back to St. Laurent: the Royal Mail became Canada Post, Dominion Day was renamed Canada Day, and the Dominion Government was changed to the Government of Canada. There had been some protest, but it was muted and came largely from the periphery. Even the amalgamation of the three armed services branches, from 1964 to 1968, while correct in concept but brutal in its implementation—with politicians imposing drab, look-alike uniforms and stripping the individual services of much of their traditions, heritage, and material culture—excited little interest across the country. The unification of the armed forces, which were bastions of Britishness with their close ties to the imperial forces and their eager adoption of Britain's military ways, was, in the opinion of one commentator of the time, "a healthy fillip to Canadian nationalism."[22]

THE TWO WORLD WARS HAD NOT been entirely buried in the past. The fiftieth anniversary of the start of the war, in 1964, inspired a number of new books, plays, film, and documentaries. In Britain, Alan Clark's much-discussed *The Donkeys* (1961) blamed the Western Front massacre on the donkey-like generals whose butchery had traumatized a nation. Plays like *Oh, What a Lovely War* (1963), later made into a film of the same name, were highly watchable skewerings that portrayed generals like Sir Douglas Haig as homicidal incompetents. The BBC's multi-part *The Great War*

(1964) drew astonishingly large crowds of viewers—about one fifth of all adults in Britain watched it, and it was also broadcast the next year in Canada, to "loom large on CBC-TV's summer schedule," according to one television critic.[23] Its message was delivered skilfully, through evocative images and eyewitness accounts, and though the series' writers tried to offer a balanced narrative, there was a visceral reaction by the viewing public, who focused on the futility and horror of the war.[24] The anniversary feature article in *The Globe and Mail* on August 1, 1964, noted that the war "was a comprehensive and indiscriminate slaughter . . . it was a war of inept generalship on all sides."[25]

In anticipation of the fiftieth anniversary of the start of the Great War, CBC Radio engaged in one of its most ambitious programs up to that point in its history. Through 1962 and 1963, researchers interviewed some 600 veterans to capture their experiences on 800 hours of tape. These were presented in seventeen one-hour programs in a series called *Flanders' Fields*. One of the producers of the series, A.E. Powley, who had served with CBC Radio at the front during the Second World War, wrote that the corporation sought to archive these important memories and "preserve them for all time."[26]

Two main intentions emerge from a reading of the series' transcripts: to show the experience of the war from the perspective of the rank and file, with a focus on the horror and deprivation of battle, and also to draw out the achievements of the Canadian Corps as an elite fighting force. Vimy was especially important to the second of these intentions, as it was revealed to be the defining moment in the story of Canada's emergence as an identifiable nation. As one of the researchers later noted, Vimy "recurs and recurs in the tapes we've gathered so far. That was the big one.

The first great battle that the Canadian Corps fought as one cohesive force; supported by their own artillery, their own machine guns and ancillaries; planned by Canadian officers; rehearsed again and again, and fought through to victory by Canadians on their own."[27] Much of the British support in the victory had been sandblasted from the narrative of Vimy in the shaping of the nationalistic story.

The introductory episode of *Flanders' Fields* was aired on Remembrance Day, November 11, 1964, and was followed by sixteen additional episodes on subsequent Sundays. Vimy was highlighted as a turning point in the war. The message was best captured by E.W. Russenholt, a wartime lieutenant in the 44th Battalion, who commented, "I have always felt that Canadian nationality was born on the top of Vimy Ridge. There was a feeling that we had mastered this job and that we were the finest troops on earth. This is where nationality first came together when all of us were fused or welded, if you like, into a unity."[28] These interviews, and the quotations extracted from them, tell about the experience of Canadians in the war, but perhaps even more about the time at which the interviews were conducted. The major themes of the series were the brutality of combat and the shaping of a nation. And it was Vimy that was heralded as the turning point. Vimy's meaning went beyond that of a battle, and the series emphasized that it was more "sacred to the memory of the Canadian Corps" than any other site in Europe.[29]

THE FIFTIETH ANNIVERSARY OF THE Great War sparked a renewed interest on the part of Canadian writers and publishers in capitalizing on the memory of the war. Veteran and journalist

Gregory Clark commented on the deluge of books, articles, television shows, and radio programs about the war, with most of the works centred on "the folly and stupidity of the field marshals and generals, on all sides. But that isn't war, as we old fellows remember."[30] For Clark, it was the camaraderie and the characters with whom he served in the trenches that mattered most. The war sat uneasily in the memory of men like Clark, as it did for the nation. It had been a relentless slaughter, but many survivors remembered it with nostalgia and felt years later that it was a key event in forcing Canada to come of age.

Though the official navy, air force, and Duguid's First World War history programs had been discontinued in 1947, the Princeton professor and Second World War army official historian Colonel Charles Stacey was able to marshal enough support and resources to keep the army program alive. Through his skilled oversight of a group of narrators who drafted chapters from the wartime records, with Stacey providing final authorship, he produced several overview and specialized histories of the Canadian Army. The success of these award-winning books allowed him to siphon off resources to enable Colonel Gerald Nicholson, a prewar school principal and an accomplished historian, to begin work on a one-volume Great War history. While Duguid's three decades of research had amassed an enormous amount of material, there were few draft chapters, and Nicholson had to start almost from scratch.[31] Mobilizing a team of writers and with his own considerable talent, Nicholson published in 1962 a 600-page brick of an operational history, *Canadian Expeditionary Force, 1914–1919*.

"In the hearts and minds of Canadian veterans of the First World War there has lurked a resentment, or at the least a slightly cynical feeling of hurt, over the fact that no official history of the performance of the half million men in the Canadian Expeditionary Force was ever produced," wrote Gregory Clark upon publication of the history. "It seemed to us old soldiers, sailors and airmen that it was a queer thing that our own nation, whom we helped to waken to consciousness as a nation, our fellow countrymen, did not think we were worth a history we could give our grandsons. . . ."[32] Nicholson's history was met with wide acclaim, reviewed positively, and lauded by veterans. The nation finally had its Great War history.

A handful of other historians took advantage of the anniversary and the renewed interest in the war. In Canada, the tone of the histories was more positive than in other countries. While the war had led to the deaths of 60,000 during wartime, with 6,000 more succumbing in its aftermath, the Canadian Corps had earned a stellar battlefield record. From 1914 to 1918, Canadian units had fought as part of the British Expeditionary Force, and Canadians had had no say in the strategic direction of the war. With British historians and filmmakers now fighting and refighting these old issues, in Canada the story of war was at the tactical or personal level. However, it was also clear that the success of the Canadian Corps on the Western Front had provided Ottawa with the leverage to demand a signature at Versailles and to begin negotiations with London to secure full autonomy over foreign affairs. The dual messages of loss and coming of age—but not futility—ran through many of the books of the anniversary years. The almost redeeming narrative of a colony emerging as a nation was deeply linked to the Battle of Vimy Ridge. "As the years passed," wrote one Canadian veteran, "the significance of Vimy to Canada became more apparent as her status among the nations increased."[33] The idea of Vimy being linked to nationhood had matured. As Canadians looked back on signpost events, many chose Vimy as the one to mark a change in Canada's standing within the British Empire.

If there was any doubt about Vimy's renewed importance fifty years after the battle, four new books signalled its status. In the anniversary period, two Canadians and two British historians offered detailed accounts of the Vimy battle. While Nicholson's official history had focused on attacking units and the role of commanders, these new books offered powerful eyewitness accounts by surviving Great War veterans. Their interviews and reminiscences were interspersed through the larger narrative of preparation and battle to provide a human face for Vimy.

The best of the Vimy histories was Herbert Fairlie Wood's *Vimy!* (1967). Colonel Wood, a veteran of the Korean War, delved lightly into German, British, and Canadian records, but augmented the narrative with dozens of veterans' stories. Fifty years on, he linked Vimy to the centennial anniversary of Confederation, emphasizing that the battle had been a defining moment for the nation. Vimy "marked a point of no return" for Canada, declared Wood, and it was as important to Canadian history as Agincourt was to the British: "no more, and no less." The foreword to the book, written by decorated Great War veteran and Second World War divisional commander Major-General F.F. Worthington, was even more lavish in claiming Vimy's place in history. Vimy, believed Worthington, was "not only the story of a successful battle but the story of a people on the way to becoming a nation." The victory was the "the first battle in which Canadian divisions fought as a whole, and in a purely Canadian effort, planned and fought on their own." Capturing that ridge fostered a "national spirit."[34]

British historians Kenneth Macksey and Alexander McKee wrote Vimy histories in 1965 and 1966, volumes that were available in British, Canadian, and American markets.[35] They were mass produced and sold in pocket-book form at newsstands and drugstores, and as selections for book clubs.[36] McKee was particularly taken with the apparently classless Canadian Corps that produced better, tougher, and more independent soldiers. Lord Beaverbrook would have been proud. While Vimy had been a signal victory, McKee worried that the battle's impact had been forgotten in the tide of anger and antipathy towards the Great War since the 1930s.[37] A reviewer of McKee's book asserted, "Vimy has become a noble part of Canadian folklore," but felt that it meant little to the youth of the nation to whom the battle was "as remote as Waterloo."[38]

D.E. Macintyre, a wartime veteran and one of the organizers of the 1936 pilgrimage, offered his own account of the battle in his memoir, *Canada at Vimy* (1967). A full-page advertisement in *The Legionary* claimed in a boldfaced title that at Vimy, "Canada wins her nationhood."[39] In a foreword to the book, Brigadier Alexander Ross, the former head of the Legion, recounted that when the Canadians captured Vimy Ridge, "It was Canada from the Atlantic to the Pacific on parade. I thought then that in those few minutes I witnessed the birth of a nation."[40]

The phrase "birth of a nation"—or the comparable "birth of the nation"—would be repeated time and time again, and ascribed to the battle in countless reports and media stories. But it is crucial to note that Ross and Worthington used it in 1967, not 1917. That doesn't mean that either man, or other Canadians, did not believe this sentiment in 1917, but much time had passed. The media often neglected to note that Ross, who was at Vimy, said that crucial phrase far from the bloody ridge. To the survivors, the year 1967—a period when Canada was changing and adopting new national symbols—was an ideal time to reassert the central importance of Vimy in the nation's history.

There were other important histories published in or around the centennial year of 1967 and, according to Pierre Berton, the national celebrations "turned many Canadians into history buffs— an enthusiasm that carried over into the next decade."[41] Many of these histories, such as bestsellers by Ralph Allen and J.M.S. Careless, argued that Canada had been forged in the fire of war.[42] The Great War, they emphasized, had been a turning point in the nation's history, although the battlefield exertions had, with the conscription crisis and the other strains of the war, sharpened the divide between English and French. Donald Creighton, Canada's most prominent historian after his award-winning biography of Sir John A. Macdonald, was no less given to finding meaning in the Great War. He wrote in a centennial history of Canada: "The War of 1914–1918 was the greatest experience that the Canadian people had ever known, or would ever know."[43] Up to this point in Canada's history, a hundred years on, the most influential historians in the nation believed that it was the trauma and heroism of the Great War that had forever shaped Canada, putting it on a new path towards full independence. And if one had to point to a single critical moment in the war that opened this path, it was Vimy—the fulcrum upon which the country had turned, moving from colony to nation.

THE FIFTIETH ANNIVERSARY OF THE BATTLE was marked on April 9, 1967, by a joint ceremony, one part in Ottawa attended by Prime Minister Pearson and the other at Vimy, where a contingent of veterans represented their comrades, dead and living. As early as 1965, the Opposition was asking the government in the House of Commons about the plans for the Vimy anniversary, and the Liberals could offer no coherent message.[44] The Legion was anxious to see Vimy commemorated and it also wished to play a part in the planning, as it had successfully done in 1936. A Canadian parliamentary committee made up of members of Parliament from all parties visited the battlefields in July 1966. After hearing that 250,000 people visited Vimy each year, admittedly most of them British, the MPs urged that a museum be built.[45] Their suggestion went unheard. The Legion's desire to organize a new pilgrimage was also ignored. The Department of Veterans Affairs refused to relinquish control of the planning and, when the tour to Vimy was finally set, invitations to veterans were sent out in March 1967, a mere six weeks before the ceremony on the ridge.[46]

Far worse, officials at Veterans Affairs blundered in dealing with French president Charles de Gaulle. Relations between Ottawa and Paris had been steadily souring since de Gaulle's return to power in May 1958. France had faced reversal and decline on many fronts, especially after its humiliation during the Second World War was followed by defeat in Indochina and a protracted and ugly war in Algeria. The proud and arrogant de Gaulle refused to accept his nation's misfortune and he ached to see France return as a great power, one that might unite the French-speaking world and act as a neutral nation in the Cold War between the West and the Soviet Union.

After years of prickliness, de Gaulle shocked the world in February 1966 when he demanded that NATO remove its forces from French soil. The Western allies were furious, having bled for

France's liberation only twenty years earlier and believing that collective defence against the Soviets was the only means of keeping the Red Army from marauding through Europe. The normally staid Pearson was apoplectic over the eviction, and in an uncharacteristically blunt remark to one senior member of the French embassy in Canada, he inquired whether Canadians "should take our hundred thousand dead with us to German territory."[47]

Ottawa was particularly wary of de Gaulle since he had been actively meddling in Canadian separatist politics in Quebec. He made a point of ignoring, sidelining, and snubbing Canadian federal diplomats and ambassadors in favour of provincial representatives from Quebec.[48] In preparing for the 1967 Vimy visit, Veterans Affairs had asked the Queen to speak at the ceremonies. When she was unable to attend, the Queen sent her husband, Prince Philip. De Gaulle was offended. In his eyes, the invitation should have come from him since Vimy Ridge was on French soil, regardless of the 1921 agreement with Canada. De Gaulle was also in a nasty struggle with Britain, having blocked that nation's bid to join the European Union, and he wished the Vimy affair to be a ceremony that included only Canada and France. The Canadian ambassador to France reported back to Ottawa that a conversation with the French deputy foreign minister in February 1967 revealed that, "Their preference was for Prince Philip not to come."[49] It was extraordinary that de Gaulle thought he could dictate to the Canadians who would be at the ceremony, but it was also surprising that Canadian authorities did not want to go forward with the event to mark their coming-of-age battle without a British monarch present.

A more civil and less churlish world leader would have let the matter go, but de Gaulle was looking to embarrass Ottawa, even to the point of dishonouring surviving veterans of the Great War who had fought to liberate his nation.[50] De Gaulle publicly called the Canadian invitation to the Queen a "fantastic oversight," even after the Department of External Affairs, which had taken over the debacle from Veterans Affairs, offered to scrap the Vimy plans and work with the French on a compromise.[51] De Gaulle's public tantrum was made worse when, out of spite, he ordered that no senior-ranking French political or military official would attend the Vimy ceremony, and even denied a French honour guard. Montreal's *The Gazette* reported that this hurt Canada and veterans, especially since "Vimy was a stunning victory, a climactic event in Canadian nationhood and a turning point in the First World War."[52] Pearson bit back his anger, especially after the leader of the Opposition, Diefenbaker, needled him on the issue in the House of Commons by declaring that it was "impossible to understand" de Gaulle's actions "on an occasion to commemorate a battle that helped make Canada as a nation," and demanding to know why Pearson did not publicly rebuke the French president.[53]

FOR THE APRIL 9 EVENT AT the memorial, 72 veterans had been flown over two days earlier on an RCAF Yukon transport to represent the 17,000 surviving Great War veterans.[54] The pilgrims were now officially known as "survivors."[55] They arrived at Vimy after a series of ceremonies, including the passing of a miner's lamp, lit from the 1967 centennial flame on Parliament Hill, to French counterparts at Notre Dame de Lorette Cemetery, where tens of thousands of French were buried near Vimy. At that April 8 event, one of the survivors, upon hearing the French band play both "O Canada" and "La Marseillaise," wrote of it being one of

Canadians have returned to the Vimy Memorial
in increasing numbers since the 1936 pilgrimage.

those rare experiences in his life where the "sensation of Patriotism" provoked "pins and needles up and down your spine. . . . I was proud to be a Canadian."[56]

On another cold April day, 72 aged Canadian veterans stood on the ridge to honour their fallen comrades, while thousands of other Canadians were encircling the National War Memorial in Ottawa. A crowd of 20,000 French civilians honoured the old soldiers.[57] With the temporary stands filled with onlookers, Lieutenant-General E.L.M. Burns, the Great War veteran and Second World War corps commander who was the leader of the group, described the scene: "What touched us most was the immense crowd of the French people from the surrounding villages and towns, who thus showed that they did not forget the Canadians who had come over the sea and fought and died by the side of the sons of France."[58] The senior Canadian politician was Léo Cadieux, the associate minister of national defence, and he later recounted that the French brigadier in attendance, embarrassed by de Gaulle's unseemly diplomatic row, apologized for the lack of an honour guard and noted that "the twenty thousand ordinary citizens who lined the route truly represented the honour of France."[59]

Broadcast by the CBC to televisions across Canada, Prince Philip spoke of the Canadian fight for freedom in the war. A fly-over of RCAF planes dropped red poppies and a hundred French schoolchildren laid flowers and sang songs.[60] However, it was Prime Minister Lester B. Pearson—whose words were read by Cadieux—who offered the most inspiring thoughts: "In the broad and colourful pageant of Canadian history past and yet to be enacted, the Battle of Vimy Ridge will stand as a benchmark of courage, gallantry and sacrifice—the crucible which brought forth and tempered the Canadian identity."[61] Pearson continued on Vimy's significance: "It was the birth of a nation, and it is appropriate that as we celebrate the centennial anniversary of the creation of our country, we should recognize the one event which above all others made it a nation, half a century later."[62]

The phrase "birth of a nation," and the powerful sentiment it induced, provided official sanction and sanctity to Vimy. As cold winds invoked the ghosts of the past, the nation-building narrative of the Great War seemed particularly stirring. Vimy had been framed as Canada's birthplace, albeit one hundred years after Confederation and fifty years after the battle.[63]

THE VIMY AFFAIR CONTRIBUTED TO THE ever-worsening relations between Canada and France, and matters came to a head a few months later, in July 1967. De Gaulle was visiting Canada on a state trip to celebrate the Canadian centennial and to see Expo 67. The French president sought to offer a dramatic overture to French Canadians, who had increasingly begun to push for greater rights within Confederation. A growing number of separatists were also anxious to form an independent Quebec nation. Starting in 1963, the terrorist group the FLQ—Front de libération du Québec—had shattered the statue of General James Wolfe standing on the Plains of Abraham, blown up federal mailboxes, killed a Québécois security guard, and destroyed other symbols of what they saw as English control over French Canada. The FLQ were separatist extremists and they did not reflect the mindset of the six million French Canadians in the country, but they were a sign—the most radical one—that the relationship between Quebec and the rest of Canada had to change.

On July 21, the French cruiser *Colbert* weighed anchor off the French-owned island of Saint-Pierre, near the coast of Newfoundland. De Gaulle, in his words, sought to "strike a strong blow" in support of French-Canadian aspirations.[64] He had refused to go to Ottawa first, as the Pearson cabinet requested, and upon setting foot on Quebec soil, he was greeted by adoring crowds. After several high-profile speeches, in which he extolled French Canada for surviving in a sea of English North America, he travelled on July 24 by open Lincoln Continental convertible from Quebec City to Montreal. He was cheered by large crowds along the route. When word passed through the city that de Gaulle had arrived, thousands thronged outside the Hôtel de Ville to catch sight of him. A roar went up from the crowd when de Gaulle appeared on a balcony to give an address. Now was the time for his grand gesture.

Still standing on the balcony, he began a short speech, claiming that "an immense emotion fills my heart in seeing before me the French city of Montreal." Arms raised, and urging Quebeckers to embrace their destiny, de Gaulle said that France had confidence that French Canada could stand on its own. The crowd roared with delight. Swept onwards, de Gaulle finished his speech, shouting, "Vive Montréal! Vive le Québec!" And then, with a dramatic pause, "Vive le Québec . . . *libre!*" The crowd was stunned into silence, and then thundered its approval.

"Vive le Québec libre" was the slogan of the separatists, and Ottawa was outraged by de Gaulle's provocation. The prime minister later wrote, "I could hardly believe my ears." And Pearson knew that the phrase was preplanned: "He was not the sort of man to do or say things without careful thought."[65] The next day, Pearson delivered a live-televised scolding to de Gaulle, whose words he described, in diplomatic language, as being "unacceptable." To drive home the point, Pearson rightly noted, "The people of Canada are free. Every province is free. Canadians do not need to be liberated. Indeed, many thousands of Canadians gave their lives in two world wars in the liberation of France and other European countries. Canada will remain united and will reject any effort to destroy her unity."[66] De Gaulle was not one to accept rebukes, and he went home without visiting Ottawa. World opinion was firmly against de Gaulle, and many French newspapers, usually sympathetic to the president, believed that he had grossly overstepped diplomatic bounds. De Gaulle was unrepentant. The Vimy insult in April had been just one of the many incidents leading up to the speech, but the episode in Montreal had revealed that the French president was willing to turn his back on his liberators, and perhaps on history.

THE IDEA THAT VIMY CHANGED CANADA was freely articulated in 1936 at the memorial's unveiling, but Allward's vision was not of martial birth, and his work instead focused on the emergence of Canada's soul from the sacrifice of its fallen soldiers. This concept was well situated in a world that trembled at the rise of the dictators and the winds of a new war. In 1967, however, as Canada turned firmly to peace and as it cast away its old symbols, Vimy came for many to represent the "birth of the nation." Vimy was an origin story that firmly placed Canada's starting point as a modern nation on that ridge and in the terrible war. Vimy was also a battle that evoked martial pride, but that pride was never fully articulated, partly because the values of the Great War generation were not the same as those that prevailed in 1967. Nonetheless, the "birth of a nation" idea was grounded in the desire to remind new generations of the tremendous sacrifice and service of the previous generation in the war, as well as the nation's military strength and its ability to deliver a clear-cut victory. The capture of Vimy was also the result of a unified assault that included Canadians from across the country, but most importantly, both English and French. That idea, in 1967, seemed perhaps most crucial as the Canadian union was under tremendous strain from French Canada's demands for greater autonomy.

Vimy remained an important icon for many Canadians, especially veterans. The prime minister understood that, even as he tried to lead Canada forward with a new flag and symbols. As Pearson told Vimy veterans in Ottawa, whom he fêted on April 9, 1967, "Vimy was more than a battle. It has become for Canada a symbol. It is . . . a coming of age of Canada as a nation, a nation which was brought to birth in the emotion of that time with a unity sealed in blood."[67] Pearson had affirmed Vimy's place in Canadian

Canada Bereft *laments her fallen sons. She will not forget them;
but perhaps Canadians, by the 1960s, were turning away.*

consciousness, but in this claim he was echoing and amplifying a message consistently delivered by soldiers, scholars, journalists, and opinion makers since 1936, and emphatically since 1964. As the old flag was downed, the idea behind the Vimy memorial was elevated. Vimy became the new standard for many Canadians.

But Vimy did not resonate in all parts of Canada or with all Canadians. Few symbols do. In the decade of discord that was the 1960s, Vimy was a bulwark for older Canadians; for veterans; and for that sizeable number of Canadians who continued to have strong connections to the British Empire, who saw war as being integral to Canada's development, and who felt their authority challenged in the 1960s rights revolution. For the new Canada emerging in that decade—a country with its own flag, a renewed emphasis on easing French–English relations, and a new desire to erase some of the British symbols of the past—Vimy did not carry such weighted meaning. The Vimy legend provided meaning for some Canadians as one that marked the birth of a new nation after the Great War. But the 1960s saw the rise of a "newer" Canada, with its own icons and symbols, and the concept of Vimy was increasingly sidelined within a Canada that was developing, maturing, and navigating nationhood.

CHAPTER 13

VIMY CONTESTED

The legend of Vimy started with the memory of a bloodbath on a ridge in France in 1917. It was furthered by the need to make sense of the war in the 1920s, cemented by a celebrated memorial, fed by a pilgrimage, and honed by cultural endeavours that marked the battle and monument. The Vimy idea found fertile ground as veterans and other like-minded Canadians sought to protect or shape the memory of the war. But Vimy gradually lost its meaning for most Canadians after the Second World War, as a new Canada was born in the search for peace and prosperity. The Vimy legend was re-energized in the 1960s during Canada's centennial era, when the victory was recast as a seminal moment in Canadian history. At the same time, it was marked by a steadily dwindling minority of Canadians, and increasingly associated with an older Canada. The Vimy idea seemed destined to die out, like others from the early twentieth century. Why did it not?

"We live in an age of denigration," observed the prolific Canadian War Museum historian John Swettenham when writing about how the Great War had been reduced in memory to a "brutish slogging match marked by a complete absence of intelligence by the leaders on both sides."[1] Around the same time that he was pleading for a more nuanced understanding of the war, Swettenham wrote a fine history of the Canadian Corps, *To Seize the Victory* (1965). With Canadians losing their grasp on their own history, Swettenham argued, an added "danger now lies in the flood of literature, television features and movies prepared in the United States for American readers and viewers, which are pouring across our borders. These give an inadequate and sometimes distorted picture of Canada's part in the First World War, and it is vital for Canadians of the present day, particularly young people, to be reminded of the facts."[2] While most Canadians found that the world wars were no longer the central symbols for the nation, the Great War, and Vimy specifically, remained a touchstone in the history texts that took a longer and more thoughtful view of how Canada had changed in the 100 years since Confederation.

By 1967 it was not just a few exuberant veterans—Ross or Worthington, or perhaps Pearson, trying to find favour with those who served their country—who believed that Vimy had led to the "birth of the nation." Having buried many of the old symbols, historians and politicians found a still useful one in Vimy. The careful and judicious Canadian historian Colonel Charles Stacey wrote in the centennial year that the creation of the Canadian Corps was "perhaps the greatest thing she has done to this day," and that the capture of Vimy was an icon "to mark the progress on the road to national maturity."[3] *General Mud*, Lieutenant-General E.L.M. Burns's 1970 memoir, also framed Vimy, a battle at which he had served six decades earlier, as an event of powerful influence: "Canadians who fought in World War I took more pride in the conquest of Vimy Ridge than in any other of their battles in the four long and bloody years." There were other victories more important to the war's outcome, like the Hundred Days campaign, but, Burns noted, "No other battle stands out so eminently as the Canadian victory as does Vimy Ridge."[4] The idea of Vimy continued to offer meaning in a significant and symbolic way to most of the 845,000 veterans of the two world wars and the Korean War, their families, and many others across the nation.[5] The power of the Vimy legend derived from the patriotic story that had evolved over time, first in the 1920s within the context of a Canada slowly inching to nationhood, and later, in the 1960s, as an enduring idea that linked the Canada of the past to the present.

Vimy's iconic status rose and fell. The vocal antiwar movement of the mid-1960s carried forward into the 1970s, especially among intellectuals and university students. Turnouts for Remembrance Day ceremonies were diminishing and *The Legion* magazine worried about the "dwindling effectiveness of the present pattern of Remembrance Day ceremonies."[6] There was even talk of cancelling the ceremonies due to Canadians' general apathy.[7] Great War veterans were passing away in significant numbers, and the reunions were cancelled and the regimental organizations shuttered. Some peace activists argued that honouring the fallen on Remembrance Day was akin to a militaristic act that only encouraged war-mongering. Veterans' medals could be found in pawnshops for a few dollars, as soldiers died off and their children sold off their belongings.[8] For many Canadians, the wars and their memory, as well as veterans, were not part of the social discourse or cultural environment. They were best shunted to the dusty pages of the history books. And in parts of the country, particularly French Canada, Vimy, the Great War—indeed, all war—was seen as a disunifying cataclysm.

IF VIMY IS THE STORY OF THE NATION coming together to achieve something great, then the 1918 Easter Riots in Quebec City signify the opposite. They are the bloody manifestation of French Canada's ostracism from the rest of Canada because of the 1917 conscription crisis.[9] For several decades, in history, school texts, and plays, French Canadians were taught about the oppressive Great War in which an English-Canadian majority humiliated French Canadians by enacting legislation to force their brothers and sons to fight against their will in an English army. The story of the 22nd Battalion, the French-Canadian infantry regiment, was all but ignored in French Canada, though several thousand French Canadians had died in service of King and country.[10]

By the 1950s, historians such as Guy Fregault, Maurice Seguin, and Michel Brunet were established in universities and were writing Quebec's history.[11] Their collective works emphasized how, since the Conquest of 1763, defeat, occupation, and subjugation had stymied French Canada's development. There was a strong current of victimization within the emerging historiography, and a blaming of the other—the British, English Canada, Americans, and, eventually, the Church.[12] This deeply ingrained grievance was set against a growing movement for change in the 1960s. The Quiet Revolution encompassed cultural, political, economic, and linguistic awakenings. With much of industry controlled by American or English-Canadian corporations, Quebec politicians, academics, students, and business leaders pushed for greater autonomy. The creation of Hydro-Québec in 1963, and the Québec Pension Plan the next year, were important signs that French Canada was reclaiming its destiny. The all-encompassing influence of the Catholic Church was steadily diminishing. Women pushed back against the paternalism of the state and church. New films, novels, and music revealed the vibrancy and uniqueness of French Canada.

In the political arena, successive Quebec premiers made demands to Ottawa for greater rights. Militant separatists, best exemplified by the FLQ, turned to violence to achieve their goal of secession from Canada. The culmination of increasingly militant acts was the kidnapping by one FLQ terrorist cell of British diplomat James Cross on October 5, 1970, followed by the abduction and murder of Pierre Laporte, the provincial minister of labour. The FLQ went too far for most Québécois, who recoiled from the unlawful actions. As the October Crisis unfolded, the hard-headed Prime Minister Pierre Trudeau refused to bend to the terrorists' demands, and the Quebec premier, Robert Bourassa, lost control of the situation and pleaded for help. Trudeau invoked the War Measures Act. Fear and uncertainty drove the actions of the politicians. As in 1918, there were rumours of armed insurrection, made more plausible by wildcat strikes of police and firefighters in Montreal the previous year, and now the political assassination had heightened tensions. Thousands of soldiers stood sentry in the cities, and some 400 Québécois were rounded up and held without trial. While polls showed that Trudeau's actions were supported by a strong majority of French Canadians, all despaired at the rapid degeneration of "peace, order, and good government."[13] The FLQ was stamped out, but the sight of soldiers in the streets was a disturbing symbol of federal control, and one not easily forgotten. There seemed uncanny parallels in 1970 to the Easter Riots in Quebec City in 1918.

In the aftermath of the FLQ crisis, Quebec historian Jean Provencher published *Québec: sous la loi des mesures de guerre 1918* (1971). The 1918 Easter Riots protesting conscription had been largely forgotten in Quebec society, with most of the school texts and general historical readers offering little mention of the shootings until the late 1950s.[14] Provencher's work followed in the vein of the emerging historiography and was likely influenced by Albert Tessier's textbook *Quebec–Canada: Histoire du Canada* (1959). *Quebec–Canada* made no mention of the war overseas, including Vimy, and even the French-Canadian 22nd Battalion was ignored. Instead, the focus was on the effects of the war on Quebec, with an emphasis on federal oppression.[15] The book received a favourable review by the influential historian Lionel Groulx.[16] A more strident work appeared seven years later, from Joseph Costilla. Riding the revolutionary spirit in Quebec, Costilla claimed that those French Canadians who had served overseas, and those at home who had supported the war effort, were sellouts and traitors.[17]

Provencher's history depicted innocent French Canadians standing up for their rights in 1918 and being shot down in the streets for it.[18] The four dead were martyrs to the cause of liberty, as they had protested draconian federal measures. Provencher's book became an influential bestseller. The provocative story drew the attention of the media, and the historian became a frequent commentator on television. In 1973, Provencher wrote a play called *Quebec, Printemps 1918*, which opened in October 1973 and ran for a month, ending on November 11, 1973—fashioning a counter-narrative to the Canada-wide one of remembrance. The production, with its depiction of the riots and the divergent views surrounding the coroner's inquest and the dum dum bullet scandal, drew favourable reviews from French papers. It would be mounted several times over the years.[19] Provencher's message became all the more powerful after the Kent State killings of four students on May 4, 1970, when the Ohio National Guard fired on unarmed demonstrating university students. Though the Kent State and Quebec City protests were very different—especially given that in 1918 some of the protestors were shooting at the soldiers—the two incidents were easily conflated. Provencher's influential view of the riots, which saw Quebeckers as the victimized and martyred, has shaped collective memory in Quebec.

AFTER THE BRIEF BURST OF CENTENNIAL interest in the Great War from 1964 to 1968, the topic again sank into historical oblivion. Even academic historians, who could now access the Canadian official war records, which had been opened to the public over the previous decade, did little to avail themselves of them, and few histories were produced. The most impressive and original were two scholarly works that offered new perspectives on the impact of the war on Canada's home front. Robert Brown and Ramsay Cook's *A Nation Transformed* (1974) explored many aspects of the conflict, from the wartime economy to women's roles, while J.L. Granatstein and J.M. Hitsman's *Broken Promises* (1977), a study of conscription in the two world wars, made it clear that the casualties at Vimy had led to conscription. Internationally, Paul Fussell's *The Great War and Modern Memory* (1975) and John Keegan's *The Face of Battle* (1976), attracted critical and popular success, reaching far into the book-buying public. Fussell returned to the British poets of the war to provide a vivid and moving account of the Western Front through their word-pictures that revealed the poets' shock and horror. Keegan's book drilled down deep, from the generals to the warriors at the front, emphasizing all the fear, misery, exhilaration, and chaos that came with the experience of combat. His account of the first day of the Somme, the notorious July 1, 1916, when close to 60,000 British and dominion troops were cut down in sickening fire, provided a new window into the massacre. By the 1970s, few could imagine that earlier generations had believed that the Great War was a just war in defence of Belgium and in support of Britain against an expansionist and aggressive Germany. The motivation for going to war back then was blotted out by the suffering of the trench soldiers.

Timothy Findley's novel *The Wars* (1977) played a significant role in shaping the memory of the Great War. One of Canada's most celebrated writers, Findley created Robert Ross, a naive and sensitive officer who, on the Western Front, encounters cruelty everywhere and rapidly loses his innocence. Findley stressed that there was no escaping the brutalizing, unending nightmare. *The Wars* propelled war novels back into the literary mainstream, and emphasized the personal trauma of the trenches.[20] While wholly original, Findley's novel was part of a war book genre, begun in the 1920s, in which the soldiers were nothing more than victims.

If an idea had been born at Vimy that a new Canada had emerged in the fire of war, by the 1970s the mainstream media were giving little coverage to the battle or to Vimy as a nation-building event.[21] The "birth" that had been evident to many in 1967, in that patriotic moment and in the search for our origins, no longer held sway even a decade later. Though the sixtieth anniversary of the battle excited some interest, with a *Globe and Mail* editorial opining, "No accounting of our evolution to full nationhood can ignore that battle," the piece also noted that the "memories of Vimy have faded."[22] *The Legion* magazine barely mentioned the battle any longer, and in 1977, the only article was by David Moir, who served as a machine-gunner in the 3rd Infantry Division. Though the editors added a subtitle to Moir's piece—"Vimy was the time the country grew from a colony to a nation"—the article mainly recounted the preparation, the accidental death of comrades, and then the fury of the battle. While Moir noted Vimy was a "famous victory," he emphasized that the success came at a cruel cost, and, quoting from Gray's "Elegy," intoned, "The paths of glory lead but to the grave."[23]

Vimy had been a touchstone in the history of the nation up to the 1960s. But the complexity of a changing country suggested that the battle was no longer appropriate as a nation-building symbol as Canada entered its second century of existence. New histories and novels provided a more nuanced view of the war, one that moved beyond the battles and into the social and cultural impact of conflict. Could Vimy be considered the birth of the nation if it had left a traumatized and fractured country in its wake?

DURING THE 1970S AND MID-1980S, THOUGH most schoolchildren across the country learned about Vimy, there was no significant national event to reinvigorate the Vimy story. Then came Pierre Berton's *Vimy*, published in 1986. The writer, broadcaster, and social commentator was the country's foremost popularizer of history. Berton was drawn to epic Canadian stories—the War of 1812, the building of the Canadian Pacific Railway, the settlement of the West, and the irresistible lure of the North—and Vimy fit well in this nation-building canon. With his pulpit and platforms of magazine, newspaper, and television programs to spread the good word, Berton was the voice of Canada.

The Vimy narrative of all four Canadian divisions taking the impregnable ridge, and of heroic sacrifice by the underdogs, was repackaged for a new generation. Berton's researcher drew upon the CBC's *Flanders' Fields* interviews and conducted another seventy interviews with surviving veterans. Soldiers' letters and diaries were newly unearthed, and Berton was captivated by the heroic Canadians struggling in the maw of battle. The book's first draft was a mess, written in an exuberant Kipling-esque style of adventure and derring-do. Editor Janice Tyrwhitt, according to Berton biographer A.B. McKillop, was "horrified." She toned down the writing, restructured the story, and asked for major rewrites. Berton obliged, especially given Tyrwhitt's admonishment that, for most Canadians, Vimy was "meaningless."[24]

Berton's subsequent drafts focused on the personal stories of Canadians in battle, as well as providing vivid depictions of death and destruction. When the book hit the stores, it was, like almost all of Berton's work, a massive bestseller. Within two years, it had sold 70,000 hardcover copies and 100,000 paperbacks.[25] *Vimy* raised the profile of the battle, and for many young Canadians, this author included, it was one of their first forays into the Great War. Berton's antiwar attitudes, shaped by his extensive reporting on war and the disaster of the Vietnam War, were tempered by the nation-building narrative of Vimy. As part of the media deluge around the book, Berton wrote in the *Toronto Star* about how Vimy "created Canadians." "In the measured march toward Canadian autonomy," he observed, "Vimy was always seen as a turning point."[26]

While Berton offered a twist at the end of the book—noting that despite the victory, the battle was not worth the cost in lives— the monumental success of *Vimy* pushed the legend to a new level of Canada-wide consciousness. Some reviewers derided Berton's "overkill" in describing the "grisly and the gory," while professional historians noted factual errors in the book. But generally it was accepted that Vimy was, as the *Alberta Report* enthused, "the battle that forged a nation."[27] There were many positive reviews, almost all of them noting how Berton had elevated the story to match other founding Canadian myths, like the construction of the railways. But no history book, not even a Berton chronicle, can single-handedly craft a national iconic experience. Berton's two volumes on the War of 1812, for example, did not succeed in making that war a foundational story of Canada. His *Vimy* resounded so strongly because it built upon seven decades of belief that Vimy was already an important event. Yet perhaps Berton's greater achievement was in bringing to the fore the many strands of memory that celebrated Vimy, retrieved from older Canadians and veterans, and presenting them front and centre to a new generation.[28] The Vimy legend had atrophied since the 1960s, but with his book, Canada's most important historian had reinvigorated it as a founding myth.

"IN RECENT TIMES, THE VIMY MEMORIAL has come to symbolize Canada's long commitment to peace in the world, as well as its stand against aggression, and for liberty and the rule of law," claimed a 1992 Veterans Affairs publication. "The Canadian tradition of asking its servicemen and women to defend and restore peace has evolved into a long commitment of peacekeeping under the aegis of the United Nations. To date, Canada has contributed 80,000 troops to more than thirty peacekeeping operations. Canadians have demonstrated their valour on many battlefields, but today the message of the Vimy Memorial is one of peace—upheld for Canada by the Canadian Armed Forces. The message of Vimy is, in fact, a deterrent to war."[29] Memorials' meanings change over time, and are often twisted to meet contemporary government objectives. But to link Vimy with peace is simply wrong, and to link peacekeeping with the memorial is utterly incoherent. While the battle and the memorial were at odds—one representing costly victory and the other staggering loss—the idea of Vimy was malleable, affording different interpretations over the years to be channelled into a more usable narrative. The Veterans Affairs publication also declared that the battle marked the birth of the nation. "It is part of the very fabric of our nationhood, for, at Vimy, our soldiers brought both pride and unity to the Canada of its day. In some senses, we became a nation because of what they accomplished."[30]

The framing of Vimy as a unifying episode in our history was a worthwhile aim in 1992, the seventy-fifth anniversary of the battle, as the country appeared to be coming apart at the seams. The 1992 Vimy ceremony was an opportunity for France and Canada to celebrate their shared history, forged in war and peace, and to engage in what scholars call "memorial diplomacy"—the bringing together of nations through commemoration of the fallen at intricately choreographed public events.[31] An estimated 2,000 French visitors trekked up the ridge, and, in contrast to the snubbing from de Gaulle in 1967, French President François Mitterand and an honour guard were in attendance on April 9, 1992, to join Prime Minister Brian Mulroney. History and heritage were interwoven at the memorial site, where the past could be repurposed to inform the present. This occasion was particularly relevant because Canada was passing through a difficult period. Mulroney had rolled the dice in trying to heal the wounds in Quebec and bring that province back into the fold, with a promise to recognize Quebec as a distinct society. Yet he had failed after two rounds of divisive constitutional debate culminating in the 1990 Meech Lake Accord and the 1992 Charlottetown Accord. The country was angry and unsure of its future, and old wounds had been reopened.

On the anniversary, Prime Minister Mulroney stood on the historic ridge that had seen Canadians from across the country—English, French, Aboriginal, and new immigrants—die for victory. The ridge was a perfect place to invoke ideals of national harmony. Mulroney believed that the sacrifices in April 1917 "made to strengthen the unity of one of the world's most admired nations were not made in vain."[32] There was, of course, not a single Canadian at Vimy seventy-five years earlier who had unity on his mind as he prepared for battle and his own possible death, but the sacred ridge allowed for the uttering of such wishful statements. The "birth of the nation" idea was supple enough to be used in yet another dire period in Canadian history, and it allowed Mulroney and others to project current beliefs and aspirations onto the ridge. It is not surprising that Mulroney made no mention of the legacy of conscription. Seventy-five years later, the subject still evoked fear and resentment of an English majority exerting control over French Canada's destiny. The Vimy monument, again, became more than a marker for the dead or a place of military pride. It was a politicized site and a performative space that allowed Mulroney to use it for a grand vision: a symbol of unity that might bind together the fragmented nation.

The seventy-fifth anniversary of Vimy received significant coverage in the newspapers, and the ceremony was broadcast live on television. The Vimy legend was being repurposed in a new age. Canada was again in need of an idea, place, and event that represented service, unity of purpose, and victory. In support of the legend, the Department of National Defence's Directorate of History and Heritage published a comprehensive history of the battle by two leading official historians, Brereton Greenhous and Stephen Harris. The minister of national defence, Marcel Masse, was keen to share the rich military history of the nation, to inspire pride, and perhaps to provide an anchor for all Canadians, through the publication's bilingual format, to explore their shared past.[33] In *Canada and the Battle of Vimy Ridge, 9–12 April 1917*, the authors described the battle's meaning in guarded terms, without resorting to the "birth of the nation" phrase. However, they did turn to Colonel Charles Stacey's words in the final paragraph, noting, "If a single milestone is needed to mark progress on the road to national maturity, one might do much worse than nominate that famous Easter Monday."[34] More far-reaching was the Veterans Affairs "Canada Remembers" program, which put teaching materials and posters into classrooms across the country. Vimy was one of the key battles emphasized. But it took some time for these programs to influence hearts and minds. Journalist Tom Clark, whose grandfather and uncle served at Vimy, wrote on Remembrance Day 1993, "Not many Canadians go to Vimy these days, not in the numbers that they used to 60 years ago when the country was young and proud."[35]

CANADA HAD IGNORED ITS VETERANS FOR YEARS. The half century of warfare that had so profoundly shaken the nation on all fronts had been replaced by the comfortable image of the peacekeeper. Canada had earned a distinguished reputation through mediating conflict and volunteering its soldiers to serve in peace-keeping missions. Canada's pride in peacekeeping, expressed in various ways—from images of the blue-helmeted soldiers on the ten-dollar bill to the national memorial built in 1992—reinforced the notion, revealed in many polls, that Canadians believed that peacekeeping was the primary focus of Canada's armed forces. The legacy lived on, long after peacekeeping died on the killing fields of Rwanda and Somalia in the early 1990s, when peace-keepers failed at their impossible tasks in lawless and murderous environments.

The fiftieth anniversary of the Second World War stimulated renewed interest in Canada's martial accomplishments, and those of other Allied nations such as the United States and Britain. About 15,000 Canadian veterans were welcomed back to Europe as liberators, in 1994 for the anniversary of the D-Day landings and in 1995 to mark the end of the war.[36] With the return receiving widespread media coverage from the two national television net-works, Canadians found to their surprise that the Western world was thanking the veterans they had for so long ignored. Shame mixed with pride, and Canadians turned to honouring their debt to veterans, as well as those who had passed away with little rec-ognition. From 1995 onward, the number of people attending Remembrance Day ceremonies spiked. Some of this renewed inter-est was also attributable to the fact that Second World War veter-ans were dying in larger numbers as the millennium came to a close. With the passing of the elderly warriors, more Canadians came out to their local memorials to pay homage to their aged or deceased family members. At the same time, many of the protestors from the 1960s antiwar generation had grown up, lived rich lives, and found that now they were more willing to reflect on the nation's history and the impact of the world wars.

Canadians had also emerged battered from the 1995 Quebec referendum. The Parti Québécois government of Jacques Parizeau, riding a wave of disaffection and anger over Mulroney's failed constitutional accords, set the stage for a second referendum to determine if Quebec should separate from the rest of Canada. Late in the hour, as a separatist victory looked unnervingly possible, English Canadians rallied to plead with and bribe French Canadians to remain within Confederation. The country was nearly lost on October 30, 1995, as Quebeckers voted narrowly to remain in Canada. The referendum provoked a series of existential questions about the Confederation project. For too long, Canadians had given little thought to what bound the nation together, or had been too focused on the Quebec question, the defining issue for Canadian federalism and identity from the late 1960s to 1995. One of the narratives that emerged from the referendum and its near dismemberment of Canada, coinciding as it did with the fiftieth anniversary of the Second World War, was a *cri de coeur* that the nation put so little stock in its shared history. Collective reflection and angst mingled in a resurgence of efforts to honour veterans and remember the past.

IN 1997, THE GOVERNMENT OF CANADA opened an interpretation centre at Vimy Ridge. It was a year after Vimy and Beaumont Hamel were designated as Canadian national historic sites, the only two such sites located outside Canada. At Vimy, the interpretation centre sits on the western slope of the ridge. Visitors walk up the boundary between the 3rd and 4th Division's route of advance during the battle to arrive at the clearing at the top, in close proximity to Hill 145, where the memorial rests. The interpretation centre contextualizes the memorial, as do Canadian students who conduct guided tours. The ridge has its own narrative, moreover, with its concrete trenches, shell craters, tunnels, and, of course, the memorial. Brian Bethune, a journalist for *Maclean's*, observed that Vimy received a staggering 750,000 visitors a year around the turn of the current century, but only about 3 percent were Canadian.[37] If the roughly 22,500 Canadians are only a small minority of visitors, what does that say about Vimy? The memorial is as much a site of remembrance for Canadians as it is a silent Canadian ambassador to Europeans. Vimy is the face of Canada in Europe, when it comes to war, sacrifice, and commemoration.

Most of the roughly thirty million Canadians in the late twentieth century would never visit the memorial in France. They were much more likely to encounter the legend in the four-part National Film Board production *Battle of Vimy Ridge* (1997). Narrated by actor Paul Gross, the film laid out the Vimy story through historical footage, re-enactments, and soldiers' eyewitness accounts. The script emphasized the innovative Canadian tactics and pre-battle preparation that led to the fierce fight for the ridge, where the Canadians "transform[ed] a field of slaughter into a field of glory."[38] After covering the Vimy victory, the film focused on the rise of Sir Arthur Currie as one of the finest generals of the war, twinning his wartime accomplishments with Vimy. As one reviewer noted, after years of NFB films that questioned Canada's effort in the world wars, especially *The Valour and the Horror* (1992), this film offered a "properly reverential view of the Great War. . . . In *The Battle of Vimy Ridge*, the battle is recalled in order to represent not only the best traditions of the Canadian military, but the birth of Canadian consciousness itself. . . . We should celebrate that achievement, though perhaps without accepting the grand claims made for the battle's significance."[39]

While some Canadians no doubt learned of Vimy's importance from the film, which was shown on television and later in schools, others found little value in the old battle. On September 3, 1998, in Quebec City's Saint-Sauveur neighbourhood, a modest crowd of 100 people attended the unveiling of *Québec, Printemps 1918*, a monument to the victims of the 1918 Easter Riots. Designed by Aline Martineau, the 3.5-metre-high memorial, consisting of a rectangular stone embossed with a metal stem leading up to a flower head, represents the people's spontaneous resistance. Its plaque commemorates the four French Canadians killed on April 1, 1918. For those who encounter the memorial without knowledge of the war, or for those who have learned about the event in Quebec's classrooms over the years, the story of the Easter Riots has been reduced to a tale of freedom-seeking French Canadians pushing back against an oppressive English federal law—conscription—and being martyred by bullets.[40] This Easter Riots narrative, inspired by Provencher's simple retelling of the complex riots, remains dominant in Quebec, although it gets little attention in English Canada, just as Vimy remains a foreign battle for most French Canadians. There are different war narratives for French and English Canada, and there are also different monuments to codify those stories.

There were other symbols that were more universally accepted across the country. Remembrance Day, the two minutes of silence, and John McCrae's "In Flanders Fields" all remained poignant signs of recollection and commemoration. War heroes like Billy Bishop remained cultural figures of some renown, but most of those who served had been lost to time, including the senior commanders Byng and Currie. While both of these generals had schools, roads, and places named after them, their accomplishments and relevance were more difficult to grasp in the new Canada. Why was a corps commander important, and what did he represent? While throughout the interwar period, the name Viscount Byng of Vimy was well-known across the country, as both the general at Vimy and a postwar governor general, the forgetting of the Great War after 1945 led to the introduction of a curious mistake into Canadian textbooks. Ramsay Cook, one of Canada's finest historians, wrote erroneously in the 1977 textbook *Canada: A Modern Study* that Currie was in command of the Corps at Vimy (instead of being one of the four divisional major-generals).[41] The next year, in a 1978 textbook, *Canada's Century*, the error was repeated.[42] To this day, it is common to hear ill-informed pundits in the media talk about Currie's expert planning at Vimy—as if he was acting on his own—that delivered victory, or, equally common, how Currie led the Corps there in battle. It must have been perplexing for some folks to wonder why Sir Julian Byng, when he was made a baron, took as his lordly title Baron Byng of Vimy!

Historical understanding of the Vimy battle was not helped by the popular, far-reaching, and generally informative *Heritage Minutes* series. These one-minute short films, conceived and produced since the 1990s by Historica Canada, a not-for-profit historical organization seeking to enrich Canadians' knowledge about their past, bring to life dozens of important historical events. The films have an enormous reach as they play on television and in movie theatres, and are included as part of educational packages for teachers.

Since its inception, Historica Canada had been polling Canadians about their understanding of the past. The polls were always temporary blows to Canada's collective self-esteem as they revealed Canadians' lack of knowledge of most events in the past. While the surveys, usually consisting of multiple-choice questions, were not the most effective way to gauge knowledge, they provided predictably grim reading. Knowledge of Vimy was polled, too, and in 1997 only about a dismal one-third of Canadians, and a smaller proportion of younger Canadians, had any idea of what Vimy was or what its relationship was to Canada.[43] And so one of the earliest *Heritage Minutes* films highlighted the Battle of Vimy Ridge.

The supporting educational material on Historica's website claimed that Vimy was "One of the greatest battles in Canadian history" and was "considered the turning point of WWI." The one-minute recreation featured Currie planning the battle and included no mention of Byng, and the accompanying website text erroneously noted that the Corps of four divisions was "led by Sir Arthur William Currie, who was the first Canadian-appointed commander of the Canadian Corps."[44] The *Minute* had a profound effect on the memory of the battle. Byng of Vimy was cast aside. The British general, it would seem, did not fit into the national myth of the Corps' battlefield exploits leading to the birth of the nation. In this defining moment, how could the commander of the Corps be British? The need for a national commander for Canada's premier national battle seemed to override the need for historical accuracy or, perhaps, it was simply assumed that Canada's most important battle, in which the nation supposedly came of age, had to be a place where a Canadian was in command.

From the 1990s onward, the military history profession expanded rapidly, with students and scholars in the field producing dozens of new academic books and articles that re-examined many aspects of military history and the Great War. Yet few of these interpretations worked their way into public consciousness. This new scholarship had begun to question all aspects of the war, including tactics, the role of generals, the social history of soldiers, and the role of families on the home front, based on newly uncovered archival evidence and eyewitness accounts. Yet the dominant interpretation remained that of a war of senseless slaughter, with the butchers and bunglers in command sending off the brave victims to be gunned down in the barbed wire to join the legion of corpses.

Despite the new and burgeoning field of Great War studies, the most important shaper of memory remained literature. Throughout the 1990s and into the new century, a number of poignant novels, plays, and history-inspired personal explorations offered insight into the war. British author Pat Barker's *Regeneration* series and Sebastian Faulks's *Birdsong* were international bestsellers, while acclaimed Canadian works including David Macfarlane's *The Danger Tree* (1991), Jack Hodgins's *Broken Ground* (1998), R.H. Thomson's *The Lost Boys* (2000), Alan Cumyn's *The Sojourn* (2003), Frances Itani's *Deafening* (2003), and Joseph Boyden's *Three Day Road* (2005) were all critical and often commercial successes.[45] The horror of warfare and the traumatizing effect on soldiers were central to the stories. Few soldiers in literature escaped unscathed, being killed in horrific ways or haunted forever as they carried the war back with them to Canada. The trope of shellshock—the wound to the mind—was prevalent in almost every work. The war that destroyed bodies with reckless abandon also shattered souls.

Vimy was not overtly represented in any of the literary efforts in this period, save for one bestseller. Jane Urquhart's novel *The*

Stone Carvers (2001), nominated for the Man Booker Prize, and a finalist for both the Giller Prize and the Governor General's Award, told the complicated story of families and bloodlines set against the backdrop of the Vimy Memorial. The story follows Klara Becker, whose lover is lost in the war and who strives to make new meaning in its aftermath by helping to carve stone at the Vimy Memorial. History haunts and is passed down through generations; Vimy, too, is bequeathed from the last to the next. Urquhart captures the power of the stone, and its carving becomes a means of laying to rest the ghosts of the past and, at the same time, resurrecting them. One effusive reviewer of *The Stone Carvers* called it "an epic portrait of a nation's birth," observing too that, "To write the Great Canadian Novel, it helps to find a setting that, in a uniquely Canadian way, marries tragedy and redemption, devastation and beauty, myth and reality."[46] Vimy Ridge provided that crucial metaphor.

IN SEVENTY COUNTRIES AROUND THE WORLD, and in hundreds of Commonwealth War Graves Cemeteries, more than 110,000 Canadians lie buried.[47] Most are identified and interred on the battlefields or named on memorials, but 6,846 are unknown soldiers from the Great War. *A Canadian Soldier of the Great War—Known Unto God.* Those chilling words are carved into the headstones. Under the maple leaf symbol that unifies these Canadians who serve forever in this silent army are Canada's sons, those whose bodies were so badly mangled in battle that in death they could not be identified. To have lost one's life is to have given everything one can give. But to lose one's name and to be lost forever to one's family is something unimaginably terrible.

Most nations have tombs for a single unknown soldier to signify all of his comrades, although this is very much a twentieth-century form of war commemoration.[48] On the second Armistice Day, November 11, 1920, the British buried one of their unknown soldiers. In London, the Unknown Warrior, as he was official named, was entombed at Westminster Abbey by King George V with Britain's kings, bishops, poets, and writers. An unknown soldier, likely a private drawn from the British working class, or from one of the colonies or dominions, represented 908,000 dead from Britain and its empire. One hundred widows who had lost their husbands during the war were present at the entombing ceremony as the living face of grief. Eleanor Watson was one Canadian mother whose son had been killed in the war and lay buried with no known grave. She confided to her diary that when visiting the Westminster Unknown Warrior as part of the 1936 Vimy pilgrimage, she was moved by "a wonderful feeling and I suppose each of us thought that 'he' may have been our dear 'missing one.'"[49]

At the time, Canada did not demand the return of one of its own unknown soldiers. Along with the governments of other dominions—Australia, South Africa, Newfoundland, and New Zealand—Ottawa was content to let the Westminster Abbey soldier stand for all. There was, interestingly, a prevalent misconception in Canada in the 1930s that the Unknown Soldier was entombed within the Memorial Chamber of the Parliament Buildings. The Legion was forced to publish an article in 1937 righting this notion.[50] Decades later, in 1993, Australia brought home one of its unknown soldiers to rest in a shrine at the Australian War Memorial in Canberra. This was a powerful, nationalizing event, and the Tomb of the Unknown Soldier has become a pilgrimage site for Australians.

The return of Canada's Unknown Soldier in May 2000 was a moving event that led to many Canadians' re-engagement with the Great War.

Spurred on by Australia's actions, the success of the 1995 Second World War commemorations, and the approaching turn of the millennium, the Royal Canadian Legion began to lobby in 1996 for the return of one of Canada's unknown soldiers.[51] Canadian officials and the Legion worked with the Commonwealth War Graves Commission to select one of the fallen. Perhaps not surprisingly, they chose a lost Canadian from Cabaret-Rouge British Cemetery in Souchez, near Vimy Ridge.[52] The cemetery contains 1,603 unknown Canadians killed between 1916 and 1918, although most fell during the April 1917 Vimy battle. In a ceremony at Cabaret-Rouge on May 25, 2000, the nameless Canadian was disinterred from Plot 8, Row E, Grave 7, and laid in a casket of silver-maple wood. The body was taken to Vimy Ridge for a ritual service and then flown back to Canada, where, from May 25 to 28, an estimated 15,000 Canadians silently passed by the soldier who lay in state in the Memorial Chamber of the Peace Tower.

More than 20,000 Canadians attended the interment ceremony in Ottawa, while all Canadians could watch the nationally televised event. The tomb and sarcophagus, upon which lies a sword, helmet, and branches of maple and laurel leaves, were added to the National War Memorial. Weighing about 10,000 kilograms and composed of Caledonia granite, the tomb contained the body, surrounded by soil from the original grave in France as well as from all the Canadian provinces and territories. Grand Chief Howard Anderson laid a golden eagle feather upon the soil, a symbol of strength and loyalty among First Nations warriors. Canadians were transfixed by 100-year-old Paul Métivier, one of the last Canadian Great War veterans, and Ernest "Smokey" Smith, a Victoria Cross recipient from the Second World War, as they read poet Laurence Binyon's stirring words, "At the going down of the sun, and in the morning, we will remember them." One lost soldier, taken from his family and his nation, was returned home and transfigured in a symbolic representation. He was "known" once again.

THE RETURN OF THE UNKNOWN SOLDIER in 2000 was a notable event in Canadian public life. Along with the fiftieth anniversary of the end of the Second World War five years earlier, it signalled a significant shift in public conception of the past. There was a perceptible sea change of thought at the end of the twentieth century, as more Canadians paid greater attention to the country's military history and its veterans. This shift was underscored by the stirring of powerful emotions at the Unknown Soldier ceremony.

Along with this development came a renewed emphasis on educating Canadians about how war has shaped the nation. Unfortunately, one of the most important venues for this sharing of stories was the dilapidated Canadian War Museum. Established in 1942, it had suffered for decades from an inadequate budget, and was in desperate need of an upgrade.[53] Its exhibitions were stale and outdated, and it was less a museum and more a mausoleum.

In 1998, military historian J.L. Granatstein was appointed to lead the museum into a new century.[54] The author of dozens of books on Canadian military, political, and diplomatic history, Granatstein had also recently published a national bestseller, *Who Killed Canadian History?*, which condemned the lacklustre and uninspired way that Canadians taught and were taught history.[55] Granatstein brought dynamism and expertise to the task, hired a number of new historians, and set about revitalizing and redoing the exhibitions. The Jean Chrétien government, having weathered the financial crisis of the mid-1990s, put aside millions of dollars for a new building, eventually to be opened in Ottawa on the LeBreton Flats.

To generate interest in the new museum project, the Canadian War Museum and the Canadian Museum of Civilization mounted a major exhibition in 2000 to showcase the neglected First World War art. *Canvas of War: Masterpieces from the Canadian War Museum* drew from its collection of over 1,000 works. The priceless art, which included works by painters A.Y. Jackson, Maurice Cullen, Arthur Lismer, and key members of several art movements in the early twentieth century, had remained unseen in storage for much of that century. *Canvas of War*, curated by Laura Brandon, toured the country. Coming as it did on the heels of the renewed interest by Canadians in their veterans and military history, the exhibition drew large crowds, with the number of visitors reaching more than 280,000 at the Museum of Civilization, and half a million in total in all the galleries.[56]

The Ottawa exhibition also featured three of Allward's maquettes that he had created in his London studios and then transferred to Vimy for the sculptors to use as a guide in carving stone statues. The story of their survival was improbable, and several times they had been nearly destroyed.[57] Crated up and forgotten for decades, they remained unseen until the late 1990s, when the museum restored them for the *Canvas of War* show. After the successful exhibition, they were put on permanent display as crucial artifacts in the Hall of Remembrance at the new Canadian War Museum. The Battle of Vimy Ridge, moreover, is one of the central components of the Great War exhibition space, with artifacts, an animated map, and an examination of the memorial.[58]

Canvas of War contributed to the revitalization of Walter Allward's connection to Vimy. In 2001, journalist Brian Bethune lamented in *Maclean's* that the sculptor "never got his due."[59] A year after Allward's death in 1955, he was recognized as a potential person of national historic significance, but nothing was done about it and in 1973 the designation was rescinded without explanation, along with sixty-eight others.[60] It appears that a backlog in processing the historical plaques led to the mass dropping of individuals from the designation list. There was no outcry on Allward's behalf. But like his sculptures, which gained in importance over time, the memory of the sculptor's contributions was invigorated after *Canvas of War*, and in 2002 he was designated a "person of national significance." The Historic Sites and Monuments Board of Canada eventually erected a plaque at his Bell Memorial in Brantford.

"VIMY; VIDI; VICHY—DOES IT REALLY MATTER?" scoffed journalist Arthur Weinreb.[61] He was mocking the minister of national
defence, John McCallum, who, in a September 1, 2002, letter to
the *National Post* trying to justify a previous slip-up over his apparent ignorance of the August 1942 Dieppe raid, confused Vimy with
Vichy, the seat of the French government that collaborated with
the Nazis during the occupation of France in the Second World
War. The *Post* could barely contain its glee at receiving such a
gift, and the minister was roundly condemned for the humiliating
slight. However, one wonders how many Canadians would have
noticed the error without the newspaper's prompting, since the
public's ignorance of Vimy had been documented only a few
months earlier. A Dominion Institute survey asked Canadians to
identify the famous First World War victory where the Canadian
army captured a "key ridge."[62] Despite the blatant hint, only 36
percent knew the site was Vimy Ridge.

Not only was the Vimy idea flickering in and out of Canadian
consciousness, but Allward's memorial to the ages was in peril.
Memorials of stone and mortar are not imperishable. Tourists
and time can destroy sites. In the case of Vimy, however, the stone
remained strong but the joints in between were weak. Even a few
decades after the memorial's erection, its faulty construction left
it marred with lime deposits and cracked masonry. The Department
of Veterans Affairs, which had cared for Vimy since 1951, had
made periodic repairs to the memorial over the years, but those
were band-aid solutions.[63] Canada's national overseas memorial
had been allowed to decay.

The big push for a major structural upgrade to the memorial
occurred in 1997, when Vimy Ridge was designated as a national
historic site. But there were no new funds coming from Parliament.

Two years later, an exposé in the *Ottawa Citizen* on August 8, 1999, revealed that the Vimy memorial was falling apart, its stones disfigured. Parts of it were cordoned off, the base was crumbling, and the sculptures were covered in black and green mould. Many of the 11,285 names had been obliterated by water damage. The missing who had once been reclaimed from the battlefield were missing again.

Aged veterans called for an intervention, and Pierre Berton went on record to say that it would be "insane" to allow the memorial to further crumble due to political inactivity.[64] The Chrétien government was eventually shamed into action, and in 2002, all parties voted to free up thirty million dollars to repair the overseas memorials.[65] The problem could now be addressed, but Canadians seemed to have lost the connection to the memorial, the battle, and what it stood for. The 2002 Remembrance Day issue of *The Legion* reported that six in ten Canadians failed a three-question quiz testing their awareness of Vimy Ridge and the Great War. Rudyard Griffiths, executive director of the Dominion Institute and a champion of Canadian history, noted wistfully, "That history seems to be slipping away."[66]

IF WE REBUILD IT, THEY MIGHT come—or so it was hoped. Ottawa architect Julian Smith, starting in 2003, spent four years leading the restoration team at the Vimy memorial. To combat the ravages of time and weather would require a new army of specialists—from seismic crews to engineers, as well as stonemasons and forestry and landscape experts. Heritage-building renovations are difficult; saving a sacred site requires a leap into the unknown. Allward had been a visionary in his construction of the memorial, its sculptures, and its place in the Vimy warscape, but he had brought to the project little experience as an engineer. He had used reinforced concrete for the memorial's base and core, a new approach at the time, and the Seget stone cladding was added to the concrete as the finish. To create the impression of a continuous surface and of a single stone face, Allward planned for narrow joints—only a few millimetres wide—between the cladding stone. But over the years the concrete expanded and contracted with temperature fluctuations, cracking the stone. Water also permeated the porous stone, migrating through the concrete and mortar. Calcium leached from the interior of the monument through the facing stone and then obscured the names of the fallen. There was no easy fix. As the names ran through and along the mortar joints and blocks of stone, it was hard to replace damaged pieces without further obliterating the record of the fallen. The restoration of the stone required that the memorial be shrouded and hidden for two years. Much of the monument was taken apart, piece by piece, using hydraulic-powered diamond stone saws. Vimy was skinned of its stone: the Seget limestone was stripped off, cleaned, and then returned to its place with the addition of an impervious backing membrane. When some of the older stone could not be restored, new stone was pulled from the original Croatian quarry.[67] For Vimy to be saved, it had first to be destroyed.

The Vimy national park also underwent restoration. While much of the ridge was forested and labelled a red zone, meaning that visitors were not allowed to walk on it because of the danger posed by tens of thousands of unexploded ordnance, the sheep of Vimy strolled about the park, munching on the grass. There were also a number of still-standing regimental and divisional memorials from the war, although the 44th Battalion's memorial on the

Pimple had degraded to the point that it had become a hazard and was destroyed in 2004.[68] Seismic studies revealed a 14-kilometre maze of Allied tunnels, most of it unexplored. Underground, unexploded ordnance from the battle, soldiers' wartime graffiti, and even footprints from hobnailed boots were found. The ghosts of the past own the subterranean space.

"I FELT MY PULSE QUICKEN," RECOUNTED Stanley Sislowski, a Second World War veteran, upon a visit to Vimy Ridge. "We had our first view of the famous Memorial of Vimy Ridge that most Canadians of our era cannot fail but to recognize."[69] Sislowski's generation knew of Vimy, but by the twenty-first century many veterans and other concerned citizens worried that most Canadians had no meaningful connection to the battle or what it represented. A Dominion Institute survey in 2007 demonstrated that only 46 percent of Canadians could correctly identify Vimy Ridge as "Canada's most famous victory in the First World War which consisted of the capture of a key ridge on the Western Front." This seemingly low figure was an improvement on the 36 percent reported half a decade earlier, and was encouraging for those who cared— except in Quebec. In that province, only a dismal 8 percent could correctly answer the question. Years of provincial governments excluding the Great War and Vimy from school curriculums, and of schools only teaching about Quebec's oppression through conscription or about the Easter Riots, had produced this depressing result.[70] As one historian remarked of the location of Vimy in the cultural and historical landscape, "it was unheard of in Quebec."[71]

In 2007, the ninetieth anniversary of the battle, the Conservative government of Stephen Harper planned a large-scale pilgrimage to the memorial site. Canada's Queen would attend as well, but with only a handful of Canadian Great War veterans still alive, and all of them over 100 years old, there would be no eyewitnesses from the battle. The last Vimy veteran, Clifford Holliday, an underage soldier who served with the 43rd Battalion, had died on May 4, 2004, at age 105. However, the dignitaries were to be joined by several thousand Canadian high school students.

The anniversary inspired a number of films and books. A new documentary, *Vimy Ridge: Heaven and Hell*, produced by yap films, aired on television in late March. A young-adult book by Hugh Brewster, *At Vimy Ridge*, and a history of the battle by popular writer Ted Barris, *Vimy*, were also published. A scholarly book of essays, edited by Geoffrey Hayes, Michael Bechthold, and Andrew Iarocci, offered new knowledge in key areas of the battle's preparation, the fighting for the ridge, and the war's memory.[72]

The 2007 pilgrimage to the refurbished
memorial reinvigorated the Vimy legend.

Vern Thiessen, a Governor General's Award–winning playwright, mounted a new play, *Vimy*. It shed light on the personal cost of the battle for a number of characters—all wounded in body and mind—and framed the human suffering in opposition to the idea of Vimy as a nation-building story. Curating a dramatic commemorative event, actor and writer R.H. Thomson projected the 3,602 names of Canadians killed during the Vimy battle onto the National War Memorial in Ottawa, in what was called the Vimy Vigil. The Royal Canadian Mint struck a commemorative thirty-dollar silver coin. The Canadian Forces, fighting in Afghanistan since late 2001, created a new Sacrifice Medal for killed and wounded service members. One side features an image of the Queen, whose crown incorporates a maple leaf, while the reverse bears the image of the mourning figure *Canada Bereft* from the Vimy Memorial, next to the single word "Sacrifice."

The observation and marking of Vimy continued as Parliament reaffirmed April 9 as Vimy Day and the Conservative government ordered that the Red Ensign be flown year-round at the memorial, beside the Canadian flag. Vimy was elevated again into social consciousness, in a way that it had not been seen since 1967. There was tremendous media coverage of the battle's history, Allward, the memorial, and the ceremony at the ridge. Michael Valpy, writing in *The Globe and Mail* on April 7, 2007, observed how a "minor battle for a French hill [was] transformed by alchemy into Canada's defining moment of nationhood."[73] Journalist Roy MacGregor echoed Valpy, observing, "Canada had entered the war as nothing more than part of the British Empire. Largely because of Vimy, she left the war a signatory of the Treaty of Versailles and, historians such as Pierre Berton have argued, now her own country."[74]

If anniversaries focused the attention of the media, it was further intensified, along with the interest of Canadians in general, by international events coinciding with those days of remembrance. In 1936, war in Europe seemed likely; in 1942, Vimy was occupied by the Germans in another world war; in 1967, Canadians were protesting the Vietnam War and seeking to avoid thermonuclear annihilation. Now, in 2007, the ceremony for a ninety-year-old battle was set against Canada's military operations in Afghanistan to destroy the terrorist al Qaeda and Taliban organizations, and then to try to bring some semblance of order and stability to that failed state. On April 9, 2007, there was no separating Vimy from Afghanistan, since six Canadians had been killed in combat the day before the ceremony. Canadians could not help but reflect on their own martial history of service and sacrifice.

The interplay of Vimy and Afghanistan created new meaning for the old battle, but there was an acknowledged challenge in finding a connection for Canadians when almost all the veterans who had fought in it were now dead. What were the links between the modern, multinational Canada of the twenty-first century and the mainly rural, British nation of 1917 undergoing a historic bloodletting? The inclusion of young students was important to show the relevance of the battle to a new generation and to fulfill the debt of remembrance.

In April 2007, 20,000 attendees gathered at the memorial. Several thousand were Canadian teenagers, each carrying with them the story of a soldier who fought or fell in the war. They marched up to the memorial in a long procession. The French cheered them on, and soon the Canadians cheered back. With the eyes of the nation on them, and those of much of the English-speaking world, the students acted unexpectedly. Instead of engaging in sombre reflection, thousands of young Canadians smiled, shouted, and even mugged for the cameras as they filed past and headed to the memorial to take their place. Flags were waved and some worn Superman style. Young Canadians clapped their hands and sang "O Canada."[75] Commentators were taken aback, some noting the irreverence of youth while others pronounced it disrespectful. National pride had always been on display at the memorial and in anniversary ceremonies, but never quite like this.

The formal speeches, not surprisingly, were more sombre and stately. Queen Elizabeth II rededicated the memorial, just as her uncle, Edward VIII, had unveiled it in the summer of 1936. She spoke in English and French of how "The Canadian Corps transformed Vimy Ridge from a symbol of despair into a source of inspiration." The victory at Vimy, intoned the Queen, "allowed Canada, who deserved it so much, to take its rightful place on the international scene as a proud, sovereign nation, strong and free." Prime Minister Stephen Harper greeted his fellow Canadians, reminding them, "there may be no place on earth that makes us feel more Canadian."[76] On the politicized ground of Vimy, where many of Canada's leaders in the past had framed the historic battle to meet the needs of the present, Harper similarly used his speech to link the Great War with the war in Afghanistan: "It [the memorial] reminds us of the enormity of their sacrifice and the enormity of our duty to follow their example and to love our country and defend its freedom forever."[77] Foreign Affairs Minister Peter MacKay even drew a direct association between Vimy and Afghanistan at a concurrent ceremony in Halifax: "The Vimy memorial service today will pay tribute to those fallen heroes and in Afghanistan we see the willingness of Canadians in modern times to fight for those same sacred values. The Afghan people are no less deserving of our support and protection of their rights as were the people of France and occupied Europe during the First and Second World Wars."[78] Only fifteen years earlier, Vimy had been construed as a symbol of peace and, even more perplexing, as a site associated with peacekeeping. After the events of 9/11, Canadians' outlook on war and combatting terrorism had hardened with the costly combat mission in Afghanistan. "As a country at war," wrote Lawrence Martin in *The Globe and Mail*, "we're in the mood for Vimy."[79]

The ceremony included more speeches, prayers, and wreath layings, and a lament played by Saskatchewan Métis fiddler Sierra Noble. Many Canadians at the ridge, and those watching the proceedings live in Canada, would have agreed with Liberal deputy leader Michael Ignatieff, who called it "one of the best days to be a Canadian I can remember."[80] The intricately planned and moving ceremony raised Vimy's profile, and was once again an occasion that reinforced the nation, a space where ideas of sacrifice, duty, and honour were enacted. But those sentiments, along with the sombre speeches, seemed at odds with the cheering crowds of students. While commemoration can be observed in many ways, few think of a patriotic mosh pit as means of honouring the dead. Moreover, what was to be made of the ball caps and T-shirts issued by the Legion, emblazoned with the phrase "Vimy: Birth of the Nation"? Canadians had always shown their colours at Vimy, but had these attendees gone too far? Had nationalism scrapped up against jingoism; had commemoration bled into commercialization? What exactly was happening at Vimy that day?

Clearly a mixture of emotions was on display in the national performance, and the solemnity of a significant commemorative event at a site of mourning was undercut by excited crowds of flag-waving young Canadians. These two forms of marking the past co-existed awkwardly, and there were complaints by many media commentators that the young Canadians shipped over by the thousands did not recognize the day's deep emotional significance. But while Vimy Ridge hosts a memorial devoted to the sacred, the idea of Vimy is wound around issues of nationalism. Even the first veterans to visit Vimy in 1936 had displayed a desire for nostalgia and celebration as well as sombre reflection. And since then, Vimy had become enmeshed with the "birth of the nation" idea, which was surely to be celebrated, not grieved. Perhaps it is not so surprising, then, that many Canadians draped themselves in flags and cheered as if they were attending other occasions of national pageantry, whether Canada Day or the Olympics.

"Every nation needs a creation story to tell, and the First World War and Vimy are central to that story," said Prime Minister Harper.[81] Though he did not use the phrase "birth of a nation," the sentiment of his speech quite rightly referred to an origin narrative. All nations have them. All nations need them. They are forged over time, codified in cultural products and political discourse, and passed down from generation to generation. Vimy is one of Canada's most long-lasting of these narratives, even though it is one that has ebbed and flowed over several generations, taking on new meanings and shedding old ones. In the post–Great War years, the memory of Vimy resonated with veterans and Canadians who had a direct link to the battle, or with Canadians who had an understanding of history. But it had nearly disappeared in the decades after the Second World War. In 2007, the Vimy legend returned to the mainstream, invoked as Canadians fought in another far-off war. The nation was more attuned to its debt to veterans, and perhaps more connected to the past.

The meaning of Vimy would continue to find relevance, potency, and usefulness in the twenty-first century, as an old idea was refashioned and given new life. Such is the power of legends.

CHAPTER 14

VIMY REBORN

A proud Vimy pilgrim, Frank O. Salisbury, wrote to Walter Allward in the aftermath of his 1936 voyage overseas. He was moved by the memorial—by its sublime beauty and how it captured the essence of Canada's grief. Salisbury believed, "A new host of pilgrims who visit that sacred spot will do so with a different emotion stirring their hearts and glory in the deeds of their fore-fathers. Then another generation and a vague epic of life's struggle and conquests will dominate their imagination and fire fresh endeavour."[1] Allward was stirred enough by the letter to keep it in his limited archives, hoping that Salisbury's sentiments might be prophetic. This has proven to be the case, and Canadians have continued to return over the last 100 years, engaging and re-engaging with the ridge, the memorial, and the idea of Vimy.

The ninetieth anniversary of the war years drew media and public attention, both in Canada and around the world. Canada's remembrance of the Great War was presented through the lens of the country's coming-of-age stories—with Vimy as perhaps "the" story. At the time of the Vimy battle, Canada was fifty years old, but the war pushed the country to extreme limits and demanded an exertion far beyond anything conceived of or given in the previous five decades since 1867. Nearly every Canadian family was touched by the war. The battlefield exploits and home front toils, the trauma and the suffering—these explain why the Great War was viewed as a test of fire through which the young nation passed. The symbols forged from struggle and paid for in blood often have a greater resonance than those derived from peace, compromise, or judicial decisions—likely because of the drama involved, and the high stakes. Revolutions, rebellions, and wars are heralded as the births of nations around the world, from the American Revolution and the Battle of Gettysburg in the United States, to the Russian Revolution and Stalingrad in the Soviet Union, to the Battles of Trafalgar and Waterloo and the 1940 air war to defend Britain, to the French Revolution. These life-and-death struggles are elevated in the public imagination, even though the symbols of a more political or peaceful maturity may be more important in the long run to the development of the country and its character. In Canada, medicare and the Charter of Rights and Freedoms, and before them the social security net created after the Second World War are key aspects of the social contract in modern Canada. They, too, defined the country and continue to touch the lives of millions. Yet our wars echo in different ways.

The Great War is both warp and weft in the tapestry of Canadian history and identity, and its memory has gathered in strength in the early twenty-first century. It has been kept alive in school curriculums and history books, through plays, novels, documentaries, websites, and films. In 2008, *Passchendaele*, a major film by one of Canada's most respected actors and directors, Paul Gross, depicted the horror of war and its shattering impact on individuals. The film made $4.3 million and won a number of Canadian film awards. And while it may have had too much "passion" and not enough "Passchendaele," it brought the war to a new generation of Canadians.[2] It is striking that the film was not titled *Vimy*, given the battle's cultural prominence, but Gross's emphasis was on the futility of war, and that is the narrative surrounding the October–November 1917 Passchendaele battle. The Vimy legend is about unity of purpose and an underdog victory, even though, as the story of the combat revealed, the fighting was as vicious and brutal at the sharp end as in any battle fought during the war.

The Great War, a 2007 documentary, brought descendants of soldiers back to the battlefields to viscerally experience aspects of the war. The film was produced by Brian McKenna, an award-winning director and creator of the divisive 1992 NFB TV series *The Valour and the Horror,* which had enraged Second World War veterans in its emphasis on the ineffectiveness—and, at times, immorality—of the Canadian war effort.[3] Now, with his new documentary, McKenna sought to show the transformative effects of the Great War and why it still mattered ninety years later. The series was enlivened by Justin Trudeau's portrayal of Talbot Papineau fated for death, and the Vimy segment was among the most compelling. The director asked the film's participants, all with a family link to a soldier or nurse in the war, to let out a cheer at the top of Vimy Ridge, as a celebration of the victory and a nod to the epic event that it was. But Joel Ralph, one of the participants and a keen student of history, observed that he and his fellow soldier re-enactors were humbled to be on the sacred spot where so many Canadians had been killed. Even though the filmmaker wished to see jubilation, Ralph described the scene: "As part of the filming, we, the great-grandsons and grand-nephews of those who fought, were asked to stand on Vimy Ridge after re-enacting the battle and shout 'Vive le Canada!' in celebration of the Canadian victory. Some answered the call with excitement and enthusiasm. But others resisted, doubting, despite McKenna's insistence, that their ancestors ever performed such an ardent act, concerned that this cinematic device glorified war. The result was eerily muted—a reflection, perhaps, of the number of ancestors being represented who were killed or maimed during the battle."[4] Ralph is correct in that the record is absent of any large-scale Canadian celebrations atop the ridge, partially because the battle was still raging. But more importantly, Vimy remains a contested space and idea, one that is infused with grief and sorrow and with pride and celebration. All of those emotions are present; all reside messily entangled on the ridge, in the memorial, and in our hearts.

But why Vimy? Why have Canadians singled out this battle, as opposed to the Second World War Juno Beach landings on June 6, 1944, or the air war over Germany or the Battle of the Atlantic? The battles in the air and at sea are difficult to mark with a single monument, but the D-Day landings are now commemorated by the Juno Beach Centre, erected in 2003. It is a memorial and a museum, situated on a site of memory that also includes the massive concrete defences of the German West Wall and the nearby cemetery of Bény-sur-Mer. The Juno Beach landing is more historically significant than the Battle of Vimy Ridge, with more at stake if the fighting forces had failed to secure the beachhead and drive back the Germans. Yet while Juno is a meaningful place where visitors feel pride and positive national feelings, as well as sadness and grief, it has not been woven through Canadian identity over generations in the same way as has Vimy. While it is only a little more than a decade old, the Juno Centre is clearly not the Allward memorial, and conveys none of its majesty or raw power.

It does not carry the same freight of sorrow. Perhaps that is because Vimy, in addition to being a sacred spot for the nation's dead, has come to represent the entire Canadian war effort. Juno has not yet become such a focal point for the Second World War, and it may never attain that status since that war effort encompassed the world, with Canadians fighting in multiple theatres, including off the Canadian coasts and in Hong Kong, the Pacific, Italy, and Northwest Europe. Vimy's power is derived from a decades-long process of distilling the Great War into a single event, and then representing that event through an alchemy of memory, loss, and national pride.

VIMY IS BOTH A REAL PLACE and an imagined space. As the ridge is situated thousands of kilometres from Canadian soil, there are frequent lamentations among those deeply affected by a visit to the monument that not all Canadians will, at some point in their lives, travel to the ridge. The power of the Vimy legend—including both the battle and the site of memory—has compelled some Canadians to want to replicate the memorial back in Canada. In preparation for the one hundredth anniversary of Vimy, retired Canadian senator and general Roméo Dallaire, author of a best-selling history of his personal struggle as commander of the 1994 Rwandan peacekeeping mission, proposed in March 2010 that the federal government reproduce the Vimy memorial on the Gatineau shore of the Ottawa River. The brooding figure of *Canada Bereft*, mourning her fallen sons, would stand tall there for all Canadians.[5] Somewhat surprisingly, given Dallaire's stature as a revered hero, there was little reaction to the idea, and after a brief news cycle the story died away. One wonders how many Canadians agreed with the *Ottawa Citizen*, which described the plan as "well intentioned but misguided," and argued that a replica statue in Canada would be "nothing more than a curious duplicate in a flowery park."[6] The Vimy Memorial's impact derives partly from the pilgrimage that Canadians must make to the site. The battlescape, laden with history, creates a presence not easily copied.

Since 2013, Canadians have had a far more visceral reaction to the Never Forgotten National Memorial, which was planned for the remote eastern shore of Cape Breton Island. Drawing inspiration from the Vimy Memorial, the 30-metre-tall statue of Mother Canada waits for her dead sons who will never come home. Her outstretched arms suggest a nation in mourning. The project began as a private impetus supported by a number of patriotic Canadians, but it has also received federal funding. It stirred controversy from the start and was seen by many as another attempt by Stephen Harper's Conservative government to militarize the nation's past by erecting memorials to war. Supporters argued that the memorial would attract tourists and create much-needed jobs. What is wrong with commemorating Canada's dead overseas?, shrugged many who were perplexed by the backlash. Others reviled the project for putting commemoration before the environment by placing the monument in a National Park, or were offended by the almost Stalinesque figure or the trademarking of names, such as "Mother Canada," for future commercialization. The media gleefully ran with the story until Parks Canada cancelled the group's permit to locate the statue in the National Park in February 2016, all but killing the project. The memorial's planners tried to bottle lightning a second time with their proposal to build a Vimy-like memorial on Canadian soil. What the conflict and controversy reveals, however, is that the Vimy monument is unique in time and place.

The lack of other memorials of its size and grandeur to mark the Second World War, Korea, or the Afghanistan war suggests that even the Vimy Memorial, as iconic as it is today, might not have found footing if the idea had been proposed even a decade later; in the financially strapped 1930s Depression era, it would have surely been a source of controversy.

EVERY FEDERAL GOVERNMENT IN CANADIAN HISTORY has had its own agenda-driven method of promoting Canada. Most recently, the Conservative government of Stephen Harper, which came to power in January 2006, offered a different vision of Canada from that upheld during the previous decade and a half of rule under the Liberal governments of Jean Chrétien and Paul Martin. Few expected the Conservative minority government to last long, but guided by Prime Minister Harper, the Conservatives survived through compromise and tenacity, eventually following through on their promise to reduce the influence of government in the lives of Canada by cutting taxes.[7] There was no shortage of criticism over the scrapping of the gun registry and the curtailing of the national census, but some of the fiercest attacks accused the Conservatives of tampering with Canadian history. The Harperites, they said, wanted to remake the nation and its collective belief system into something more warlike.

One of Harper's long-term goals was to shift some of the firm beliefs in Canadian society that had been created and codified by previous generations of Liberal governments.[8] The severing of the British connection, the promulgation of multiculturalism, and the embracing of peacekeeping over fighting wars were all signs, in the Conservatives' thinking, of narrow selectivity regarding

Canadian identity. Harper emphasized a more aggressive version of Canadian history, one that highlighted Canada as a proud member of allied forces and even resurrected the War of 1812 as an event that shaped the destiny of the future Canada. The government rewrote its citizenship guide, which now said of Vimy, "The Canadian Corps captured Vimy Ridge in April 1917, with 10,000 killed or wounded, securing the Canadians' reputation for valour as the 'shock troops of the British Empire.' One Canadian officer said: 'It was Canada from Atlantic to the Pacific on parade. . . . In those few moments I witnessed the birth of the nation.'" That the Harper government had a different idea of what to promote in Canadian history is not surprising, despite the widespread negative reaction it elicited from academics and journalists. The idea of Canada is constantly reconfigured and changed; it is imagined and negotiated, and the process is ongoing and at times confrontational. The new Liberal government of Justin Trudeau, elected in October 2015, has begun to reverse some of the Conservatives' policies, while also offering new ones, with an emphasis on reconciliation with First Nations and resettlement of Syrian refugees. Governments pick and choose what they prioritize; they all do it.

Vimy was one of the icons used by the Conservatives to support the notion that Canada was a country not just of peacekeepers but also of warriors. In addition to scores of journalists who scoffed at the Harper government's transparent actions, the most prominent critics were historians Ian McKay and journalist Jamie Swift, and cultural commentator and filmmaker Noah Richler. McKay and Swift accused the Conservatives of reshaping Canada into a "warrior nation," while Richler was equally adamant that Canada should not turn its back on its proud peacekeeping traditions.[9] In contrast, others warmly applauded the Conservatives' actions to

Cartoonist Raeside captures the politicized nature of the Vimy legend.

show that Canada was a country that had been forged in war and been irrevocably changed by it throughout the twentieth century.

The desire to nurture the story of Vimy was not unique to Ottawa. Groups like the Vimy Foundation seek to propagate the story. This private organization has worked in recent years to send students overseas and, more ambitiously, to raise millions of dollars to build a new interpretation centre at Vimy to be opened in 2017. The Vimy Foundation had some sway with the Harper government, and the new twenty-dollar bill, issued in 2012, features the Vimy Ridge Memorial. As part of the fundraising campaign, the Vimy Foundation asked all Canadians to donate a "Vimy" (twenty dollars).

In 2012, a few days before Vimy Day, the influential hockey commentator Don Cherry, who wears his nationalism as proudly as his signature suits, spoke from his pulpit on CBC's *Hockey Night in Canada*. Leading off his segment by showing a baseball cap imprinted with "Vimy: Birth of the Nation, 1917 to 2007," he enthused about the importance of educating his considerable audience about Vimy: "I know the Lefties don't like that, but it made us a nation." He summoned the familiar narrative of the French and British armies failing to capture the ridge despite sustaining horrendous casualties and, drawing on an oft-repeated and erroneous assumption, repeated how Sir Arthur Currie gathered his four divisions to take the position. He asserted, "Everybody says, it is the birth of the nation." And then, cleverly, he held up a hockey jersey with the Vimy memorial on the chest and noted, "This was the first Team Canada."[10] Cherry, whose grandfather had served at Vimy, was giving voice to what many Canadians believed.

A few days later, on Vimy Day 2012, Governor General David Johnston declared more solemnly, and with a prepared text, that Vimy represented the "birth of the nation."[11] The next year, on April 9, the only day of the year when the media focuses on Vimy, in a letter to the *National Post*, Joe O'Connor claimed that Vimy resonated because our "boring history," as he characterized it, of "maintaining law and order" paled in comparison to the American history of civil wars and revolutions. As a foil to this, Vimy Ridge leapt "off the pages of our sleep-inducing Grade 10 history textbooks."[12] Not everyone would agree with this characterization of Canadian history as dull, save for the war parts, or that this is the reason behind Vimy's appeal. But many more Canadians probably have no opinion either way, lacking much sense of the broad or narrow contours of Canadian history. For them, the past is just that—the past.

Moreover, it is important to note that such debates do not occur in Quebec. Vimy simply has little relevance there, and if it ever mattered, it has long since been left in the past. Symbols, icons, legends, and myths bind a nation together through an imagined community. They can also divide, deepen fissures, and stir anger. If Vimy represents the colony-to-nation arc in parts of English Canada, then it is an aggravating icon to those in French Canada who see the war as an event of disunity. During the war, Vimy could not be separated from conscription or, in Quebec, from the 1918 Easter Riots. However, the shaping of Vimy in the postwar years into a meaningful event, and later a nation-building one, required that conscription be shorn from the memory of Vimy and, for that matter, from social memory in English Canada. In Quebec, the opposite occurred, as conscription remained crucial to understanding French Canada's war and took on its own meaning in the politicized educational arena from the 1960s onward. The Easter Riots resonated fiercely in Quebec in the aftermath of the October Crisis, and they have been a staple in the long list of grievances of that province towards English Canada.

Never did the phrase "birth of the nation" find any purchase in Quebec schools, books, plays, or discourse. This stark difference between English and French Canada's perspectives was plainly evident in June 2016, when the Montreal borough of Outremont sought to change the name of one of its parks. The greenspace had been named Vimy Park in 1933 and now some residents proposed renaming it Jacques Parizeau Park. Parizeau, the key leader and architect of the Quebec sovereignty movement for the previous four decades before his death in 2015, was a divisive and reviled figure throughout much of the country, having made it his life's mission to tear Canada apart. A national controversy erupted over the insult of dropping the Vimy name, a symbol of unity, martial might, and shared history in the rest of the country. Historian Desmond Morton called the move a "political jab trying to stir up the English community,"[13] while long-time politician Bob Rae labelled it as an "insult pure and simple."[14] The online commentary surrounding the incident was predictably furious, swiping at Quebec's disrespectful desire to replace a tribute to the sacrifice of soldiers with the name of a traitor to the nation. While it appeared to Canadians outside Quebec, and Anglos within it, that the act was nothing short of offensive, it also revealed that the Vimy legend simply had little resonance in large parts of Quebec. The promise to name another public space in Montreal after Vimy did little to assuage critics' concerns, and the controversy revealed, again, how the Great War and Vimy continue to provoke both unity and division.

Despite the varying levels of interest in the idea of Vimy over time, the legend is not going to fade away any time soon. The one hundredth anniversary of the battle is in 2017, which is also the sesquicentennial (hundred and fiftieth anniversary) of Confederation. Tens of millions of dollars have been allocated to celebrate this anniversary of the nation's founding. Not to be outdone, groups like the Vimy Foundation and schools across the country, with government funding and private donations, are preparing to take several thousand teenagers overseas on a pilgrimage to the ridge. A new interpretation centre is to be opened around that time too, and there will be intense media coverage of the one hundredth anniversary. No veterans from the war remain, but the torch has been passed to a new generation that will possibly reinvent the idea of Vimy.

THE BATTLE OF VIMY RIDGE IS almost entirely ignored in the narratives of most nations. The Germans barely acknowledge it, or even try to frame it as part of a victory (in that the Arras offensive was stopped). This is, of course, nonsense, as the German loss of Vimy at that time was a clear-cut tactical defeat. The British, who fought on the ridge and to the south, grudgingly accept that Vimy was largely a Canadian battle, with the Corps' infantry and machine-gunners doing almost all of the fighting for the ridge. And the French have countless other battles that matter far more to them. Yet Canadians embrace Vimy as an event that matters to them, not because it does or doesn't resonate with the British, but because it is ours. This is similar to how Gallipoli belongs in constructed memory to the Australians and New Zealanders rather than to the British or French who committed far more soldiers to the campaign, and lost more too. That Canadians have elevated a battle that they deemed to be important at the time, and ever since, does not amount to a fallacy or an exercise in national navel-gazing. All nations have founding myths and enduring narratives. Vimy is one of our strongest.

Sir Ian Hamilton, British Great War army general, observed, "On the actual day of battle naked truths may be picked up for the asking; by the following morning they have already begun to get into uniforms."[15] One wonders, then, about "naked truths" 100 years later. They have not only changed uniforms many times but have also marched off in all directions. Canada's pains and efforts during the Great War have long since firmed up into a number of accepted narratives, and the importance ascribed to Vimy has become shorthand for the colony-to-nation arc. The pride of the Canadian Corps' battlefield prowess during and after the war led in turn to an inspiring story that bolstered the idea of the country and its people as different from Britain and other nations.

Vimy grew in importance over time, even though there were a handful of other crucial battles, especially Second Ypres, which also could have been woven into the story of how the war made Canada. Vimy became prominent not because Canada was born on that captured ridge. We can put that to rest. It was not. But there is no denying the impact of the Great War: it shook Canada to the core. Canadians sacrificed and bled like never before, and never again. The Second World War had a greater impact on the development of Canada, but that first catastrophe could never be equalled. The pride in the success of the Canadian Corps galvanized the disparate regions of Canada, and Canadians from across the Dominion were brought together in the Corps. The loyalty within the brotherhood of the trenches was a unifying force of great power. All of these things had to be marked and honoured.

Canada's struggle during the war fed into the protracted political evolution and constitutional reform throughout the 1920s that culminated in the Statute of Westminster. But the slower development of an English-Canadian sense of identity separate from Britain was a more gradual progression. It was driven by many aspects, such as the fear of an American cultural invasion, the development of national institutions and symbols, and a growing list of Canadian accomplishments. Canada struggled to find its way forward, but Vimy was not, initially, a beacon of nationhood. In the 1920s, Canada did not need the national unifying idea of Vimy, as the war was viewed most forcefully through the local experience, with the memorials and the names of the fallen dotting the country's towns and cities.

By the late 1920s, the idea of the war as a just and necessary sacrifice was threatened by the General Currie trial of 1928, American claims to victory, a resurgent peace movement, and the 1929 war books boom. This multi-pronged threat troubled many Canadians, who refused to let the war be cast as futile. The long delay to complete Allward's memorial excited little controversy, but the anticipation of its unveiling gathered in strength during the despair of the Depression. The 1936 pilgrimage was a crucial moment for the Vimy idea: it was propelled forward—by the King's speech, Empire-wide media coverage, and the material culture and memories it generated or simulated—to a celebrated place in Canadian history. Canadians imprinted on Vimy what they needed, and this impulse continued after 1936. The dull prose of the Great War gave way to the evocative poetry of Vimy.

The memorial that was raised to the dead had new values grafted onto it. Allward's sculptures and design spoke little to nation-building or an emerging Canadian sense of identity, but

Vimy became the new stalking horse for some nationalists who found idealized meanings in its bloody origins and, later, in its constructed memorial. The battle had all the right ingredients to fulfill a message of togetherness and nationalism. The unified assault on Vimy, with English, French, First Nations, and New Canadians taking part, was a story that, over time, gained in importance, perhaps because Canada struggled so fiercely with identity and language issues.

All nations seek out, create, elevate, and actively shape narratives on which to hang national stories or aspirations. As such a narrative, Vimy appeared, for a time, destined to have only a one-generation lifespan, as it lost relevance in the 1950s and early 1960s. With Canadians looking forward and not backwards for inspiration, Vimy was neither needed nor germane to the new Canada that arose out of the Second World War. And even that war, with its unambiguous meanings—the need to fight the murderous ideology of Fascism and the moral imperative to prevent another Holocaust—was largely pushed to the periphery as Canadians accepted the nation's new mantle as peacemaker. The celebration of military history and even the honouring of veterans became even more toxic in the late 1960s and early 1970s, despite a brief Great War resurgence during the fiftieth anniversary.

The Vimy idea resonated more strongly from the mid-1980s onward, driven by Berton's *Vimy* and Urquhart's *The Stone Carvers*, and it again found a prominent place in Canadian history, heritage, and identity. The legend of the battle and the memorial conflated over time with an emerging sense of nationalism and a desire to find icons from the past. Key anniversaries in 1967, 1992, and 2007 have also coincided with the anniversaries of Confederation. The twinning of these anniversaries—Canada's true, shaky birth in 1867 and its supposed rebirth in the cauldron of battle at Vimy fifty years later—allowed for the infusion and commingling of the one with the other. The long-lasting fascination with Vimy on the part of many Canadians was furthered by a resurgence of interest in the Great War, first in scholarship and study from the 1980s, both in Canada and internationally, and then as part of a broader reawakening since the fiftieth-anniversary celebrations of the Second World War in 1995. At that point, Canadians began to pay more attention to veterans and their military history. Vimy stormed back into public consciousness in 2007, as history bled into the present, and as Canadians drew upon their past for a renewed sense of identity and citizenship in the new century.

A different view of Canadian identity also emerged after the demise of traditional peacekeeping in the 1990s, with high-profile disasters in Somalia and Rwanda. And, more recently, Canadians have been more receptive to thinking about the Canadian Forces as consisting of both peacemakers and warriors after the ten-year-long war in Afghanistan.

To return to those hats and T-shirts at Vimy in 2007: the "birth of a nation" story was not a twenty-first-century fabrication but an idea with many rich meanings that stretched back to 1967, and to an era before that in different ways, through the pilgrimage and to the muddy slopes of Vimy in April 1917. The refurbishment of the Vimy memorial in 2007 allowed for a recasting of the Vimy legend to meet the spirit of a new age. Now, ten years later, as Canada closes upon the one hundredth anniversary of the battle and the sesquicentennial, Vimy remains a touchstone of remembrance and pride in large parts of the country.

THAT THE VICTORY AT VIMY RIDGE required a heartrending loss of lives further entrenched the idea of Vimy in the Canadian story. If we had not bled for Vimy, it would not matter today. Its enduring power is also tied up with layers of identity, contestations over the fears of a changing country, and nostalgia for a simple symbol of unity and martial power. A symbol's decline within a society usually occurs when the symbol is no longer useful to that society. Vimy has undergone rise and fall, but never to the point that it has been buried and lost. It cannot be, for Vimy, as captured in the memorial, represents the sacred dead who were scattered and then found. Vimy was not just associated with the old Canada or an embracing of Britishness. In places, it underpins Canadian nationalism. The Vimy legend was fused into the cultural landscape of not just war but identity. At the same time, the shaping of the public memory of Vimy cannot be attributed solely to government influence or to a concentrated effort to privilege the memory of the battle. Nor is it right to ascribe Vimy's endurance solely to the memorial, the King's 1936 speech, or Pearson's giving voice to the "birth of the nation" phrase. One critic of the Vimy myth believed that it could be laid firmly at the feet of Pierre Berton, remarking, "Berton's execrable [book] . . . has distorted this battle beyond anyone's ability to repair the damage."[16] This is not right either, as no book can have such an immense impact. Veterans, mythmakers, government officials, historians, playwrights, writers, and teachers, and over multiple generations, have all elevated Vimy into representing a crucial milestone in our development as a nation. The battle for Vimy Ridge lasted four days; the battle to shape the memory surrounding Vimy Ridge has endured for 100 years.

To stand on Vimy Ridge in the shadow of the memorial is to recognize that few other places in the world can make Canadians feel so proud. One also feels the weight of history and the presence of the dead. There is a palpable confluence of what we would like to forget and what we must remember. The ghosts walk this soil, as they did in Allward's dream, through the claustrophobic tunnels, treading carefully across the cratered battlegrounds, and with the faint touch of fingers on engraved names of the fallen. Vimy is also a place of enormous beauty. The pylons soar to the blue beyond, and the sculptures are intricate in their lines and evocative in their meanings. The creamy white and warm stone provokes strong emotion. The historical inscriptions are minimal, but the names of the missing 11,285 are monumental. Those searing marks in honour of the fallen are thousands of small scars on the stone, a reminder of the terrible loss and grief of the Great War. Tears come easily while standing on the memorial. These are not tears of uncontrollable grief but tears of something else, something more profound. They are the tears invoked by the memory of a grandfather, by a few lines from McCrae's "In Flanders Fields," and even by a surprising flash of patriotism. There is a power in the Vimy legend—the ridge, the memorial, the meaning—that is not easily put into words. The memorial is for the dead, but it is remade generation after generation by the living. Canada was indeed forever changed by the Great War, but Vimy did not make the nation. It was the nation that made Vimy.

ENDNOTES

CHAPTER 1: VIMY: BATTLE AND LEGEND

1. See Anna Grey, "Will Longstaff's Menin Gate at Midnight," *Journal of the Australian War Memorial* 12 (April 1988) 47–9.
2. Steven E. Sawell (ed.), *Into the Cauldron: Experiences of a CEF Infantry Officer during the Great War: Memoirs of Edward Stanley Sawell, M.C., V.D.* (Burlington, Ont.: self-published, 2009) 58.
3. Brian Douglas Tennyson, *Percy Willmot: A Cape Bretoner at War* (Sydney, N.S.: Cape Breton University Press, 2007) 159.
4. Donald Goodspeed, *The Road Past Vimy: The Canadian Corps, 1914–1918* (Toronto: Macmillan, 1969) 93.
5. CWM, PAM NA 9330 .F8 C2 L5, Col. D.C. Unwin Simson, *Little Known Facts and Difficulties in the Construction of the Canadian Memorial on Vimy Ridge, and Other Memorials in France and Belgium,* 17.

CHAPTER 2: VIMY BATTLEGROUND

1. A.F. Duguid, "Canada on Vimy Ridge" (Ottawa: *Canada Year Book*, 1936) 5.
2. Jonathan Krause, "The French Battle for Vimy Ridge, Spring 1915," *Journal of Military History* 77 (January 2013) 95.
3. Anthony Clayton, *Paths of Glory: The French Army, 1914–18* (London: Cassell, 2003) 70.

4. Joseph Hayes, *The Eighty-Fifth in France and Flanders* (Halifax: Royal Print and Litho, 1920) 39.

5. R.G. Moyle and Doug Owram, *Imperial Dreams and Colonial Realities* (Toronto: University of Toronto Press, 1988) 37–40.

6. J.C. Hopkins (ed.), *The Empire Club of Canada: Speeches, 1910–11* (Toronto: 1912) 110–16.

7. W.S. Wallace, "The Growth of Canadian National Feeling," *The Canadian Historical Review* 1.2 (June 1920) 136.

8. For the First Contingent, see Andrew Iarocci, *Shoestring Soldiers: The 1st Canadian Division at War, 1914–1915* (Toronto: University of Toronto Press, 2008).

9. Sylvie Lacombe, *La Rencontre de deux peuples élus: Comparaison des ambitions nationale et impériale au Canada entre 1868 et 1920* (Sainte-Foy, Qué.: Presses de l'Université Laval, 2002).

10. Desmond Morton, "French Canada and the Canadian Militia, 1868–1914," *Social History* 3 (June 1969) 32–50.

11. J.L. Granatstein and Desmond Morton, *Canada and the Two World Wars* (Toronto: Key Porter Books, 2003) 25.

12. *Chris Sharpe*, "Enlistment in the Canadian Expeditionary Force 1914–1918: A Re-Evaluation," *Canadian Military History* 24.1 (2015) 32–4; Elizabeth Armstrong, *The Crisis of Quebec 1914–1918* (New York, 1937) 39; Jonathan F. Vance, "Provincial Patterns of Enlistment in the Canadian Expeditionary Force," *Canadian Military History* 17.2 (Spring 2008) 75–8.

13. Peter Broznitsky, "For King, Not Tsar: Identifying Ukrainians in the Canadian Expeditionary Force, 1914–1918," *Canadian Military History* 17.3 (2008) 21–30; Timothy Winegard, *For King and Kanata: Canadian Indians and the First World War* (Winnipeg: University of Manitoba Press, 2012).

14. Peter G. Rogers (ed.), *Gunner Ferguson's Diary* (Hantsport, N.S.: Lancelot Press, 1985) 19.

15. George Goodwin, *Why Stay We Here?: Odyssey of a Canadian Infantry Officer in France in World War I* (Victoria, B.C.: Godwin Books (reprint), 2002) 45.

16. Colonel George Nasmith, *Canada's Sons in the World War*, volume I (Toronto: The John C. Winston Co., 1919), foreword by Arthur Currie, iv.

17. See Tim Cook, "Documenting War & Forging Reputations: Sir Max Aitken and the Canadian War Records Office in the First World War," *War in History* 10.3 (2003) 265–95.

18. Desmond Morton, *When Your Number's Up: The Canadian Soldier in the First World War* (Toronto: Random House of Canada, 1993) 278. Also see, *James Wood, Militia Myths: Ideas of the Canadian Citizen Soldier, 1896–1921* (Vancouver: UBC Press, 2010).

19. See Carolyn Holbrook, *ANZAC: The Unauthorised Biography* (Canberra: University of New South Wales, 2014).

20. Tim Cook, "Wet Canteens and Worrying Mothers: Soldiers and Temperance Groups in the Great War," *Social History* 35.70 (June 2003) 311–30; Tim Cook, "Black-Hearted Traitors, Crucified Martyrs, and the Leaning Virgin: The Role of Rumor and the Great War Canadian Soldier," in Michael Neiberg and Jennifer Keene (ed.), *Finding Common Ground: New Directions in First World War Studies* (Leiden: Brill Academic Publishers, 2010) 21–42.

21. LAC, MG 30 E52, Talbot Papineau collection, v. 2, Talbot Papineau to Mother, 23 April 1915.

22. McGill University Archives, Arthur Currie/ Hugh Urquhart collection, MG4027, box 1, file 13, Response to Circular letter, Ox Webber, n.d. [ca. 1934].

23. For Gallipoli, see Tim Travers, *Gallipoli 1915* (London: Tempus, 2001).

24. Jeffrey Williams, *Byng of Vimy: General and Governor General* (London: Leo Cooper in association with Secker & Warburg, 1983) 115.

25. CWM, 20040015-005, Lawrence Rogers papers, letter, 9 June 1916.

26. Tim Cook, *At the Sharp End: Canadians Fighting the Great War, 1914–1916* (Toronto: Viking, 2007) 351.

27. War Diary [hereafter WD], Canadian Corps Artillery, June 1916, Report of Operations of Artillery Canadian Corps, various appendices.

28. Susan McGrath (ed.), *The Long Sadness: World War I Diary of William Hannaford Ball* (Thousand Oaks: Seanachie Press, 2014) 32–3.

29. Tennyson, *Percy Willmot: A Cape Bretoner at War*, 140.

30. G.W.L. Nicholson, *Canadian Expeditionary Force, 1914–1919: Official History of the Canadian Army in the First World War* (Ottawa: Queen's Printer, 1962) 172.

31. David Charles Gregory Campbell, "The Divisional Experience in the C.E.F.: A Social and Operational History of the 2nd Canadian Division, 1915–1918," (PhD dissertation: Calgary University, 2003) 44.

32. Library Archives Canada [hereafter LAC], RG 9, v. 4044, 3/5, Notes on Recent Operations, 29 October 1915.

33. McGrath (ed.), *The Long Sadness*, 47–8.

34. R.G. Kentner, *Some Recollections of the Battles of World War I* (self-published, 1995) 18.

35. Alexander McKee, *Vimy Ridge* (London: Souvenir Press, 1966) 33.

36. Canada's History, http://greatwaralbum.ca/Great-War-Album/About-the-Great-War/Unrest-on-the-homefront/Francis-Cumming

37. G.R. Stevens, *A City Goes to War* (Brampton, Ont: Charters Pub, 1964) 31.

38. Charles S. Cameron, *War! What of It!* (self-published, 2008) 23.

39. Bill Rawling, *Surviving Trench Warfare: Technology and the Canadian Corps, 1914–1918* (Toronto: University of Toronto Press, 1992).

40. A.M.J. Hyatt, *General Sir Arthur Currie: A Military Biography* (Toronto: University of Toronto Press, 1987) 60–1.

41. RG 9, v. 4142, 6/2, "Notes on French Attacks," [Currie's report].

42. Robert Doughty, *Pyrrhic Victory: French Strategy and*

Operations in the Great War (Cambridge: Belknap Press of Harvard University Press, 2005) 1.

43. David Woodward, *Lloyd George and the Generals* (London: Associated University Press, 1983) 136.

44. Jeremy Black, *The Great War and the Making of the Modern World* (London: Continuum, 2011) 134.

45. John Grigg, *Lloyd George: War Leader, 1916–1918* (London: Penguin Books, 2003) 40–3; Andrew Suttie, *Rewriting the First World War: Lloyd George, Politics and Strategy, 1914–18* (Basingstoke: Palgrave Macmillan, 2005) 99–119.

46. Don Farr, *The Silent General: Horne of the First Army* (Solihull, U.K.: Helion and Company, 2006) 150; R.C. Fetherstonhaugh, *The 24th Battalion, CEF, Victoria Rifles of Canada, 1914–1919, Regimental History* (Montreal: Gazette Printing Company 1930) 142; D.J. Corrigall, *The History of the Twentieth Canadian Battalion (Central Ontario Regiment) Canadian Expeditionary Force, in the Great War, 1914–1918* (Toronto : Stone & Cox, 1935) 109; Gary Sheffield, *The Chief: Douglas Haig and the British Army* (London: Aurum Press Ltd, 2011) 204.

47. Ernst Junger, *The Storm of Steel* (London: Chatto & Windus, 1929) 126.

48. Rupprecht von Bayern, Eugeun von Frauenholz, *Mein Kriegstage-buch: Vol. II* (Munich: Deutsher National Verlag, 1929) 138.

49. McKee, *Vimy Ridge*, 75.

50. Brereton Greenhous and Stephen J. Harris, *Canada and the Battle of Vimy Ridge, 9–12 April 1917* (Montreal: Art Global, 1992) 70.

51. Heinz Hagenlucke, "The German High Command," Peter Liddle, *Passchendaele in Perspective* (London: Leo Cooper, 1997) 48.

CHAPTER 3: PREPARING THE ASSAULT

1. Douglas E. Delaney, "Mentoring the Canadian Corps: Imperial Officers and the Canadian Expeditionary Force, 1914–1918." *Journal of Military History*, Vol. 77, No. 3 (July 2013), 931–53.

2. William F. Stewart, *The Embattled General: Sir Richard Turner and the First World War* (Montreal: McGill-Queen's University Press, 2015).

3. Patrick Brennan, "Major-General David Watson: A Critical Appraisal of Canadian Generalship in the Great War," in Andrew B. Godefroy (ed.), *Great War Commands: Historical Perspectives on Canadian Army Leadership, 1914–1918* (Kingston: Canadian Defence Academy Press, 2010).

4. McGill University Archives, Arthur Currie/ Hugh Urquhart collection, MG4027, General Ironside Comments, 18 December 1934, 12.

5. Patrick Brennan, "Julian Byng and Leadership in the Canadian Corps," in Geoffrey Hayes, Andrew Iarocci, Mike Bechthold (eds.), *Vimy Ridge: A Canadian Reassessment* (Waterloo: Wilfrid Laurier University Press, 2007) 90.

6. Brennan, "Julian Byng and Leadership in the Canadian Corps," in Hayes, et al., *Vimy Ridge*, 91.

7. Sanders Marble Paul Harris, "British Military Thought and Operational Method on the Western Front, 1915-1917," *War in History* 15.1 (2008): 34.

8. RG 9, v. 4136, 24/3, Canadian Corps G. 340, 27 December 1916.

9. Charles S. Cameron, *War! What of It!* (self-published, 2008) 17.

10. Aaron Taylor Miedema, *Bayonets and Blobsticks: The Canadian Experience of Close Combat, 1915–1918* (Kingston: Legacy Books Press, 2011).

11. Bruce Cane (ed.), *It Made You Think of Home: The Haunting Journal of Deward Barnes, CEF 1916–1919* (Toronto: Dundurn Press, 2004) 64.

12. WD, 4th Division, Appendix II, Report of Operations, 1.

13. "Editorial," *Canadian Defence Quarterly* 2.4 (July 1925) 322.

14. John Swettenham, *McNaughton,* volume I (Toronto: Ryerson Press, 1968), 136.

15. Albert Palazzo, "The British Army's Counter-Battery Staff Office and Control of the Enemy in World War I," *The Journal of Military History* 63 (1999) 55–74.

16. For Canadian flyers in the Great War, see S.F. Wise, *Canadian Airmen and the First World War* (Toronto: University of Toronto Press, 1980).

17. Canadian Bank of Commerce, *Letters from the Front: being a record of the part played by officers of the Bank in the Great War, 1914–1919* (Toronto: Southam Press, 1920) 197.

18. See RG 9, III, v. 3922, 8/4, Notes on Counter Battery Work in Connection with the Capture of Vimy Ridge.

19. Jonathan Nicholls, *Cheerful Sacrifice: The Battle of Arras, 1917* (London: Cooper, 1993) 36.

20. CWM, 20110042-002, Robert Miller, diary, 22 March 1917.

21. See Peter Hart, *Bloody April: Slaughter over the Skies in Arras 1917* (London: McArthur & Company, 2005).

22. CWM, 20030153-001, Lieutenant J.W. McClung, diary, 6 April 1917.

23. Simon Robbins, *The First World War Letters of General Lord Horne* (Stroud: The History Press for the Army Records Society, 2009), 1–4; David Monger, "'No mere silent commander'? Henry Horne and the Mentality of Command during the First World War," *Historical Research*, 82:216 (2007), 341–4.

24. Robbins, *Letters of General Lord Horne*, 3. Simon Robbins, *British Generalship during the Great War: The Military Career of Sir Henry Horne (1861–1929)* (Farnham, U.K.: Ashgate, 2010).

25. CWM, MHRC, *First Army Administrative Report on the Vimy Ridge Operations*, 26.

26. Duguid, "Canada on Vimy Ridge," 12.

27. Lt. Col. C.S. Grafton, *The Canadian "Emma Gees": A History of the Canadian Machine Gun Corps* (London, Ont.: Canadian Machine Gun Corps Association, 1938) 63.

28. [no author], *The Story of the Sixty-Sixth C.F.A.* (Edinburgh: Turnbull & Spears for the Sixty-Sixth Battery, C.F.A., 1919) 47.

29. CWM, MHRC, *First Army Administrative Report on the Vimy Ridge Operations*, 11.

30. LAC, RG 24, v. 1834, file 8-41, Report on Ordnance of Canadian Corps; Ibid., 1st Tramway Company, Historical Record.

31. Robbins, *Letters of General Lord Horne*, 7.

32. CWM, MHRC, *First Army Administrative Report on the Vimy Ridge Operations*, 19.

33. Greenhous and Harris, *Vimy*, 74.

34. Andrew Scott McEwen, "'Maintaining the Mobility of the Corps': Horses, Mules, and the Canadian Army Veterinary Corps in the Great War," (PhD dissertation: Calgary University, 2016) 325–9.

35. CWM, 20110042-002, diary, 1 March 1917 (page 47).

36. RG 9, III, v. 3846, folder 51, file 5, Report on Operations of Canadian Corps against Vimy Ridge, 9.

37. Milly Walsh and John Callan (eds.), *We're Not Dead Yet: The First World War Diary of Private Bert Cooke* (Vanwell, 2004) 103.

38. There were thirteen tunnels on the Canadian front, and another one, the Souchez tunnel under the northern end of the Ridge, was on the 24th British Infantry Division's front.

39. Michael Boire, "The Underground War: Military Mining Operations in Support of the Attack on Vimy Ridge, 9 April 1917," *Canadian Military History* 1. 1–2 (1992) 16–19.

40. WD, 4th Division, Appendix II, Report of Operations, 2.

41. Len Willans, *The Lost Memoirs of a Canadian Soldier: World War I Diary Entries and Letters* (Unknown place of publication: Gail Booth, 2012) 33.

42. A.J. Kerry and W.A. McDill, The *History of the Corps of Royal Canadian Engineers* (Ottawa: Military Engineers Association of Canada, 1962) 123.

43. Robert F. Zubkowski, *As Long as Faith and Freedom Last* (Calgary: Bunker to Bunker, 2003) 251.

44. Bill Freeman and Richard Nielsen, *Far from Home: Canadians in the First World War* (Toronto: McGraw-Hill Ryerson, 1999) 102.

45. CWM, MHRC, *SS143, Instructions for the Training of Platoons for Offensive Action*, and *SS144, The Normal Formation for the Attack*.

46. See, for example, CWM, Sir Arthur Currie papers, 58A.1.59.4, Report of Operations Carried Out by the 1st Canadian Division, April 9th–May 5th, 1917.

47. S.G. Bennett, *The 4th Canadian Mounted Rifles, 1914–1919* (Toronto: Murray Printing Co., 1926) 47.

48. LAC, MG 30 E300, Victor Odlum papers, v. 21, Odlum to Nelson, 4 November 1917.

49. RG 24, v. 1820, file GAQ 5-3, The Battle of Vimy Ridge, 9–14th April, 1917.

50. Robert England, M.C., *Recollections of a Nonagenarian of Service in the Royal Canadian Regiment (1916–19)* (self-published, 1983) 2.

51. Greenhous and Harris, *Vimy*, 83.

52. WD, 4th Division, Appendix II, Report of Operations, 5.

53. Willans, *The Lost Memoirs*, 37.

54. LAC, MG 30 E241, D.E. Macintyre papers, diary, 13 March 1917.

55. For raiding, see Colin Garnett, "Butcher and Bolt: Canadian Trench Raiding during the Great War," (Master's thesis: Carleton University, 2011).

56. RG 24, v. 1826, GAQ 5-89, Raids, Canadian Corps, Summary of Raids.

57. Harold Peat, *Private Peat* (New York: Grosset and Dunlap Pub., 1917) 114–15.

58. H.F. Wood, *Vimy!* (Toronto: Macmillan of Canada, 1967) 29.

59. E.L.M. Burns, *General Mud: Memoirs of Two World Wars* (Toronto: Clarke, Irwin, 1970), 40.

60. Victor W. Wheeler, *The 50th Battalion in No Man's Land* (Ottawa: CEF Books, 2000) 71.

61. RG 9, IIII, v. 3858, 83/4, Preliminary Report on the 4th Canadian Division Gas Raid.

62. For these failures, see Tim Cook, "A Proper Slaughter: The March 1917 Gas Raid," *Canadian Military History* 8.2 (Spring 1999) 7–23.

63. McKee, *Vimy Ridge*, 74.

64. CWM, 19990026-016, Captain Keith Campbell Macgowan, letter to mother, 2–3 April 1917.

65. Farr, *The Silent General*, 153.

66. Roy Ito, *We Went to War: The Story of the Japanese Canadians Who Served during the First and Second World Wars* (Stittsville, Ont.: Canada's Wings, 1984) 55.

67. Bennett, *The 4th Canadian Mounted Rifles*, 51.

68. RG 9, v. 4958, WD, Royal Artillery, Canadian Corps, Artillery Instructions No. 1, 28 March 1917.

69. RG 9, v. 3846, Report of Operations of Canadian Corps against Vimy Ridge, Appendix A, Artillery Plan.

70. RG 9, v. 3846, Report of Operations of Canadian Corps against Vimy Ridge, Appendix A, Artillery Plan, Appendix G.1.

71. Swettenham, *McNaughton*, 90; Duguid, "Canada on Vimy Ridge," 12.

72. A.G.L. McNaughton, "The Development of Artillery in the Great War," *Canadian Defence Quarterly* VI.2 (January 1929) 164.

73. Tim Cook, "The Gunners of Vimy," in Hayes, et al., *Vimy Ridge*, 113.

74. LAC, MG 30 E50, Battle of Arras, 1917, by the German General Staff, translated by Elmer Jones.

75. Thomas Weber, *Hitler's First War: Adolf Hitler, the Men of the List Regiment, and the First World War* (Oxford: Oxford University Press, 2011).

76. RG 24, v. 1825, file GAQ 5-64, Army Historical Section, "The Significance of Vimy," (1935) 10.

77. RG 9, v. 3846, 51/7, Notes on the Vimy Ridge Operations by General Radcliffe, 19; RG 24, v. 1819, file 5-2, Canadian Corps Operations.

78. CWM, 19810467-005, Second-Lieutenant Victor John Nixon, Daily Reminder, 8 April 1917.

79. RG 9, v. 3846, folder 51, file 5, Report on Operations of Canadian Corps against Vimy Ridge, 10.

80. See the DVD, *One of Our Mines Is Missing*, by the Durand Group. Phillip Robinson and Nigel Cave, "The Vimy Subways and Grange Tunnel," The Western Front Association *Stand To!* 99, 20.

81. WD, 4th Division, Appendix B, Report of the 4th Division at Vimy, 21.

82. LAC, R 8258, Gregory Clark papers, v. 4, file 4-5, Gregory to father, 6 April 1917.

83. Canadian Letters and Images Project [hereafter CLIP], David McLean, letter, 5 April 1917.

CHAPTER 4: OVER THE TOP

1. WD, 5th CMR, 8 April 1917.

2. General Sir Martin Farndale, *History of the Royal Regiment of Artillery, Western Front, 1914–1918* (London: The Royal Artillery Institution, 1986) 175.

3. Tennyson, *Percy Willmot*, 161.

4. McKee, *Vimy Ridge*, 48.

5. Sawell (ed.), *Into the Cauldron*, 62.

6. Cook, *At the Sharp End*, 440.

7. WD, 12th Infantry Brigade, April 1917, Appendix 1, First Army diary log.

8. LAC, MG 30 E379, Hubert Morris papers, memoir, "The Story of My 3½ Years in World War I," 25.

9. William D. Mathieson, *My Grandfather's War: Canadians Remember the First World War, 1914–1918* (Toronto: Macmillan of Canada, 1981) 116.

10. Lt. Col. C.S. Grafton, *The Canadian "Emma Gees,"* 65–6; WD, 4th Division, Appendix II, Report of Operations, 4.

11. WD, Report of Operations of Canadian Corps against Vimy Ridge, 5.

12. Burns, *General Mud*, 43.

13. CWM, 20070073-042 (stored in file 20070073-007), letter, April 13 1917.

14. RG 9, v. 3922, 8/2, Notes on Counter Battery Work in Connection with the Capture of Vimy Ridge.

15. Bernd Ulrich and Benjamin Ziemann, *German Soldiers in the Great War: Letters and Eyewitness Accounts* (London: Pen & Sword, 2010) 75.

16. Greenhous and Harris, *Vimy*, 90.

17. RG 9, v. 4051, 19/2, 15th Summary of Operations, from 9 to 20 April 1917.

18. Nicholls, *Cheerful Sacrifice*, 79.

19. Kim Beattie, *48th Highlanders of Canada, 1891–1928* (Toronto: Southam Press, 1932) 225–6.

20. Tim Cook, *Shock Troops: Canadians Fighting the Great War, 1917–1918* (Toronto: Viking, 2008) 103.

21. WD, 14th Battalion, Report of Operations, 25 April 1917.

22. WD, 14th Battalion, Report of Operations, 25 April 1917.

23. R.C. Fetherstonhaugh, *The Royal Montreal Regiment, 1883–1933* (Westmount: The Regiment, 1936) 148.

24. Ulrich and Ziemann, *German Soldiers in the Great War*, 75.

25. WD, 16th Battalion, 11 April 1917.

26. Daniel Dancocks, *Gallant Canadians: The Story of the Tenth Canadian Infantry Battalion, 1914–1919* (Toronto: Penguin, 1990) 115.

27. *Letters from the Front*, 202.

28. WD, 5th Battalion, Summary of Operations, 9 April 1917.

29. WD, 5th Battalion, Summary of Operations, 9 April 1917.

30. WD, 5th Battalion, Summary of Operations, 9 April 1917.

31. RG 24, v. 20409, 958.009 (D40), Transcripts with Archie McWade, n.d. [early 1960s].

32. Armine Norris, *Mainly for Mother* (Toronto: Ryerson Press, 1919) 117.

33. David Campbell, "2nd Canadian Division: A 'Most Spectacular Battle,'" in Hayes, et al., *Vimy Ridge*, 172.

34. Generalleutnant Alfred Dieterich, "The German 79th Reserve Infantry Division in the Battle of Vimy Ridge, April 1917," *Canadian Military History* 15.1 (Winter 2006) 76.

35. LAC, MG 30 E156, Robert N. Clements, "Merry Hell: The Story of the 25th Battalion," 255.

36. WD, 5th Brigade, Summary of Battle, 8–18 April 1917.

37. Peter Barton and Jeremy Banning, *Vimy Ridge and Arras* (Toronto: Dundurn, 2010) 111.

38. Dancocks, *Gallant Canadians*, 114.

39. Sawell (ed.), *Into the Cauldron*, 58.

40. Stephen J. Nichols, *Ordinary Heroes: Eastern Ontario's 21st Battalion C.E.F. in the Great War* (Almonte, Ont: Nichol, 2008) 115.

41. Sawell (ed.), *Into the Cauldron*, 59–60.

42. Nicholson, *CEF*, 255.

43. WD, 22nd Battalion, 9 April 1917.

44. F.B. MacDonald and John J. Gardiner, *The Twenty-Fifth Battalion: Nova Scotia's Famous Regiment in World War One* (Sydney, N.S.: J. Chadwick, 1985) 25.

45. RG 9, v. 3846, 51/7, Notes on the Vimy Ridge Operations by General Radcliffe, 14.

46. James MacGregor, *MacGregor, V.C.* (Victoria, B.C.: Victoria Pub., 2002) 66–7.

47. WD, 2nd CMR, Operations against Vimy Ridge.

48. Wood, *Vimy!*, 142.

49. WD, 1st CMR, Report of Operations; WD, 1st CMR, 12 April 1917.

50. WD, 4th CMR, Preliminary Instructions for Attack.

51. LAC, R 8258, Gregory Clark papers, v. 2, file 2-3, memoir/diary, Vimy section, unnumbered.

52. Greenhous and Harris, *Vimy*, 100.

53. CWM, 20030153-001, John Wesley McClung, diary, 9 April 1917.

54. WD, 42nd Battalion, 9 April 1917.

55. WD, 42nd Battalion, 9 April 1917; WD, Royal Canadian Regiment, 9 April 1917.

56. Sawell (ed.), *Into the Cauldron*, 64.

57. Robbins, *Letters of General Lord Horne*, 209–11.

58. LAC, MG 30 E300, Victor Odlum papers, v. 20, Battle of Vimy Ridge, 26 and 67; Geoffrey Jackson, "The British Empire on the Western Front: A Transnational Study of the 62nd West Riding Division and the Canadian 4th Division" (PhD dissertation: Calgary University, 2013) 141, 149.

59. L.M. Gould, *From B.C. to Baisieux: Being the Narrative of the 102nd Battalion* (Victoria: Thos. R. Cusack Presses, 1919) 50.

60. WD, 54th Battalion, 9 April 1917; WD, Report of Operations of Canadian Corps against Vimy Ridge, 12.

61. Wood, *Vimy!*, 140–1.

62. WD, 4th Canadian Division, April 1917, Report of Operations, Appendix B.

63. Andrew Godefroy, "The 4th Canadian Division: Trenches Should Never Be Saved," in Hayes, et al., *Vimy Ridge*, 219.

64. Sheldon and Cave, *The Battle for Vimy Ridge, 1917*, 151.

65. RG 9, v. 4943, War Diary, Report of Operations, 78th Battalion.

66. CWM, 58 A 1 141.3, "The Story of the Fourth Overseas Siege Battery in the Great War," 8.

67. WD, 4th Division, Appendix II, Report of Operations, 5.

68. Greenhous and Harris, *Vimy*, 114.

69. See Tim Cook, "The Politics of Surrender: Canadian Soldiers and the Killing of Prisoners in the Great War," *Journal of Military History* 70.3 (July 2006) 637–65; Wood, *Vimy!*, 130.

70. LAC, MG 30 E430, William Green memoirs, 4.

71. WD, 3rd Battalion, Narrative of Operations against Vimy Ridge.

72. Nicholls, *Cheerful Sacrifice*, 80.

73. WD, 1st Division, 9 April 1917.

74. H.R.N. Clyne, *Vancouver's 29th: A Chronicle of the 29th in Flanders Fields* (Vancouver, B.C.: Tobin's Tigers Association, 1964) 31–2.

75. Marjorie Barron Norris (ed.), *Medicine and Duty: The World War I Memoir of Captain Harold W. McGill, Medical Officer,*

31st Battalion, C.E.F. (Calgary: University of Calgary Press, 2007) 268.

76. WD, 31st Battalion, Report of Operations, 9 April 1917.
77. CWM, 20110042-002, Robert Miller collection, diary, 10 April 1917.
78. Sheldon and Cave, *The Battle for Vimy Ridge, 1917*, 98.
79. Norris (ed.), *Medicine and Duty*, 261.
80. Greenhous and Harris, *Vimy*, 98.
81. LAC, RG 41, v. 11. 27th Battalion, W.J. Sheppard, 1/9–10.
82. Wood, *Vimy!*, 141.
83. CWM, 19990026-016, Captain Keith Campbell Macgowan, letter to mother, 15 April 1917.
84. Lt. Col. Joseph Hayes, *The 85th in France and Flanders* (Halifax: Royal Print, 1920) 53.
85. London Gazette, No. 30234, Order 1074, 17 September 1917.
86. Hayes, *The 85th in France and Flanders*, 54.
87. Lieutenant-Colonel Robert William, "The 85th Canadian Infantry Battalion and First Contact with the Enemy at Vimy Ridge, 9–14 April 1917," *Canadian Army Journal* 8.1 (Winter 2005) 80.
88. Nicholson, *CEF*, 261; also Sheldon and Cave, *The Battle for Vimy Ridge, 1917*, 36.
89. RG 24, v. 20409, 958.009 (D40), Diary of A.F. Brayman.

CHAPTER 5: VIMY AFTERMATH
1. CWM, 20100067-002, Albert Percy Menzies, letter to Garnet Menzies, 17 April 1917.
2. J. Clinton Morrison, *Hell Upon Earth: A Personal Account of Prince Edward Island Soldiers in the Great War, 1914–1918* (Summerside: self-published, 1995) 119.
3. CLIP, Maurice Bracewell, memoir, unpaginated.
4. Barton and Banning, *Vimy Ridge and Arras*, 114.
5. Mathieson, *My Grandfather's War*, 119.
6. CWM, 19800218-014, Joseph Harrison MacFarlane, diary, 9 April 1917.

7. RG 24, v. 1834, file 8-41, Extract from War Diary of the Chief Engineer, April 1917.

8. CWM, 20060105-001, Private Andrew Coulter, diary, 9 April 1917.

9. Veterans Affairs Canada, http://www.veterans.gc.ca/eng/ remembrance/those-who-served/diaries-letters-stories/first-world-war/Bellenden.

10. CWM, 19910028-001, Howard Scott, diary, 9–12 April 1917.

11. CLIP, Amos William Mayse to Betty and children, 5 July 1917.

12. LAC, MG 30 E379, Hubert Morris papers, memoir, "The Story of My 3½ Years in World War I," 25.

13. Reginald Roy (ed.), *The Journal of Private Fraser* (Victoria: Sono Nis Press, 1985) 268.

14. Hayes, *The 85th in France and Flanders*, 55.

15. Philip Longworth, *The Unending Vigil: A History of the Commonwealth War Graves Commission* (London: Constable, 1967) 22.

16. Dancocks, *Gallant Canadians*, 115.

17. Wilfrid Bovey, "Vimy—The Battle and the Cost," *The Legionary* (May 1954) 16.

18. Nicholson, *CEF*, 265.

19. LAC, MG 30 E241, D.E. Macintyre papers, diary, 11 April 1917.

20. Grafton, *The Canadian "Emma Gees,"* 68.

21. Duguid, "Canada on Vimy Ridge," 11; WD, 2nd Canadian Divisional Artillery, 10 April 1917.

22. Valerie Teed (ed.), *Uncle Cy's War* (Fredericton, N.B.: Goose Lane Editions and New Brunswick Military Heritage Project, 2009) 193.

23. CWM, 20080132-001, Leonard Cuff, letter, 28 April 1917.

24. Thomas Smith, "Curley Christian," *The Canadian Encyclopedia*, accessed online.

25. Wheeler, *The 50th Battalion in No Man's Land*, 95.

26. WD, Report of Operations of Canadian Corps against Vimy Ridge, 17.

27. Kentner, *Some Recollections of the Battles of World War I*, 41.

28. Jack Sheldon, *The German Army on Vimy Ridge, 1914–1917* (Barnsley: Pen and Sword, 2008) 320.

29. James McWilliams and R. James Steel, *The Suicide Battalion* (Edmonton: Hurtig, 1978) 84.

30. Wheeler, *The 50th Battalion in No Man's Land*, 99.

31. McWilliams and Steel, *The Suicide Battalion*, 84.

32. CWM, 19810467-005, Victor John Nixon, Daily Reminder diary, 12 April 1917.

33. Wood, *Vimy!*, 160.

34. RG 24, v.1819, file 5-2, extract from memoir of Marshal von Hindenburg and Ludendorff's *My Memoirs, 1914–1918*.

35. Farr, *The Silent General*, 157.

36. Gary Sheffield, "Haig and the British Expeditionary Force in 1917," in Gary Sheffield, *Command and Morale: The British Army on the Western Front, 1914–1918* (Barnsley: Praetorian Press, 2014) 104.

37. Lawrence James, *Imperial Warrior: The Life and Times of Field Marshal Viscount Allenby, 1861–1936* (London: Weidenfeld and Nicolson, 1993) 101.

38. Clayton, *Paths of Glory*, 125.

39. Doughty, *Pyrrhic Victory*, 353–4.

40. Gary Sheffield and John Bourne, *Douglas Haig: War Diaries and Letters, 1914–1918* (London: Weidenfeld and Nicolson, 2005) 285.

41. Farr, *The Silent General*, 164.

42. Clayton, *Paths of Glory*, 130.

43. See Leonard Smith, *The Embattled Self: French Soldiers' Testimony of the Great War* (Ithaca: Cornell University Press, 2007) 161-2; Guy Pedroncini, *Les mutineries de 1917* (Paris: Presses universitaires de France, 1967).

44. Nicholls, *Cheerful Sacrifice*, 210–11.

CHAPTER 6: VIMY'S IMPACT

1. Dale McClare (ed.), *The Letters of a Young Canadian Soldier During World War I* (Kentville: Brook House Press, 2000) 107.

2. A.F. Duguid, *Official History of the Canadian Forces in the Great War, 1914–1919* (Ottawa: King's Printer, 1938) 701.

3. CWM, 20050172-004, Horace Hubert Forster Dibblee, diary, April 1917.

4. CWM, 19730295-007, Walter Draycot papers, The Story of Vimy Ridge, 1.

5. CLIP, G.H. Tripp, letter, 19 April 1917.

6. Jeffrey Booth (ed.), *Opened by Censor* (St. Thomas, Ont.: Elgin Military Museum, 2008) 149.

7. CWM, 20030142-001, William Hendrie Hay papers, Pile to Hay, 23 February 1917.

8. WD, Report of Operations of Canadian Corps against Vimy Ridge, 31.

9. Nicholls, *Cheerful Sacrifice*, 89.

10. C.B. Topp, *The 42nd Battalion, CEF: Royal Highlanders of Canada in the Great War* (Montreal: Gazette Printing, 1931) 237.

11. Nicholson, *CEF*, 261

12. RG 24, v. 1819, file 5-2, Canadian Corps Operations; RG 24, v. 1844, file GAD 11-11D, Total Casualties, All Units, Canadian Corps, April 1917.

13. CWM, 19820623-002, 58A 1 31.13, Watson to Rowley, 14 April 1917.

14. Nichols, *Ordinary Heroes*, 118.

15. *Letters from the Front*, 204.

16. RG 24, v. 4628, file 7-1.3, Memorial Cross, 27 June 1924.

17. *Letters from the Front*, 227.

18. *Edmonton Journal*, 9 April 1917.

19. *The Globe*, 10 April 1917; Vancouver *Sun*, 10 April 1917.

20. Jonathan Vance, "Battle Verse: Poetry and Nationalism after Vimy Ridge," in Hayes, et al., *Vimy Ridge*, 265.

21. *Le Devoir*, 10 April 1917.

22. Michael Valpy, "Setting Legend in Stone," *The Globe and Mail*, 7 April 2007, F5.

23. CWM, 20080038-003, William Antliff, letters from mother, 9 and 12 April 1917.

24. Ito, *We Went to War*, 63.

25. Kevin R. Shackleton, *Second to None: The Fighting 58th Battalion of the Canadian Expeditionary Force* (Toronto: Dundurn Press, 2002) 130.

26. O.C.S. Wallace (ed.), *From Montreal to Vimy Ridge and Beyond* (Toronto: McClelland, 1917) x.

27. RG 24, v.1819, file 5-2, Extract of Sir Douglas Haig's Despatch.

28. Duguid, "Canada on Vimy Ridge," 13.

29. Black, *The Great War and the Making of the Modern World*, 145.

30. CWM, 20080132-001, Leonard Cuff, 28 April 1917.

31. W.R. Young, "Conscription, Rural Depopulation, and the Farmers of Ontario, 1917–19," *Canadian Historical Review* 53.3 (1972) 289–320.

32. Robert Borden, *Robert Laird Borden: His Memoirs* (Toronto: Macmillan Co. of Canada, 1938) volume II, 678.

33. Robert MacGregor Dawson, *The Development of Dominion Status, 1900–1936* (London: Frank Cass, 1965).

34. Margaret MacMillan, "Sibling Rivalry: Australia and Canada from the Boer War to the Great War," in Margaret MacMillan and Francine McKenzie (eds.), *Parties Long Estranged: Canada and Australia in the Twentieth Century* (Vancouver: UBC Press, 2003) 20.

35. J.L. Granatstein and J.M. Hitsman, *Broken Promises: A History of Conscription in Canada* (Toronto: Oxford University Press, 1977) 32; Robert Bothwell, *The Penguin History of Canada* (Toronto: Penguin Canada, 2006) 293.

36. Desmond Morton, *Fight or Pay: Soldiers' Families in the Great War* (Vancouver: UBC Press, 2004) 178.

37. Montreal *Gazette*, 29 August 1917; Alan Gordon, "Lest We Forget: Two Solitudes in War and Memory," in Chapnick and Hillmer (eds.) *Canadas of the Mind*, 161.

38. Martin Auger, "On the Brink of Civil War: The Canadian Government and the Suppression of the 1918 Quebec Easter Riots," *The Canadian Historical Review* 89.4 (December 2008), 503–40.

39. LAC, Sir Robert Borden papers, MG 26 H, diary, 25 September 1917.

40. Donald Creighton, *Canada's First Century* (Toronto: Macmillan, 1970) 152.

41. Granatstein and Hitsman, *Broken Promises*, 85.

42. Patrick Bouvier, *Déserteurs et insoumis. Les Canadiens français et la justice militaire (1914–1918)* (Outremont 2003).

43. Cook, *Shock Troops*, 389.

44. See RG 24, v. 4517-8, military reports.

45. Chris Young, "'Sous les balles des troupes fédérales': Representing the Quebec City Riots in Francophone Quebec (1919–2009)" (Master's thesis: Concordia University, 2009) 37; Brock Millman, *Polarity, Patriotism, and Dissent in Great War Canada, 1914–1919* (Toronto: University of Toronto Press, 2016) 183–7.

46. See RG 24, v. 4517-8, military reports.

47. *Le Devoir*, 1 April 1918.

48. *Le Devoir*, 1 April 1918.

49. Young, "'Sous les balles des troupes fédérales,'" 49; *Le Devoir*, 2 April 1918.

50. Hansard, 1918, volume I, 418.

51. RG 24, v. 4517-18, Proceedings of a Military Court of Inquiry, 3 April 1918.

52. Hansard, 1918, volume I, 441.

CHAPTER 7: COMMEMORATING THE FALLEN

1. See Cook, *Shock Troops*, 611–20.

2. Benjamin Isitt, *Victoria to Vladivostok: Canada's Siberian Expedition, 1917–19* (Vancouver: UBC Press, 2010).

3. See Adrian Gregory, *The Silence of Memory: Armistice Day, 1919–1946* (Oxford: Berg Publishers, 1994).

4. "King's Request Well Observed Over Dominion," *The Globe*, 12 November 1919, 7.

5. Amanda Betts (ed.), *In Flanders Fields: 100 years: Writing on War, Loss and Remembrance* (Toronto: Knopf, 2015).

6. David Crane, *Empires of the Dead: How One Man's Vision Led to the Creation of WW1's War Graves* (London, England: William Collins, 2013) 141.

7. Reginald Blomfield, *Memoirs of an Architect* (London: Macmillan, 1932) 181.

8. Fabian Ware, *The Immortal Heritage: An Account of the Work and Policy of the Imperial War Graves Commission During Twenty Years, 1917–1937* (Cambridge: The University Press, 1937) 30.

9. Bart Ziino, *A Distant Grief: Australians, War Graves and the Great War* (Crawley: University of Western Australia Press, 2007) 2–3; and Lisa M. Budreau, *Bodies of War: World War I and the Politics of Commemoration in America, 1919–1933* (New York and London: New York University Press, 2010) 21.

10. LAC, Sir Robert Borden papers, C-4316, Perley's report from France, 7 May 1919, 37912; Ibid., Ware to Perley, 1 July 1920, 38007.

11. Philip Longworth, *The Unending Vigil: A History of the Commonwealth War Graves Commission, 1917–1984* (London: Leo Cooper, 1985) 130.

12. Booth (ed.), *Opened by Censor*, 158.

13. For the idea of emotional investment, see Audoin-Rouzeau and Annette Becker, *14–18: Understanding the Great War* (London: Profile, 2002) 92.

14. Veterans Affairs Canada, *Canadian Forces Advisory Council: The Origins and Evolution of Veterans Benefits in Canada, 1914–2004* (Ottawa: Government publication, 2004) 3.

15. On veterans, see Desmond Morton and Glenn Wright, *Winning the Second Battle: Canadian Veterans and the Return to Civilian Life: 1915–1930* (Toronto: University of Toronto Press, 1987).

16. Joan Sangster, "Mobilizing Canadian Women for War," in David Mackenzie (ed.), *Canada and the First World War* (Toronto: University of Toronto Press, 2005) 157–94.

17. William and Jeannette Raynsford, *Silent Casualties: Veterans' Families in the Aftermath of the Great War* (Madoc, Ont.: The Merribrae Press, 1986) 8.

18. Walter S. Woods, *The Men Who Came Back* (Toronto: The Ryerson Press, 1956) 83.

19. See Desmond Morton, "The Canadian Veterans' Heritage from the Great War," in Peter Neary and J.L. Granatstein (eds.), *The Veterans Charter and Post–World War II Canada* (Montreal: McGill-Queen's University Press, 1998) 15–31.

20. Stevens, *A City Goes to War*, 155.

21. See Jonathan Vance, *Death So Noble: Memory, Meaning, and the First World War* (Vancouver: UBC Press, 1997); and Mark Connelly, *The Great War, Memory and Ritual: Commemorations in the City and East London, 1916–1939* (Woodbridge: Boydell Press, 2002). For some examples of unveilings, see RG 24, v. 4262, file 1-107-1.

22. Vance, *Death So Noble*, 147.

23. For trophies, see Jonathan Vance, "Tangible Demonstrations of a Great Victory: War Trophies in Canada," *Material History Review* 42 (fall 1995) 47–56; Edward Atkinson, "Colonel Doughy and the War Museum," *The Archivist* 16 (July–August 1989) 4, 7–8.

24. E.S. Russenholt, *Six Thousand Men* (Winnipeg: Printed to the order of Forty-Fourth Battalion Association by the Montfort Press, 1932) 139.

25. See Robert Shipley, *To Mark Our Place: A History of Canadian War Memorials* (Toronto: NC Press Limited, 1987); and Alex King, *Memorials of the Great War in Britain: The Symbolism & Politics of Remembrance* (Oxford: Berg Publishers, 1998), 11–12.

26. Mark David Sheftall, *Altered Memories of the Great War: Divergent Narratives of Britain, Australia, New Zealand and Canada* (London: I.B. Tauris, 2009) 130.

27. James Wood, *Militia Myths: Ideas of the Canadian Citizen Soldier, 1896–1921* (Vancouver: UBC Press, 2010) 18.

28. See Alan Young, "We Throw the Torch: Canadian Memorials of

the Great War and the Mythology of Historical Sacrifice," *Journal of Canadian Studies* (1989–90) 5–28.

29. Jay Winter, *Sites of Memory, Sites of Mourning: The Great War in European Cultural History* (Cambridge: Cambridge University Press, 1995) 7.

30. Alan Gordon, "Lest We Forget: Two Solitudes in War and Memory," in Adam Chapnick and Norman Hillmer (eds.), *Canadas of the Mind* (Montreal: McGill-Queen's University Press, 2007) 165.

31. Ziino, *A Distant Grief*, 3–4; Thomas W. Laqueur, "Names, Bodies and the Anxiety of Erasure," *The Social and Political Body*, Theodore R. Schatzki and Wolfgang Natter (eds.) (New York: The Guilford Press, 1996) 129–30.

32. For some of these challenges, see the correspondence in RG 24, v. 4454, file 24-1-72, Duguid to MD, No. 3, 28 October 1924. Also see Jessica Emma Sandy, "Names in Stone: War Memorials as Commemorative Intermediaries," (Master's thesis: University of Calgary, 2015) 39–40.

33. Vance, *Death So Noble*, 119.

34. Tim Cook, *The Madman and the Butcher: The Sensational Wars of Sam Hughes and General Arthur Currie* (Toronto: Allen Lane, 2010).

35. CWM, George Metcalf Archival Collection, 1990-0066-015, "Canada's Battlefield Memorials," undated monograph.

36. CWM, 20030088-028, S. C. Mewburn, *Battlefield Memorials: Report of the Special Committee* (Ottawa: King's Printer, 1920).

37. Ian Ross Robertson, *Sir Andrew Macphail: The Life and Legacy of a Canadian Man of Letters* (Montreal and Kingston: McGill-Queen's University Press, 2008) 153, 226.

38. Mewburn, *Battlefield Memorials: Report of the Special Committee*, 5. Also see, LAC, Sir Arthur Currie papers, MG 30 E100, v. 11, file 33, Currie to A.C. Macdonell, 19 April 1922.

39. Mewburn, *Battlefield Memorials: Report of the Special Committee*, Appendix C, "Evidence of General Sir Arthur Currie and Prof. Nobbs."

40. Mewburn, *Battlefield Memorials: Report of the Special Committee*, Appendix C, "Evidence of General Sir Arthur Currie and Prof. Nobbs."

41. *Debates*, House of Commons, 28 April 1920.

42. LAC, RG 38, v. 419, file Canadian Battlefields Memorials Commission, pt. 1, 1920–1924, PC 2334 (8 November 1919) and PC 2146 (30 August 1920). Also see Canadian Battlefields Memorials Commission, *Canadian Battlefield Memorials* (Ottawa: King's Printer, 1929) 9.

43. RG 38, v. 419, PC 2334. Also see Alexandra Holland, "Canadian Memorialization at Vimy Ridge: The 'Vimy Myth,'" (University of Ottawa: major research paper, 2010).

44. RG 38, v. 419, "Conditions of Open Preliminary Competition for the Selection of Designers for Eight (8) Canadian Battlefields Memorial Monuments in France and Belgium," 5.

45. RG 38, v. 419, file Canadian Battlefields Memorials Commission, pt. 1, 1920–1924, "Conditions of Open Preliminary Competition for the Selection of Designers for Eight (8) Canadian Battlefields Memorial Monuments in France and Belgium"; Ibid., Expenditure in Sight, [nd., ca. 1920].

46. RG 24, v. 1825, file 11-28, Terms of the Competition, n.d. [May 1921]; Lane Borstad, "Walter Allward: Sculptor and Architect of the Vimy Ridge Memorial," *Journal of the Society for the Study of Architecture in Canada* 33.1 (2008) 38.

47. RG 38, v. 419, Agenda, 2nd Meeting of the Canadian Battlefields Memorials Commission, 21 April 1921.

48. RG 38, v. 419, Agenda, 3rd Meeting of the Canadian Battlefields Memorials Commission, 4 October 1921.

49. A.Y. Jackson letter to editor, *Canadian Forum* 11.18 (March 1922) 559.

50. RG 38, v. 419, Agenda, 3rd Meeting of the Canadian Battlefields Memorials Commission, 4 October 1921.

51. See the poster on the cover of Iarocci, *Shoestring Soldiers*.

52. "St Julien: A Glorious Page in Canadian History," *The Globe*, 22 April 1916, 17.

53. B.A. Garnell, *History of Canada* (Toronto: W.J. Gage and Company, 1926) 266.

54. W. Stewart Wallace, *A New History of Great Britain and Canada* (Toronto: The Macmillan Company, 1929) 195.

55. Jenny Macleod, *Great Battles: Gallipoli* (Oxford: Oxford University Press, 2015).

56. RG 38, v. 419, Minutes of Proceedings of 5th Meeting of the CBMC, 26 April 1922.

57. *Debates*, House of Commons, 22 May 1922, 2101.

58. RG 24, v. 6298, file 40-1-2, pt.2, Canada, Treaty Series, 1922, Supplement No. 1, *Agreement Between Canada and France Respecting the Cession to Canada of the Use of a Tract of Land on Vimy Ridge (Pas-De-Calais), December 5, 1922*, trans. (Ottawa, 1944) 3.

59. LAC, William Lyon Mackenzie King diaries, 5 December 1922.

60. *Debates*, House of Commons, 1923, 181.

CHAPTER 8: CONSTRUCTING MEMORY

1. For a variation of the dream, see CWM, Artist File, Walter Allward, volume I, *Military Gazette*, 13 June 1922.

2. Lane Borstad, "Walter Allward: Sculptor and Architect of the Vimy Ridge Memorial," *JSSAC / JSEAC* 33.1 (2008) 31.

3. Anne Anderson Perry, "Walter Allward: Canada's Great Sculptor," *National Pictorial* (1 March 1922) 8–9, 55.

4. O.J. Stevenson, *A People's Best* (Toronto: The Musson Book Company, 1927) 32.

5. "Mr. Allward's Designs," *The Globe*, 9 July 1904, 24; "Memorial to Canadians who fell in the war in South Africa," *Canadian Architect and Builder*, XVIII (January 1905) 8.

6. Hansard, House of Commons Debates, 13 March 1900, 1848.

7. Borstad, "Walter Allward: Sculptor and Architect of the Vimy Ridge Memorial," 26.

8. *The Globe*, 28 May 1910.

9. Queen's University Archives (QUA), Walter Seymour Allward fonds, 5055, box 2, file: "Bell Memorial, Brantford."

10. Augustus Bridle, *Sons of Canada: Short Studies of Characteristic Canadians* (Toronto, London and Paris: J.M. Dent & Sons, 1916) 123–9.

11. *Saturday Night* (13 November 1920) 5.

12. Anne Anderson Perry, "Walter Allward: Canada's Great Sculptor," *National Pictorial* (1 March 1922) 8.

13. *The Globe and Mail*, 15 September 1950, 5; Perry, "Walter Allward: Canada's Great Sculptor," 8.

14. QUA, Allward papers, box 1, file 1921–1924, Allward to Osborne, 16 December 1921; Dennis Duffy, "Among the Missing: Mass Death & Canadian Nationalism at the Vimy Memorial," *disClosure: A Journal of Social Theory* 18.10 (2009) 161.

15. CWM, Artist File, Walter Allward, volume I, *Military Gazette*, 13 June 1922.

16. H.C. Osborne, "British Cemeteries and Memorials of the Great War," *AACS—Proceedings of the 44th Annual Convention, Toronto, Ontario, Canada, September 8, 9, 10 and 11, 1930.*

17. Sir Max Aitken, *Canada in Flanders: The Official Story of the Canadian Expeditionary Force*, volume I (Toronto: Hodder and Stoughton, 1916) 81.

18. Canadian Battlefields Memorials Commission, *Canadian Battlefield Memorials* (Ottawa: King's Printer, 1929) 11. Also see RG 38, v. 419, Minutes of Proceedings of 9th Meeting of the CBMC, 6 December 1923.

19. RG 24, v. 1751, file DHS 7-10, pt. 1, Osborne to Duguid, 15 November 1924.

20. RG 38, v. 419, Minutes of Proceedings of 9th Meeting of the CBMC, 6 December 1923.

21. RG 24, v. 1751, file DHS 7-10, pt. 1, *The Evening Standard*, 14 August 1923.

22. CWM, PAM NA 9330 .F8 C2 L5, Col. D.C. Unwin Simson, *Little Known Facts and Difficulties in the Construction of the Canadian Memorial on Vimy Ridge, and Other Memorials in France and Belgium*, 7.

23. H.C. Osborne, "Allward of Vimy," *The Legionary* 12.9 (April 1937) 15.

24. Allward interview, London *Observer*, 31 May 1936; QUA, Allward papers, box 1, file 1921–1924, Allward to Mewburn, 13 October 1924.

25. CWM, PAM NA 9330 .F8 C2 L5, Simson, *Little Known Facts*, 6.

26. LAC, RG 25, v. 337, file W 18/26, Larkin to Osborne, 16 January 1924.

27. CWM, PAM NA 9330 .F8 C2 L5, Simson, *Little Known Facts*, 9.

28. CWM, PAM NA 9330 .F8 C2 L5, Simson, *Little Known Facts*, 9; CWM, Artist File, Walter Allward, volume III, The Vimy Memorial, Report by SMAR Roberts [Department of Veterans Affairs, November 1965] 4.

29. Canadian Battlefields Memorials Commission, *Canadian Battlefield Memorials* (Ottawa: King's Printer, 1929) 39.

30. Simson, *Little Known Facts*, 9

31. "Premier Baldwin Sees Vimy Ridge," *The Globe and Mail*, 3 July 1928.

32. Ziino, *A Distant Grief*, 98.

33. RG 38, v. 419, Minutes of Proceedings of 7th Meeting of the CBMC, Commemoration of the Missing [ca. October 1922].

34. It was initially thought that there were 14,000 missing. For the 20,000 figure, see RG 38, v. 419, Minutes of Proceedings of 7th Meeting of the CBMC, Commemoration of the Missing [ca. October 1922].

35. Longworth, *The Unending Vigil*, 103.

36. RG 38, v. 419, file: C.B.C. pt. 1., H. C. Osborne, Commemoration of Canadian Missing, Report to the Chairman and Members of the Canadian Battlefields Memorials Commission, 10 January 1923.

37. Duffy, "Among the Missing," 171; RG 38, v. 419, Chief Engineer to Commission, 1 December 1922.

38. QUA, Allward papers, box 1, file 1926, letter to W. S. Allward from H. C. Osborne, 2 September 1926, and Allward to Osborne, 27 September 1926.

39. QUA, Allward papers, box 1, file 1927, Imperial War Memorials Committee meeting, 8 November 1927, and Allward to Osborne, 27 September 1926.

40. QUA, Allward papers, box 1, file 1926, Allward to Osborne, 27 September 1926.

41. CWM, Artist File, Walter Allward, volume II, Allward to Mewburn, 7 November 1924.

42. QUA, Allward papers, box 1, file 1921–1924, 11 January 1924. And RG 38, v.419, Minutes of Proceedings of 9th Meeting of the CBMC, 6 December 1923.

43. CWM, Artist File, Walter Allward, volume I, Allward to Mewburn, 13 October 1924.

44. CWM, Artist File, Walter Allward, volume I, no title [typed series of statements] n.d. [ca. 1924].

45. CWM, Artist File, Walter Allward, volume II, Rodolphe Lemieux to G.N. Gordon, 29 July 1925.

46. Jacqueline Hucker, "The Vimy Memorial: The Role of the Stone," [unpublished report, 10 March 1999] 5–6.

47. QUA, Allward papers, box 1, file 1930, Allward to Osborne, 29 September 1930; RG 38, v. 419, file CBC, vol. 2, Minutes of Proceedings of the 15th Meeting of the Canadian Battlefields Memorials Commission held in Ottawa, 18 May 1926.

48. Laura Brandon, "Making Memory: Canvas of War and the Vimy Sculptures," in Briton Busch (ed.), *Canada and the Great War* (Montreal: McGill-Queen's University Press, 2003) 206.

49. RG 24, v. 6298, file 40-1-2, pt. 1, Osborne to Deputy Minister, 11 May 1934.

50. See Paul Fussell, *The Great War and Modern Memory* (New York: Oxford University Press, 1975).

51. Jay Winter, *Sites of Memory, Sites of Mourning: The Great War in European Cultural History* (Cambridge: Cambridge University Press, 1995) 5.

52. Quoted in John Pierce, "Constructing Memory: The Vimy Memorial," *Canadian Military History* 1.1 (1992) 6. For other interpretations, see Jill Scott, "Vimy Ridge Memorial: Stone with a Story," *Queen's Quarterly* 114.4 (Winter 2007) 509–10, 512; Dennis Duffy, "Complexity and Contradiction in Canadian Public Sculpture: The Case of Walter Allward," *American Review of Canadian Studies* 38.2 (Summer 2008); Katrina Bormanis, "The Monumental Landscape: Canadian, Newfoundland, and Australian Great War Capital and Battlefield Memorials and the Topography of National Remembrance," (PhD dissertation: Concordia University, 2010); John Burge, *Three Soldiers and the Ethos of Service* (self-published, 2016) 55–80.

53. See Hucker, "Vimy: A Monument," Mewburn to Prime Minister Bennett, 13 February 1932. Pierre De La Ruffiniere Du Prey, "Allward's Figures, Lutyens's Flags and Wreaths," *JSSAC / JSEAC* 33.1 (2008) 62.

54. Jill Scott, "Vimy Ridge Memorial: Stone with a Story," *Queen's Quarterly* 114.4 (Winter 2007) accessed at www.thefreelibrary.com, no pages.

55. QUA, Allward papers, box 1, file 1926, Allward to Andre Ventre, 12 April 1926. For the French worry, see Joan Beaumont, "Australia's Global Memory Footprint: Memorial Building on the Western Front, 1916–2015," *Australian Historical Studies* 46.1 (2015) 55.

56. QUA, Allward papers, box 1, file 1926, Allward to Andre Ventre, 12 April 1926.

57. Canadian Battlefields Memorials Commission, *Canadian Battlefield Memorials* (Ottawa: King's Printer, 1929) 7, 33.

58. "Leading Canadian Artist," *The Globe*, 19 July 1930, 23

59. Hansard, Debates, 1929, III, 3612; See RG 24, v. 1872, file 14, clipping, *Ottawa Citizen*, 7 March 1930.

60. See RG 24, v. 1872, file 14, clipping, *Ottawa Citizen*, 7 March 1930.
61. On the cost, see Government of Canada, *Canada in the First World War and the Road to Vimy Ridge* (Ottawa: Minister of Supply and Services, 1992); on veterans' pressure, see Hale, *Branching Out*, 40.
62. QUA, Allward papers, box 1, file 1921–1924, Osborne to Allward, 23 March 1931.
63. "The Missing Monument," *The Globe*, 5 September 1932; "Work on Memorial Expedited at Vimy," *The Globe*, 11 July 1932.
64. On Osborne, see "Work on Memorial Expedited at Vimy," *The Globe*, 11 July 1932.
65. "Huge War Memorial Placed on Vimy Ridge Soon Will Be Ready," *The Globe*, 5 December 1933.
66. QUA, Allward papers, box 1, file 1931, Allward to Osborne, 23 March 1931 and 16 June 1931; Ibid., file 1932–1936, Osborne to Allward, 21 January 1932; RG 38, v. 419, v.3, Minutes of the Proceedings, 21st Meeting July 15th, 1931.
67. Laura Brandon, *Art or Memorial?: The Forgotten History of Canada's War Art* (Calgary: University of Calgary Press, 2006) 11.
68. London *Observer*, 31 May 1936.
69. QUA, Allward papers, box 2, file "Vimy Clippings 1936," Lemieux to the Secretary of the Canadian Battlefields Memorials Commission, 25 February 1935.

CHAPTER 9: THE GREAT WAR CONTESTED

1. John W. Dafoe, *Over the Canadian Battlefields: Notes of a Little Journey in France, in March, 1919* (Toronto: Thomas Allen, 1919) 83–4.
2. Desmond Morton, "'Junior by Sovereign Allies': The Transformation of the Canadian Expeditionary Force, 1914–1918," in Norman Hillmer and Philip Wigley (eds.), *The First British Commonwealth* (London: Frank Cass, 1980) 57.

3. Cook, *Warlords*, 141.

4. See Margaret MacMillan, "Canada and the Peace Settlements," in David Mackenzie (ed.), *Canada and the First World War* (Toronto: University of Toronto Press, 2005) 379–408.

5. W.S. Wallace, "The Growth of Canadian National Feeling," *The Canadian Historical Review* 1.2 (June 1920) 161.

6. Jeremy Black, *The Great War and the Making of the Modern World* (London: Continuum, 2011) 240.

7. LAC, William Lyon Mackenzie King, diary, 30 May 1919.

8. Alan Bowker, *A Time Such as There Never Was Before: Canada After the Great War* (Toronto: Dundurn Press, 2014) 278.

9. Arthur R.M. Lower, *My First Seventy-Five Years* (Toronto: Macmillan, 1967) 139.

10. Susan Mann Trofimenkoff, *The Dream of a Nation: A Social and Intellectual History of Quebec* (Toronto: Macmillan, 1982) 201; Peter Gossage and J.I. Little, *An Illustrated History of Quebec: Tradition and Modernity* (Toronto: Oxford University Press, 2012) 174–5.

11. David Bercuson, *True Patriot: The Life of Brooke Claxton, 1898–1960* (Toronto: University of Toronto Press, 1993) 59.

12. Chris Champion, *The Strange Demise of British Canada: The Liberals and Canadian Nationalism, 1964–68* (Montreal: McGill-Queen's University Press, 2010) 94.

13. Norman Hillmer, *O.D. Skelton: A Portrait of Canadian Ambition* (Toronto: University of Toronto Press, 2015) 105.

14. Norman Ward (ed.), *A Party Politician: The Memoirs of Chubby Power* (Toronto: Macmillan of Canada, 1966) 115.

15. CWM, MHRC, *Catalogue of the Canadian Official War Photographs, Second Exhibition* (16 July 1917).

16. Lieutenant-Colonel J.N. Gunn, *Historical Records of No. 8 Canadian Field Ambulance* (Toronto: The Ryerson Press, 1920) 37.

17. Vance, "Battle Verse," in Hayes, et al., *Vimy Ridge*, 265–78.

18. *The Globe*, 8 April 1922.

19. Paul Litt, "The War, Mass Culture, and Cultural Nationalism," in David Mackenzie (ed.), *Canada and the First World War*, 335.

20. Pat Jalland, *Death in War and Peace: Loss and Grief in England, 1914–1970* (Oxford: Oxford University Press, 2010) 69.

21. Dafoe, *Over the Canadian Battlefields*, 13, 15, 16.

22. Frank Fox, *The Battle of the Ridge Arras-Messines, March–June 1917* (London: C. Arthur Pearson, 1918) 18–9.

23. George Ralphson, *Over There with the Canadians at Vimy Ridge* (Chicago: M.A. Donohue and Company, 1919).

24. For the impact of Beaverbrook, see Tim Cook, "Documenting War & Forging Reputations: Sir Max Aitken and the Canadian War Records Office in the First World War," *War in History* 10.3 (2003) 265–95.

25. Colonel George Nasmith, *Canada's Sons in the World War*, volume I (Toronto: The John C. Winston Co., 1919) 333.

26. Allan Donnell, "Vimy Ridge," *Canada in the Great War*, volume IV (Toronto: United Publishers of Canada Limited, 1920) 164.

27. W.L. Grant, *History of Canada* (London: William Heinemann, 1923) 368.

28. David Merritt Duncan, *The Story of the Canadian People* (Toronto: Macmillan, 1919) 250.

29. "Comrades All," *The Globe*, 10 April 1922.

30. Jeffrey Williams, *Byng of Vimy: General and Governor General* (Toronto: University of Toronto Press, 1992) 312–13.

31. "Gather to Celebrate Vimy Ridge Capture," *The Globe*, 9 April 1923.

32. LAC, Sir Arthur Currie papers, MG 30 E100, v. 11, Currie to MacBrien, 2 March 1927. I thank Glenn Wright for sharing this letter with me.

33. Vance, *Death So Noble*, 233.

34. Eugene Forsey, *The Royal Power of Dissolution of Parliament in the British Commonwealth* (Toronto: Oxford University Press, 1943); and Roger Graham, *The King–Byng Affair, 1926: A Question of Responsible Government* (Toronto: Copp Clark, 1967).

35. Ward (ed.), *A Party Politician*, 112–13.

36. T.H.E. Travers, "Allies in Conflict: The British and Canadian Official Historians and the Real Story of the Second Ypres," *Journal of Contemporary History* 24. 2 (April 1989); Wes Gustavson, '"Fairly Well Known and Need Not Be Discussed": Colonel A.F. Duguid and the Canadian Official History of the First World War,' *Canadian Military History* 10.2 (Spring 2001) 41–54.

37. Cook, *Clio's Warriors*, 78–99.

38. S.F. Wise, "Canadian Official Military History," in Jeffrey Grey (ed.), *The Last Word?: Essays on Official History in the United States and British Commonwealth* (Westport, CT: Greenwood, 2003), 11.

39. Will Bird, *The Communication Trench* (Montreal: Perreault, 1932) preface. On Bird, see Ian McKay and Robin Bates, *In the Province of History: The Making of the Public Past in Twentieth-Century Nova Scotia* (Montreal: McGill-Queen's University Press, 2010) 133.

40. Pierre Berton, *Hollywood's Canada: The Americanization of Our National Image* (Toronto: McClelland and Stewart Ltd., 1975).

41. Wade Rowland, *Canada Lives Here: The Case for Public Broadcasting* (Westmount: Linda Leith Publishing, 2015) 29; Mary Vipond, "Canadian Nationalism and the Plight of Canadian Magazines in the 1920s," *The Canadian Historical Review* LVIII.1 (March 1977) 43–4.

42. Bowker, *A Time Such as There Never Was Before*, 46.

43. Vance, *Death So Noble*, 178–9.

44. Cook, *Clio's Warriors*, 71.

45. For the interwar years, see Stephen Harris, *Canadian Brass: The Making of a Professional Army, 1860–1939* (Toronto: University of Toronto Press, 1988).

46. See Thomas P. Socknat, *Witness Against War, Pacifism in Canada, 1900–1945* (University of Toronto Press, 1987) 90–161.

47. Jonathan Vance, "Remembering Armageddon," David Mackenzie (ed.), *Canada and the First World War* (Toronto: University of Toronto Press, 2005) 427.

48. Socknat, *Witness Against War*, 112.

49. Cynthia Commachio, "Challenging Strathcona: The Cadet Training Controversy in English Canada, 1920–1950," in Lara Campbell, Michael Dawson, and Catherine Gidney (eds.), *Worth Fighting For: Canada's Tradition of War Resistance from 1812 to the War on Terror* (Toronto: Between the Lines, 2015) 79–92.

50. Terry Copp, *No Price Too High: Canadians and the Second World War* (Toronto: McGraw-Hill Ryerson, 1996) 15.

51. Maria Tippett, *Art at the Service of War: Canada, Art, and the Great War* (Toronto: University of Toronto Press, 1984) 89–90.

52. *The Globe*, 23 September 1919.

53. David Lloyd, *Battlefield Tourism: Pilgrimage and the Commemoration of the Great War in Britain, Australia and Canada, 1919–1939* (Oxford: Berg Publishers, 1998) 103.

54. Edward Peter Soye, "Canadian War Trophies: Arthur Doughty and German Aircraft Allocated to Canada after the First World War," (Master's thesis: Royal Military College of Canada, 2009); Brandon, *Art or Memorial?*, 3.

55. Laura Brandon, "The Canadian War Memorial That Never Was," *Canadian Military History* 7.4 (Autumn 1998) 45–54.

56. McGill University Archives, Arthur Currie/ Hugh Urquhart collection, MG4027, box 1, file 12, Currie to Gregory, 31 May 1919; Cook, *The Madman and the Butcher*, 273.

57. Tim Cook, "Sir Arthur Currie," *Dictionary of Canadian Biography*, online.

58. Cook, *The Madman and the Butcher*, 362.

59. Lloyd, *Battlefield Tourism*, 101.

60. Samuel Hynes, *A War Imagined: The First World War and English Culture* (London: Bodley Head, 1990) 283.

61. RG 24, v. 1740, DHS 4-4. Pt 4, "Nova Scotian Tells of War as It Was on the Western Front," 13 December 1930.

62. On Harrison's novel, see Jonathan Vance, "The Soldier as Novelist: Literature, History and the Great War," *Canadian Literature: A Quarterly of Criticism and Review* 179 (Winter 2003) 22–37.

63. G.R. Stevens, *A City Goes to War* (Brampton, Ont.: Charters Pub. Co., 1964) 171.

64. Hall, *Branching Out*, 30.

65. "The Funeral of General Sir Arthur Currie," *Canadian Defence Quarterly* 11.2 (1934) 156–8.

66. "Canada Remembers," *The Legionary* (November 1921) 6.

67. Glenn R. Iriam (ed.), *In the Trenches, 1914–1918* (Kenora: self-published, 2008) 264.

68. R. Douglas Francis, *Frank H. Underhill: Intellectual Provocateur* (Toronto: University of Toronto Press, 1986) 97.

69. Frank Underhill, "The Canadian Forces in the War," in C.A. Lucas (ed.), *The Empire at War* (London, 1923) 285–6.

CHAPTER 10: THE 1936 VIMY PILGRIMAGE

1. W.W. Murray, "The Vimy Pilgrimage," *Canadian Geographic Journal* 13.8 (December 1936) 409.

2. John Hundevad, "Pilgrimages, Then and Now," *The Legionary* 37.1 (June 1962) 10.

3. Lloyd, *Battlefield Tourism*, 103.

4. John Pegum, "The Old Front Line: Returning to the Battlefields in the Writings of Ex-Servicemen," Jessica Meyer (ed.), *British Popular Culture and the First World War* (Leiden, Netherlands: Brill, 2008) 218.

5. Angela Duffett, "Memory, Myth and Memorials: Newfoundland's Public Memory of the First World War" (Master's thesis: Carleton University, 2010) 50–2; Thomas Nangle, "Newfoundland Memorial Park: Beaumont Hamel," *The Veteran* 5.3 (May 1926) 8, 13.

6. Budreau, *Bodies of War*.

7. W.W. Murray, *The Epic of Vimy* (Ottawa: The Legionary, 1936) 6–7.

8. *The Legionary*, III (July 1928) 19.

9. Murray, *The Epic of Vimy*, 7.

10. Will Bird, *Thirteen Years After* (Toronto: The Maclean Publishing Company, 1932) 79.

11. "Ages-Old Art Of Sculpture Vividly Seen: Miss Frances Loring Gives Impressive Review of Subject at Art Gallery," *The Globe and Mail*, 2 April 1932, 16.

12. Jonathan Vance, "'Today they were alive again': The Canadian Corps Reunion of 1934," *Ontario History Magazine* LXXXVII. 4 (December 1995) 327–43.

13. CWM, MHRC, *Behind the Lines* (pamphlet, 1934) 2.

14. Tim Cook, "Canada's Great War on Film: *Lest We Forget* (1935)," *Canadian Military History* 14.3 (Summer 2005) 5–20.

15. *The Legionary* 10.1 (January 1935) 10.

16. *The Legionary* 10.1 (January 1935) 10.

17. "Lest We Forget," *The Legionary* 10.3 (March 1935) 8.

18. A.F. Duguid, "Canadians in Battle, 1915–1918," *Canadian Historical Association Report* (1935) 42; Hyatt, *General Sir Arthur Currie*, 67.

19. A.F. Duguid, "Canadians in Battle: An Epic Achievement," *The Legionary* 11.12 (July 1936) 4.

20. *The Legionary* 9.7 (July 1934) 9.

21. Murray, *The Epic of Vimy*, 12.

22. *The Legionary* 10.1 (January 1935) 13.

23. For unemployment figures, see Shaun R.G. Brown, "Re-establishment and Rehabilitating: Canadian Veteran Policy, 1933–1946," (PhD dissertation: Western University, 1995) 35.

24. RG 24, v.1753, file DHS-7-29, *The Canadian Veteran* (March 1935), unpaginated page pasted in file. Also see "Vimy and the Veterans," *The Globe*, 19 June 1936, 4.

25. *Debates*, 1936, v. III, 2281; *Debates*, 1936, v. III, 3079.

26. William Lyon Mackenzie King diaries, 26 May 1936; also King's public statement in *Debates*, v. IV, 23 June 1936, 4122.

27. For a printed condemnation of King's actions, see *The Legionary* 10.6 (June 1935) 7.

28. *The Gazette* (Montreal), 9 April 1967.

29. Holland, "Canadian Memorialization at Vimy Ridge: The 'Vimy Myth,'" 45.

30. A.G.L. "Vimy Anniversary: A Few Reflections," *The Legionary* 10.4 (April 1935) 5.

31. Elaine Young, "Being 'Over There': Veterans, Civilians, and the Vimy Pilgrimage of 1936," (Master's thesis: York University, 2008) 11; RG 24, v. 6298, file 40-1-2, pt. 1, Vimy Pilgrimage, Treatment Facilities, 29 May 1936.

32. *The Legionary* 11.1 (January 1936) 13.

33. "Mothers and Widows," *The Globe and Mail*, 30 March 1935.

34. Harry Hillard, "A Little Lady of the East," *The Legionary* 12.4 (December 1936) 7. For Silver Cross mothers, see Suzanne Evans, *Mothers of Heroes, Mothers of Martyrs: World War I and the Politics of Grief* (Montreal: McGill-Queen's University Press, 2007).

35. "Clark, Scott and Halton Will Describe Unveiling," *The Toronto Daily Star,* 25 July 1936, 16.

36. Herb Morden, *The Vimy Pilgrimage, July 1936: Experiences— Impressions and Some Random Jottings* (self-published, no date) 16.

37. David Pierce Beatty, *The Vimy Pilgrimage 1936* (Port Elgin, N.B.: D.P. Beatty, 1987) 17–18.

38. "The Significance of Vimy: An Address by the Venerable Archdeacon F.G. Scott, C.M.G, D.S.O., D.D., D.C.L., LL.D.," Toronto Empire Club of Canada, 22 October 1936, 4.

39. Beatty, *The Vimy Pilgrimage 1936*, 21.

40. John Hundevad, *Guidebook of the Pilgrimage to Vimy and the Battlefields, July–August, 1936* (Ottawa: Published on behalf of the Vimy Pilgrimage Committee by *The Veteran*, 1936) 15.

41. "Canada's Salute," *The Legionary* 12.1 (August 1936) 4.

42. Beatty, *The Vimy Pilgrimage 1936*, 64. For the importance of songs to soldiers, see Tim Cook, "The Singing War: Soldiers' Songs in the Great War," *American Review of Canadian Studies* 39.3 (September 2009) 224–41.

43. Young, "Being 'Over There,'" 45.

44. Capt J.G. Bisset, "All At Sea," *The Legionary* 12.3 (October 1936) 5.

45. Beatty, *The Vimy Pilgrimage 1936*, 22.

46. "The Significance of Vimy," 4.

47. *Toronto Daily Star,* 25 July 1936, 1.

48. CWM, 20100116-003, Mary Botel diary, 25 July 1936.

49. Morden, *The Vimy Pilgrimage,* 22.

50. Beatty, *The Vimy Pilgrimage,* 23.

51. CWM, 20100116-003, Mary Botel diary, 26 July 1936.

52. *Gloucester Citizen,* 5 August 1936.

53. "The Significance of Vimy," 5.

54. LAC, MG 30 E379, Hubert Morris papers, memoir, "The Story of My 3½ Years in World War I," 26.

55. Murray, *The Epic of Vimy,* 70.

56. *The Legionary* spoke of 100,000 visitors, but other Canadians remarked that this number was likely too high. Whatever the figure, the ridge was filled with spectators. "Canada's Salute," *The Legionary* 12.1 (August 1936) 1.

57. D.E. Macintyre, "The Vimy Pilgrimage," *The Legionary* (July 1961) 13; Murray, *The Epic of Vimy,* 18–19.

58. RG 38, v. 419, Minutes of Proceedings of 11th Meeting of the CBMC, 4 July 1924.

59. Lloyd, *Battlefield Tourism,* 203.

60. "Broadcast from Vimy," *Winnipeg Free Press,* 25 July 1936, 16; "The Vimy Memorial," *Winnipeg Free Press,* 27 July 1936, 11.

61. CWM Archives, 1982-602/18, Diary of Katherine R. de la Bruère Girouard, 26 July 1936.

62. *Toronto Daily Star,* 27 July 1936, 2.

63. There is some debate, even controversy, over the number of sons who were killed. The most coherent story is a series of posts on the CEF Study Group website: cefresearch.ca.

64. M.H. Halton, "Winnipeg Mother Who Sent 11 Sons to War, Meets the King," *Winnipeg Free Press,* 28 July 1936, 1.

65. Murray, *The Epic of Vimy*, 92.
66. Murray, *The Epic of Vimy*, 93–4.
67. Murray, *The Epic of Vimy*, 93–4. For Lapointe in the crisis, see Lita-Rose Betcherman, *Ernest Lapointe: Mackenzie King's Great Quebec Lieutenant* (Toronto: University of Toronto Press, 2002).
68. Murray, *The Epic of Vimy*, 94.
69. "Canada's Salute," *The Legionary* 12.1 (August 1936) 1.
70. *The Canadian Veteran* 8 (July 1936) 3.
71. Harold Davidson, "A Vimy Memory," *The Legionary* 12.9 (April 1937) 12.
72. "Mrs. Jackson Speaks of Vimy and Pilgrimage," *The Globe*, 26 September 1936.
73. Bill Garvock, "From Vimy to Ypres: Pilgrimage Musings," *The Legionary* 12.2 (September 1936) 1.
74. Hundevad, *To Vimy and the Battlefields*, 44.
75. Walter S. Woods, *The Men Who Came Back* (Toronto: The Ryerson Press, 1956) 106.

CHAPTER 11: FORGING AN ICON

1. LAC, Sir Robert Borden papers, Borden to Laura Borden, 1 August 1936.
2. Stuart Armour, *A Pilgrim's Progress* (Cobourg, Ont.: Frank W. Lapp, 1936) 17.
3. *The Legionary* 12.1 (August 1936) 4.
4. *Our Empire* 12.4 (July 1936) 9–10.
5. Woods, *The Men Who Came Back*, 115.
6. Gregory Clark, *War Stories* (Toronto: Ryerson Press, 1964) 32.
7. "Dominion President's Notes," *The Legionary* (July 1936) 21.
8. "The Significance of Vimy," 1.
9. Ibid., 7–8.
10. *The Legionary* 12.1 (August 1936).
11. RG 24, v. 6298, F.G. Goddard to DND, 9 September 1936; and Ibid., L. Staines to DND, 22 September 1936.
12. *The Legionary* 12.2 (September 1936) 1.

13. *The Legionary* 12.1 (August 1936) 23.

14. The CWM MHRC holds at least 10 scrapbooks.

15. Morden, *The Vimy Pilgrimage,* 7–8, 12.

16. "The Vimy Film," *The Legionary* 12.9 (April 1937) 25. "Who's Who in Civil Defence," *The Civil Defence Bulletin* 3.6 (September 1944) 4. There were also at least two informal films made of the pilgrimage. The Kirkland Lake branch of the Canadian Legion sponsored Oliver Blais to film the trip across the Atlantic and the unveiling, although his footage does not appear to have been used in Badgley's official film. A second film by an Ontario judge, James C. McRuer, who served as a lieutenant in the Canadian Field Artillery during the war, captured the unveiling on 8mm footage. See CWM, 20070063-001; Archives of Ontario, F 1329-7, J.R. McRuer fonds, film, European trip, 1936.

17. RG 24, C-8320, Sound film of the unveiling of the Vimy Memorial and the Canadian Legion pilgrimage to the battlefields in 1936—"Salute to Valour."

18. Tim Travers, "Canadian Film and the First World War," Michael Paris (ed.), *The First World War and Popular Cinema: 1914 to the Present* (New Brunswick, N.J.: Rutgers University Press, 2000) 108.

19. "Rambling with Roly," *The Globe and Mail,* 10 July 1937; "Vimy Memorial in Pictures," *The Globe and Mail,* 22 June 1937. No copies of the film are known to exist.

20. RG 24, v. 6298, fie 40-1-2, pt. 3, Middleton to Dear Sirs, 25 September 1936; Ibid., Staines to Dear Sirs, 22 September 1936.

21. Brian Bethune, "Monumental Obsession: The Man behind the Vimy Ridge Memorial Never Got His Due," *Maclean's,* 16 April 2001, 56.

22. *Halifax Weekly Courier,* 1 August 1936.

23. "Among Ourselves," *The Globe,* 9 October 1936, 12.

24. *Saturday Night,* 1 August 1946, 1.

25. Harold Hessler, *War Interlude, 1916–1919* (Bloomington, Ind.: iUniverse, 2011) 90–1.

26. Vance, *Death So Noble*, 68.

27. Bertie Black, "Vimy 1936: A July Retrospect," *The Legionary* (July 1952) 7.

28. Siegfried Sassoon, "On Passing the New Menin Gate," *The Norton Anthology of English Literature* (New York: W.W. Norton and Company, 1986) 1900–1901.

29. QUA, Allward papers, box 1, file clippings, *The Globe and Mail*, 10 February 1937.

30. H.C. Osborne, "Allward of Vimy," *The Legionary* 12.9 (April 1937) 15.

31. H.C. Osborne, "Allward of Vimy," *The Legionary* 12.9 (April 1937) 25.

32. William Lyon Mackenzie King Diaries, online, 8 September 1936, item 17182.

33. Denis Duffy, "The Grandfathering of William Lyon Mackenzie King," *The American Review of Canadian Studies* (Winter 2002) 594.

34. Alexandra Mesquin, "Walter Allward, Submission Report," *Historic Sites and Monuments Board Canada*, 3.

35. *The Legionary* 12.9 (June 1937) 12.

36. *The Legionary* 12.2 (September 1936) 1.

37. Advertisement, *The Legionary* 12.9 (April 1937) 21; "A Vimy Reunion," *The Legionary* 12.10 (May 1937) 20.

38. Suzanne Kingsmill, *Francis Scrimger: Beyond the Call of Duty* (Toronto: Dundurn, 1991) 62.

39. D.E. Macintyre, "The Vimy Sector: In War and Peace," *The Legionary* 14.9 (April 1939) 7.

40. "The Vimy Spirit Lives," *The Globe and Mail*, 10 April 1939.

41. H.F. Angus (ed.), *Canada and Her Great Neighbor: Sociological Surveys of Opinion and Attitudes in Canada Concerning the United States* (Toronto: Ryerson Press, 1938) 116.

42. The *Globe*, 4 August 1927.

43. RG 24, v. 1751, file DHS 7-12, pt. 1, Duguid to High Commissioner for Canada, July 1926.

44. RG 24, v. 1881, CEF 6-10, The Canadian Book of Remembrance, n.d. [1943].

45. Katie FitzRandolph, "Strength, honesty: Canadian symbol," *Ottawa Citizen*, 11 November 1977. Also see, Malcolm Ferguson, "The Response: Canada's National War Memorial," (Master's thesis: Carleton University, 2010).

46. Natascha Morrison, "Looking Backwards, Looking Forwards: Remembrance Day in Canada, 1919–2008," (Master's thesis: Carleton University, 2010) 43.

47. Vincent Massey, *What's Past Is Prologue: The Memoirs of the Right Honourable Vincent Massey* (Toronto: Macmillan, 1963) 331.

48. *Montreal Daily Star*, 1 June 1940.

49. "Vimy Memorial Bombed," *The Globe and Mail*, June 3, 1940, 9.

50. QUA, Allward papers, box 1, file 1921-1924, Allward to Mewburn, 13 October 1924.

51. "Vimy Memorial Bombed," *The Globe and Mail*, June 3, 1940, 9.

52. Serge Durflinger, "Safeguarding Sanctity: Canada and the Vimy Memorial during the Second World War," in Hayes, et al., *Vimy Ridge*, 294.

53. *Montreal Daily Star*, 3 June 1940.

54. H.F. Wood, "Adolph Hitler's Vimy 'Pilgrimage,'" *The Legionary* 39.3 (August 1964) 14.

55. "Vimy Ridge Caretaker Is Through with Europe," *The Globe and Mail*, 16 March 1948; H.F. Wood, "Adolph Hitler's Vimy 'Pilgrimage,'" 14.

56. CWM, 19780056-041, E.C. Forrest papers, Douglas R. Oliver, "The Vimy Guardians," 3.

57. Douglas Oliver, "New Defenders of Vimy," *The Globe and Mail*, 8 August 1959.

58. "Churchill Tells Faith in Canada," *The Globe and Mail*, 2 June 1941.

59. "1,100 Veterans Parade Here," *The Globe and Mail*, 13 April 1942.

60. "What Price Vimy?" *The Legionary* 18.10 (April 1943), 23.

61. "Vimy Redeemed," *The Legionary* 20.4 (October 1944) 67.

62. Richard Malone, *A World in Flames: A Portrait of War* (Toronto: Collins, 1984) 106–7.

63. For Crerar's battles with Montgomery, see Paul Dickson, *A Thoroughly Canadian General: A Biography of General H.D.G. Crerar* (Toronto: University of Toronto Press, 2007).

64. Durflinger, "Safeguarding Sanctity," 301–2.

65. "A 'Presence' at Vimy," *The Legionary* 42.7 (December 1967) 5.

66. Macintyre, *Canada at Vimy*, 202–204.

CHAPTER 12: BIRTH OF THE NATION

1. RG 24, v. 1881, file CEF 6-10, Duguid to Osborne, 4 March 1947.

2. Viscountess Byng of Vimy, *Up the Stream of Time* (Toronto: The Macmillan Company of Canada Limited, 1946) 118.

3. The exception was Burns, *General Mud*.

4. Inglis, *Vimy Ridge: 1917–1992*, 79–80.

5. See "School Children Bring Flowers," *The Globe and Mail*, 12 November 1955; "Legion Asks for Annual Service at Vimy Ridge," *The Globe and Mail*, 30 May 1958.

6. Hugh A. Urquhart, *Arthur Currie: The Biography of a Great Canadian* (Vancouver: J.M. Dent and Sons, 1950).

7. "Walter Seymour Allward: His Dream Led to Vimy Memorial," *The Globe and Mail*, 25 April 1955, 14.

8. "Walter Seymour Allward," *The Globe and Mail*, 26 April 1955, 6.

9. CWM, 19780056-041, E.C. Forrest papers, Douglas R. Oliver, "The Vimy Guardians," 7.

10. "April the Ninth," *The Globe and Mail*, 9 April 1962.

11. George Stanley, *Canada's Soldiers: The Military History of an Unmilitary People* (Toronto: The Macmillan Company of Canada, 1960) 315.

12. See Antony Anderson, *The Diplomat: Lester Pearson and the Suez Crisis* (Fredericton, N.B.: Goose Lane, 2015).

13. José Igartua, *The Other Quiet Revolution: National Identities in English Canada, 1945–1971* (Vancouver: University of British Columbia Press, 2006), chapter five.

14. See David J. Bercuson and J.L. Granatstein, *War and Peacekeeping: From South Africa to the Gulf—Canada's Limited Wars* (Toronto: Key Porter Books, 1991).

15. Quoted in Philip Massolin, *Canadian Intellectuals, the Tory Tradition and the Challenge of Modernity, 1939–70* (Toronto: University of Toronto Press, 2001) 263.

16. Andrew Cohen, *Lester B. Pearson* (Toronto: Penguin, 2008) 154.

17. John English, *The Worldly Years: The Life of Lester Pearson, Volume II: 1949–1972* (Toronto: A.A. Knopf Canada, 1992) 289; Richard Snell, "'Private' Pearson salutes Vimy Men," *Toronto Daily Star*, 10 April 1967, 21.

18. Champion, *The Strange Demise of British Canada*, 3.

19. For the flag story, John Ross Matheson, *Canada's Flag: A Search for a Country* (Boston, Mass.: G. K. Hall, 1980).

20. Brian Palmer, *Canada's 1960s: The Ironies of Identity in a Rebellious Era* (Toronto: University of Toronto Press, 2009) 5.

21. Paul Litt, "Trudeaumania: Participatory Democracy in the Mass-Mediated Nation," *The Canadian Historical Review* 89:1 (March 2008) 27–53.

22. Champion, *The Strange Demise of British Canada*, 197.

23. Emma Hanna, *The Great War on the Small Screen* (Edinburgh: Edinburgh University Press, 2009) 21; "Keeping Tab on TV," *The Globe and Mail*, 16 April 1965.

24. See Dan Todman, *The Great War: Myth and Memory* (London: Hambledon, 2005); Brian Bond, *The Unquiet Western Front: Britain's Role in Literature and History* (Cambridge: Cambridge University Press, 2002).

25. "The First Great War," *The Globe and Mail*, 1 August 1964.

26. A.E. Powley, "Flanders' Fields," *Radio-TV* (October 1964) no pagination. Also see Teresa Iacobelli, "A Participant's History?: The CBC and the Manipulation of Oral History," *Oral History Review* 38/2 (Fall–Winter 2011) 331–48.

27. A.E. Powley, 'Flanders' Fields,' *Radio-TV* (October 1964) no pagination.

28. MHRC, *Flanders' Fields* transcripts, episode 9, page 11.

29. MHRC, *Flanders' Fields* transcripts, episode 9, page 1.

30. Clark, *War Stories,* 160.

31. See the new introduction by Mark Humphries to Nicholson's reissued history. G.W.L. Nicholson, *Canadian Expeditionary Force, 1914–1919: Official History of the Canadian Army in the First World War,* (Montreal: McGill-Queen's University Press, 2015).

32. LAC, G.W.L. Nicholson Papers, MG31 G19, v.6, CEF, 1914–19, clipping, Gregory Clark, [ca. 1962].

33. D.E. Macintyre, "The Vimy Pilgrimage," *The Legionary* (July 1961) 8.

34. Herbert Fairlie Wood, *Vimy!* (Toronto: Macmillan of Canada, 1967) foreword.

35. Kenneth Macksey, *The Shadow of Vimy Ridge* (London: William Kimber and Company, 1965); Alexander McKee, *The Battle of Vimy Ridge* (New York: Stein and Day, 1966).

36. Jeremy Black, *Rethinking Military History* (London: Routledge, 2004) 215.

37. McKee, *The Battle of Vimy Ridge,* 227.

38. "Bleating Memories of Old Soldiers," *The Globe and Mail,* 8 April 1967.

39. *The Legionary* 41.12 (May 1967) 7.

40. D.E. Macintyre, *Canada at Vimy* (Toronto: Peter Martin Associates Limited, 1967) viii.

41. Pierre Berton, *1967: The Last Good Year* (Toronto: Doubleday, 1967) 48.

42. Ralph Allen, *Ordeal by Fire: Canada, 1910–1945* (Toronto: Doubleday Canada, 1961) 1, 142–144; J.M.S. Careless, *Canada: A Story of Challenge* (Toronto: Macmillan, 1963) 328.

43. Donald Creighton, *Canada's First Century,* 132.

44. "Centennial Salute," *The Legionary* 42.1 (June 1967) 9; "The V.C. and G.C. Reunion," *The Legionary* 42.2 (July 1967) 15.

45. "Touring MP to urge Vimy Ridge Museum," *The Globe and Mail,* 13 July 1966.

46. Mallory White, "The Vimy 'Snub': How the Politics of Commemoration Affected the 50th Anniversary Observance of the Battle of Vimy Ridge," (Carleton University: MRE, 2015).

47. John A. Munro and Alex I. Inglis, eds., *Mike: The Memoirs of the Right Honourable Lester B. Pearson, Volume 3: 1957–1968* (Toronto: University of Toronto Press, 1975), 264.

48. On the colonies, see Robin Gendron, "The two faces of Charles the Good: Charles de Gaulle, France, and decolonization in Quebec and New Caledonia," *International Journal* 69(1) 2014, 94–109. Also see, David Meren, *Friends Like These: Entangled Nationalisms in the Canada-Quebec-France Triangle, 1945–1970* (Vancouver: UBC Press, 2012).

49. LAC, RG 25, v. 10333, file 27-10-11-2-1-1967, "Memorandum for the Prime Minister, February 28, 1967 from Paul Martin, Secretary of State for External Affairs—Vimy Ceremony."

50. Ibid.

51. *The Gazette* (Montreal), 13 April 1967; LAC, RG 25, v. 10333, file 27-10-11-2-1-1967, "Memorandum for the Prime Minister, February 28, 1967 from Paul Martin, Secretary of State for External Affairs—Vimy Ceremony." Munro and Inglis (eds.), *Mike*, volume III, 264.

52. *The Gazette* (Montreal), 6 April 1967.

53. "Parliament Questions" *The Globe and Mail*, 7 April 1967; English, *The Worldly Years*, 330; A. Munro Inglis, eds., *Mike*, 264.

54. CWM, 19780056-041, E.C. Forrest papers, "Administrative Information: 50th Anniversary Ceremonies Vimy Memorial," 1; "Vimy Celebrations in Ottawa," *The Legionary* 41.12 (May 1967) 30.

55. D.E. Macintyre, "Return to Vimy Fifty Years Later," *Legionary* 41.12 (May 1967) 16.

56. CWM, 19780056-041, E.C. Forrest papers, untitled account written by one of the survivors, 11.

57. CWM, 19780056-041, E.C. Forrest papers, 50th Anniversary Ceremony, 18 April 1967, 4; Charles Hargrove, "Canadians Return to Vimy Ridge," *The Times*, 10 April 1967, 5.

58. Burns, *General Mud*, 50.

59. Dale Thomson, *Vive le Québec Libre* (Ottawa: Deneau, 1988) 189.

60. CWM, 19780056-041, E.C. Forrest papers, Martin Dunsford, "Return to Vimy Ridge," undated clipping.

61. *The Gazette* (Montreal), 10 April 1967.

62. Charles Hargrove, "Canadians Return to Vimy Ridge," *The Times*, 10 April 1967, 5.

63. The Legion produced a colour film of the Survivors, *That Other April* (1968). See *The Legionary* 42.8 (January 1968) 31.

64. Thomson, *Vive le Québec Libre*, 199. For de Gaulle's plan to do something dramatic in Canada, see Bernard Lachaise, «De Gaulle et le Québec libre en 1967,» *Proceedings of the Western Society for French History* 36 (2008) 327.

65. Munro and Inglis (eds.), *Mike*, volume III, 267. This is also the conclusion drawn in J.F. Bosher, *The Gaullist Attack on Canada, 1967–1997* (Montreal: McGill-Queen's University Press, 2000) 40–2.

66. Munro and Inglis (eds.), *Mike*, volume III, 268.

67. Lester B. Pearson, *Words and Occasions: An Anthology of Speeches and Articles Selected from His Papers* (Toronto: University of Toronto Press, 1970) 264.

CHAPTER 13: VIMY CONTESTED

1. John Swettenham, "The Battle of Hill 70," *The Legionary* 42.4 (September 1967) 31.

2. John Swettenham, *To Seize the Victory: The Canadian Corps in World War I* (Toronto: Ryerson Press, 1965), preface.

3. C.P. Stacey, "Nationality: The Experience of Canada," Canadian Historical Association, *Historical Papers*, 1967, 12.

4. Burns, *General Mud*, 32.

5. Peter Neary, *Reference Paper: The Origins and Evolution of Veterans Benefits in Canada 1914–2004* (Veterans Affairs Canada: March 2004) 25.

6. "Remembrance Day," *The Legion* (January 1970) 3.

7. For the rise, fall, and rise again of Remembrance Day, see Natascha Morrison, "Looking Backwards, Looking Forwards: Remembrance Day in Canada, 1919–2008" (Master's thesis: Carleton University, 2010).

8. "What Price Glory?" *The Legionary* (October 1969) 34.

9. Beatrice Richard, "La mémoire collective de la guerre au Québec: un espace de résistance politique?," *Canadian Issues/Themes canadiens* (2004) 2.

10. Geoff Keelan, "'Il a bien merité de la Patrie': The 22nd Battalion and the Memory of Courcelette," *Canadian Military History* 19.3 (Summer 2010) 28–40.

11. Ronald Rudin, *Making History in Twentieth-Century Quebec* (Toronto: University of Toronto Press, 1997) 95.

12. Jocelyn Letournea, *A History for the Future: Rewriting Memory and Identity in Quebec* (Montreal: McGill-Queen's University Press, 2004) 4.

13. Dominique Clement, *Human Rights in Canada: A History* (Waterloo: Laurier University Press, 2016) 73.

14. See Rudin, *Making History in Twentieth-Century Quebec*; Mourad Djebabla-Brun, *Se souvenir de la Grande Guerre: la mémoire plurielle de 14–18 au Québec* (Montreal: VLB, 2004); Mourad Djebabla, "Historiographie francophone de la Première Guerre mondiale: écrire la Grande Guerre de 1914–1918 français au Canada et au Québec," *The Canadian Historical Review* 3.95 (September, 2014) 407–16.

15. Albert Tessier, *Québec–Canada: Histoire du Canada* (Quebec: Pelican, 1958) 253.

16. Lionel Groulx, *Revue d'histoire de l'Amérique française*, 12.4 (1959) 591–3.

17. Joseph Costilla, *Le people de la nuit* (Montreal: Editons Chenier, 1965) 101–5.

18. Young, "'Sous les balles des troupes fédérales,'" 70–80.

19. Robert Comeau, "L'Opposition à la conscription au Québec," in

Legault and Lamarre (eds.), *La Premiere Guerre Mondiale et le Canada* (Montreal: Meridien, 1999) 96.

20. Zachary Abram, "The Knights of Faith: The Soldier in Canadian War Fiction," (PhD dissertation: University of Ottawa, 2016) 155.

21. Inglis, *Vimy Ridge: 1917–1992*, 95.

22. "60 Years on," *The Globe and Mail*, 9 April 1917.

23. David Moir, "At What Price?" *The Legion* (1977).

24. A.B. McKillop, *Pierre Berton: A Biography* (Toronto: McClelland and Stewart, 2008) 591–4.

25. Michele Landsberg, "It's not easy explaining Canadian culture," *The Globe and Mail*, 19 March 1988.

26. Pierre Berton, "Vimy: World War I Battle 'Created' Canadians," *Toronto Star*, 6 April 1986.

27. William French, "Purple Writing for Vimy Ridge," *The Globe and Mail*, 6 September 1986; Brereton Greenhous, "War Stories to Further Our Social Mythology," *Quill and Quire* (August 1986); Stephen Weatherbee, "The Battle That Forged a Nation," *Alberta Report* (1 September 1986).

28. Pierre Berton, *Vimy* (Toronto: McClelland and Stewart, 1986) 294.

29. Government of Canada, *Canada in the First World War and the Road to Vimy Ridge* (Ottawa: Minister of Supply and Services, 1992) 20.

30. Stephen Ward, "Veterans of Vimy recall the horror; Mulroney says country they fought for will remain united," *The Gazette*, April 10, 1992, B1.

31. Matthew Graves, "Memorial Diplomacy in Franco-Australian Relations"; in Shanti Sumartojo and Ben Wellings (eds.), *Nation, Memory and Great War Commemoration Mobilizing the Past in Europe, Australia and New Zealand* (Bern: Peter Lang, 2014) 182.

32. Patrick Doyle, "Vimy Ridge 'Sacrifice' forged unity PM Declares," *Toronto Star*, 10 April 1992, A3. For Mulroney's use of other historical allusions, especially Sir John A. Macdonald's legacy, see Patrice Dutil and Sean Conway, "A Legacy Lost: Macdonald in the Memory of His Successors," in Patrice Dutil and Roger Hall

(eds.), *Macdonald at 200: New Reflections and Legacies* (Toronto: Dundurn, 2014) 397.

33. Interview with Dr. Roger Sarty, 1 May 2016.

34. Brereton Greenhous and Stephen J. Harris, *Canada and the Battle of Vimy Ridge* (Montreal: Art Global, 1992) 148.

35. Tom Clark, "Echoes from the Killing Fields," *The Globe and Mail*, 11 November 1993.

36. For a larger discussion, see Tim Cook, *Fight to the Finish: Canadians Fighting the Second World War* (Toronto: Allen Lane, 2015).

37. Brian Bethune, "It's Sublime and Deadly," *Maclean's* v.118, issue 27/28 (2005) 30–2; also see, for the figure of 750,000, Natalie Salat, "A Monumental Task," *The Legion* (November–December 2002) 15.

38. As cited in Jeffrey Keshen, "The Great War Soldier as Nation Builder," Briton C. Busch (ed.) *Canada and the Great War: Western Front Association Papers*, 15.

39. Peter Steven, "The Battle of Vimy Ridge," *The Beaver* 79.1 (February 1999) 45–6.

40. Gerald Filteau, *Le Québec, le Canada et la guerre 1914–1918* (Montreal: Les Editions de l'Aurore, 1977) 160.

41. Ramsay Cook, *Canada: A Modern Study* (Toronto: Clarke, Irwin, and Company, 1977) 187.

42. Allan S. Evans and I.L. Martinello, *Canada's Century* (Toronto: McGraw-Hill Ryerson, 1978) 158.

43. Historica Canada, Remembrance Day Poll, 12 November 1997.

44. https://www.historicacanada.ca/content/heritage-minutes/vimy-ridge. The error was still there as of August 2016.

45. See Sherrill Grace, *Landscapes of War and Memory: The Two World Wars in Canadian Literature and the Arts, 1977–2007* (Edmonton: University of Alberta Press, 2014).

46. Paul Gessel, "Urquhart's latest an epic portrait of a nation's birth," *Ottawa Citizen*, 31 March 2001.

47. H.F. Wood and John Swettenham, *Silent Witnesses* (Toronto: Hakkert, 1974) 1.

48. K.S. Inglis, "Entombing Unknown Soldiers: From London to Paris to Baghdad," *History & Memory* 5.2 (1993) 7–31.

49. Cecilia Morgan, *Commemorating Canada: History, Heritage, and Memory 1850s–1990s* (Toronto: University of Toronto Press, 2016) 90.

50. Ernie Pye, "Shrine of the Nations: The Unknown Warrior," *The Legionary* 13.4 (November 1937) 13.

51. Katrina Bormanis, "What Remains: Repatriating and Entombing a Canadian Unknown Soldier of the Great War in the Nation's Capital," *War & Society* 35.3 (August 2016) 219–40.

52. Dan Black, "Canada's Unknown Soldier: The Tomb of the Unknown Soldier," *The Legion* (1 September 2000) online.

53. Roger Sarty, "The Nationalization of Military History: Scholarship, Politics, and the Canadian War Museum," in Chapnick and Hillmer, *Canadas of the Mind*, 121–2.

54. See Norman Hillmer, "The Canadian War Museum and the Military Identity of an Unmilitary People," *Canadian Military History*, 19.3 (Summer 2010) 19–26.

55. J.L. Granatstein, *Who Killed Canadian History?* (Toronto: Harper Collins, 1998).

56. Laura Brandon, "Making Memory: Canvas of War and the Vimy Sculptures," in Briton Busch (ed.), *Canada and the Great War*, 215; Brandon, *Art or Memorial*, xix.

57. CWM, Artist File, Walter Allward, volume 4, Brian Arthur and Charles Hett, "An Approach to the Conservation of 13 Plaster Models for the War Memorial at Vimy Ridge. . . . ," (1998).

58. The gallery was curated by this author.

59. Brian Bethune, "Monumental Obsession: The Man behind the Vimy Ridge Memorial Never Got His Due," *Maclean's* (16 April 2001) 56.

60. Alexandra Mesquin, "Walter Allward, Submission Report," *Historic Sites and Monuments Board Canada* (Ottawa: Parks Canada, 2001) 1.

61. Arthur Weinreb, "Vimy Vidi Vichy," *Canadian Free Press*, 16 September 2002.

62. Susan Martinuk, "A nation that doesn't know Vichy from Vimy," *National Post*, 5 September 2002.

63. CWM, Artist File, Walter Allward, volume III, Report, The Vimy Memorial, 1961–51, n.d. [ca 1965].

64. Alan Freeman, "Canada's 'disgrace' on Vimy Ridge," *The Globe and Mail*, 13 May 2000, 1.

65. Salat, "A Monumental Task," 16.

66. "A once-proud history, slipping away," *The Globe and Mail*, 9 April 2002.

67. *Ottawa Citizen*, 6 July 2002; Jacqueline Hucker and Julian Smith, *Vimy: Canada's Memorial to a Generation* (Ottawa: Sanderling Press, 2012) 98.

68. Sheldon and Cave, *The Battle for Vimy Ridge, 1917*, 38.

69. Stanley Sislowski, "Vimy Ridge," no editor listed, *Canadian Veterans' Stories, Special Edition* (self-published, 2007) 18.

70. Dominion Institute, *Vimy Ridge 2007 Survey*, March 29, 2007, http://www.dominion.ca/DominionInstitute_VimyPoll_April9.pdf.

71. Jean Martin, "Vimy, April 1917: The Birth of Which Nation?" *Canadian Military Journal* 11.2 (Spring 2011) 32.

72. Hayes, Iarroci, and Bechthold (eds.), *Vimy Ridge*.

73. Michael Valpy, "The Making of a Myth," *The Globe and Mail*, 7 April 2007, F4.

74. Roy MacGregor, "Like pressed heather . . .", *The Globe and Mail*, 20 March 2007.

75. Canwest News Service, "Vimy Ridge monument shines through the ages," Canada.com, 9 April 2007.

76. Canwest News Service, "Vimy Ridge monument shines through the ages," Canada.com, 9 April 2007.

77. Stephen Harper, Prime Minister's Speech at Vimy Ridge Memorial, France (9 April 2007). Cited in Danielle Teillet, "The Commemoration of the Battle of Vimy Ridge: History, Remembrance, and National Identity" (Master's thesis: Royal Military College of Canada, 2011).

78. "Foreign Affairs Minister MacKay draws link between Vimy and Afghanistan," *Canadian Press NewsWire*, 9 April 2007.

79. Lawrence Martin, "As a country at war, we're in the mood for Vimy," *The Globe and Mail*, 5 April 2007, A19.

80. Canwest News Service, "Vimy Ridge monument shines through the ages," Canada.com, 9 April 2007.

81. Ibid.

CHAPTER 14: VIMY REBORN

1. QUA, Allward papers, box 1, file 1932–36, "Vimy Ridge—An Appreciation," 27 July 1936.

2. See Tim Cook and Christopher Schultz, "New Theatres of War: An Analysis of Paul Gross's Passchendaele, *Canadian Military History*, 19.3 (Summer 2010) 51–6; Mary Vipond, *The Mass Media in Canada*, 4th edition (Toronto: Lorimer, 2011) 63.

3. Graham Carr, "Rules of Engagement: Public History and the Drama of Legitimation," *The Canadian Historical Review* 86.2 (June 2005) 317–54.

4. Joel Ralph, "Vimy Revisited," *The Beaver* 87 (2), 2007, 36–41.

5. Bryn Weese, "Dallaire eyes Gatineau shore for Vimy Memorial," *Edmonton Sun*, 12 March 2010.

6. Joshua Dauphinee, "We must not replicate Vimy Memorial Statues," *Ottawa Citizen*, 19 March 2010, A11; *The Globe and Mail*, 3 April 2007.

7. Jordan Michael Smith, "Reinventing Canada: Stephen Harper's Conservative Revolution," *World Affairs Journal*, online.

8. See Brooke Jeffrey, *Dismantling Canada: Stephen Harper's New Conservative Agenda* (Montreal: McGill-Queen's University Press, 2015); Michael Eamon, "The War Against Public Forgetfulness: Commemorating 1812 in Canada," *London Journal of Canadian Studies*, 29.1 (November 2014) 134–185.

9. Ian McKay and Jamie Swift, *Warrior Nation: Rebranding Canada in an Age of Anxiety* (Toronto: Between the Lines, 2012);

Noah Richler, *What We Talk About When We Talk About War* (Fredericton, N.B.: Goose Lane Editions, 2012).

10. CBC Television, http://www.cbc.ca/player/Shows/ID/2220528646.

11. "Vimy Ridge marked Canada's birth as a nation," *Postmedia News*, 9 April 2012.

12. Joe O'Connor, "How Vimy Ridge made Canada into a country of heroes," *The National Post*, 8 April 2013.

13. Sabrina Marandola, "Montreal's Outremont borough moves to rename Vimy Park after Jacques Parizeau," *CBC News*, 15 June 2016.

14. "Critics slam Montreal's plan to rename Vimy Park after Jacques Parizeau," *CBC News*, 16 June 2016.

15. Cook, *Clio's Warriors*, 123.

16. Major John R. Grodzinski, "The Use and Abuse of Battle: Vimy Ridge and the Great War over the History of the First World War," *Canadian Military Journal* 10.1 (2009) 85.

ACKNOWLEDGMENTS

Canadian military historians are a generous group, and I was able to call upon friends and colleagues to read the manuscript. Dr. Laura Brandon, a former colleague at the Canadian War Museum, offered insight into Allward and his monument. I also benefited greatly from Laura's research files on Allward. Dr. Pat Brennan, professor of history at the University of Calgary, read the entire manuscript and marked it up with expertise and wit. Eric Brown, a volunteer at the CWM and co-author of a previous venture into unpacking the Vimy legend, provided a thorough edit and valued advice, as he has done for my previous three books. Dr. Nic Clarke, a fellow historian at the CWM, shared his experience, while prodding me on a number of issues. Robert Fisher, a former official historian, an archivist at Library Archives Canada, and a long-time friend, read an early draft and gave an important critique. Dr. J.L. Granatstein, Canada's foremost historian, pointed out errors of interpretation and fact, and offered good advice, as he has done for my previous six books. Dr. Steve Harris, the director general of the Directorate of History and Heritage, my former PhD supervisor and a life-long supporter who has edited and commented on all nine of my major books, again shared his deep knowledge of war, public history, and commemoration. Dr. Mark Humphries, professor of history at Laurier University and director of the Laurier Centre for Military Strategic and Disarmament Studies, passed along good advice and caution, especially with regard to framing aspects of Canadian nationalism. Dr. Cameron Pulsifer, retired historian of the CWM, provided a thorough edit of an early draft and was a sounding board for machine-gun tactics, one of his many areas of specialization. Dr. Bill Stewart, one of Canada's leading experts on the Canadian Corps' tactics and command, offered penetrating insight on the Vimy battle and its constructed memory. Dr. Norman Hillmer, professor of history at Carleton and one of the country's finest historians and editors, read the manuscript, shared his expertise, and provided good cheer over many walks. Dr. Roger Sarty, professor of history at Laurier University and former director at the CWM, offered very useful information on the place of Vimy in post-1945 Canada. Glenn Wright read the chapters and offered good advice and caution in several critical areas.

I thank Fiona Anthes, Carol Reid, Susan Ross, and Maggie Arbour at the Canadian War Museum's Military History Research Centre, and Sonia Doyon at the Ottawa Public Library, for their sharing of information, supply of books, and access to archival material.

I have had the pleasure of working at the CWM with a number of first-class colleagues, many of whom helped me sharpen my thinking about Vimy. I especially thank Molly McCullough, Marie-Louise Deruaz, Eric Fernberg, and Patricia Grimshaw. My colleagues at the CWM teach me something new every day, and it is a pleasure to work in this important institution. For this book, as in my previous ones, I have had the ongoing support of senior managers Mark O'Neill, Stephen Quick, James Whitham, Tony Glen, and Dr. Peter MacLeod.

My fellow historians at the CWM are an inspiring group with deep knowledge and enormous passion for military history and material culture. I have thanked Dr. Nic Clarke above, but I also wish to thank Dr. Mélanie Morin-Pelletier, with whom I have had many conversations about the nature of commemoration and the memory of the war in French Canada. Dr. Peter MacLeod and Dr. Andrew Burtch have been steadfast friends and brilliant colleagues of mine for over twelve years, and both have read and commented on many of my books and papers.

Years before the writing of this project, Sarah Cook conducted important research into newspapers and revealed to me the untapped information contained within. Matt Moore and Eliza Richardson carried out additional research into newspapers. All three located stories and nuances related to the Vimy legend. Trevor Ford came in the late innings to compile a bibliography. As a research fellow at the Laurier Centre for Military Strategic and Disarmament Studies, I gratefully acknowledge the support from that fine institution that does so much to encourage scholarship, especially through the flagship journal *Canadian Military History*. I also gratefully acknowledge support from the City of Ottawa through the Creation and Production Fund for Professional Artists. Dr. Mike Bechthold has been a friend for over two decades and he provided a number of key images of the Vimy monument.

Publishing Director Diane Turbide has been my champion at Penguin Random House Canada for a decade and I am grateful for her ongoing support and friendship. Diane and the large team there work diligently on behalf of authors. They are an inspiration. My friend and agent, Rick Broadhead, has been an ongoing source of support, keeping in touch throughout my illness and working tirelessly on my behalf. In our seventh book together, Tara Tovell provided her usual brilliant line and copy editing. Tara always gets me at the end of the long writing process, and with this being my sixth book in eight years, I did not have a lot left in the tank. But Tara inspired me to dig deep, and her careful and precise work makes my books better. I am very lucky to work with her.

The oncologists and nurses at the Ottawa Hospital have been unfailingly professional and supportive in treating me over the past several years. In addition to their prodigious skills and know-ledge, their compassion and optimism during dark times have given me hope to keep going.

Many friends have kept up my spirits and reminded me that there might be an end to this very long battle. Dr. Serge Durflinger has been a friend for a long time, sharing wisdom and positive thoughts on many things related to history, friendship, health, and fatherhood, including his considerable knowledge of Vimy. The Trent University crowd of Rachel, John, Lucy, Rick, Staci, Brien, and Gesa have been there through thick and thin. Friends in Manor Park, throughout Ottawa, and around the world have provided kind words and welcome aid.

I am lucky to have a strong and resilient family. Dr. Sharon Cook is a wise academic, loving mom, and super-fun grandmother. She and Clifford are a crucial part of our family. Together, we all miss my dad, Dr. Terry Cook, who did so much for the historical and archival profession, and who, more than anyone, guided me along the path to being a professional historian.

I always welcome a wry email or call from my brother, Graham, whose sharp advice and pointed humour give the Cook household much laughter. We are proud of him as a lawyer and author. Sam,

ACKNOWLEDGMENTS

Graham, Calla, and Redden Shantz, as well as Jennifer Klotz, have all been there for us. We are a happy bunch when we get together.

Emma, Paige, and Chloe are a daily delight for Sarah and me. We watch them grow and take on vibrant personalities. Every day is an adventure with them, and Sarah and I are lucky to share our lives with these wonderful girls. I would not have been able to fight so hard or for so long without the love of Sarah. She picks up the pieces, time and time again, and puts us all back together. Her deep knowledge and curiosity about history makes our life at home and abroad one that is filled with exploration, knowledge, discovery, and life-long education. She is my best friend and love.

SELECT BIBLIOGRAPHY

Library and Archives Canada, Government Records
RG 2, Records of the Privy Council Office
RG 9, Records of the Department of Militia and Defence
RG 24, Records of the Department of National Defence
RG 25, Records of the Department of External Affairs
RG 38, Records of the Department of Veterans Affairs

Library and Archives Canada, Private Records
Lord Beaverbrook papers, MG 27 II-G-1
R.G. Bennett papers, MG 26 K
Sir Robert Borden papers, MG 26 H
E.L.M. Burns papers, MG 31 G6
Gregory Clark papers, R8258 08E
Robert N. Clements papers, MG 30 E156
Sir Arthur Currie papers, MG 30 E100
William Green papers, MG 30 E430
Elmer Watson Jones papers, MG 30 E50
William Lyon Mackenzie King Diaries, MG 26 J13
D.E. Macintyre papers, MG 30 E241
Andrew McNaughton papers, MG 30 E133
Hubert Morris papers, MG 30 E379
G.W.L. Nicholson Papers, MG 31 G19

Victor Odlum papers, MG 30 E300
Talbot Mercer Papineau papers, MG 30 E52

Library and Archives Canada, War Diaries
Unit war diaries, available online

Canadian War Museum
William Antliff papers, 20080038-003
Mary Botel papers, 20100116-003
Andrew Coulter papers, 20060105-001
Leonard Cuff papers, 20080132-001
Sir Arthur Currie papers, 19801226-286
W.M.L. Draycott papers, 19730295-007
E.C. Forrest papers, 19780056-041
Horace Hubert Forster, Dibblee, 20050172-004
Katherine R. de la Bruère Girouard papers, 19820602-017
William Hendrie Hay papers, 20030142-001
Joseph Harrison MacFarlane papers, 19800218-014
Keith Campbell Macgowan papers, 19990026-016
J.W. McClung papers, 20030153-001
Albert Percy Menzies papers, 20100067-002
George Metcalf papers, 1990-0066-015
S.C. Mewburn papers, 20030088-028
Robert Miller papers, 20110042-002
Victor John Nixon papers, 19810467-005
Lawrence Rogers papers, 20040015-005
Howard Scott papers, 19910028-001
Richard Turner papers, 19710147-001
David Watson papers, 19820623-002

Canadian War Museum, Military History Research Centre
First Army Administrative Report on the Vimy Ridge Operations
Behind the Lines (1934)
Catalogue of the Canadian Official War Photographs, Second Exhibition

Flanders' Fields transcripts

Col. D.C. Unwin Simson, "Little Known Facts and Difficulties in the Construction of the Canadian Memorial on Vimy Ridge, and Other Memorials in France and Belgium"

SS143, Instructions for the Training of Platoons for Offensive Action

SS144, The Normal Formation for the Attack

Queen's University Archives

Walter Seymour Allward papers

National Gallery of Canada

Walter Allward papers

McGill University Archives

Hugh Urquhart papers

Published Government Documents

Canadian Battlefields Memorial Commission. *Canadian Battlefield Memorials*. Ottawa: King's Printer, 1929.

Government of Canada. *Canada in the First World War and the Road to Vimy Ridge*. Ottawa: Minister of Supply and Services, 1992.

Hansard, 1917–1939.

Mesquin, Alexandra. "Walter Allward, Submission Report," *Historic Sites and Monuments Board Canada* (Ottawa, 2001).

Newspapers and Media

Canada.com; CBC Television; *Daily Province*; *Edmonton Journal*; *The Globe*; *The Globe and Mail*; *Gloucester Citizen*; *Le Devoir*; *London Gazette*; *Military Gazette*; *Montreal Gazette*; *Ottawa Citizen*; *Toronto Daily Star*; *Winnipeg Free Press*.

Websites

Canada's Great War Album: http://greatwaralbum.ca/Great-War-Album/About-the-Great-War/Unrest-on-the-homefront/Francis-Cumming

CEF Study Group: http://cefresearch.ca

Canadian Images and Letters Project
David McLean, Maurice Bracewell, Amos William Mayse, G.H. Tripp

ARTICLES

Atkinson, Edward. "Colonel Doughy and the War Museum," *The Archivist* 16.4 (July–August 1989) 7–8.

Auger, Martin. "On the Brink of Civil War: The Canadian Government and the Suppression of the 1918 Quebec Easter Riots," *The Canadian Historical Review* 89.4 (December 2008) 503–40.

Baker, Marilyn. "To Honor and Remember: Remembrances of the Great War. The Next-of-Kin Monument in Winnipeg," *Manitoba History* 2 (1981) 8–11.

Bechthold, Mike. "In the Shadow of Vimy Ridge: The Canadian Corps in April and May 1917," in Geoffrey Hayes, Andrew Iarocci, and Mike Bechthold (eds.), *Vimy Ridge: A Canadian Reassessment* (Waterloo, Ontario: Laurier Centre for Military Strategic and Disarmament Studies and Wilfrid Laurier University Press, 2007) 239–64.

Black, Dan. "Canada's Unknown Soldier: The Tomb of the Unknown Soldier," *The Legion* (1 September 2000) online.

Boire, Michael. "The Underground War: Military Mining Operations in Support of the Attack on Vimy Ridge, 9 April 1917," *Canadian Military History* 1.1–2 (1992) 15–24.

Bormanis, Katrina. "What Remains: Repatriating and Entombing a Canadian Unknown Soldier of the Great War in the Nation's Capital," *War & Society* 35.3 (August 2016) 219–40.

Borstad, Lane. "Walter Allward: Sculptor and Architect of the Vimy Ridge Memorial," *Journal of the Society for the Study of Architecture in Canada* 33.1 (2008) 23–38.

Brandon, Laura. "Making Memory: Canvas of War and the Vimy Sculptures," in Briton Busch (ed.), *Canada and the Great War* (Montreal: McGill-Queen's University Press, 2003) 203–15.

Brandon, Laura. "The Canadian War Memorial That Never Was," *Canadian Military History* 7.4 (Autumn 1998) 45–54.

Brennan, Patrick. "Julian Byng and Leadership in the Canadian Corps," in Geoffrey Hayes, Andrew Iarocci, and Mike Bechthold (eds.), *Vimy Ridge: A Canadian Reassessment* (Waterloo, Ontario: Laurier Centre for Military Strategic and Disarmament Studies and Wilfrid Laurier University Press, 2007) 87–104.

Brennan, Patrick. "Major-General David Watson: A Critical Appraisal of Canadian Generalship in the Great War," in Andrew B. Godefroy (ed.), *Great War Commands: Historical Perspectives on Canadian Army Leadership 1914–1918* (Kingston: Canadian Defence Academy Press, 2010) 111–43.

Broznitsky, Peter. "For King, Not Tsar: Identifying Ukrainians in the Canadian Expeditionary Force, 1914–1918," *Canadian Military History* 17.3 (2008) 21–30.

Budreau, Lisa M. "The Politics of Remembrance: The Gold Star Mothers' Pilgrimage and America's Fading Memory of the Great War," *The Journal of Military History* 72 (April 2008) 371–411.

Campbell, David. "2nd Canadian Division: A 'Most Spectacular Battle,'" in Geoffrey Hayes, Andrew Iarocci, and Mike Bechthold (eds.), *Vimy Ridge: A Canadian Reassessment* (Waterloo, Ontario: Laurier Centre for Military Strategic and Disarmament Studies and Wilfrid Laurier University Press, 2007) 171–92.

Carr, Graham. "Rules of Engagement: Public History and the Drama of Legitimation," *The Canadian Historical Review* 86.2 (June 2005) 317–54.

Champion, C.P. "A Very British Coup: Canadianism, Quebec, and Ethnicity in the Flag Debate, 1964–1965," *Journal of Canadian Studies* 40.3 (2006) 68–99.

Chapman, Paul. "The Spirit of Canada—Uncloaked," *Stand To: The Journal of the Western Front Association* 51 (1990) 31–2.

Churchill, David S. "Draft Resisters, Left Nationalism, and the Politics of Anti-Imperialism," *Canadian Historical Review* 93.2 (June 2012) 227–60.

Cole, Douglas. "John S. Ewart and Canadian Nationalism," *Historical Papers* 4.1 (1969) 62–73.

Comeau, Robert. "L'Opposition à la conscription au Québec," in Legault and Lamarre (eds.), *La Premiere Guerre Mondiale et le Canada* (Montreal: Meridien, 1999).

Commachio, Cynthia. "Challenging Strathcona: The Cadet Training Controversy in English Canada, 1920–1950," in Campbell et al. (eds.), *Worth Fighting For: Canada's Tradition of War Resistance from 1812 to the War on Terror* (Toronto: Between the Lines, 2015) 79–92.

Cook, Tim. "A Proper Slaughter: The March 1917 Gas Raid," *Canadian Military History* 8.2 (Spring 1999) 7–23.

Cook, Tim. "Black-Hearted Traitors, Crucified Martyrs, and the Leaning Virgin: The Role of Rumor and the Great War Canadian Soldier," in Michael Neiberg and Jennifer Keene (eds.), *Finding Common Ground: New Directions in First World War Studies* (Leiden: Brill Academic Publishers, 2010) 21–42.

Cook, Tim. "Canada's Great War on Film: *Lest We Forget* (1935)," *Canadian Military History* 14.3 (Summer 2005) 5–20.

Cook, Tim. "Documenting War and Forging Reputations: Sir Max Aitken and the Canadian War Records Office in the First World War," *War in History* 10.3 (July 2003) 265–95.

Cook, Tim. "Literary Memorials: The Great War Regimental Histories, 1919–1939," *Journal of the Canadian Historical Association* (2002) 167–90.

Cook, Tim. "Quill and Canon: Writing the Great War in Canada," *The American Review of Canadian Studies* 35.3 (Autumn 2005) 503–30.

Cook, Tim. "Sir Arthur Currie," *Dictionary of Canadian Biography*, online.

Cook, Tim. "The Gunners of Vimy," in Geoffrey Hayes, Andrew Iarocci, and Mike Bechthold (eds.), *Vimy Ridge: A Canadian Reassessment.* (Waterloo, Ontario: Laurier Centre for Military Strategic and Disarmament Studies and Wilfrid Laurier University Press, 2007) 105–24.

Cook, Tim. "The Politics of Surrender: Canadian Soldiers and the Killing of Prisoners in the Great War," *Journal of Military History* 70.3 (July 2006) 637–65.

Cook, Tim. "The Singing War: Soldiers' Songs in the Great War," *American Review of Canadian Studies* 39.3 (September 2009) 224–41.

Cook, Tim. "Through Clouded Eyes: Gas Masks and the Canadian Corps in the First World War," *Canada Science and Technology Museum* 47 (Spring 1998) 4–20.

Cook, Tim and Christopher Schultz. "New Theatres of War: An Analysis of Paul Gross's Passchendaele," *Canadian Military History*, 19.3 (Summer 2010) 51–6.

Delaney, Douglas E. "Mentoring the Canadian Corps: Imperial Officers and the Canadian Expeditionary Force, 1914–1918," *Journal of Military History* 77.3 (July 2013) 931–53.

Dieterich, Generalleutnant Alfred. "The German 79th Reserve Infantry Division in the Battle of Vimy Ridge, April 1917," *Canadian Military History* 15.1 (Winter 2006) 69–85.

Djebabla, Mourad. "Historiographie francophone de la Première Guerre mondiale: écrire la Grande Guerre de 1914–1918 français au Canada et au Québec," *The Canadian Historical Review* 3.95 (September 2014) 407–16.

Donnell, Allan. "Vimy Ridge," in *Canada in the Great War*, volume IV (Toronto: United Publishers of Canada Limited, 1920).

Duffy, Dennis. "Among the Missing: Mass Death & Canadian Nationalism at the Vimy Memorial," *disClosure: A Journal of Social Theory* 18.10 (2009) 159–80.

Duffy, Dennis. "Complexity and Contradictions in Canadian Public Sculpture: The Case of Walter Allward," *American Review of Canadian Studies* 38 (Summer 2008) 189–206.

Duffy, Dennis. "The Grandfathering of William Lyon Mackenzie King," *The American Review of Canadian Studies* (Winter 2002) 581–608.

Duffy, Dennis. "Memorial as Expression of National Consciousness: The Canadian Vimy World War I Memorial," *Competitions* 15.3 (2005) 53–9.

Duguid, A. Fortesque. "Canada on Vimy Ridge," *The Canada Year Book* (1936).

Duguid, A. Fortesque. "Canadians in Battle: An Epic Achievement," *The Legionary* 11 (July 1936).

Du Prey, Pierre De La Ruffinière. "Allward's Figures, Lutyens's Flags and Wreaths," *JSSAC / JSEAC* 33.1 (2008) 57–64.

Durflinger, Serge. "Safeguarding Sanctity: Canada and the Vimy Memorial during the Second World War," in Geoffrey Hayes, Andrew Iarocci, and Mike Bechthold (eds.), *Vimy Ridge: A Canadian Reassessment*, (Waterloo: Laurier Centre for Military Strategic and Disarmament Studies and Wilfrid Laurier University Press, 2007) 291–312.

Dutil, Patrice A. "Against Isolationism: Napoléon Belcourt, French Canada, and 'La grande guerre,'" in David Mackenzie (ed.), *Canada and the First World War: Essay in Honour of Robert Craig Brown*. (Toronto: University of Toronto Press, 2005) 115–20.

Dutil, Patrice and Sean Conway. "A Legacy Lost: Macdonald in the Memory of His Successors," in Patrice Dutil and Roger Hall (eds.), *Macdonald at 200: New Reflections and Legacies* (Toronto: Dundurn, 2014) 379–404.

Eamon, Michael. "The War Against Public Forgetfulness: Commemorating 1812 in Canada," *London Journal of Canadian Studies*, 29.1 (November 2014) 134–85.

Fetherstonhaugh, R.C. "The Funeral of General Sir Arthur Currie," *Canadian Defence Quarterly* 11.2 (1934) 156–8.

Flanagan, Luke. "Canadians in Bexhill-on-Sea during the First World War: A Reflection of Canadian Nationhood?" *British Journal of Canadian Studies* 27.2 (2014) 131–48.

Flavelle, Ryan B. "The Second Battle of Ypres," *Canadian Military History* 24.1 (2015) 209–45.

Gammel, Irene. "The Memory of St. Julien: Configuring Gas Warfare in Mary Riter Hamilton's Battlefield Art," *Journal of War & Culture Studies* 9.1 (2016) 20–41.

Garvock, Bill. "From Vimy to Ypres: Pilgrimage Musings," *The Legionary* 12.2 (September 1936) 1.

Gendron, Robin. "The Two Faces of Charles the Good: Charles de Gaulle, France, and Decolonization in Quebec and New Caledonia," *International Journal* 69.1 (2014) 94–109.

Godefroy, Andrew. "The 4th Canadian Division: Trenches Should Never be Saved," in Geoffrey Hayes, Andrew Iarocci, and Mike Bechthold (eds.), *Vimy Ridge: A Canadian Reassessment.* (Waterloo, Ontario: Laurier Centre for Military Strategic and Disarmament Studies and Wilfrid Laurier University Press, 2007) 211–24.

Gordon, Alan. "Lest We Forget: Two Solitudes in War and Memory," in Adam Chapnick and Norman Hillmer (eds.), *Canadas of the Mind: The Making and Unmaking of Canadian Nationalisms in the Twentieth Century* (Montreal: McGill-Queen's University Press, 2007) 159–73.

Granatstein, J.L. "Conscription in the Great War," in David Mackenzie (ed.), *Canada and the First World War: Essays in Honour of Robert Craig Brown* (Toronto: University of Toronto Press, 2005) 62–75.

Graves, Matthew. "Memorial Diplomacy in Franco-Australian Relations," in Shanti Sumartojo and Ben Wellings (eds.), *Nation, Memory and Great War Commemoration Mobilizing the Past in Europe, Australia and New Zealand* (Bern: Peter Lang, 2014).

Grey, Anna. "Will Longstaff's Menin Gate at Midnight," *Journal of the Australian War Memorial* 12 (April 1988) 47–9.

Grodzinski, Major John R. "The Use and Abuse of Battle: Vimy Ridge and the Great War over the History of the First World War," *Canadian Military Journal* 10.1 (2009) 83–6.

Gustavson, Wes. "'Fairly Well Known and Need Not Be Discussed': Colonel A.F. Duguid and the Canadian Official History of the First World War," *Canadian Military History* 10.2 (Spring 2001) 41–54.

Hagenlucke, Heinz. "The German High Command," in Peter H. Liddle (ed.), *Passchendaele in Perspective: The Third Battle of Ypres* (London: Leo Cooper, 1997) 45–58.

Hale, Katherine. "Walter S. Allward, Sculptor," *The Canadian Magazine* 52.3 (January 1919) 783–8.

Harris, Paul and Sanders Marble. "The 'Step-by-Step' Approach: British Military Thought and Operational Method on the Western Front, 1915–1917," *War in History* 15.1 (2008) 17–42.

Harris, Stephen. "From Subordinate to Ally: The Canadian Corps and National Autonomy, 1914–1918," *Revue Internationale d'Histoire Militaire* 54 (1982) 109–30.

Hillmer, Norman. "The Canadian War Museum and the Military Identity of an Unmilitary People," *Canadian Military History*, 19.3 (Summer 2010), 19–26.

Hucker, Jacqueline. "'After the Agony in Stony Places': The Meaning and Significance of the Vimy Monument," in Geoffrey Hayes, Andrew Iarocci, and Mike Bechthold (eds.), *Vimy Ridge: A Canadian Reassessment*. (Waterloo, Ontario: Laurier Centre for Military Strategic and Disarmament Studies and Wilfrid Laurier University Press, 2007) 279–90.

Hucker, Jacqueline. "'Battle and Burial': Recapturing the Cultural Meaning of Canada's National Memorial on Vimy Ridge," *The Public Historian* 31.1 (February 2009) 89–109.

Hucker, Jacqueline. "The Vimy Memorial: The Role of the Stone," unpublished report (10 March 1999).

Humphries, Mark. "War's Long Shadow: Masculinity, Medicine and the Gendered Politics of Trauma, 1914–1939," *Canadian Historical Review* 91.3 (2010) 503–31.

Hundevad, John. "Pilgrimages, Then and Now," *The Legionary* 37.1 (June 1962) 10.

Iacobelli, Teresa. "A Participant's History?: The CBC and the Manipulation of Oral History," *Oral History Review* 38.2 (Fall–Winter 2011) 331–48.

Inglis, K.S. "Entombing Unknown Soldiers: From London to Paris to Baghdad," *History & Memory* 5.2 (1993) 7–31.

Jackson, A.Y. *Canadian Forum* 11.18 (March 1922) 559.

Keelan, Geoff. "Il a bien merité de la Patrie: The 22nd Battalion and the Memory of Courcelette," *Canadian Military History*, 19.3 (Summer 2010) 29–40.

Keshen, Jeffrey. "The Great War Soldier as Nation Builder," in Briton C. Busch (ed.), *Canada and the Great War* (Montreal: McGill-Queen's University Press, 2003) 3–26.

Krause, Jonathan. "The French Battle for Vimy Ridge, Spring 1915," *Journal of Military History* 77 (January 2013) 91–113.

Lachaise, Bernard. "De Gaulle et le Québec libre en 1967," *Proceedings of the Western Society for French History* 36 (2008) 323–35.

Laqueur, Thomas W. "Names, Bodies and the Anxiety of Erasure," in Theodore R. Schatzki and Wolfgang Natter (eds.), *The Social and Political Body* (New York: The Guilford Press, 1996) 123–61.

Litt, Paul. "The War, Mass Culture, and Cultural Nationalism," in David Mackenzie (ed.), *Canada and the First World War: Essays in Honour of Robert Craig Brown* (Toronto: University of Toronto Press, 2005) 339–44.

Litt, Paul. "Trudeaumania: Participatory Democracy in the Mass-Mediated Nation," *The Canadian Historical Review* 89.1 (March 2008) 27–53.

Macintyre, D.E. "The Vimy Sector: In War and Peace," *The Legionary* 14.9 (April 1939).

Macleod, Jenny. "The Fall and Rise of Anzac Day: 1965 and 1990 Compared," *War in Society* 20.1 (May 2002) 149–68.

MacMillan, Margaret. "Canada and the Peace Settlements," in David Mackenzie (ed.), *Canada and the First World War: Essays in Honour of Robert Craig Brown* (Toronto: University of Toronto Press, 2005) 379–408.

Martin, Jean. "Vimy, April 1917: The Birth of *Which* Nation?" *Canadian Military Journal* 11.2 (Spring 2011) 32–8.

McNaughton, A.G.L. "The Development of Artillery in the Great War," *Canadian Defence Quarterly* 6.2 (January 1929) 160–71.

McPherson, Kathryn. "Carving Out a Past: The Canadian Nurses' Association War Memorial," *Histoire sociale/Social History* 29.58 (November 1996) 418–29.

Monger, David. "'No mere silent commander'? Henry Horne and the Mentality of Command during the First World War," *Historical Research,* 82.216 (2009) 340–59.

Morton, Desmond. "French Canada and the Canadian Militia, 1868–1914," *Social History* 3 (June 1969) 32–50.

Morton, Desmond. "'Junior by Sovereign Allies': The Transformation of the Canadian Expeditionary Force, 1914–1918," in Norman Hillmer and Philip Wigley (eds.), *The First British Commonwealth* (London: Frank Cass, 1980) 56–67.

Morton, Desmond. "The Canadian Veterans' Heritage from the Great War," in Peter Neary and J.L. Granatstein (eds.), *The Veterans Charter and Post–World War II Canada* (Montreal: McGill-Queen's University Press, 1998) 15–31.

Morton, Desmond and Glenn Wright. "The Bonus Campaign, 1919–21: Veterans and the Campaign for Re-establishment," *Canadian Historical Review* 64.2 (1983) 147–67.

Nangle, Lieutenant-Colonel T. "Newfoundland Memorial Park: Beaumont Hamel," *The Veteran* 5.3 (May 1926) 8–13.

Neary, Peter. "'Without the stigma of pauperism': Canadian Veterans in the 1930s," *British Journal of Canadian Studies* 22.1 (2009) 31–62.

Neiberg, Mike. "'What True Misery Is': France's Crisis of Morale 1917," in Peter Dennis and Jeffrey Grey (eds.), *1917: Tactics, Training and Technology, Proceedings of the 2007 Chief of Army's Military History Conference* (Canberra: Australian Military History Publications, 2007) 105–24.

Nicholson, Colonel G.W.L. "The Second Battle of Ypres," *Canadian Military History* 24.1 (2015) 183–207.

Oliver, Dean F. "Vimy Ridge Day, 2012," *Canadian Military History* 21.3 (2015) 49–57.

Osbourne, B.S. "Warscapes, Landscapes, Inscapes: France, War, and Canadian National Identity," in A.R.H. Baker (ed.), *Place, Culture and Identity: Essays in Historical Geography in Honour of Alan R.H. Baker.* (Québec: Les Presses de L' Université Laval, 2001) 311–33.

Osborne, H.C. "Allward of Vimy," *The Legionary* (April 1937).

Osborne, H.C. "British Cemeteries and Memorials of the Great War," in *AACS—Proceedings of the 44th Annual Convention, Toronto, Ontario, Canada, September 8, 9, 10 and 11, 1930.*

Palazzo, Albert. "The British Army's Counter-Battery Staff Office and Control of the Enemy in World War I," *The Journal of Military History* 63 (1999) 55–74.

Pegum, John. "The Old Front Line: Returning to the Battlefields in the Writings of Ex-Servicemen," in Jessica Meyer (ed.), *British Popular Culture and the First World War* (Leiden: Brill, 2008) 217–36.

Perry, Anne Anderson. "Walter Allward: Canada's Great Sculptor," *National Pictorial* (1 March 1922) 8–9.

Pierce, John. "Constructing Memory: The Vimy Memorial," *Canadian Military History* 1.1 (1992) 5–8.

Powley, A.E. "Flanders' Fields," *Radio-TV: The Canadian Broadcasting Corporation Staff Magazine* (October 1964) no pagination.

Ralph, Joel. "Vimy Revisited," *The Beaver* 87.2 (2007) 36–41.

Richard, Beatrice. "La mémoire collective de la guerre au Québec: Un espace de résistance politique?," *Canadian Issues/Themes canadiens* (2004) 383–92.

Roy, Reginald. "The Canadian Military Tradition," in Hector J. Massey (ed.), *The Canadian Military: A Profile* (Toronto: Copp Clark Publishing, 1972) 6–48.

Sangster, Joan. "Mobilizing Canadian Women for War," in David Mackenzie (ed.), *Canada and the First World War* (Toronto: University of Toronto Press, 2005) 157–94.

Sarty, Roger. "The Nationalization of Military History: Scholarship, Politics, and the Canadian War Museum," in Chapnick and Hillmer (eds.), *Canadas of the Mind*, 110–33.

Sassoon, Siegfried. "On Passing the New Menin Gate," *The Norton Anthology of English Literature* (New York: W.W. Norton and Company, 1986) 1900–1.

Scott, F.G. "The Significance of Vimy: An Address by the Venerable Archdeacon F.G. Scott, C.M.G, D.S.O., D.D., D.C.L., LL.D.," Toronto Empire Club of Canada, 22 October 1936.

Scott, Jill. "Vimy Ridge Memorial: Stone with a Story," *Queen's Quarterly* 114.4 (Winter 2007): 506–20.

Scott, John. "'Three Cheers for Earl Haig': Canadian Veterans and the Visit of Field Marshal Sir Douglas Haig to Canada in the Summer of 1925," *Canadian Military History* 5.1 (1996) 35–40.

Sharpe, Chris A. "Enlistment in the Canadian Expeditionary Force 1914–1918: A Regional Analysis," *Journal of Canadian Studies* 18 (1984) 15–29.

Sharpe, Chris A. "Enlistment in the Canadian Expeditionary Force 1914–1918: A Re-Evaluation," *Canadian Military History* 24.1 (2015) 17–60.

Sheffield, Gary. "Haig and the British Expeditionary Force in 1917," in Gary Sheffield, *Command and Morale: The British Army on the Western Front, 1914–1918* (Barnsley, United Kingdom: Praetorian Press, 2014).

Sheffield, Gary. "Vimy Ridge and the Battle of Arras," in Geoffrey Hayes, Andrew Iarocci, and Mike Bechthold (eds.), *Vimy Ridge: A Canadian Reassessment* (Waterloo, Ontario: Laurier Centre for Military Strategic and Disarmament Studies and Wilfrid Laurier University Press, 2007) 15–30.

Smith, Jordan Michael. "Reinventing Canada: Stephen Harper's Conservative Revolution," *World Affairs Journal*, online.

Stacey, C.P. "Nationality: The Experience of Canada," Canadian Historical Association, *Historical Papers* (1967) 10–19.

Stewart, William F. "'Byng Boys': A Profile of Senior Commanders of Canadian Combat Units on the Somme, 1916," *War in History* 23.1 (January 2016) 55–78.

Stewart, William F. "Frustrated Belligerence: The Unhappy History of the 5th Canadian Division in the First World War," *Canadian Military History* 2.4 (2015) 31–47.

Swettenham, John. "The Battle of Hill 70," *The Legionary* 42.4 (September 1967).

Thomson, Denise. "National Sorrow, National Pride: Commemoration of the War in Canada, 1918–1945," *Journal of Canadian Studies* 30.4 (1995/1996) 5–27.

Todman, Daniel. "'Sans peur et sans reproche': The Retirement, Death, and Mourning of Sir Douglas Haig," *Journal of Military History* 67.4 (2003) 1083–6.

Travers, T.H.E. "Allies in Conflict: The British and Canadian Official Historians and the Real Story of the Second Ypres," *Journal of Contemporary History* 24.2 (April 1989) 301–13.

Travers, Tim. "Canadian Film and the First World War," in Michael Paris (ed.), *The First World War and Popular Cinema: 1914 to the Present* (New Brunswick, New Jersey: Rutgers University Press, 2000).

Underhill, Frank H. "The Political Ideas of John S. Ewart," *Report of the Annual Meeting of the Canadian Historical Association* 12.1 (1933) 23–32.

Vance, Jonathan. "An Open Door to a Better Future: The Memory of Canada's Second World War," in Geoffrey Hayes, Mike Bechthold, and Matt Symes (eds.), *Canada and the Second World War: Essays in Honour of Terry Copp* (Waterloo, Ontario: Wilfrid Laurier University Press, 2012) 461–77.

Vance, Jonathan. "Battle Verse: Poetry and Nationalism after Vimy Ridge," in Geoffrey Hayes, Andrew Iarocci, and Mike Bechthold (eds.), *Vimy Ridge: A Canadian Reassessment* (Waterloo, Ontario: Laurier Centre for Military Strategic and Disarmament Studies and Wilfrid Laurier University Press, 2007) 265–77.

Vance, Jonathan. "Provincial Patterns of Enlistment in the Canadian Expeditionary Force," *Canadian Military History* 17.2 (Spring 2008) 75–8.

Vance, Jonathan. "Remembering Armageddon," in David Mackenzie (ed.), *Canada and the First World War: Essays in Honour of Robert Craig Brown* (Toronto: University of Toronto Press 2005) 409–33.

Vance, Jonathan. "Tangible Demonstrations of a Great Victory: War Trophies in Canada," *Material History Review* 42 (Fall 1995) 47–56.

Vance, Jonathan. "The Soldier as Novelist: Literature, History and the Great War," *Canadian Literature: A Quarterly of Criticism and Review* 179 (Winter 2003) 22–37.

Vance, Jonathan. "'Today they were alive again': The Canadian Corps Reunion of 1934," *Ontario History* 87.4 (December 1995) 327–43.

Vipond, Mary. "Canadian Nationalism and the Plight of Canadian Magazines in the 1920s," *The Canadian Historical Review* 58.1 (March 1977) 43–63.

Wallace, W.S. "The Growth of Canadian National Feeling," *Canadian Historical Review* 1.2 (June 1920) 136–65.

"Walter S. Allward, Sculptor and Architect of Vimy Memorial Honoured by R.A.I.C.," *The Journal of the Royal Architectural Institute of Canada* 14.3 (March 1937) 36–7, 40–1, 43.

William, Lieutenant-Colonel Robert. "The 85th Canadian Infantry Battalion and First Contact with the Enemy at Vimy Ridge, 9–14 April 1917," *Canadian Army Journal* 8.1 (Winter 2005) 73–82.

Wood, H.F. "Adolph Hitler's Vimy 'Pilgrimage,'" *The Legionary* 39.3 (August 1964).

Young, Alan. "'We throw the torch': Canadian Memorials of the Great War and the Mythology of Heroic Sacrifice," *Journal of Canadian Studies* 24.4 (1990) 5–28.

Young, W.R. "Conscription, Rural Depopulation, and the Farmers of Ontario, 1917–19," *The Canadian Historical Review* 53.3 (1972), 289–320.

Zucchero, Jim. "The Canadian National War Memorial: Metaphor for the Birth of a Nation," in D.M.R. Bentley (ed.), *Mnemographia Canadensis: Essays on Memory, Community, and Environment in Canada*, vol. 2 (London, Ontario: Canadian Poetry Press, 1999) 143–73.

Monographs and Books

Aitken, Sir Max. *Canada in Flanders: The Official Story of the Canadian Expeditionary Force*, Volume I. Toronto: Hodder and Stoughton, 1916.

Allen, Gene and Daniel J. Robinson, eds. *Communicating in Canada's Past: Essays in Media History*. Toronto: University of Toronto Press, 2006.

Allen, Ralph. *Ordeal by Fire: Canada, 1910–1945.* Toronto: Doubleday Canada, 1961.

Anderson, Antony. *The Diplomat: Lester Pearson and the Suez Crisis.* Fredericton, New Brunswick: Goose Lane, 2015.

Angus, H.F., ed. *Canada and Her Great Neighbor: Sociological Surveys of Opinion and Attitudes in Canada Concerning the United States.* Toronto: Ryerson Press, 1938.

Armour, Stuart. *A Pilgrim's Progress.* Cobourg: Frank W. Lapp, 1936.

Armstrong, Elizabeth. *The Crisis of Quebec 1914–1918.* New York: Columbia University Press, 1937.

Audoin-Rouzeau, Stéphane and Annette Becker. *14–18: Understanding the Great War.* New York: Hill and Wang, 2014.

Barton, Peter and Banning Banning. *Vimy Ridge and Arras: The Spring 1917 Offensive in Panoramas.* Toronto: Dundurn Publishers, 2010.

Bayern, Rupprecht von. *Eugeun von Frauenholz, Mein Kriegstagebuch,* volume II. Munich: Deutsher National Verlag, 1929.

Beach, Jim. *Haig's Intelligence: GHQ and the German Army, 1916–1918.* New York: Cambridge University Press, 2013.

Beattie, Kim. *48th Highlanders of Canada, 1891–1928.* Toronto: Southam Press, 1932.

Beatty, David, ed. *The Vimy Pilgrimage, July 1936 from the Diary of Florence Murdock, Amherst, Nova Scotia.* Amherst: Acadian, 1919.

Bennett, Stewart Gordon. *The 4th Canadian Mounted Rifles, 1914–1919.* Toronto: Murray Print Co., 1926.

Bercuson, David Jay. *True Patriot: The Life of Brooke Claxton, 1898–1960.* Toronto: University of Toronto Press, 1993.

Bercuson, David J. and J.L. Granatstein. *War and Peacekeeping: From South Africa to the Gulf—Canada's Limited Wars.* Toronto: Key Porter Books, 1991.

Berton, Pierre. *1967: The Last Good Year.* Toronto: Doubleday, 1967.

Berton, Pierre. *Vimy.* Toronto: McClelland & Stewart, 1986.

Betts, Amanda, ed. *In Flanders Fields: 100 Years.* Toronto: Alfred A. Knopf, 2015.

Bird, Will. *The Communication Trench*. Montreal: Perreault, 1932.

Bird, Will. *Thirteen Years After*. Toronto: The Maclean Publishing Company, 1932.

Black, Jeremy. *The Great War and the Making of the Modern World*. London: Continuum, 2011.

Blomfield, Reginald. *Memoirs of an Architect*. Toronto: Macmillan Publishers, 1932.

Boff, Jonathan. *Winning and Losing on the Western Front: The British Third Army and the Defeat of Germany in 1918*. Cambridge: Cambridge University Press, 2012.

Bond, Brian. *The Unquiet Western Front: Britain's Role in Literature and History*. Cambridge: Cambridge University Press, 2002.

Booth, Jeffrey, ed. *Opened by Censor*. Aylmer, Ontario: Aylmer Express Ltd., 2008.

Borden, Robert. *Robert Laird Borden: His Memoirs*. Edited by Henry Borden. 2 vols. London: Macmillan, 1938.

Bosher, J.F. *The Gaullist Attack on Canada, 1967–1997*. Montreal: McGill-Queen's University Press, 2000.

Bothwell, Robert. *The New Penguin History of Canada*. Toronto: Penguin Canada, 2006.

Bouvier, Patrick. *Déserteurs et insoumis. Les Canadiens français et la justice militaire (1914–1918)*. Outremont, Quebec: Athéna Editions, 2003.

Bowering, Clifford H. *Service: The Story of the Canadian Legion 1925–1936*. Ottawa: Dominion Command, Canadian Legion, 1960.

Bowker, Alan. *A Time Such as There Never Was Before: Canada After the Great War*. Toronto: Dundurn Publishers, 2014.

Brandon, Laura. *Art or Memorial: The Forgotten History of Canada's War Art*. Calgary: University of Calgary, 2006.

Bridle, Augustus. *Sons of Canada: Short Studies of Characteristic Canadians*. Toronto: J.M. Dent & Sons, 1916.

Budreau, Lisa M. *Bodies of War: World War I and the Politics of Commemoration in America, 1919–1933*. New York: New York University Press, 2010.

Burge, John. *Three Soldiers and the Ethos of Service.* Self-published, 2016.

Burns, E.L.M. *General Mud: Memoirs of Two World Wars.* Toronto: Clarke, Irwin, 1970.

Cameron, Charles S. *War! What of it! His Memoirs While Serving with the 16th Battalion (Canadian Scottish).* Victoria, British Columbia: A. Craig Cameron, 2008.

Campbell, Lara A., Dominique Clément, and Greg Kealey, eds. *Debating Dissent: Canada and the 1960s.* Toronto: University of Toronto Press, 2012.

Canadian Bank of Commerce. *Letters from the Front: Being a record of the part played by officers of the Bank in the Great War, 1914–1919.* Toronto: Southam Press, 1920.

Canadian Veterans' Stories, Special Edition (no editor listed). Self-published, 2007.

Cane, Bruce, ed. *It Made You Think of Home: The Haunting Journal of Deward Barnes, CEF: 1916–1919.* Toronto: Dundurn Publishers, 2004.

Careless, J.M.S. *Canada: A Story of Challenge.* Toronto: Macmillan, 1963.

Champion, Christian P. *The Strange Demise of British Canada: The Liberals and Canadian Nationalism, 1964–68.* Montreal: McGill-Queen's University Press, 2010.

Chapnick, Adam and Norman Hillmer, eds. *Canadas of the Mind: The Making and Unmaking of Canadian Nationalisms in the Twentieth Century.* Montreal: McGill-Queen's University Press, 2007.

Clark, Gregory. *War Stories.* Toronto: Ryerson Press, 1964.

Clayton, Anthony. *Paths of Glory: The French Army, 1914–18.* London: Cassell, 2003.

Clement, Dominique. *Human Rights in Canada: A History.* Waterloo: Wilfred Laurier University Press, 2016.

Clyne, Henry Randolph Notman. *Vancouver's 29th: A Chronicle of the 29th in Flanders Fields.* Vancouver: Tobin's Tiger Association, 1964.

Cohen, Andrew. *Lester B. Pearson.* Toronto: Penguin, 2008.

Connelly, Mark. *The Great War, Memory and Ritual: Commemorations in the City and East London, 1916–1939*. Woodbridge, Ontario: Boydell Press, 2002.

Cook, Tim. *At the Sharp End: Canadians Fighting the Great War 1914 to 1916, Volume One*. Toronto: Viking Canada, 2007.

Cook, Tim. *Clio's Warriors: Canadian Historians and the Writing of the World Wars*. Vancouver: University of British Columbia Press, 2006.

Cook, Tim. *Fight to the Finish: Canadians Fighting the Second World War 1944–1945*. Toronto: Allen Lane, 2015.

Cook, Tim. *Shock Troops: Canadians Fighting the Great War 1917–1918, Volume Two*. Toronto: Penguin Canada, 2009.

Cook, Tim. *The Madman and the Butcher: The Sensational Wars of Sam Hughes and General Arthur Currie*. Toronto: Penguin Canada, 2011.

Cook, Tim. *Warlords: Borden, Mackenzie King, and Canada's World Wars*. Toronto: Allen Lane, 2012.

Copp, Terry and Richard Nielsen. *No Price Too High: Canadians and the Second World War*. Toronto: McGraw-Hill Ryerson Trade, 1995.

Cormier, Jeffrey. *The Canadianization Movement: Emergence, Survival, and Success*. Toronto: University of Toronto Press, 2004.

Corrigall, Major D.J. *History of the 20th Battalion CEF*. Toronto: Stone and Cox Ltd., 1936.

Corrigall, Major D.J. *The History of the Twentieth Canadian Battalion (Central Ontario regiment) Canadian Expeditionary Force: In the Great War, 1914–1918*. Toronto: Stone and Cox Ltd., 1936.

Costilla, Joseph. *Le people de la nuit*. Montreal: Éditions Chénier, 1965.

Crane, David. *Empires of the Dead: How One Man's Vision Led to the Creation of WWI's War Graves*. Glasgow: United Kingdom, 2013.

Creighton, Donald. *Canada's First Century*, 2nd ed. Don Mills, Ontario: Oxford University Press, 1970 (reprint 2012).

Dafoe, John W. *Over the Canadian Battlefields: Notes of a Little Journey in France, in March, 1919*. Toronto: Thomas Allen, 1919.

Dancocks, Daniel G. *Gallant Canadians: The Story of the Tenth Canadian Infantry Battalion, 1914–1919.* Toronto: Penguin Books Canada, 1990.

Dancocks, Daniel G. *Sir Arthur Currie: A Biography.* Toronto: University of Toronto Press, 1987.

Dawson, Robert MacGregor. *The Development of Dominion Status, 1900–1936.* London: Frank Cass, 1965.

Dickson, Paul Douglas. *A Thoroughly Canadian General: A Biography of General H.D.G. Crerar.* Toronto: University of Toronto Press, 2007.

Djebabla-Brun, Mourad. *Se souvenir de la Grande Guerre: la mémoire plurielle de 14–18 au Québec.* Montreal: VLB, 2004.

Doughty, Robert. *Pyrrhic Victory: French Strategy and Operations in the Great War.* Cambridge, Massachusetts: Belknap Press of Harvard University Press, 2005.

Duguid, A.F. *Official History of the Canadian Forces in the Great War, 1914–1919.* Ottawa: King's Printer, 1938.

Duncan, David Merritt. *The Story of the Canadian People.* Toronto: The Macmillan Co. of Canada, Ltd. 1919.

Durflinger, Serge. *Lest We Forget: A History of the Last Post Fund, 1909–1999.* Montreal: Last Post Fund, 2000.

Durflinger, Serge. *Veterans with a Vision: Canada's War Blinded in Peace and War.* Vancouver: UBC Press, 2010.

Edwardson, Ryan. *Canadian Content: Culture and the Quest for Nationhood.* Toronto: University of Toronto Press, 2008.

England, M.C., Robert. *Recollections of a Nonagenarian of Service in the Royal Canadian Regiment (1916–19).* Self-published, 1983.

English, John. *The Worldly Years: The Life of Lester Pearson, Volume II: 1949–1972.* Toronto: A.A. Knopf Canada, 1992.

Evans, Suzanne. *Mothers of Heroes, Mothers of Martyrs: World War I and the Politics of Grief.* Montreal: McGill-Queen's University Press, 2007.

Farndale, General Sir Martin. *History of the Royal Regiment of Artillery, Western Front, 1914–1918.* London: The Royal Artillery Institution, 1986.

Farr, Don. *The Silent General: Horne of the First Army.* Solihull: Helion and Company, 2006.

Fetherstonaugh, R.C. *The Royal Montreal Regiment, 14th Battalion, C.E.F., 1914–1925.* Montreal: Gazette Print Co. Limited, 1927.

Fetherstonhaugh, R.C. *The 24th Battalion, CEF, Victoria Rifles of Canada, 1914–1919.* Montreal: Gazette Printing Company, 1930.

Filteau, Gerald. *Le Québec, le Canada et la guerre 1914–1918.* Montreal: Les Éditions de l'Aurore, 1977.

Forsey, Eugene. *The Royal Power of Dissolution of Parliament in the British Commonwealth.* Toronto: Oxford University Press, 1943.

Fox, Frank. *The Battle of the Ridge Arras–Messines, March–June 1917.* London: C. Arthur Pearson, 1918.

Francis, R. Douglas. *Frank H. Underhill: Intellectual Provocateur.* Toronto: University of Toronto Press, 1986.

Fraser, Donald and Reginald H. Roy. *The Journal of Private Fraser, 1914–1918, Canadian Expeditionary Force.* Victoria, British Columbia: Sono Nis Press, 1985.

Freeman, Bill and Richard Nielson. *Far from Home: Canadians and the First World War.* New York: McGraw-Hill Ryerson Trade, 1999.

Fussell, Paul. *The Great War and Modern Memory.* New York: Oxford University Press, 1975.

Garnell, B.A. *History of Canada.* Toronto: W.J. Gage and Company, 1926.

Godwin, George. *Why Stay We Here?: Odyssey of a Canadian Infantry Officer in France in World War I.* Victoria, British Columbia: Godwin Books, (1930) 2002.

Goodspeed, Donald. *The Road Past Vimy: The Canadian Corps, 1914–1918.* Toronto: Macmillan Publishers, 1969.

Gordon, Alan. *Making Public Pasts: The Contested Terrain of Montreal's Public Memories, 1891–1930.* Montreal: McGill-Queen's University Press, 2001.

Gossage, Peter and J.I. Little. *An Illustrated History of Quebec: Tradition and Modernity.* Don Mills, Ontario: Oxford University Press, 2012.

Gould, L.M. *From B.C. to Baisieux: Being the Narrative of the 102nd Battalion.* Victoria, British Columbia: Thos. R. Cusack Presses, 1919.

Grace, Sherrill. *Landscapes of War and Memory: The Two World Wars in Canadian Literature and the Arts, 1977–2007.* Edmonton: University of Alberta Press, 2014.

Grafton, Lt. Col. C.S. *The Canadian "Emma Gees": A History of the Canadian Machine Gun Corps.* London, Ontario: Hunter Printing Company, 1938.

Graham, Roger. *The King–Byng Affair, 1926: A Question of Responsible Government.* Toronto: Copp Clark, 1967.

Granatstein, J.L. *Who Killed Canadian History?* Toronto: Harper Collins, 1998.

Granatstein, J.L. and J. M. Hitsman. *Broken Promises: A History of Conscription in Canada.* Oxford: Oxford University Press, 1977.

Granatstein, J.L. and Desmond Morton. *Canada and the Two World Wars.* Toronto: Key Porter Books, 2003.

Grant, W.L. *History of Canada.* London: William Heinemann, 1923.

Graves, Dianne. *A Crown of Life: The World of John McCrae.* St. Catharines, Ontario: Vanwell, 1997.

Greenhous, Bereton and Stephen J. Harris. *Canada and the Battle of Vimy Ridge.* Ottawa: Canadian Government Publication Centre, 1992.

Gregory, Adrian. *The Silence of Memory: Armistice Day, 1919–1946.* Oxford: Berg Publishers, 1994.

Grigg, John. *Lloyd George: War Leader, 1916–1918.* London: Penguin Books, 2003.

Grout, Derek. *Thunder in the Skies: A Canadian Gunner in the Great War.* Foreword by Brigadier General Ernest Beno. Toronto: Dundurn Publishers, 2015.

Gunn, Lieutenant-Colonel J.N. *Historical Records of No. 8 Canadian Field Ambulance.* Toronto: The Ryerson Press, 1920.

Hale, James. *Branching Out: The Story of the Royal Canadian Legion.* Ottawa: Royal Canadian Legion, 1995.

Hale, Katherine. *Canada's Peace Tower and Memorial Chamber.* Oshawa, Ontario: Mundy-Goodfellow, 1935.

Hanna, Emma. *The Great War on the Small Screen.* Edinburgh: Edinburgh University Press, 2009.

Harris, J.P. *Douglas Haig and the First World War*. Cambridge: Cambridge University Press, 2008.

Harris, Stephen J. *The Making of a Professional Army 1860–1939*. Toronto: University of Toronto Press, 1988.

Hart, Peter. *Bloody April: Slaughter over the Skies in Arras 1917*. London: McArthur & Company, 2005.

Hayes, Geoffrey, Andrew Iarocci and Mike Bechthold, eds. *Vimy Ridge: A Canadian Reassessment*. Waterloo, Ontario: Laurier Centre for Military Strategic and Disarmament Studies and Wilfrid Laurier University Press, 2007.

Hayes, Joseph. *The Eighty-Fifth in France and Flanders*. Halifax: Royal Print & Litho Limited, 1920.

Hessler, Harold. *War Interlude, 1916–1919*. Bloomington, IUniverse, 2011.

Hillmer, Norman. *O.D. Skelton: A Portrait of Canadian Ambition*. Toronto: University of Toronto Press, 2015.

Holbrook, Carolyn. *ANZAC: The Unauthorised Biography*. Canberra: University of New South Wales, 2014.

Hucker, Jacqueline and Julian Smith. *Vimy: Canada's Memorial to a Generation*. Ottawa: Sanderling Press, 2012.

Hundevad, John. *Guide Book of the Pilgrimage to Vimy and the Battlefields*. Ann Arbor, Michigan: University of Michigan Press, 1936.

Hutchison, Bruce. *The Unknown Country: Canada and Her People*. Don Mills, Ontario: Oxford University Press, 1942.

Hyatt, A.M.J. *General Sir Arthur Currie: A Military Biography*. Toronto: University of Toronto Press in collaboration with Canadian War Museum and National Museums of Canada, 1987.

Hynes, Samuel. *A War Imagined: The First World War and English Culture*. New York: Collier Books, 1990.

Iarocci, Andrew. *Shoestring Soldiers: The 1st Canadian Division at War, 1914–1915*. Toronto: University of Toronto Press, 2008.

Igartua, José. *The Other Quiet Revolution: National Identities in English Canada, 1945–1971*. Vancouver: University of British Columbia Press, 2006.

Inglis, Ken. *Sacred Places: War Memorials in the Australian Landscape.* Carlton, Victoria: The Miegunyah Press, 1998.

Iriam, Glenn R. *In the Trenches, 1914–1918.* Bloomington, Indiana: Trafford Publishing, 2008.

Isitt, Benjamin. *Victoria to Vladivostok: Canada's Siberian Expedition, 1917–19.* Vancouver: UBC Press, 2010.

Ito, Roy. *We Went to War: The Story of the Japanese Canadians Who Served During the First and Second World Wars.* Stittsville, Ontario: Canada's Wings, 1985.

Jalland, Pat. *Death in War and Peace: A History of Loss and Grief in England, 1914–1970.* Oxford: Oxford University Press, 2010.

James, Lawrence. *Imperial Warrior: The Life and Times of Field Marshal Viscount Allenby, 1861–1936.* London: Weidenfeld and Nicolson, 1993.

Jeffrey, Brooke. *Dismantling Canada: Stephen Harper's New Conservative Agenda.* Montreal: McGill-Queen's University Press, 2015

Junger, Ernst. *The Storm of Steel.* London: Chatto & Windus, 1929.

Kentner, Robert George. *Some Recollections of the Battles of World War I.* Fredonia, New York: Irene Kentner Lawson, 1995.

Kerry, A.J. and W. A. McDill. *History of the Corps of Royal Canadian Engineers: Volume I, 1749–1939.* Ottawa: Military Engineers Association of Canada, 1962.

King, Alex. *Memorials of the Great War in Britain: The Symbolism & Politics of Remembrance.* Oxford: Berg Publishers, 1998.

Kingsmill, Suzanne. *Francis Scrimger: Beyond the Call of Duty.* Toronto: Dundurn, 1991.

Knowles, Norman. *Inventing the Loyalists: The Ontario Loyalist Tradition and the Creation of Usable Pasts.* Toronto: University of Toronto Press, 1997.

Lacombe, Sylvie. *La Rencontre de deux peuples élus: Comparaison des ambitions nationale et impériale au Canada entre 1868 et 1920.* Sainte-Foy, Quebec: Presses de l'Université Laval, 2002.

Letournea, Jocelyn. *A History for the Future: Rewriting Memory and Identity in Quebec.* Montreal: McGill Queen's University Press, 2004.

Lloyd, David William. *Battlefield Tourism: Pilgrimage and the Commemoration of the Great War in Britain, Australia and Canada, 1919–1939*. New York: Bloomsbury Publishing, 1998.

Longworth, Philip. *The Unending Vigil: A History of the Commonwealth War Graves Commission*. London: Constable, 1967.

Lower, Arthur R.M. *My First Seventy-Five Years*. Toronto: Macmillan, 1967.

Lucas, C.A. (ed.). *The Empire at War*. London: Oxford University Press, 1923.

Malone, Richard. *A World in Flames: A Portrait of War*. Toronto: Collins, 1984.

Massey, Vincent. *What's Past Is Prologue: The Memoirs of the Right Honourable Vincent Massey*. Toronto: Macmillan, 1963.

Massolin, Philip. *Canadian Intellectuals, the Tory Tradition and the Challenge of Modernity, 1939–70*. Toronto: University of Toronto Press, 2001.

Matheson, John Ross. *Canada's Flag: A Search for a Country*. Boston: G.K. Hall, 1980.

MacDonald, F.B. and John J. Gardiner. *The Twenty-Fifth Battalion: Nova Scotia's Famous Regiment in World War One*. Sydney, Nova Scotia: J.A. Chadwick, 1983.

MacGregor, James G. *MacGregor V.C.: Goodbye Dad: Biography of the Man Who Won More Awards for Valour Than Any Other Canadian Soldier*. Victoria, British Columbia: Victoria Publication, 2002.

Macksey, Kenneth. *The Shadow of Vimy Ridge*. London: William Kimber and Company, 1965.

Macleod, Jenny. *Great Battles: Gallipoli*. Oxford: Oxford University Press, 2015.

MacMillan, Margaret and Francine McKenzie, eds. *Parties Long Estranged: Canada and Australia in the Twentieth Century*. Vancouver: UBC Press, 2003.

Mathieson, William. *My Grandfather's War: Canadians Remember the First World War, 1914– 1918*. Toronto: Macmillan Canada, 1981.

McClare, Dale, ed. *The Letters of a Young Canadian Soldier During World War I*. Dartmouth, Nova Scotia: Brook House Press, 2000.

McGrath, Susan, ed. *The Long Sadness: World War I Diary of William Hannaford Ball*. Thousand Oaks, California: Seanachie Press, 2014.

McKay, Ian and Jamie Swift. *Warrior Nation: Rebranding Canada in an Age of Anxiety*. Toronto: Between the Lines, 2012.

McKee, Alexander. *Vimy Ridge*. London: Pan Books, 1968.

McKernan, Michael. *Here Is Their Spirit: A History of the Australian War Memorial, 1917–1990*. St. Lucia, Queensland: University of Queensland Press, 1991.

McKillop, A.B. *Pierre Berton: A Biography*. Toronto: McClelland & Stewart, 2008.

McWilliams, James and R. James Steel. *The Suicide Battalion*. Edmonton, Alberta: Hurtig, 1978.

Meren, David. *Friends Like These: Entangled Nationalisms in the Canada-Quebec-France Triangle, 1945–1970*. Vancouver: UBC Press, 2012.

Miedema, Aaron Taylor. *Bayonets and Blobsticks: The Canadian Experience of Close Combat 1915–1918*. White Plains, New York: Legacy Books Press, 2011.

Millman, Brock. *Polarity, Patriotism, and Dissent in Great War Canada, 1914–1919*. Toronto: University of Toronto Press, 2016.

Montague, Charles Edward. *Disenchantment*. London: Chatto and Windus, 1922.

Morden, Herb. *The Vimy Pilgrimage, July 1936: Experiences—Impressions and Some Random Jottings*. Vancouver: Self-published, no date.

Morgan, Cecilia. *Commemorating Canada: History, Heritage, and Memory 1850s–1990s*. Toronto: University of Toronto Press, 2016.

Morrison, J. Clinton. *Hell Upon Earth: A Personal Account of Prince Edward Island Soldiers in the Great War, 1914–1918*. Summerside, Prince Edward Island: Self-published, 1995.

Morton, Desmond. *Fight or Pay: Soldiers' Families in the Great War*. Vancouver: University of British Columbia Press, 2004.

Morton, Desmond. *When Your Number's Up: The Canadian Soldier in the First World War*. Toronto: Random House of Canada Ltd., 1993.

Morton, Desmond and Glenn Wright. *Winning the Second Battle: Canadian Veterans and the Return to Civilian Life, 1915–1930.* Toronto: University of Toronto Press, 1987.

Munro, John A. and Alex I. Inglis, eds. *Mike: The Memoirs of the Right Honourable Lester B. Pearson, Volume 3: 1957–1968.* Toronto: University of Toronto Press, 1975.

Murray, W.W. *The Epic of Vimy.* Ottawa: The Legionary, 1936.

Nasmith, Colonel George. *Canada's Sons in the World War,* volume I. Toronto: The John C. Winston Co., 1919.

Neary, Peter. *Reference Paper: The Origins and Evolution of Veterans Benefits in Canada 1914–2004.* Ottawa: Veterans Affairs Canada, 2004.

Nicholls, Jonathan. *Cheerful Sacrifice: The Battle of Arras 1917.* Barnsley, United Kingdom: Pen & Sword, 2008.

Nichols, Stephen J. *Ordinary Heroes: Eastern Ontario's 21st Battalion C.E.F. in the Great War.* Almonte, Ontario: S.J. Nichol, 2008.

Nicholson, G.W.L. *Canadian Expeditionary Force, 1914–1919: Official History of the Canadian Army in the First World War.* Introduction by Mark Humphries. Montreal: McGill-Queen's University Press, 2015.

Nicholson, G.W.L. *Gunners of Canada: The History of the Royal Regiment of Canadian Artillery.* Toronto: McClelland & Stewart, 1967.

Nicholson, Colonel G.W.L. *Official History of the Canadian Army in the First World War: Canadian Expeditionary Force 1914–1919.* Ottawa: Queen's Printer and Controller of Stationery, 1962.

Norris, Armine. *Mainly for Mother.* Toronto: Ryerson Press, 1919.

Norris, Majorie Barron, ed. *Medicine and Duty: The World War I Memoir of Captain Harold W. McGill, Medical Officer, 31st Battalion C.E.F.* Calgary, Alberta: University of Calgary Press, 2007.

Owram, Doug and R. F. Moyles. *Imperial Dreams and Colonial Realities.* Toronto: University of Toronto Press, 1988.

Palk, Helen. *The Book of Canadian Achievement.* Toronto: Dent, 1951.

Palmer, Brian. *Canada's 1960s: The Ironies of Identity in a Rebellious Era.* Toronto: University of Toronto Press, 2009.

Pearson, Lester B. *Words and Occasions: An Anthology of Speeches and Articles Selected from His Papers*. Toronto: University of Toronto Press, 1970.

Peat, Harold. *Private Peat*. New York: Grosset and Dunlap, 1917.

Pedroncini, Guy. *Les mutineries de 1917*. Paris: Presses universitaires de France, 1967.

Power, Charles G. *A Party Politician: The Memoirs of Chubby Power*. Toronto: Macmillan, 1966.

Ralphson, George. *Over There with the Canadians at Vimy Ridge*. Chicago: M.A. Donohue and Company, 1919.

Rawling, Bill. *Surviving Trench Warfare: Technology and the Canadian Corps, 1914–1918*. Toronto: University of Toronto Press, 1992.

Raynsford, William. *Silent Casualties: Veterans' Families in the Aftermath of the Great War.* Madoc, Ontario: The Merribrae Press, 1986.

Robbins, Simon. *British Generalship during the Great War: The Military Career of Sir Henry Horne (1861–1929)*. Farnham, Surrey: Ashgate, 2010.

Robbins, Simon. *The First World War Letters of General Lord Horne*. Stroud, United Kingdom: The History Press for the Army Records Society, 2009.

Robertson, Ian Ross. *Sir Andrew Macphail: The Life and Legacy of a Canadian Man of Letters*. Montreal: McGill-Queen's University Press, 2008.

Rogers, Peter G., ed. *Gunner Ferguson's Diary*. Hantsport, Nova Scotia: Lancelot Press, 1985.

Rowland, Wade. *Canada Lives Here: The Case for Public Broadcasting*. Westmount: Linda Leith Publishing, 2015.

Rudin, Ronald. *Making History in Twentieth-Century Quebec*. Toronto: University of Toronto Press, 1997.

Russenholt, Edgar Stanford, ed. *Six thousand Canadian men: Being the history of the 44th Battalion Canadian Infantry, 1914–1919*. Winnipeg, Manitoba: 44th Battalion Association, 1932.

Sawell, Edward Stanley and Steven E. Sawell, ed. *Into the Cauldron: Experiences of a CEF Infantry Officer During the Great War:*

Memoirs of Edward Stanley Sawell, M.C., V.D. Burlington, Ontario: S.E. Sawell, 2009.

Scates, Bruce. *Return to Gallipoli: Walking the Battlefields of the Great War.* New York: Cambridge University Press, 2006.

Shackleton, Kevin R. *Second to None: The Fighting 58th Battalion of the Canadian Expeditionary Force.* Toronto: Dundurn Publishers, 2002.

Sheffield, Gary. *The Chief: Douglas Haig and the British Army.* London: Aurum Press Ltd., 2012.

Sheffield, Gary and John Bourne. *Douglas Haig: War Diaries and Letters, 1914–1918.* London: Weidenfeld and Nicolson, 2005.

Sheftall, Mark David. *Altered Memories of the Great War: Divergent Narratives of Britain, Australia, New Zealand and Canada.* London: I.B. Tauris, 2009.

Sheldon, Jack. *The German Army on Vimy Ridge, 1914–1917.* Barnsley, United Kingdom: Pen & Sword, 2008.

Sheldon, Jack and Nigel Cave. *The Battle for Vimy Ridge, 1917.* Barnsley, United Kingdom: Pen & Sword, 2007.

Sherman, Daniel J. *The Construction of Memory in Interwar France.* Chicago and London: The University of Chicago Press, 1999.

Shipley, Robert. *To Mark Our Place: A History of Canadian War Memorials.* Toronto: NC Press Limited, 1987.

Smith, Leonard. *The Embattled Self: French Soldiers' Testimony of the Great War.* Ithaca: Cornell University Press, 2007.

Socknat, Thomas P. *Witness Against War, Pacifism in Canada, 1900–1945.* Toronto: University of Toronto Press, 1987.

Stanley, George. *Canada's Soldiers: The Military History of an Unmilitary People.* Toronto: The Macmillan Company of Canada, 1954 (1960).

Stevens, G.R. *A City Goes to War: History of the Loyal Edmonton Regiment.* Brampton, Ontario: Charters Publication Co. Ltd., 1964.

Stevenson, O.J. *A People's Best.* Toronto: The Musson Book Company, 1927.

Stewart, William F. *The Embattled General: Sir Richard Turner and the First World War.* Montreal: McGill-Queen's University Press, 2015.

Suttie, Andrew. *Rewriting the First World War: Lloyd George, Politics and Strategy, 1914–18.* Basingstoke, United Kingdom: Palgrave Macmillan, 2005.

Swettenham, John. *McNaughton.* Toronto: Ryerson Press, 1968.

Swettenham, John. *To Seize the Victory: The Canadian Corps in World War I.* Toronto: Ryerson Press, 1965.

Teed, Valerie, ed. *Uncle Cy's War: The First World War Letters of Major Cyrus F. Inches.* Fredericton, New Brunswick: Goose Lane Editions and the New Brunswick Military Heritage Project, 2009.

Tennyson, Brian Douglas. *Percy Willmot: A Cape Bretoner at War.* Sydney, Nova Scotia: Cape Breton University Press, 2007.

Tessier, Albert. *Quebec–Canada: Histoire de Canada.* Quebec: Pelican, 1958.

The Story of the Sixty-Sixth C.F.A. Edinburgh: Turnbull & Spears, 1919.

Thomson, Dale. *Vive le Québec Libre.* Ottawa: Deneau, 1988.

Tippett, Maria. *Art at the Service of War: Canada, Art, and the Great War.* Toronto: University of Toronto Press, 1981.

Todman, Dan. *The Great War: Myth and Memory.* London: Hambledon, 2005.

Topp, Lieut.-Colonel C. Beresford. *The 42nd Battalion, C.E.F. Royal Highlanders of Canada.* Montreal: Gazette Printing Limited, 1931.

Travers, Tim. *Gallipoli 1915.* London: Tempus, 2001.

Trofimenkoff, Susan Mann. *The Dream of a Nation: A Social and Intellectual History of Quebec.* Montreal: McGill-Queen's University Press, 1982.

Trout, Steven. *On the Battlefield of Memory: The First World War and American Remembrance, 1919–1941.* Tuscaloosa, Alabama: University of Alabama Press, 2010.

Ulrich, Bernd and Benjamin Ziemann. *German Soldiers in the Great War: Letters and Eyewitness Accounts.* Barnsley, United Kingdom: Pen & Sword, 2010.

Urquhart, Hugh. *Arthur Currie: The Biography of a Great Canadian.* Toronto: J.M. Dent, 1950.

Vance, Jonathan. *Death So Noble: Memory, Meaning, and the First World War.* Vancouver: UBC Press, 1997.

Vipond, Mary. *The Mass Media in Canada*, 4th Edition. Toronto: Lorimer, 2011.

Viscountess Byng of Vimy. *Up the Stream of Time.* Toronto: The Macmillan Company of Canada Limited, 1946.

Wallace, O.C.S., ed. *From Montreal to Vimy Ridge and Beyond.* Toronto: McClelland, 1917.

Wallace, W. Stewart. *A New History of Great Britain and Canada.* Toronto: The Macmillan Company, 1929.

Walsh, Milly and John Callan, eds. *We're Not Dead Yet: The First World War Diary of Private Bert Cooke.* St. Catharines, Ontario: Vanwell, 2004.

Ward, Norman, ed. *A Party Politician: The Memoirs of Chubby Power.* Toronto: Macmillan of Canada, 1966.

Ware, Fabian. *The Immortal Heritage: An Account of the Work and Policy of the Imperial War Graves Commission During Twenty Years, 1917–1937.* Cambridge: The University Press, 1937.

Watkins, Ernest. *Prospect of Canada.* London: Secker & Warburg, 1954.

Weber, Thomas. *Hitler's First War: Adolf Hitler, the Men of the List Regiment, and the First World War.* Oxford: Oxford University Press, 2011.

Wheeler, Victor W. *The 50th Battalion in No Man's Land.* Ottawa: CEF Books, 2000.

Willans, Len. *The Lost Memoirs of a Canadian Soldier: World War I Diary Entries and Letters.* Edmonton, Alberta: Bobair Media Inc., 2012.

Williams, David. *Media, Memory and the First World War.* Montreal: McGill-Queen's University Press, 2009.

Williams, Jeffery. *Byng of Vimy, General and Governor General.* London: Leo Cooper in Association with Secker & Warburg, 1983.

Winegard, Timothy. *For King and Kanata: Canadian Indians and the First World War*. Winnipeg: University of Manitoba Press, 2012.

Winter, Jay. *Sites of Memory, Sites of Mourning: The Great War in European Cultural History*. Cambridge: Cambridge University Press, 1995.

Wise, S.F. *Canadian Airmen and the First World War: The Official History of the Royal Canadian Air Force*. Toronto: University of Toronto Press, 1980.

Wood, H.F. and John Swettenham. *Silent Witnesses*. Toronto: Hakkert, 1974.

Wood, Herbert Fairlie. *Vimy!* Toronto: Macmillan, 1967.

Wood, James. *Militia Myths: Ideas of the Canadian Citizen Soldier, 1896–1921*. Vancouver: UBC Press, 2010.

Woods, Walter S. *The Men Who Came Back*. Toronto: The Ryerson Press, 1953.

Woodward, David. *Lloyd George and the Generals*. London: Associated University Press, 1983.

Ziino, Bart. *A Distant Grief: Australians, War Graves and the Great War*. Crawley, Australia: University of Western Australia Press, 2007.

Ziino, Bart, ed. *Remembering the First World War*. New York: Routledge, 2015.

Zubkowski, Robert. *As Long as Faith and Freedom Last: Stories from the Princess Patricia's Canadian Light Infantry from June 1914 to September 1919*. Calgary, Alberta: Bunker to Bunker Publications, 2003.

Theses and Dissertations

Abram, Zachary. "The Knights of Faith: The Soldier in Canadian War Fiction." PhD dissertation: University of Ottawa, 2016.

Bormanis, Katrina. "The Monumental Landscape: Canadian, Newfoundland, and Australian Great War Capital and Battlefield Memorials and the Topography of National Remembrance." PhD dissertation: Concordia University, 2010.

Brown, Shaun R.G. "Re-establishment and Rehabilitating: Canadian Veteran Policy, 1933–1946." PhD dissertation: Western University, 1995.

Campbell, David Charles Gregory. "The Divisional Experience in the C.E.F.: A Social and Operational History of the 2nd Canadian Division, 1915–1918." PhD dissertation: University of Calgary, 2003.

Duffett, Angela. "Memory, Myth and Memorials: Newfoundland's Public Memory of the First World War." Master's thesis: Carleton University, 2010.

Ferguson, Malcolm. "The Response: Canada's National War Memorial." Master's thesis: Carleton University, 2010.

Garnett, Colin. "Butcher and Bolt: Canadian Trench Raiding during the Great War." Master's thesis: Carleton University, 2011.

Holland, Alexandra. "Canadian Memorialization at Vimy Ridge: The 'Vimy Myth.'" Master's research essay: University of Ottawa, 2010.

Inglis, Dave. "Vimy Ridge: 1917–1992: A Canadian Myth Over Seventy-Five Years." Master's thesis: Simon Fraser University, 1995.

Jackson, Geoffrey. "The British Empire on the Western Front: A Transnational Study of the 62nd West Riding Division and the Canadian 4th Division." PhD dissertation: University of Calgary, 2013.

McEwen, Andrew Scott. "'Maintaining the Mobility of the Corps': Horses, Mules, and the Canadian Army Veterinary Corps in the Great War." PhD dissertation: University of Calgary, 2016.

Morrison, Natascha. "Looking Backwards, Looking Forwards: Remembrance Day in Canada, 1919–2008." Master's thesis: Carleton University, 2010.

Sandy, Jessica Emma. "Names in Stone: War Memorials As Commemorative Intermediaries." Master's thesis: University of Calgary, 2015.

Soye, Edward Peter. "Canadian War Trophies: Arthur Doughty and German Aircraft Allocated to Canada after the First World War." Master's thesis: Royal Military College of Canada, 2009.

Teillet, Danielle. "The Commemoration of the Battle of Vimy Ridge: History, Remembrance, and National Identity." Master's thesis: Royal Military College of Canada, 2011.

White, Mallory. "The Vimy 'Snub': How the Politics of Commemoration Affected the 50th Anniversary Observance of the Battle of Vimy Ridge." Master's research essay: Carleton University, 2015.

Young, Chris. "'Sous les balles des troupes fédérales': Representing the Quebec City Riots in Francophone Quebec (1919–2009)." Master's thesis: Concordia University, 2009.

Young, Elaine. "'Over There': Veterans, Civilians, and the Vimy Pilgrimage of 1936." Master's thesis: York University, 2008.

INDEX

Note: Page references in *italics* denote a photograph.

Acland, Peregrine, 244
Afghanistan, 360, 361, 362, 363, 372, 382
air force
   British compared to German, 48–50
   Canadians join British, 48
   casualties in, 48, 50
   life expectancy of new pilots, 49
Airmen's Monument, 204
airplanes
   and intelligence gathering, 47–48, 50
   use of, 124, 134
Aitken, Sir Max, 38, 195–96, 229–30. *See also* Beaverbrook, Lord
Alderson, E.A.H., 18
Algeria, 318–19
All Else Is Folly (Acland), 244
Allen, Ben, 255
Allen, Ralph, 317
Allenby, Sir Edmund, 30, 60, 133–34, 148
All Quiet on the Western Front (Remarque), 243–44, 287
Allward, Donald, 270
Allward, Margaret Kenney, 195

Allward, Walter, *182, 189, 192, 283*
   assessment of Vimy site, 199
   background, 192
   building materials used in memorial, 356–57
   carving methods, 210, *211*
   contracts after Vimy Memorial, 284–85
   death, 302
   design style, 193
   display of maquettes in 2000, 354
   figures in memorial, 210–12, *211*
   honours and awards to, 283–84
   and issue of names of missing soldiers, 205–7
   lack of recognition for, 282–83
   memorials and monuments designed, 192–94
   physical appearance, 194–95
   reaction to Vimy Memorial damage, 293
   recognition of, 354
   renewed interest in, 360
   role and aides, 197–98
   and *Salute to Valour* film, 280
   signs contract, 187
   slow progress of Vimy Memorial, 208, 214, 215
   stone for memorial, 199–200, 207–10, 212
   symbolism in monument, 216–17

and Vimy Memorial unveiling,
266, 270, 282–83
Vimy pilgrim writes to, 366
vision for Vimy Memorial, 191–
92, 213–14, 216
wins competition for memorial,
183–85
Anderson, Howard, 352
Anderson, Percival, 110, 111
And We Go On (Bird), 244
Antliff, Will, 146
armistice, 163, 164
Armistice Day, 166–67, 238, 243,
246, 350. *See also*
Remembrance Day
Armour, Stuart, 274
Arras Memorial, 204
Artillerie Weg, 94
Artois offensive, 9
Asquith, Herbert, 28
Association of Canadian Clubs, 223
Atholstan, Lord, 154
At Vimy Ridge (Brewster), 359
Auchincloss, W.J., 203
Australia
casualties, 186
and "dummy graves," 203
at Gallipoli, 186–87
memorials and monuments, 180,
204
and unknown soldiers, 350
Australian War Memorial, 350

Badgley, Frank C., 279, 280
Bairnsfather, Bruce, *130*
Baldwin, Robert, *194*
Baldwin, Stanley, 275
Balfour, Lord, 225
Balfour Declaration, 225
Ball, William, 20, 23
Bapty, Walter, 118
barbed wire, 26, 52, 62, 66, 67
identified from the air, 48
at Vimy Ridge, 43, 46
Barclay, Gregor, 243
Barker, Pat, 348

Barris, Ted, 359
Batter Trench, 98
Battle Exploits Memorials
Commission, 179
battlefield
changes in fighting methods,
26–27
conditions, 26
training, 90
Battle of Amiens, 106, 163
Battle of Arras, 4, 30. *See also* Battle
of Vimy Ridge
British difficulty in, 133–34
compared to Battle of Vimy
Ridge, 229
preparations, 54–60
shut down, 137
tactics, 135
Battle of Cambrai, 106
Battle of Caporetto, 150
Battle of Hill 70, 149
Battle of Mount Sorrel, 18, 20, 21,
39, 51, 140, 141, 148, 179,
185, 187
Battle of Second Marne, 163
Battle of Second Ypres (1915), *16*,
185–86, *197*, 204
compared to Gallipoli, 187
importance of, 195–96, 231, 379
pride in, 138, 148
St. Julien as site of memorial, 179
use of gas at, 4, 16
Vimy battle overshadows, 273,
285
Battle of St. Eloi, 18
*The Battle of the Ridge Arras-
Messines* (Fox), 229
Battle of the Somme, 20–22, 274
casualties, 22–23
Battle of Thiepval Ridge, 22
Battle of Vimy Ridge. *See also* Battle
of Arras
anniversaries, 232–33, 234, 295,
302, 318, 335–36, 339–40,
358–59, 361–64, 366, 370,
377, 381–82

artistic celebration of, 226–27, 227

as birth of a nation, 325–27 (*See also* "birth of a nation" concept)

books about, 227–30, 230–31, 278, 315–17, 336–38, 341, 348–49, 359

Canadian divisions in, 61

Canadian pride in success, 130–31, 138–40

Canadians' knowledge of, 358

casualties, 78, 79, 81, 82, 83, 95, 99, 100, 101, 113, 123, 142

changing perception of, 328–29

commemorations of, 360

compared to Juno Beach, 369

creation of legend, 6–7

described in citizenship guide, 373

effect of on morale, 150

eve of, 68–71, 72

fading of relevance, 301–2

as *Heritage Minutes* subject, 347

historical assessment of by Duguid, 254

importance of, 148, 276–77, 284, 286–87, 314–15, 379, 383–84

importance of tactics, 149

lack of recognition by other countries, 378

memorials to, 142

movies and TV shows about, 279–80, 346, 368

newspaper coverage of success, 144

noise of, 75

praise for Canada, 151–52

preparation for, 62–63

public ignorance of, 355

relevance in post-war years, 301

renewed interest in, 358–60, 374–75

significance of, 322

as symbol, 295, 327, 329–30, 336

weapons used in, 72

zero hour, 74–75

Battle of Vimy Ridge (film), 344–45

Bean, Charles, 186–87

Beaverbrook, Lord, 38, 239, 240, 253, 316. *See also* Aitken, Sir Max

Bechthold, Michael, 359

Belgium

cemeteries in, 255

defence of and war, 335

invasion of, 12

and memorial sites, 180, 182

post-war tours to, 249

Bell, Alexander Graham, 194

Bennett, R.B., 214, 215

Bennett, S.G., 59

Berton, Pierre, 317, 336–38, 356, 360, 381, 383

Bethune, Brian, 344, 354

Binyon, Laurence, 352

Bird, Will, 235, 244, 252

Birdsong (Faulks), 348

"birth of a nation" concept, 3, 272, 316–17, 322, 325, 327, 329, 336, 339, 340, 341, 347, 364, 375, 376, 382, 383

Bishop, Billy, 345

Black Line, 77–78, 81, 82, 84, 86, 87, 88, 89, 91, 93, 96, 97, 98–99, 101–2

Blaikie, Harry, 91

Blomfield, Reginald, 168

Blue Line, 77, 83, 84, 103, 104–5, 106

Bonar, Arthur, 58

Books of Remembrance, 289, 300

Borden, A.H., 110

Borden, Sir Robert, 5, 13, 150, 151–53, 155, 156, 157, 158, 159, 161–62, 170–71, 219, 266, 274

Botel, Frances, 261

Botel, Harry, 261

Botel, Mary, 261, 262

Bourassa, Robert, 332

Bovey, Wilfrid, 123

Boyden, Joseph, 348

Brandon, Laura, 353
Brayman, A.F., 113
Brewster, Hugh, 359
British Broadcasting Corporation,
    265
British Expeditionary Force (BEF),
    17, 25, 149, 291, 292, 314
British Legion, 275
British Third Army, 60
Broken Ground (Hodgins), 348
Broken Promises (Granatstein and
    Hitsman), 334
"Brooding Soldier" (Clemesha), *183,
    184, 196, 197, 273*
Brooke, Alan, 44, 45–46, 66, 67,
    74–75
Brown, Robert, 334
Brown Line, 77, 84, 104–5, 106, 108
Brunet, Michel, 331
Brute Force (Allward), 194
burials, 168–69. *See also* cemeteries
Burns, E.L.M., 75, 321–22, 329–30
Burstall, Henry, 37, 61, 84
Burton, James, 202–3
Byng, Sir Julian, 4, *18,* 232
    admiration for, 221
    background and experience,
        17–18
    and Battle of Vimy Ridge, 62
    and Battle of Vimy Ridge suc-
        cess, 131, 132
    and Canadian Corps, 18–19
    comments on Vimy Ridge battle,
        301
    effect of Vimy win on, 148–49
    encourages troops, 58
    first battle with Canadian Corps,
        19
    and Gallipoli campaign, 17–18
    as governor general, 231–32
    and Horne, 50–51, 54
    and King, 233, 234, 256
    legacy of, 346
    methods, 26, 27
    and Mount Sorrel battle, 20
    overlooked in history, 346, 347

personnel changes made by, 38–39
plan for Vimy assault, 51
and pre-battle raids, 67
regard for veterans, 232
relationship with Currie, 37
success at Courcelette, 22
Byng, Viscountess, 300–301

Cadieux, Léo, 322
Cameron, Charles, 25, 41
Canada. *See also* "birth of a nation"
    concept; French Canada;
    Quebec
    in Afghanistan, 361, 362–63
    aftermath of the war, 164–66,
        170
    anger at Quebec, 151
    anti-conscription riots, 158–62
    and autonomy, 225–26
    backlash against farmers, 151,
        155, 165
    books about the war, 227–31,
        234–35, 244–45, 289
    centennial, 323
    change in status, 218
    changing role in world, 304–5
    connection with Britain, 221–22
    conscription, 150, 153–55,
        156–59
    creation of army, 13
    declares war on Germany (1939),
        290
    defining elements of, 367
    desire to honour dead in Europe,
        179
    effect of war on nationalism,
        222–24
    enters war, 12–13
    establishment of Order of
        Canada, 309
    exhibition of war images and
        artefacts, 239–40
    growing sense of identity, 380
    and Imperial War Cabinet, 152
    and independence as country,
        218–19

links to Great Britain, 305–6, 310
makeup of forces, 13–15
national anthem, 309
and nationhood, 152–53, 220,
221
new flag, 307–8
1917 election, 155–56
and 90th anniversary of Vimy,
358–65
October Crisis, 332, 376
pacifism in, 238–39
as peacekeeper, 304–5, 341–42
population in 1911, 11
in post-war years, 247
pride in Canadian Corps, 379
Quebec referendum, 343
recruitment, 150
relationship with France, 322–24
relationship with U.S., 236–37
self-comparison to U.S., 11
service exemptions, 156, 157–58
and 75th anniversary of Vimy,
339
status as nation, 224
and Treaty of Versailles, 219–20
Unknown Soldier, *351*, 352
view of world wars, 329, 330
war as divisive event, 222
war debt, 165
war film collection, 253
War Measures Act, 332
Canada: A Modern Study (Cook),
346
*Canada and the Battle of Vimy
Ridge, 9–12 April 1917*
(Brereton and Harris), 341
Canada at Vimy (Macintyre), 316
Canada Bereft (Allward), 208, 211,
270, 326, 360, 370
Canada in Flanders (Aitken),
229–30
Canada in the Great War (Drew),
237
Canada's Century (book), 346
Canada's Hundred Days (Livesay),
230

*Canada's Soldiers: The Military
History of an Unmilitary
People* (Stanley), 303
Canada's Sons in the World War
(Nasmith), 230
Canada Year Book, 1936, 154
Canadian Artillery, 142
Canadian Battlefields Memorials
Commission, 181–82, 196,
217
Canadian Cemetery, 143
Canadian Cemetery No. 2, 203
Canadian Corps, 14
ammunition requirements, 55
arrives at Somme, 21
battlefield conditions, 26
and Battle of Arras, 60–61, 136
and Battle of St. Eloi, 18
book on history of, 329
and Byng, 18–19
capture of weapons and prisoners, 140
casualties, 1, 22, 65, 79, 81, 83,
91, 95, 113, 142, 163, 240
clothing and protective gear,
72–73
creation of, 16–17
distinctiveness of, 220, 221
effect of success on Canada, 379
and effect of Vimy battle, 3
and anniversary of Great War,
311–12
first battle under Byng, 19
food supplies, 73–74
4th Canadian Infantry Division
joins, 25
German opinion of, 63, 68
and Hundred Days campaign
(Amiens), 163
importance of Vimy to, 148
leadership of, 149
makeup of, 69
map preparation and use, 60, 61
official history of, 154
opinions of, 17
position at Vimy Ridge, 24

pre-battle raids, 63–65
prisoners of war taken, 140
public attention to, 36
recognition given to, 147
reputation of, 4, 314
and Royal Flying Corps, 48–49
size, 1, 36
at the Somme, 20–21
structure, 36–37, 40, 42–43
successes of, 5
tactics, 39–40, 42, 46, 51–52,
    59–60, 66, 88
veterans and Byng, 232
and Vimy success, 132–33
weapons used, 40, 52–53, 67, 82,
    85
zero hour in Vimy Ridge battle,
    74–75
Canadian Counter Battery Office, 45
Canadian Expeditionary Force
    (CEF), 14–15, 228
    film about, 253
Canadian Expeditionary Force,
    1914–1919 (Nicholson),
    313–14
Canadian Forces, 360
Canadian Government Motion
    Picture Bureau, 252–53, 279
Canadian Grenadier Guards. See
    87th Battalion
Canadian Historical Association,
    154
Canadian Institute of International
    Affairs, 223
Canadian League, 223
Canadian Machine Gun Brigade, 53
Canadian Museum of Civilization,
    353, 354
Canadian National Vimy Memorial.
    See Vimy Memorial
Canadian Pacific Steamships, 255
Canadian Radio Broadcasting
    Commission (CRBC), 265
The Canadian Veteran (magazine),
    255–56, 270
Canadian War Museum, 328, 353

Canadian War Records Office, 239
Canvas of War: Masterpieces from
    the Canadian War Museum
    (exhibition), 353–54
Careless, J.M.S., 317
casualties
    in air force, 50
    from assault on Pimple, 129
    Australian, 186
    at Battle of Arras, 136
    British, 10
    at Brown Line, 104
    Canadian, 16, 22, 48, 65, 78, 95,
        103, 138–39, 142, 155, 164,
        240
    challenges of identifying and
        compiling list of, 122, 123
    of 87th Battalion, 99
    families' reaction to, 146–47
    in 5th Battalion, 83
    of 4th Division, 22
    French, 9, 10, 27, 28, 135
    German, 9, 27, 100, 140–41, 163
    at Hill 145, 113
    during the Hundred Days, 163
    at Mount Sorrel, 20
    of 72nd Battalion, 101
    of 78th Battalion, 100
    of 102nd Battalion, 98
    at the Somme, 22–23
    of 3rd Battalion, 103
    3rd Canadian Division, 19
    in 3rd Division, 19
    of 25th Battalion, 22
    at Verdun, 27
    at Vimy Ridge battle, 79, 81, 82,
        83, 91, 104, 123
CBC Radio, 311
cemeteries
    in Belgium, 255
    Borden visit to, 274
    exhumation and reinterment,
        167–68
    Givenchy Road Canadian, 203
    headstones in, 168
    requirements of, 168

unknown soldiers, 349–50, 351
visited by veteran pilgrims, 261–
62, 274
Chanak Crisis, 224
Charles, E.P., 48
Charlottetown Accord, 340
Chemin des Dames, 29
Cherry, Don, 374–75
Chisholm, Gordon, 78
chlorine gas. *See* gas
Chrétien, Jean, 353, 372
Christian, Ethelbert "Curley," 125,
267
Churchill, Winston, 295
Clark, Alan, 310
Clark, Gregory, 70, 94, 258, 261,
275, 313
Clark, S.D., 287–88
Clark, Tom, 341
Claxton, Brooke, 223
Clémenceau, Georges, 219
Clements, Robert, 88
Clemesha, Frederick Chapman, *183,*
184, 185, 196
Colpitts, Laurence, 129
Commonwealth War Graves
Cemeteries, 349
Commonwealth War Graves
Commission, 167, 351
conscription, 5, 13, 150, 153–55,
156–62, 222, 251, 332, 334,
376
Cook, C.C., 74
Cook, Ramsay, 334, 346
Cooke, Bert, 56
Costilla, Joseph, 333
Coulter, Andrew, 119
Courcelette, 21–22, 37, 139
creeping barrage, 46, 47
Creighton, Donald, 317
Crerar, Harry, 291, 297, 299
Cross, James, 332
Crossby, Jimmy, 271
Cross of Sacrifice, 168
Cruikshank, William, 192
Cuff, Leonard, 125, 148

Cullen, Maurice, 353
Cumming, Francis, 24
Cumyn, Alan, 348
Cunard–White Star Line, 255
Cunard–White Star Shipping
Company, 285
Currie, Sir Arthur, 221, 228
appearance and personality,
19–20
attack on reputation of, 240–43,
287
and Battle of Vimy Ridge, 61
biography of, 302
comments on anti-war books, 244
death, 246, 252
knighting of, 149
libel trial, 242–43, 287, 380
and memorial site selection, 179,
180–81
on nature of Canadians, 14
published errors about, 346, 347,
375
recognition of Canadian identity,
220, 233, *241*
relationship with Byng, 37
role in Vimy attack, 77
as successor to Byng, 149
tactics, 51
training tactics, 26–27
treatment in *Battle of Vimy
Ridge,* 344
and veterans' groups, 172
CWGC Halifax Memorial, 204

Dafoe, J.W., 218, 228–29
Dallaire, Roméo, 370
The Danger Tree (Macfarlane), 348
Darling, Frank, 182
Davidson, B.B., 79
Davidson, Harold, 285
dead, honouring of, 167–69. *See
also* memorials and
monuments
Deafening (Itani), 348
de Gaulle, Charles, 318–20, 322,
323–24, 339

Department of External Affairs, 320
Department of Militia and Defence, 234
Department of National Defence, 252–53, 277, 279, 280, 281, 341
Department of Soldiers' Civil Re-establishment, 172
Department of Veterans Affairs, 318, 319, 320, 341, 355
Depression, the Great, 245–46, 251, 252, 255
Dibblee, Hubert Forster, 139
Diefenbaker, John, 307, 320
Distinguished Conduct Medal, 93, 142
Dominion Institute, 355, 356, 358
The Donkeys (Clark), 310
Donnell, Allan, 230
Draycot, Walter, 138–39
Drew, George, 235, 237
Duguid, Archer F., 154, 234–35, 237, 289, 300, 313
Dunbar, John, 81
Duncan, D.M., 231
d'Urbal, Victor, 9
Dynamite Gang, 154

Easter Riots, 1918, 331, 332, 333, 345, 358, 376
Edward VIII, King of England, 256, 266–68, 267, 269, 269–70, 272, 275, 280, 362
8th Battalion, 81, 147
8th Brigade, 92
XVII Corps, 18
18th Battalion, 85, 86, 87
18th Infantry Division, 131
85th Battalion, 10, 110–11, 113, 121
87th Battalion (Canadian Grenadier Guards), 97, 99, 100
Eiserner Kreuz Weg (trench), 78
11th Brigade, 97, 100
11th Company, 98
Elizabeth, Queen, 287, 288

Elizabeth II, Queen of England, 319, 320, 359, 362
Ellis, W.E., 298–99
England, Robert, 60
The Epic of Vimy (Murray), 278
Expo 67, 323

The Face of Battle (Keegan), 334–35
Fall Alberich, 31
Fallis, George, 268
Farbus Wood, 61, 77, 84, 104, 105, 107
Fassbender, Karl Ritter von, 33, 34
Faulks, Sebastian, 348
Ferguson, Frank, 14
5th Battalion, 77, 81, 82, 83
5th Brigade, 85
5th British Division, 105
5th British Divisional Artillery, 85
5th British Infantry Division, 69, 84
5th Canadian Mounted Rifles, 72
Fifth Army, 157
15th Battalion, 77–78, 102–3, 202
50th Battalion, 65, 113, 126, 127, 128
51st British Infantry Division, 81
51st Highland Division, 77
54th Battalion, 97, 98–99
Findley, Timothy, 335
1st Battalion, 103, 104, 105
1st Battalion (German), 95
1st Bavarian Reserve Corps, 9, 33, 140–41
1st Bavarian Reserve Division, 34, 84
1st Brigade, 83, 103
1st Canadian Heavy Battery, 125
1st Canadian Infantry Division, 16, 16, 77, 291
1st Canadian Mounted Rifles (CMR), 19, 92, 93, 94
1st Division, 61, 83, 91, 96, 102, 104, 143, 276
1st Guards Reserve Division, 131
1st Infantry Brigade, 172
First Army (British), 30, 54, 60–61, 96, 147

First Canadian Army, 291, 297
First Contingent, 13
I British Corps, 62
First Nations, 352, 373
  serving in army, 14
First World War
  books about, 313, 334–35, 348
  casualties, 314
  effect on Canada, 317
  50th anniversary, 311–22
  meaning for Canada, 367
  renewed interest in history of, 347–48
  TV series about, 310–11, 368
Flanders' Fields (radio series), 311–12, 337
FLQ. *See* Front de libération du Québec
Foch, Ferdinand, 195
Fort Douaumont, 28
Fortescue, Den, 148
The Forty-Niner, 245
Foster, W.W., 293
4th Battalion (Mad Fourth), 103, 104
4th Brigade, 85
4th Canadian Infantry Division, 38, 61, 62, 64, 65, 132, 197
  joins Canadian Corps, 25
4th Canadian Mounted Rifles, 70–71
4th Canadian Mounted Rifles (CMR), 19, 59, 92, 94
4th Canadian Siege Battery, 100
4th Division, 22, 92, 95, 96, 102, 109, 112, 124, 126
4th Field Company of Canadian Engineers, 143
4th Guards Infantry Division, 127
4th Infantry Brigade, 104
14th Battalion, 77, 78, 79, 102–3
42nd Battalion, 92, 95, 141
42nd Highlanders, 95
43rd Battalion, 359
44th Battalion, 126, 127, 143, 174–75, 263–64, 312, 357–58

46th Battalion, 24, 109, 127, 129, 143
47th Battalion, 109
48th Highlanders of Canada, 202
49th Battalion, 172, 173, 245
Fox, Frank, 229
France
  and Battle of Arras, 134–35, 136–37
  casualties, 23, 27, 28, 135, 136
  declares war on Germany (1939), 290
  German defeat of (1940), 291
  gift of Vimy Memorial site, 189
  gratitude to Canadian Corps, 147
  lack of importance of Vimy battle to, 378
  and memorial sites, 180
  opposition to Germany, 12
  post-Second World War, 318
  relationship with Canada, 322–24
  Resistance movement, 294
  and 75th anniversary of Vimy, 339
Franco-Prussian War, 12
Franz Ferdinand, Archduke, 12
Fraser, Donald, 120
Fregault, Guy, 331
French Canada. *See also* Quebec
  in British Canada, 11
  Catholic Church in, 222, 306, 331
  changes in, 331–32
  and conscription, 222, 331
  and makeup of army, 13–14
  and rest of Canada, 331
  view of First World War, 5
French Foreign Legion, 9
French Tenth Army, 8–9
  Moroccan Division, 9
Front de libération du Québec, 323, 332
Fussell, Paul, 334

Gallipoli campaign, 186–87
    Byng's role, 17–18
Garnell, B.A., 186
Garvock, Bill, 72, 277, 285
gas, use of, 4, 16, *16*, 64, 96
General Mud (Burns), 329
Generals Die in Bed (Harrison), 244
George V, King of England, 147,
    166, 256, 350
George VI, King of England, 287,
    288, 289–90, 383
German Sixth Army, 33–34
Germany
    acknowledgement of Vimy battle,
        378
    air power, 48–49
    casualties, 23, 27, 100, 163
    defeats France in World War !!,
        291
    destroyed weapons, 67
    first day of Vimy Ridge battle,
        76–77
    French opposition to, 12
    invades Poland, 290
    rearming of, 286
    response to Vimy defeat, 132
    Russia surrenders to, 157
    and Vimy Memorial damage,
        292–93
    warfare tactics, 32–33, 34–35
    weapons used, 65
    Week of Suffering, 67–69
The Ghosts of Vimy Ridge, 1–2
Gibson, Henry, 192
Girouard, Katherine de la Bruère,
    266
Givenchy Road Canadian Cemetery,
    203
Goddard, F.G., 277
Goerne, Wilhelm von, 97
Goodspeed, Donald, 3
Gough, Hubert, 22
Gould, L. McLeod, 98
Grafton, C.S., 53
Granatstein, J.L., 334, 353
Grant, George, 306

Grant, W.L., 231
Great Britain
    acknowledgement of Vimy battle,
        378
    Asquith as prime minister, 28
    and the Battle of Arras, 135–36
    casualties at Arras, 136
    declares war on Germany (1939),
        290
    Dunkirk, 292
    effect of Passchendaele on, 150
    enters war, 12–13
    links with Canada, 305–6, 310
    pacifist movement in, 237–38
    war tactics, 39–40
The Great Response, 290
The Great War (TV series), 310–11,
    368
*The Great War and Modern
    Memory* (Fussell), 334
Great War Veterans Association,
    172
Green, William, 103
Greenhous, Brereton, 341
Grenadier Guards. *See* 87th
    Battalion
Griesbach, William, 38, 83, 172–73
Grieving Man (Allward), 216
Grieving Woman (Allward), 211
Griffiths, Rudyard, 356
Gross, Paul, 344, 367
Groulx, Lionel, 333
Group Vimy, 34, 35
Gunn, J.N., 226

Hagemann (German soldier), 95
Haig, Sir Douglas, 17, 250, 310
    and attack on Vimy Ridge,
        30–31
    and Battle of Arras, 60, 85, 135,
        137
    and command of Canadians, 18,
        36
    disagreements with Lloyd
        George, 29–30
    King George congratulates, 147

Lloyd Douglas opinion of, 29
  as mentor to Horne, 50
  opinion of Canadians, 219
  promotes Byng, 148–49
  response to Vimy victory, 132
Haller, Art, 129
Haller, Harry, 128–29
Hamilton, Sir Ian, 379
Hara, Shinkichi, 146
Harper, Stephen, 358–59, 362, 364,
  371, 372–73
Harrington, Tim, 133
Harris, Stephen, 341
Harrison, Charles Yale, 244
Harvie, A.K., 143
Hawkes, Arthur, 10
Hayes, Geoffrey, 359
Hayes, Joseph, 10, 121
headstones, 168, 169
Heliconian Club, 281
Heritage Minute series, 346–47
Hesler, Harold, 282
Hill 62, 18, 84, 179, 185, 187, 261
Hill 135, 84, 105, 107, 108, 185, 187,
  261
Hill 145, 61
  battle for, 62, 97, 101–2, 126–27
  German control of, 34, 99, 100,
    102, 109
  Germans' partial control of, 126
  interpretation centre at, 344
  landscape of, 24
  as memorial site, 8, 143, 174,
    182, 199
  and the Pimple, 62
  taking of, 111
  Watson's pride in Canadians, 143
Hilliam, Edward, 102, 126
Hindenburg, Paul von, 32, 132, 145
Hindenburg Line (Siegfried
  Stellung), 31
Historica Canada, 346–47
Historic Sites and Monuments
  Board of Canada, 354
History of Canada (Garnell), 186
History of Canada (Grant), 231

Hitler, Adolf, 68, 247, 257, 290,
  292, 293, 301, 302
Hitsman, J.M., 334
HMCS Saguenay, 259, 265
Hockey Night in Canada, 375
Hodgins, Jack, 348
Holden, Percy, 140
Holliday, Clifford, 359
Hood, Magnus, 88
Horne, Henry, 50–51, 52, 54, 60,
  62, 96, 148
horses, 54, 55
  difficulty in mud, 125
House, John Albert, 75–76
Hughes, Garnet, 282
Hughes, Henry Thoresby, 179–80,
  182, 197, 198, 203
Hughes, Sam, 18, 37, 38, 47–48,
  179, 241, 242, 282
Hundred Days campaign (1918), 4,
  163, 179, 240, 241
Hurley, J.F., 79
Hutcheson, Bellenden, 119
Hydro-Québec, 331

Iarocci, Andrew, 359
Ignatieff, Michael, 363
Imperial Commonwealth War
  Graves Commission, 281
Imperial Conference (1923), 225
Imperial Order Daughters of the
  Empire (IODE), 175, 178
Imperial War Cabinet (IWC), 151,
  152, 219
Imperial War Graves Commission
  (IWGC), 167–68, 177, 178–
  79, 198, 199, 203, 228
Imperial War Museum, 141, 240
Inches, Cyrus, 125
India, 180
infantry
  and barbed wire, 23
  battle preparations, 58–60
  British, 84
  commanders, 39
  divisions, 16–17, 36

fighting style, 84
importance of in Vimy Ridge
    battle, 72
size of, 25
success at Courcelette, 21
tactics, 42, 51
and tunnels, 57
weapons available to, 40, 41
"In Flanders Fields" (McCrae), 167,
    186, 288–89, 295, 345, 384
injuries at Vimy, 115–16, 116, 117,
    118–19
intelligence gathering
    by on-the-ground patrollers, 62
    use of airplanes, 47–48, 50
Iriam, Frank, 246
Ironside, Edmund, 38, 64, 65
Iron Sixth, 104
Italy, losses, 150
Itani, Frances, 348

Jack, Richard, 44
Jackson, A.Y., 184–85, 221, 281, 353
Jacques Parizeau Park, 376–77, See
    also Parizeau
Jenkins, Walter, 209
Joffre, Joseph, 27
Johnston, David, 375
Junger, Ernst, 31
Juno Beach Centre, 369–70

Keegan, John, 334–35
Kennedy, Harold, 169
Kentner, Robert, 24, 128
Kent State, 333–34
King, Martin Luther, 305
King, William Lyon Mackenzie, 220
    attitude to veterans, 256
    and Byng, 233, 234, 256
    and Canadian autonomy, 224–45
    career, 187–88
    friends, 198, 200
    and Meighen, 233–34
    and Vimy Memorial delays, 214
    and Vimy memorial site selec-
        tion, 189–90
and Vimy Memorial unveiling,
    268
Viscountess Byng's hatred of, 301
and W.L. Mackenzie memorial,
    284
Kipling, Rudyard, 168
Knott, Francis, 281

Lafontaine, Sir Louis-Hippolyte,
    194
Lament for a Nation (Grant), 306
Landry, J.P., 159
Lapointe, Ernest, 161, 266, 268–69,
    277
Laporte, Pierre, 332
Larkin, Peter, 200
Laurier, Sir Wilfrid, 193
League of Nations, 225, 247, 257,
    269
League of Nations Society, 223
LeBoutillier, Leo, 142
Legion, the. See Royal Canadian
    Legion
The Legion (magazine), 253, 282,
    330, 335–36, 356
The Legionary (magazine), 254–55,
    257, 276, 277, 295, 297, 316
Lemieux, Rodolphe, 181, 188–89,
    203, 208, 217
Lessard, J.L., 159
Lest We Forget (film), 253, 278
Liddle, Gordon, 103–4
Lipsett, Louis, 37–38, 61, 91–92
Lismer, Arthur, 353
Livesay, J.F.B., 230
Lloyd George, David, 28–30, 60,
    151, 152, 153, 170, 219
Longstaff, Will, 1–2
Loomis, Frederick, 77
Loring, Frances, 252
The Lost Boys (Thompson), 348
Louden, Walter, 115, 116
Lower, Arthur, 221, 223
Ludendorff, Erich, 32, 132
Lutyens, Sir Edwin, 168, 212,
    215–16

MacBrien, James, 38, 97, 102
Macdonell, A.H., 85–86
MacDowell, Thain, 120
Macfarlane, David, 348
MacFarlane, Joseph, 118–19
Macgowan, Keith Campbell, 65, 109
MacGregor, John ("Jock"), 93
MacGregor, Roy, 360
machine guns, 44
    advantages of, 32
    German, 35, 76–77, 87, 94, 105
    Lewis, 42
    shortcomings of, 123
    used by Canadian forces, 40, 42,
        43–44, 53
    used on the Somme, 40, 43, 53
    use in Vimy Ridge battle, 74, 80,
        81, 85, 123–24, 124
Macintyre, D.E., 63, 255, 286, 316
MacKay, Peter, 362–63
Mackenzie, Ian, 256
Mackenzie, William Lyon, 284
Macksey, Kenneth, 316
Macphail, Agnes, 239
Mad Fourth. See 4th Battalion (Mad
    Fourth)
Maiden, Fred, 122–23
Malone, Richard, 297
Maple Leaf, 297
maps, preparation and use, 60, 61
Martin, Lawrence, 363
Martin, Paul, 372
Martineau, Aline, 345
Masse, Marcel, 341
Massey, Vincent, 195, 291
Massie, Roger, 44–45, 66, 67, 74
Mayse, Amos, 119
McCallum, John, 355
McClare, P. Winthrop, 138
McClung, J.W., 50, 95
McClung, Nellie, 50
McCrae, John, 167, 175, 186, 288,
    295, 345, 384
McDougall, Neil, 115
McGill, Harold, 105–6, 117
McGill, T.C., 143, 144

McGillivray, N.H., 170
McGill University, 173, 242
McKay, Ian, 373
McKee, Alexander, 316
McKenna, Brian, 368, 369
McKillop, A.B., 337
McLean, David, 70
McLeod, Neil, 128
McNaughton, Andrew, 44, 45, 51,
    66, 74, 291
McNaughton, Violet, 238
McPherson, Cleopatra (Cleo), 125
McWade, Archie, 83, 102–3
medical system, 116–18
    stretcher-bearers, 117–18, 121
Meech Lake Accord, 340
Meighen, Arthur, 154, 155, 233–34
Memorial Chamber (Peace Tower),
    288, 289, 350, 352
memorials and monuments, 173. See
    also Vimy Memorial
    aborted plans for, 289
    to Allward, 354
    in Australia, 204
    at Beaumont Hamel, 250
    Books of Remembrance, 289
    built by units, 143
    choice of site for Vimy Memorial,
        187–88
    commissioned by Canada, 196–97
    created by Allward after Vimy,
        284–85
    criticism of, 282
    design of, 181–85
    erected at Vimy, 141, 142
    erected by communities, 173–77
    erected by regiments, 143–44
    local compared to Vimy, 286–87
    Memorial Chamber, 288–89
    Menin Gate, 204
    for missing soldiers with no
        graves, 203–5
    models for overseas, 183
    Molson Stadium, 173
    names included on, 177–78,
        205–7

National War Memorial, 289–
90, 352
Never Forgotten National
Memorial, 371
in New Zealand, 204
to 1918 Easter Riots victims, 345
Peace Tower, 288
at the Pimple, 264
proposed museum, 240
register of names on Vimy
Memorial, 280–81
site selection in Europe, 179–81,
185
South African War, 193–94
St. Julien, 197
at Toronto City Hall, 177
to unknown soldiers, 349–50,
351
unveiling of National War
Memorial, 288
values attached to, 380–81
at Vimy Ridge, 357–58
visited by veteran pilgrims,
261–62
war trophies, 78, 174
in Ypres, 195, 196
Memorial University, 174
Menin Gate Memorial, 204, 205,
251, 274–75, 282
Menzies, Albert Percy, 114
Mercier, Joseph, 157–58
Métivier, Paul, 352
Mewburn, S.C., 181, 207
Michelin Company, 249
Middleton, Ethel, 281
Military Cross, 90, 93, 111, 114,
258, 278
Military Medal, 122, 140
Military Service Act, 153
Miller, Robert, 49–50, 55, 106–7
Milne, Wiliam, 80
mines, 57
Mitterand, François, 339
Moir, David, 336
Molson, Percy, 173
Molson Stadium, 173

Montgomery, Bernard, 297
Morden, Herb, 258, 261
Moro-oka, Sachimaro, 65
Morris, Hubert, 74, 120
Morrison, Edward "Dinky," 43–44,
45, 67
Morton, Desmond, 377
Morton, W.L., 305
"Mother Canada" (Allward), 208
Moule, Frances, 147
mud
horses' difficulty in, 125
and tanks, 106
Mulroney, Brian, 339–40, 343
Murdoch, Alfred, 258–59
Murdoch, Florence, 258–59, 261,
262
Murdoch, Kathleen, 259
Murdoch, Ward, 258–59
Murray, W.W., 249, 252, 278
Mussolini, Benito, 247
mutinies, 100, 136

Nangle, Thomas, 180, 250
Nasmith, George, 230
Nasser, Gamal, 304
National Film Board, 344, 368
National War Finance Committee,
295
National War Memorial, 288, 289–
90, 321, 352, 360
A Nation Transformed (Brown and
Cook), 334
Never Forgotten National
Memorial, 371
Newfoundland
decoration on headstone, 168
founding of Memorial University,
173–74
French site for memorial, 180
inability of veterans to attend
pilgrimage, 250
and memorial sites, 180
Newfoundland Regiment, 20
A New History of Great Britain and
Canada (Wallace), 186

New Zealand, honouring of dead
    soldiers, 204
Nicholson, George, 239
Nicholson, Gerald, 313, 315
9th Company, 98
19th Battalion, 85, 86, 87
93rd Army Field Artillery Brigade,
    85
Nivelle, Robert, 28, 29, 30, 31, 32,
    134, 135, 136
Nixon, Victor John, 69, 129
No. 4 Canadian Field Ambulance,
    119
No. 8 Field Ambulance, 119
No. 9 Canadian Field Ambulance,
    146
No. 9 Field Ambulance, 118–19
No. 10 Field Ambulance, 120
No. 16 Squadron, 48
Nobbs, Percy, 180, 200, 207
Nobel Peace Prize, 304
Noble, Sierra, 363
Norris, Armine, 85
Notre Dame de Lorette, 203

O'Connor, Joe, 375
Odlum, Victor, 38, 59, 97, 98, 174
Oh, What a Lovely War (play), 310
102nd Battalion, 97, 98–99, 118,
    169
Only This (Pedley), 244
Ontario Motion Picture Bureau, 253
Osborne, Henry Campbell, 197–98,
    200, 203, 205, 209, 214, 215,
    283–84
Our Empire, 275
Over the Canadian Battlefields
    (Dafoe), 228
Over There, with the Canadians at
    Vimy Ridge (Ralphson), 229
Owen, Hector, 78

Papineau, Talbot, 16, 368
Parizeau, Jacques, 343
Parks Canada, 371
Parti Québécois, 343

Passchendaele, 111, 150, 179, 185,
    196, 204, 261, 277, 368
Passchendaele (film), 367–68
Pattison, John, 126–27
Peace, 192, 193
Peace Tower, 288
Pearson, John, 288
Pearson, Lester B., 303–4, 306–7,
    309, 318, 319, 320, 322, 324,
    325, 329, 383
Peat, Harold, 63
Pedley, James, 244
Perry, Anne, 193–94
Perry, R.T., 182
Pétain, Philippe, 136–37
Philip, Prince, 319, 322
Pile, F.A., 140
pilgrimages
    to Britain, 274–75, 321, 380
    to Vimy, 257–62, 274–75, 358–
        59, 359
    to Western Front battlefields,
        249–51, 255–56
Pimple, the, 101
    battle for, 127–29
    challenge of, 62
    delay in attack on, 102, 126
    German reinforcement of, 127
    memorial at, 89, 264
Piroson, Pierre, 294, 302
Plumer, Sir Herbert, 133
poppies, 167, 238, 322
Potter, G.R.L., 278
Power, Charles "Chubby," 225
Powley, A.E., 311
Prince of Wales, 256, 288. See also
    Edward VIII, King of England
Princess of Wales' Own Regiment,
    143
Princess Patricia's Canadian Light
    Infantry (PPCLI), 50, 58, 72,
    92, 95, 138–39, 277
prisoners
    at Brown Line, 104
    Canadian, 122
    dangers to, 83

German, 63, 91, 94, 127, 133
  taken at Farbus Wood, 104
  taken by Canadian Corps, 140
Provencher, Jean, 332, 333, 334, 345
Public Archives of Canada, 141, 240

Quebec
  anger against in Canada, 151,
    156
  anti-conscription riots, 158–62
  attitude to Vimy, 376–77
  and Catholic Church, 222, 306,
    331
  changes in, 306–7
  and conscription, 153–55, 157–
    59, 332
  and de Gaulle, 323–24
  Easter Riots, 331, 332, 345, 358,
    376
  memorials erected in, 176
  Mulroney's attempts to accom-
    modate, 339–40
  October Crisis, 332
  opposition to war, 258
  Quiet Revolution, 306, 331
  referendum, 343
  separation movement in, 323,
    332
Québec, Printemps 1918 (monument), 345
Quebec, Printemps 1918
  (Provencher), 333
Quebec-Canada: Histoire du
  Canada (Tessier), 333
Québec Pension Plan, 331
Québec: sous la loi des mesures de
  guerre 1918 (Provencher), 332
Quiet Revolution, 306, 331

Radcliffe, Percy Pollexfen de
  Blaquiere, 45
Rae, Bob, 377
railways and trams, to convey the
  injured, 116, 118–19
Ralph, Joel, 368–69
Ralphson, George, 229

Red Line, 77, 78, 79, 81, 83, 84, 90,
  91, 96, 97, 102
Regeneration series (Barker), 348
regimental pipers, 95
Reid, Escott, 223
Remarque, Erich, 243–44
Remembrance Day, 167, 246, 286,
  290, 294, 299, 302, 312, 330,
  341, 342, 345
Rennie, Robert, 85
Resolution IX, 152
Richler, Noah, 373
Richthofen, Manfred Freiherr von
  ("Red Baron"), 50
Rigamonti, Luigi, 210
Riot Act, 160
Roberts, G.D., 230
Robertson, Sir William, 39
Rogers, Lawrence, 19
Rogers, Norman, 291
Ross, Alexander, 259, 316–17, 329
Ross, Arthur, 146–47
Ross, Mrs. Duncan, 146
Ross, William G., 146
Rowat, Duke, 182
Roy, Philippe, 266
Royal Canadian Engineers, 197, 198
Royal Canadian Horse Artillery
  Band, 265
Royal Canadian Legion, 235, 238,
  246, 251, 275, 278, 279, 280,
  285, 302, 318, 350
  and unknown soldiers return,
    351–52
Royal Canadian Mint, 360
Royal Canadian Regiment, 92, 95,
  202–3
Royal Commission on Bilingualism
  and Biculturalism, 306
Royal Dragoons, 160
Royal Flying Corps (RFC), 48–49
Royal Military College, 143, 303
Royal Naval Air Service, 47
Royal Navy, 221
Royal Newfoundland Regiment,
  250

Rugh, H.B., 174
Rupprecht, Crown Prindce, 131
Russenholt, E.W., 312
Russia
    effect of war on, 150
    surrender to Germany, 157

Sacrifice (Vimy Memorial), 297
Sacrifice Medal, 360
Salisbury, Frank O., 366
Salute to Valour (film), 279–80
Sassoon, Siegfried, 282
Saturday Night (magazine), 281–82
Sawell, Edward, 2, 73, 90
Schlieffen Plan, 12
Scott, F.G., 259, 262, 276–77
Scott, Howard, 119
Scrimger, Dr. Francis, 286
2nd Battalion (King's Own Scottish
    Borderers), 105, 278
2nd Brigade, 77, 81
2nd Canadian Infantry Division, 77
2nd Canadian Mounted Rifles, 73,
    92, 93
2nd Division, 56, 61, 84, 85, 86, 91,
    96, 104, 106, 125, 139
2nd Reserve Infantry Regiment, 128
Second Battle of the Scarpe, 135–36
Second Battle of Ypres, 185–86
Second British Army, 133
Second World War
    50th anniversary, 342, 352
    Great Britain declares against
        Germany, 290
    overshadowing First World War,
        301–2
Seguin, Maurice, 331
7th Battalion, 77, 81
7th Brigade, 92, 95
72nd Battalion, 97, 100, 101
72nd Reserve Infantry Division, 97
73rd Battalion, 97, 101
73rd Hanoverian Fusilier Regiment,
    31
75th Battalion, 56, 97, 140
78th Battalion, 97, 100, 125

79th Reserve Division, 34, 35, 68,
    108, 140–41
Sharpe, C.T., 302
shellshock, 120, 348
Sheppard, W.J., 108
Shinobu, Saburo, 260
Siegfried Stellung (Hindenburg
    Line), 31
Sifton, Ellis Wellwood, 87–88
Silver Cross mothers, 72, 258, 267,
    267
Simpson, Charles, 192
Simson, D.C. Unwin, 7, 198, 199,
    200, 202–3, 298
Sislowski, Stanley, 358
Sivetz, Gus, 73
6th Brigade, 104
Sixth Army, 68, 131, 132
16th Battalion, 25, 41, 77, 79–81,
    102–3
16th Bavarian Jaeger Infantry
    Division, 34
16th Bavarian Reserve Infantry
    Division, 68
60th Battalion, 57, 62
Skelton, Oscar D., 223–24
Smith, Ernest "Smokey," 352
Smith, Julian, 356
The Sojourn (Cumyn), 348
Sons of Canada, 194
South Africa, and memorial sites, 179
Spain, civil war in, 286
Spanish influenza, 163
Spiritual Triumph (Allward), 194
Stacey, Charles, 313, 329, 341
Staines, Lilian, 281
Stanley, George, 303
Statute of Westminster, 225, 226,
    380
Steele, Harwood, 24
St. Laurent, Louis, 303
The Stone Carvers (Urquhart), 348–
    49, 381
Stone of Remembrance, 168
The Story of the Canadian People
    (Duncan), 231

Stubbs, George, 294, 297
Suez Crisis, 304
surrender
    by German soldiers, 89
    politics of, 82–83
Swettenham, John, 328–29
Swift, Jamie, 373

The Taking of Vimy Ridge, Easter
    Monday, 1917, 44
tanks, 86
    in Arras assault, 85
    German response to, 85
    inadequacy at Vimy, 106
    use of, 84–85, 106
    weapons against, 106
10th Battalion, 77, 81, 115, 122
10th Brigade, 102, 126
10th Field Ambulance, 74
10th Infantry Brigade, 62
Tessier, Albert, 333
Thiepval monument, 212
Thiessen, Vern, 360
3rd Battalion, 103–4
3rd Bavarian Infantry Regiment, 78
3rd Brigade, 77
3rd Canadian Division, 19, 98
3rd Canadian Infantry Division, 34,
    37, 61
3rd Division, 91, 96, 109, 124, 143
3rd Divisional Ammunition
    Column, 282
3rd Infantry Division, 336
Third British Army, 30, 133, 136,
    148–49, 157
13th Battalion (Royal Highlanders
    of Canada), 102–3
13th British Brigade, 104
13th British Infantry Brigade, 84
31st Battalion, 104, 106, 117, 120
37th Battery, 20
38th Battalion, 97, 99, 101, 120
Thomson, R.H., 348, 360
Three Day Road (Boyden), 348
Topp, C.B, 141
Toronto Art Students' League, 192

To Seize the Victory (Swettenham),
    329
Treaty of Versailles, 219–20, 360
trenches and trench systems, 55,
    56–57, 59, 62, 78, 79, 86, 94,
    97, 98, 126, 200–202
Tripp, G.H., 138–39
Trudeau, Justin, 368, 373
Trudeau, Pierre, 307, 309–10, 332
tunnels
    Goodman, 69, 92
    Grange, 69, 92, 95, 200–201,
        201, 264, 294, 298
    use in Vimy Ridge battle, 75
Turko Graben trench, 86
Turner, Richard, 37, 181
The Turn of the Tide, 230
Tuxford, George, 77
12th Brigade, 101
12th Brigade, 97, 99
20th Battalion, 89
21st Battalion, 89, 90–91, 143
21st Reserve Battalion, 86
22nd Battalion, 21, 89, 90–91, 176,
    331, 333
24th Battalion, 85, 88, 138, 142
25th Battalion, 21, 22, 72, 88, 89,
    90–91
25th Reserve Battalion, 86
26th Battalion, 85, 88
27th Battalion, 105, 108, 271
27th Battery, Canadian Field
    Artillery, 49–50
28th Army Field Artillery Brigade, 85
28th Battalion, 104, 106–7
29th Battalion, 104, 106, 108
29th British Division, 20
261st Prussian Reserve Infantry
    Regiment, 93-94, 98, 99
263rd Reserve Regiment, 94
Tyne Cot, 204, 205
Tyrwhitt, Janice, 337

Underhill, Frank, 247
United Nations, 304–5
United Publishers, 230

United States
  dissent in in 1960s, 305
  joins war, 69
  recognition of veterans by
    French, 251
  role in war, 235–37
  strength of popular culture, 305
Up the Stream of Time (Viscountess
    Byng), 300–301
Urquhart, Hugh, 302
Urquhart, Jane, 348–49, 381

The Valour and the Horror (film),
    344, 368
Valpy, Michael, 360
Verdun campaign, 27, 28
veterans. See also pilgrimages
  and annual Vimy dinner,
    232–33
  associations, 172
  attitude to war, 245
  bitterness of treatment by
    Canada, 246, 247
  care for wounded, 171–72
  complaints about battlefield tour-
    ists, 249–50
  death of last Vimy, 359
  defence of Currie, 243
  desire for jobs, 171
  50th anniversary ceremonies,
    320–22
  health problems of, 246
  importance of pilgrimage, 287
  King's attitude to, 256
  medals, 330
  opinion of anti-war movement,
    238
  pilgrimage anniversary, 285
  pilgrimage mementoes, 279
  pride of, 247–48
  regard for Byng, 231, 232, 234
  reunion in 1934, 252
  of Second World War, 342
  tours to Western Front, 249,
    251
  treatment of, 170–73, 341, 342

Victoria Cross, 80–81, 87, 93, 111,
    119, 120, 127, 140, 181, 220,
    286, 352
Victory Loans, 295
Vien, Thomas, 162
Vietnam War, 305, 337, 361
Vimy! (Wood), 315
Vimy (Barris), 359
Vimy (Berton), 336–38, 381
Vimy (play, Thiessen), 360
Vimy Day, 294, 302, 360, 374, 375
Vimy Foundation, 374, 377
Vimy Memorial, 1, 6, 7, 308
  Allward at unveiling, 282–83
  assessment of site, 199
  attraction for soldiers in World
    War II, 298, 298–99
  caretaking of, 294, 302–3
  carving methods used, 210, 211
  choice of site, 187–88
  condition of, 355–56, 357
  cost of, 215
  creation of, 191
  criticism of, 282
  description of, 183, 262, 384
  and anniversary of First World
    War, 318
  figures in, 210–12, 211
  German damage to, 292, 292–93
  homages to in Second World
    War, 291
  as icon/symbol, 281, 286, 290,
    295, 296, 308–9, 327, 372, 373
  importance to Canadians,
    383–84
  land preparation for, 198–99
  lessening of interest in, 302–3
  Macphail questions symbolism
    of, 239
  missing soldiers, 138
  model of, 184
  names of missing soldiers, 204,
    206
  as nationalistic icon, 276, 277
  pilgrimages to, 257–62, 274–75,
    358–59, 359

as place of pilgrimage, 285
praise for, 281–82, 284
proposed reproduction of,
370–71
register of names on, 280–81
restoration of, 356–57
safety during World War II, 297,
298
search for stone, 199–200, 207–
10, 212, 284
site of, 182
size of, 212
slow progress of, 208, 214, 215
symbolism in, 205, 212–13
symbolism of, 338–39, 344
on twenty-dollar bill, 374
unveiling ceremony, 217, 251, 252,
255, 256, 263, 264–72, 269
Vimy Park, 376
Vimy Pilgrimage Medal, 259, 266
Vimy Ridge. *See also* Battle of Vimy
Ridge
commercialization of, 227–28,
228
description of, 8
importance of, 3–4, 8, 132
interpretation centre at, 343–44
landscape of, 147–48
memorials erected at, 141,
143–44
post-war condition, 182, 188,
198, 228
as site of memorial, 187
view from, 112
Week of Suffering, 67–69
Vimy Ridge: Heaven and Hell (film),
359
Vimy Vigil, 360
Visener Graben, 79
von Falkenhausen, Ludwig, 33, 68,
131, 132

Wallace, W.S., 11, 186, 219–20
Ware, Sir Fabian, 203
War Measures Act, 332
The Wars (Findley), 335

war trophies, 78, 141, 174
Watson, David, 38, 96, 102
approves use of gas, 64
and attack on Hill 145, 126
and Battle of Vimy Ridge, 61, 62
and Battle of Vimy Ridge success, 131
and pre-battle raids, 64, 65
pride in Canadian Corps, 142–43
tactics, 109–10
Watson, Eleanor, 350
weapons
ammunition requirements, 55
anti-tank, 106
bayonets, 40–41, 111–12
effect of weather on, 51
gas, 64, 65, 185
Germans' destroyed, 67
grenades, 41
lack of, 40
machine guns, 32, 40, 42, 43–44,
44, 53, 74, 76–77, 80, 81, 85,
87, 94, 105, 123–24, 124
mines, 57
rifles, 40–42
tanks, 85
used by Canadian Corps, 40,
52–53, 67, 82, 85
used by Germans, 82
used in Vimy Ridge battle, 72
weather
in battle for Hill 145, 128
effect on air reconnaissance, 134
effect on weapons, 51
at end of April 9, 123
Webber, Ox, 17
Weinreb, Arthur, 355
Wells, Clifford, 147
Wells, H.G., 237
Welsh Guards, 297
Wheeler, Victor, 126, 128–29
Who Killed Canadian History?
(Granatstein), 353
Wilhelm II, Kaiser, 12
Willans, Len, 57, 62
Williams, George, 143

Willmot, Percy, 2, 22, 72
Wilson, Woodrow, 236
Winged Canada (Allward), 193
Winged Victory, 175
Winnipeg General Strike, 165
Women's Christian Temperance
    Union, 175
Women's International League for
    Peace and Freedom, 238
Wood, Herbert Fairlie, 315
Woods, Mrs. C.S., 267–68
Woods, Walter, 272
Woodsworth, J.S., 238–39
Working Class Ex-Service Men's
    League, 238

Worthington, F.F., 315, 329
wounded soldiers. *See* injuries
Wrenn, Agnes, 258
Wrenn, Alexander, 258
Wrenn, Edward, 258
Württemberg XIII Corps, 19

yap films, 359
Yugoslavia, as supplier of stone for
    Vimy Memorial, 208–9

Zivy Cave, 56
Zwischen Stellung (Red Line), 81,
    86, 94. *See also* Red Line
Zwolfer Weg (Black Line), 77–78

CREDITS

The maps were influenced by the official maps in G.W.L. Nicholson's *Official History of the Canadian Army in the First World War: Canadian Expeditionary Force 1914–1919* (Ottawa, Queen's Printer and Controller of Stationery, 1962), the gold standard for all Canadian First World War maps, as well as Dr. Michael Bechthold's maps in Geoffrey Hayes, Andrew Iarocci, and Mike Bechthold (eds.) *Vimy Ridge: A Canadian Reassessment*. (Waterloo: Laurier Centre for Military Strategic and Disarmament Studies and Wilfrid Laurier University Press, 2007).

The author has been collecting images from multiple sources for two decades. All of the images here are his own unless otherwise stated.

Page 2: *The Ghosts of Vimy*, original held by Parliament of Canada
Page 44: *The Taking of Vimy Ridge, Easter Monday, 1917*, held by Canadian War Museum
Page 145: Victoria Daily Times, 7 May 1917
Page 216: Library Archives Canada (LAC), 066786-v8
Page 224: Halifax *Herald,* 3 August 1918.
Page 269: LAC, 148880-v8
Page 283: LAC, 103158-v8
Page 298: LAC, 010786291-v8
Page 308: Courtesy of Dr. Michael Bechthold
Page 326: Courtesy of Dr. Michael Bechthold
Page 359: Courtesy of Dr. Michael Bechthold
Page 374: Courtesy of Raeside